Approaches to Teaching
Milton's Shorter Poetry and Prose

Approaches to Teaching
World Literature

Joseph Gibaldi, series editor

For a complete listing of titles,
see the last pages of this book.

Approaches to Teaching Milton's Shorter Poetry and Prose

Edited by

Peter C. Herman

The Modern Language Association of America
New York · 2007

For information about obtaining permission to reprint material from
MLA book publications, send your request by mail (see address below),
e-mail (permissions@mla.org), or fax (646 458-0030).

Library of Congress Cataloging-in-Publication Data

Approaches to teaching Milton's shorter poetry and prose /
edited by Peter C. Herman.
p.   cm. — (Approaches to teaching world literature ; 94)
Includes bibliographical references and index.
ISBN-13:   978-0-87352-593-0 (alk. paper)
ISBN-13:   978-0-87352-594-7 (pbk. : alk. paper)
1. Milton, John, 1608–1674—Study and teaching.
I. Herman, Peter C., 1958–
PR3588 .A68 2007
821' .4–dc22   2007018480
ISSN 1059-1133

Cover illustration of the paperback edition: *The Blinding of Samson*,
by Rembrandt van Rijn. 1636. Oil on canvas.
Städel Museum, Frankfurt am Main.

Published by The Modern Language Association of America
26 Broadway, New York, NY 10004-1789
www.mla.org

CONTENTS

Preface to the Series ix

Preface to the Volume xi

PART ONE: MATERIALS
Peter C. Herman

Editions and Texts 3
Reference Works and Biographies 4
Audiovisual and Online Resources 5
Required and Recommended Reading for Students 7
The Instructor's Library 8

PART TWO: APPROACHES

Introduction: Which Courses and What Gets Taught 15

Approaching Milton's Poetry and Prose

Biographic Milton: Teaching the Undead Author 24
James Dougal Fleming

Past and Present: Memorializing the English Nation 29
Andrew Escobedo

Teaching Milton and Gender 35
Catherine Gimelli Martin

Milton and Hebraism 42
Jason P. Rosenblatt

Milton and the Undergraduate British Literature Survey Course:
 Who, Where, When, How, and, by All Means, Why? 47
Angelica Duran

Approaching Milton's Poetry

Milton and Textual Studies: Teaching "On Shakespeare"
 as a Work in Progress 54
Stephen B. Dobranski

"That Glorious Form": Teaching the Nativity Ode and
 Samson Agonistes through Visual Images 62
Wendy Furman-Adams

Teaching Theology in Milton's Shorter Poetry 74
Albert C. Labriola

Milton's Sonnets and the Sonnet Tradition   80
  Jennifer Lewin

Pursuing the Subtle Thief: Teaching Meter in Milton's Short Poems   88
  Elizabeth Harris Sagaser

Radical Politics and Milton's Civil War Verse: "Licence"
    and "Libertie"   97
  Elizabeth Sauer

Approaching Milton's Prose

Approaching the Antiprelatical Tracts   103
  John T. Shawcross

Milton and the Bible   110
  Jameela Lares

Elaborating Differences: Milton's *Areopagitica* in the
    Postmodern Classroom   114
  William Kolbrener

Teaching Milton's Late Political Tracts in a Public,
    Comprehensive University   121
  Elizabeth Skerpan-Wheeler

Discipline in the Classroom   126
  Alison A. Chapman

Milton and the Constitution, Ancient and American   132
  Peter C. Herman

Teaching Specific Texts: Poetry

Introducing John Milton: Why, When, and How to Teach
    "On the Morning of Christ's Nativity"   139
  John Rumrich

Milton and the Incarnation: Embodiment, Gender, and
    Eroticism in "On the Morning of Christ's Nativity"   145
  Richard Rambuss

The "Unowned" Lady: Teaching *Comus* and Gender   152
  Lynne A. Greenberg

Companionable Poetry: Milton's "L'Allegro" and "Il Penseroso"   156
  David Mikics

"On Shakespeare," Poetic Rivalry, and the Art of the Intertext   161
  Curtis Perry

Reading for Detail: Four Approaches to Sonnet 19   166
  Bruce Boehrer

Johnson, Genre, and "Lycidas" 171
Matthew Davis

Exploring Early Modern Homosociality: Milton's "Lycidas"
in the General Education Classroom 175
Mark K. Fulk

Teaching *Paradise Regained* 179
Barbara K. Lewalski

"By Winning Words to Conquer Willing Hearts": Teaching Miltonic
Strategies of Alliteration in *Paradise Regained* 185
R. Allen Shoaf

"Passion Spent": Teaching *Paradise Regained* and *Samson
Agonistes* as Twin Texts 189
Jeffrey Shoulson

Interpreting Dalila: *Samson Agonistes* and the Politics of Servility 194
David Loewenstein

"Ruin, Destruction at the Utmost Point": Terrorism and
Samson Agonistes 200
Joseph A. Wittreich

Teaching Specific Texts: Prose

Biography, Creation, and Authority in *The Reason of
Church Government* 205
Gardner Campbell

Areopagitica and Free Speech 211
John Leonard

Arguing about Politics in *The Tenure of Kings and Magistrates*
and Contemporary Debates 218
Gina Hausknecht

Milton versus King Charles: Re-Creating the
Debate of *Eikonoklastes* 222
Laura Lunger Knoppers

Reading Milton Reading in *The Doctrine and Discipline of Divorce*;
or, How to Make His "Wild" and "Wary" Hermeneutics
Matter in the Classroom 228
Shari A. Zimmerman

On Christian Doctrine: Teaching the Conflict and What's at Stake 235
David V. Urban

The Ready and Easy Way: Milton's Utopia? 242
Matthew Woodcock

Notes on Contributors   247

Survey Participants   253

Works Cited   255

Index of Names   277

Index of Works by Milton   283

PREFACE TO THE SERIES

In *The Art of Teaching*, Gilbert Highet wrote, "Bad teaching wastes a great deal of effort, and spoils many lives which might have been full of energy and happiness." All too many teachers have failed in their work, Highet argued, simply "because they have not thought about it." We hope that the Approaches to Teaching World Literature series, sponsored by the Modern Language Association's Publications Committee, will not only improve the craft—as well as the art—of teaching but also encourage serious and continuing discussion of the aims and methods of teaching literature.

The principal objective of the series is to collect within each volume different points of view on teaching a specific literary work, a literary tradition, or a writer widely taught at the undergraduate level. The preparation of each volume begins with a wide-ranging survey of instructors, thus enabling us to include in the volume the philosophies and approaches, thoughts and methods of scores of experienced teachers. The result is a sourcebook of material, information, and ideas on teaching the subject of the volume to undergraduates.

The series is intended to serve nonspecialists as well as specialists, inexperienced as well as experienced teachers, graduate students who wish to learn effective ways of teaching as well as senior professors who wish to compare their own approaches with the approaches of colleagues in other schools. Of course, no volume in the series can ever substitute for erudition, intelligence, creativity, and sensitivity in teaching. We hope merely that each book will point readers in useful directions; at most each will offer only a first step in the long journey to successful teaching.

Joseph Gibaldi
Series Editor

PREFACE TO THE VOLUME

Teaching Milton's shorter poetry and prose presents several obstacles beyond the usual difficulties facing teachers of early modern texts. First, there is the issue of time. As numerous survey respondents said, the primary focus of any course on Milton is going to be *Paradise Lost*, a work unmatched for its combination of length, difficulty, and rewards. Therefore, the question for the Milton instructor is not so much which of Milton's other works to teach as whether to teach them at all. How, given the amount of time that *Paradise Lost* requires and its importance to English and American literature and culture, can one justify taking time away from Milton's epic, especially since the option of a two-semester course on Milton (often offered for Shakespeare), which would give one world enough and time to teach all his works, does not exist? The problem only gets worse if one's institution is on the quarter system. Furthermore, there are special challenges in teaching this material. There are few prose stylists as difficult as Milton. His verse often participates in genres that have become alien to contemporary culture, and his prose often concerns issues and controversies far from the "knowledge base" of most contemporary students.

And yet, making the effort to include Milton's shorter poetry and prose is worthwhile for a number of reasons. First (as many respondents pointed out), the earlier works pave the way for the epic, and Milton seemed to assume that the reader of *Paradise Lost* would recognize the echoes of *The Ready and Easy Way to Establish a Free Commonwealth* in Satan's speeches, the near-quotations from *Areopagitica* in Eve's speeches on why she wants to work alone, and the resemblances between Adam's situation and the speaker of the divorce tracts. Because *Paradise Lost* is very much in conversation with the earlier works, learning about the earlier works helps students understand the epic. Furthermore, Milton also seemed to assume that the readers of *Paradise Regained* and *Samson Agonistes* (published together in 1671) would know *Paradise Lost*. Milton's final poems, in other words, comment on and revise his epic, suggesting that excluding these works would give students an incomplete picture of Milton's career as a poet. But one need not base the argument for teaching the shorter poetry and prose on their essential relation to *Paradise Lost*: the works have their own aesthetic and intellectual rewards. Reading *The Tenure of Kings and Magistrates* allows students to see some of the roots of the American Revolution, just as the anticensorship themes of *Areopagitica* remain as relevant as ever (as does Milton's commitment in his political pamphlets to the rule of law and to political accountability). The divorce tracts and *Comus* similarly continue to challenge our students' thinking about gender and about marriage. There are few poems about death and mourning as powerful as "Lycidas," and Milton's struggles with his sense of vocation in his sonnets, "Lycidas," and the companion poems "L'Allegro" / "Il Penseroso" resonate with the difficulty many students have figuring out what they want to do in life. Finally, the terrible events of 9/11 and the continuing popularity, if that is the right word, of suicide bombings have made *Samson Agonistes* intensely timely.

The purpose, therefore, of *Approaches to Teaching Milton's Shorter Poetry and Prose* is to provide, in a single volume, a map of study materials available and a collection of essays displaying a diversity of methods and critical approaches for teaching the texts. The essays in part 2 address the variety of courses that include Milton's shorter poetry and prose and present a wide range of methods. The essays are divided into five sections: three on general approaches to the poetry and prose, one on teaching specific poems, and one on teaching specific prose works.

PCH

Part One

MATERIALS

Editions and Texts

While Miltonists are fortunate to have at their disposal a good number of excellent editions for the classroom (and as we will see, the future will bring even more), the questionnaires received indicate that no one edition predominates. The standard edition of Milton's prose is the magisterial eight-volume *Complete Prose Works*, edited by Don M. Wolfe and published by Yale University Press, largely because of its introductions and annotations. Unfortunately, these volumes are out of print, although most university libraries own them. Instructors nonetheless will use excerpts for their classes. No equivalent edition exists for Milton's poetry, but that may soon change, as Oxford University Press has commissioned a new complete edition of all of Milton works, prose and poetry, under the general editorship of Thomas Corns and Gordon Campbell. The aim, according to Sharon Achinstein, who is editing the divorce tracts, "is to update the Yale Prose and consolidate the poetry too, doing a better job with textual histories for the whole thing and integrating new scholarship (though not as heavily annotated as Yale)" (E-mail). The first volume, *De Doctrina Christiana*, should appear in 2008.

At the moment, three editions of the complete poetry and selected prose are available for classroom use, and one edition is in process. The respondents generally agreed that while the *Complete Poems and Major Prose* (1957; rpt. 2003), edited by Merritt Y. Hughes, had many merits, a new edition with up-to-date bibliographies and introductions was necessary (too, the Hughes edition was out of print for many years). Hence many have opted for *The Riverside Milton* (1998), edited by Roy Flannagan,[1] despite their attachment to Hughes (which is now available in paperback from Hackett). The third of these editions is Stephen Orgel and Jonathan Goldberg's *John Milton* (1991) in the Oxford Authors series. In 2003, Oxford published a paperbound edition of this book under the title *John Milton: The Major Works*. Finally, a three-volume edition of Milton's works—*Paradise Lost*, selected prose, and the shorter poems—under the general editorship of Barbara Lewalski is forthcoming from Blackwell. (Lewalski is editing *Paradise Lost* [due out in 2007], David Loewenstein the selected prose, and Stella Revard the shorter poems [both scheduled for 2008].) Lewalski informs me that the edition is aimed at graduates and undergraduates, with appropriate introductions and annotations, and that the works will appear with their original spelling and punctuation.

There are several editions of the poetry alone (or poetry plus a small amount of the prose): *Complete English Poems, Of Education, Areopagitica* (Everyman edition), edited by Gordon J. M. Campbell; *Complete Shorter Poems* (Longman Annotated English Poets series), edited by John Carey; Paradise Lost *and Other Poems*, edited by Edward Le Comte; *The Complete Poems*, edited by John Leonard; and *The Complete Poetry of John Milton*, edited by John Shawcross. The only stand-alone edition of the prose used by respondents is

John Milton: Selected Prose, edited by C. A. Patrides. All these editions are currently in print and available.

Finally, period anthologies cover at least some of Milton's shorter poetry and prose. *The Longman Anthology of British Literature*, volume 1b (Jordan and Carroll), includes "L'Allegro" / "Il Penseroso," "Lycidas," "On the New Forcers of Conscience," sonnets 7 ("How soon hath Time"), 16 ("To the Lord General Cromwell"), 18 ("On the Massacre in Piedmont"), 19 ("When I consider"), and 23 ("Methought I saw"), along with an excerpt from *Areopagitica*. *The Norton Anthology of English Literature* (Abrams et al.) includes the same sonnets and excerpt from *Areopagitica*, adding the Nativity Ode, "On Shakespeare," and the biographical digression in *The Reason of Church Government*. *The Broadview Anthology of Seventeenth-Century Verse and Prose* (Rudrum, Black, and Nelson) gives more space to Milton's works. In addition to the expected poems (the Nativity Ode, "Lycidas," "L'Allegro" / "Il Penseroso," and sonnets 7, 18, and 19), this volume includes sonnet 12 ("I did but prompt the age"), sonnet 15 ("On the Lord General Fairfax)," and *Samson Agonistes*. The prose is represented by an excerpt from *The Reason of Church Government* and all of *Areopagitica* and *Of True Religion*. Blackwell's *Seventeenth-Century Poetry: The Annotated Anthology* (Cummings) has the Nativity Ode, the companion poems, "Lycidas," and sonnets 8, 13 ("To Henry Lawes"), 18, 19, and 23. Two works present in this anthology not included in the others are *Comus* and "The Fifth Ode of Horace, Book 1." Milton's presence in *The Penguin Book of Renaissance Verse, 1509–1659* (Norbrook and Woudhuysen) is surprisingly minimal: "Song: On May Morning," "L'Allegro" (not "Il Penseroso"), the Nativity Ode, "The Fifth Ode of Horace," and an excerpt from "At a Vacation Exercise." Finally, notice should be taken of Herschel Baker's reprinted *The Later Renaissance in England: Nondramatic Verse and Prose, 1600–1660*, as the editor gives Milton more space than any other anthology. In addition to substantial excerpts from the 1645 *Poems of Mr. John Milton*, and 1673 *Poems, & c. upon Several Occasions*, this anthology includes *Of Reformation* (complete), chapters 1 and 7 of *The Reason of Church Government*, and chapter one of *Eikonoklastes*.

Reference Works and Biographies

Teachers of Milton and their students can avail themselves of a number of excellent reference works and biographies, and as with editions, more are forthcoming in the future. Pride of place must be given to *A Milton Encyclopedia*, edited by William B. Hunter and others. This work contains articles on all Milton's major works as well as on topics essential for understanding Milton and his time (e.g., "Pastoral," "Independents," "Fall and Restoration of Mankind"). This resource will be supplemented soon with the publication of *The Milton*

Encyclopedia, edited by Thomas N. Corns. According to Corns, this volume will be informed by recent scholarship and written, for the most part, by a new generation of scholars. In other words, this will be a Milton resource for the new century. The volume will be organized more straightforwardly like an encyclopedia and will not contain the discursive articles distinguishing the older *Milton Encyclopedia* (Corns, E-mail). Students and teachers alike can also profitably consult Gordon Campbell's entry on Milton in the *Oxford Dictionary of National Biography*, the successor to the *Dictionary of National Biography* (*DNB*) edited by Leslie Stephen and Sidney Lee (this resource is available online and in print, although its cost means that only wealthier libraries can afford it), and Albert C. Labriola's entry on Milton in the *Dictionary of Literary Biography*. Two older and two more recent concordances are available: Charles Dexter Cleveland's *A Complete Concordance to the Poetical Works of John Milton* (1867); John Bradshaw's *A Concordance to the Poetical Works of John Milton* (1894); *A Concordance to Milton's English Poetry* (1972), edited by William Ingram and Kathleen Swaim; and *A Concordance to the English Prose of John Milton* (1985), edited by Laurence Sterne and Harold H. Kollmeier.

Milton criticism has grown to enormous proportions, especially since commentary starts with the publication of *Paradise Lost*. John Shawcross's volumes *Milton, 1732–1801: The Critical Heritage* and *Milton: A Bibliography for the Years 1624–1700* remain invaluable aids for older commentary, and Calvin Huckabay has done two annotated bibliographies that bring us relatively up to date: *John Milton: An Annotated Bibliography, 1929–1968* and *John Milton: An Annotated Bibliography, 1968–1988* (compiled by Huckabay and edited by Paul J. Klemp). For more current critical works, one still must consult the *MLA International Bibliography* and the two journals devoted exclusively to Milton: *Milton Studies* and *Milton Quarterly*. As for biographies, William Riley Parker's magisterial *Milton: A Biography* has been reissued in a revised version edited by Gordon Campbell, and Barbara Lewalski has published *The Life of John Milton: A Critical Biography*, which is available in paperback. Respondents also mentioned A. N. Wilson's *The Life of John Milton*, Peter Levi's *Eden Renewed: The Public and Private Life of John Milton*, and Gordon Campbell's *A Milton Chronology*.

Audiovisual and Online Resources

Most respondents used visual aids in teaching these works. The Nativity Ode in particular calls for visual supplementation in the form of various paintings of the Nativity and the Passion. As Wendy Furman-Adams's essay in this volume demonstrates, Renaissance paintings of the Samson story also work well in illuminating *Samson Agonistes*. Richard Rambuss had the wonderful suggestion of using illustrations of nineteenth-century Mardi Gras carnival materials from the Mystic Krewe of Comus for help with *Comus: A Mask*. Additionally, many respondents found it helpful to bring in photocopies of the original publications of Milton's works, a practice considerably facilitated by the online database *Early English Books Online* (*EEBO*; see below for more information on this resource). Several of the respondents suggested bringing in maps and charts of the geocentric universe and contemporary Renaissance illustrations such as those in S. K. Heninger's *Cosmographical Glass*.

Despite Milton's and his father's well-known interest in music, comparatively few respondents suggested using musical aids for teaching the shorter poems. Even so, mention was made of the Handel oratorio based on "L'Allegro" / "Il Penseroso" (which also includes "Il Moderato," thus creating an opportunity for learning how Handel's librettist understands or misunderstands Milton's poem) and the one based on *Samson*. The Nativity Ode can be supplemented by the Nativity Ode portion of Ralph Vaughan Williams's *Hodie*, and for *Comus*, there is the videotape of the production of *Comus* staged at the Seventh Annual International Milton Symposium (available from Roy Flannagan). Anthony Rooley and the Consort of Musicke's *Sitting by the Streams* (Hyperion, 2002) is an album of songs by Henry Lawes, who composed music for *Comus* and to whom Milton wrote sonnet 13.

A number of Miltonists take advantage of the various pedagogical opportunities the Web affords. A distinction, however, must be made between materials and resources open to the public and those available only by subscription. There is general agreement that Milton-L, the e-mail discussion list dedicated to Milton studies, has become an essential resource. Several respondents not only use it themselves, they also have their students subscribe to the list and report on a particularly interesting strand. The list is largely populated by an international group of graduate students, professors of all ranks, independent scholars, and the interested public, and undergraduates are welcome to submit queries and have them answered by some of the most distinguished names in the field. Subscription information as well as other links to important and useful Web sites for Milton studies can be found at the Milton-L homepage (www.richmond.edu/~creamer/milton/index.html). The *Milton Reading Room* (www.dartmouth.edu/~milton) provides online editions of Milton's poems, as does Risa Bear's *Renascence Editions* site (http://darkwing.uoregon.edu/~rbear/ren.htm). Anniina Jokinen's *Luminarium* provides a wealth of links to essays and various other online resources helpful for teaching and studying Milton (www.luminarium.org), as do Alan Liu's *Voice of the Shuttle* (http://vos.ucsb.edu/), Michael Bryson's pages on Milton (www.brysons.net/miltonweb/), and Blackwell's online literature resource site, *Literature Compass* (www.blackwell-compass.com/subject/literature/).[2] The King James Bible is available online through the Electronic Text Center at the University of Virginia (http://etext.lib.virginia.edu/kjv.browse.html).[3] While, to be sure, the public Web has become a source of misinformation, not to mention papers ready for the plagiarizing, it has also become a useful repository for hard-to-find documents (e.g., the 1649 "Statement of the Levellers") and for images to use as teaching aids (e.g., pictures of Milton, Anthony Van Dyck's portraits of Charles I, Robert Walker's portraits of Oliver Cromwell). Other resources useful for teaching Milton include sites on Renaissance emblems (e.g., Andrea Alciato's *Book of Emblems* [www.mun.ca/alciato/]; the *English Emblem Book Project*, hosted by Penn State University [http://emblem.libraries.psu.edu/] and the *Early Modern English Dictionaries Database* [www.chass.utoronto.ca/english/emed/emedd.html]).

For the institutions that have it, Blackboard is a useful tool for posting information and images as well as for creating online communities of students. In addition, the subscription database *Early English Books Online (EEBO)* constitutes a spectacular resource for scholars and students. While not complete, the *EEBO* database contains nearly every book published in England between 1475 and 1700, including the entire Thomason Tracts collection and multiple editions of Milton's works. Books can be viewed either online or downloaded as PDF files requiring Adobe Acrobat to view them. (A teacher could, for instance, present to the class both versions of *The Ready and Easy Way*). *EEBO* also runs an undergraduate essay contest (one of the 1995 winners wrote her essay on Milton's *Paradise Lost*). Finally, the online *Oxford English Dictionary* is also very useful and can be adapted for a wide variety of classroom assignments. It is, however, available only by library subscription (although some public libraries subscribe), and like the online *Oxford Dictionary of National Biography* and *EEBO*, it is expensive.

Required and Recommended Reading for Students

The respondents varied widely in the type and amount of secondary reading they assigned or recommended for students: some professors assigned a great deal of secondary source reading, and others eschewed it altogether as a distraction. One respondent wrote that "nine out of ten times, secondary material swamps [students'] critical voices." Nonetheless, almost everybody praised Dennis Danielson's *Cambridge Companion to Milton* as exceptionally helpful for undergraduates, as they did the *Milton Encyclopedia* (Hunter et al.). Other guides to Milton include Catherine Belsey's *John Milton*; Richard Bradford's *Complete Critical Guide to Milton*; *A Companion to Milton*, edited by Thomas N. Corns; J. Holly Hanford's *A Milton Handbook*; Marjorie Nicolson's *John Milton: A Reader's Guide to His Poetry*; Lois Potter's *A Preface to Milton*; and Angelica Duran's *A Concise Companion to Milton*. Most of the respondents also recommended that students consult the various guides to the historical and literary backgrounds of Milton's England: Douglas Bush's *English Literature in the Earlier Seventeenth Century*; Christopher Hill's *Milton and the English Revolution*; Graham Parry's *The Seventeenth Century: The Intellectual and Cultural Context of English Literature, 1603–1700;* Thomas Corns's *Milton Encyclopedia*; Stephen Orgel's *The Jonsonian Masque* (for *Comus*); C. A. Patrides and Raymond Waddington's *The Age of Milton*; Debora Shuger's *The Renaissance Bible*; Nigel Smith's *Literature and Revolution in England*; Lawrence Stone's *Family, Sex, and Marriage;* Michael Wilding's "John Milton: The Early Works"; and Basil Willey's *Seventeenth Century Background.*

A small minority (three respondents) required substantial secondary source readings in their Milton courses, including C. M. Bowra's *From Virgil to Milton*; Dennis Danielson's *Milton's Good God*; Stevie Davies's *Milton*; William Empson's *Milton's God*; Stephen Fallon's *Milton among the Philosophers*; Stanley Fish's *Surprised by Sin*; the debate between Christine Froula ("When Eve" and "Pechter's Specter") and Edward Pechter in the pages of *Critical Inquiry*; Richard Helgerson's *Self-Crowned Laureates*; Hill's *Milton and the English Revolution*; David Norbrook's *Writing the English Republic*; *Re-membering Milton*, edited by Mary Nyquist and Margaret W. Ferguson; John Rumrich's *Milton Unbound*; and S. E. Sprott's *A Maske*. Instructors also often refer to the introductory essays in the various editions they use for Milton's works.

The Instructor's Library

The Milton instructor's library, which several respondents said was too vast to specify, includes all the works cited above, although respondents often pointed to Hill (*Milton*); Norbrook (*Writing*), Fish (*Surprised*), Danielson (*Cambridge Companion* and *Milton's Good God*), Empson (*Milton's God*), Corns's *Milton Encyclopedia*, and Nyquist's *Re-membering Milton*. However, if there is one piece of criticism that could be called canonical, without a doubt that would be Mary Nyquist's "The Genesis of Gendered Subjectivity in the Divorce Tracts and in *Paradise Lost*," first published in *Re-membering Milton* and frequently reprinted. There is general consensus that whether one agrees with Nyquist's thesis or not, this article is essential for framing the debate over Milton and gender when teaching the shorter poems, the divorce tracts, or the epics.

Respondents pointed out the following monographs as particularly helpful. For contextual issues and Milton's politics, the reader is directed to Sharon Achinstein, *Milton and the Revolutionary Reader*; Arthur E. Barker, *Milton and the Puritan Dilemma*; Richard Helgerson, *Forms of Nationhood*; Laura Lunger Knoppers, *Historicizing Milton: Spectacle, Power, and Poetry in Restoration England*; David Loewenstein, *Representing Revolution in Milton and His Contemporaries: Religion, Politics, and Polemics in Radical Puritanism*; David Norbrook, *Poetry and Politics in the English Renaissance*; Don M. Wolfe, *Milton in the Puritan Revolution*; and Perez Zagorin, *Ways of Lying*. Stephen Dobranski's *Milton, Authorship, and the Book Trade* provides valuable material on a different context, the material culture of books, as well as a powerful analysis of *Samson Agonistes*. For the visual contexts of Milton's work, Roland M. Frye's *Milton's Imagery and the Visual Arts* is invaluable. Christopher Ricks's *Milton's Grand Style* and Rosemond Tuve's *Images and Themes in Five Poems by Milton* still offer some of the best analyses of the sinuousness and vibrancy of Milton's verse. F. T. Prince's *The Italian Element in Milton's Verse* is a good entrée into Milton's relation to continental poetry. Stimulating treatments of various theological issues can be found in Michael Fixler's *Milton and the Kingdoms of God*, William Kerrigan's *The Prophetic Milton*, and Regina Schwartz's *Remembering and Repeating: On Milton's Theology and Poetics*.

For help with Milton's prose generally, the respondents suggested Thomas Corns's introductory book *John Milton: The Prose Works* and for an important revisionary treatment of the place of sexuality in Protestantism generally and Milton's prose in particular, see James G. Turner's *One Flesh: Paradisal Marriage and Sexual Relations in the Age of Milton*.

For *Comus*, the respondents recommended Maryann Cale McGuire's *Milton's Puritan Masque*, and for *Lycidas*, the respondents suggested Scott Elledge's *Milton's "Lycidas," Edited to Serve as an Introduction to Criticism*, and C. A. Patrides, *Milton's "Lycidas": The Tradition and the Poem*. On Milton's later poetry (*Paradise Regained* and *Samson Agonistes*), the teacher is directed toward Stanley Fish's *How Milton Works*, Mary Ann Radzinowicz's *Toward Samson Agonistes: The Growth of Milton's Mind*, Ashraf Rushdy's *The Empty Garden: The Subject of Late Milton*, and Joseph A. Wittreich's magisterial books *Interpreting Samson Agonistes* and *Shifting Contexts: Reinterpreting Samson Agonistes*.

Two essay collections were consistently mentioned by the respondents as particularly helpful to teachers and students alike: *Re-membering Milton*, edited by Nyquist and Ferguson, is among the attempts to apply theory (feminism and deconstruction) to Milton; and *The Cambridge Companion to Milton*, edited by Danielson, contains superb introductory essays on all aspects of Milton's poetry and prose. The respondents also singled out these anthologies: *Politics, Poetics, and Hermeneutics in Milton's Prose*, edited by Loewenstein and Turner; *Milton and Heresy*, edited by Stephen Dobranski and John Rumrich; *Milton and Republicanism*, edited by David Armitage Armand Himy, and Quentin Skinner; *Milton and the Imperial Vision*, edited by Balachandra Rajan and Elizabeth Sauer; *Literary Milton*, edited by Diana Benet and Michael Lieb; *Achievements of the Left Hand: Essays on the Prose of John Milton*, edited by Lieb and John Shawcross; *Milton and the Terms of Liberty*, edited by Graham Parry and Joad Raymond; and *Arenas of Conflict*, edited by Kristin Pruitt and Charles Durham (see McColgan and Durham). *Critical Essays on John Milton*, edited by Christopher Kendrick, and *John Milton* (Longman Critical Readers series), edited by Annabel Patterson, reprint important articles on

Milton. Like *Re-membering Milton*, Patterson's anthology shows how contemporary theoretical developments illuminate Milton in new ways, and short introductions from the contributors detail each essay's origins and what larger point the author tried to make.

Individual respondents called attention to the following essays, which I present organized by subject.

For general background

Cedric Brown, "The Legacy of the Late Jacobean Period."

For poetry

M. H. Abrams, "Five Types of Lycidas"

Bruce Boehrer, " 'Lycidas': The Pastoral Elegy as Same-Sex Epithalamium"

Barbara Breasted, "*Comus* and the Castlehaven Scandal"

Gordon Campbell, "Shakespeare and the Youth of Milton"

Michael Dietz, " 'Thus Sang the Uncouth Swain': Pastoral, Prophecy, and Historicism in *Lycidas*"

J. Martin Evans, "The Birth of the Author: Milton's Poetic Self-Construction" and " 'Lycidas' "

Stanley Fish, chapters 10 and 11 of *How Milton Works* (for *Paradise Regained*)

Roy Flannagan, ed. Comus: *Contexts* (Special issue of *Milton Quarterly*)

Alastair Fowler, "*Paradise Regained*: Some Problems of Style"

Christine Froula, "When Eve Reads Milton: Undoing the Canonical Economy" and "Pechter's Specter: Milton's Bogey Writ Small; or, Why Is He Afraid of Virginia Woolf?"

Linda Gregerson, "Colonials Write the Nation: Spenser, Milton, and England on the Margins"

E. R. Gregory, "Milton's Protestant Sonnet Lady: Revisions in the Donna Angelicata Tradition"

Allen Grossman, "Milton's Sonnet 'On the Late Massacre in Piedmont': A Note on the Vulnerability of Persons in a Revolutionary Situation"

Randall Ingram, "The Writing Poet: The Descent from Song in *The Poems of Mr. John Milton, Both English and Latin*"

Victoria Kahn, "The Metaphorical Contract in Milton's *Tenure of Kings and Magistrates*"

Lloyd Kermode, " 'To the Shores of Life': Textual Recovery in *Lycidas*"

Douglas Lanier, "Encryptions: Reading Milton Reading Jonson Reading Shakespeare"

Leah S. Marcus, "John Milton's Voice" and "Milton's Anti-Laudian Masque"

Jerome Mazzaro, "Gaining Authority: John Milton at Sonnets"

Edward Pechter, "When Pechter Reads Froula Pretending She's Eve Reading Milton; or, New Feminist Is but Old Priest Writ Large"

Paul Stevens, "Subversion and Wonder in Milton's Epitaph 'On Shakespeare'"

Blair Worden, "Milton, *Samson Agonistes*, and the Restoration"

For prose

David Aers and Bob Hodge, "'Rational Burning': Milton on Sex and Marriage"

Thomas Corns, "Milton's Prose"

Stanley Fish, "Wanting a Supplement: The Question of Interpretation in Milton's Early Prose"

Janet Halley, "Female Autonomy in Milton's Sexual Poetics"

John F. Huntley, "The Images of Poet and Poetry in Milton's *The Reason of Church Government*"

John Illo, "The Misreading of Milton"

Laura Lunger Knoppers, "Late Political Prose"

Annabel Patterson, "'No Meer Amatorious Novel'?"

Paul Stevens, "Milton's Janus-Faced Nationalism: Soliloquy, Subject, and the Modern Nation State"

Blair Worden, "Milton and Marchamont Nedham" and "Milton's Republicanism and the Tyranny of Heaven"

Shari A. Zimmerman, "Disaffection, Dissimulation, and the Uncertain Ground of Silent Dismission: Juxtaposing John Milton and Elizabeth Cary"

NOTES

Unless indicated otherwise, all references to Milton's poetry and prose throughout this volume are to *The Riverside Milton*, edited by Roy Flannagan.

[1] The first printings of this edition were marred by significant numbers of typographical errors and omissions of lines. While these problems have been subsequently corrected, the faulty books still circulate through the used-book market, and so instructors who decide to use Flannagan should warn their students.

[2] Alan Rudrum's essay "Milton Scholarship and the *Agon* over *Samson Agonistes*" is among this site's most popular downloads.

[3] Web searches on the Vulgate and Geneva Bibles will turn up links to sites with these texts as well, but as these sites seem more inspired by religious zeal than scholarship, their probity cannot be assured.

Part Two

APPROACHES

Introduction: Which Courses and What Gets Taught

On the one hand, the surveys demonstrate that Milton's poetry and prose show up in a wide variety of undergraduate and graduate classes in a wide variety of institutions. As one might expect, these works are taught most often in senior and graduate seminars devoted exclusively to Milton, and almost every respondent stated that their institution has at least one such course. Occasionally, an institution will have more than one. Georgia State University has several (an undergraduate course, an honors seminar, a seminar for English majors, and a graduate course), as does the University of Kentucky (seminars on *Comus*, the prose, *Samson Agonistes*, and *Paradise Regained*).[1] Again, as one would expect, Milton's poetry (exclusive of *Paradise Lost*) and prose also show up in period surveys of Renaissance literature, seventeenth-century literature, seventeenth-century poetry or prose, and in various special topics courses. At Hofstra University, these works are featured in courses on the "problem" of woman in the early modern period and on women in scripture. At the University of Arizona, the poetry and prose are taught in an upper-division course on Milton, such seminars as Gender, Religion, and Politics in Early Modern England and Land, Nation, Empire, as they are at City College of New York in Spenser, Milton, and the Creation of Literary Tradition. Milton's poetry and prose also figure prominently in a number of courses at Hunter College. In addition to the period survey and the course on Milton, Hunter offers three master's courses that include Milton's works: Milton: Lyric and Dramatic Poems; Seventeenth-Century Literature; and The Renaissance Pastoral. I have offered Milton and the English Revolution at San Diego State University and at the Claremont Graduate University.

It was particularly heartening to see that Milton also has a place in introductory and composition courses. At the University of Connecticut, Milton figures in Introduction to Poetry, and the respondent from Chowan College reported that he uses some of Milton's shorter poems in his freshman introductory class on composition and literature. At Indira Gandhi National Open University in New Delhi, Milton's shorter poetry and prose figure in their undergraduate class Understanding Poetry, and the graduate course British Poetry.

However, if Milton's shorter poetry and prose have a presence in a large number of courses devoted to Renaissance literature and in a number of freshman and sophomore courses, the range of works taught is surprisingly narrow. While, as noted above, almost every university and college has a course on Milton's works, the University of Kentucky is the only institution I know of to offer courses concentrating exclusively on Milton's prose, *Comus*, *Paradise Regained*, or *Samson Agonistes*. (By way of contrast, seminars on Shakespeare's *The Tempest* are not unusual). In other words, Milton's shorter poetry and prose are, with one exception, never given a course unto themselves, never studied individually, but always as part of a larger context (usually *Paradise Lost*).

As the list below will show, the most popular of Milton's shorter poetry are, in order, "Lycidas," the Nativity Ode, *Comus*, and "L'Allegro" / "Il Penseroso" (the percentage refers to the proportion of the 46 respondents who teach the work in question):

"Lycidas," 85%

Nativity Ode, 75%

Comus, 67%

"L'Allegro" / "Il Penseroso," 57%

Samson Agonistes, 32%
sonnet 19 ("When I consider"), 32%

sonnet 7 ("How soon hath Time"), 28%
Paradise Regained, 28%
"The Passion," 28%

Ad Patrem, 25%

all the poetry, 21%

"At a Solemn Musick," 17%
sonnet 23 ("Methought I saw"), 17%
"On Shakespeare," 17%

sonnet 18 ("On the Late Massacher in Piemont"), 14%
"Upon the Circumcision," 14%

"On Time," 10%

"On the University Carrier," 7%
"Another on the Same," 7%
sonnet 8 ("Captain or Colonel"), 7%
"Damon's Epitaph," 7%
"At a Vacation Exercise," 7%

Most of the 1645 edition of *Poems of Mr. John Milton* 3%
"An Epitaph upon the Marchioness of Winchester," 3%
elegy 6 ("To Charles Diodati"), 3%
sonnet 1 ("O Nightingale"), 3%
sonnet 2 ("Beautiful Lady"), 3%
sonnet 3 ("As on a Rugged Mountain"), 3%
"On the New Forcers of Conscience," 3%

Of the prose, *Areopagitica* and *The Doctrine and Discipline of Divorce* are by far the most popular, and the biographical digression in *The Reason of Church Government* comes in a distant third:

Areopagitica, 78%

The Doctrine and Discipline of Divorce, 50%

The Reason of Church Government (biographical digression), 39%

Of Education, 32%

The Tenure of Kings and Magistrates, 28%

The Ready and Easy Way to Establish a Free Commonwealth, 25%

The Second Defense of the English People, 21%

An Apology for Smectymnuus, 14%
On Christian Doctrine, 14%

"Letter to a Friend," 7%
Eikonoklastes, 7%
Tetrachordon, 7%
Prolusions, 7%

To summarize, while a small number of Milton's shorter poems and prose are frequently taught ("Lycidas," the Nativity Ode, *Comus,* "L'Allegro" / "Il Penseroso," *Areopagitica, The Doctrine and Discipline of Divorce,* and part of *The Reason of Church Government*), the rest of Milton's considerable oeuvre appears in the classroom only sporadically. The infrequency of teachers' putting *Samson Agonistes* and *Paradise Regained* on the syllabus was especially surprising (one respondent said that she teaches one or the other, never both).

Difficulties and Approaches

Virtually all the respondents agreed that teaching Milton's shorter poetry and prose to undergraduates and graduate students alike can be ferociously difficult. And while there is some variety in the responses, overall the problems faced by students boil down to two main hurdles: students lack the requisite knowledge of biblical, classical, and historical contexts, and they lack training in close reading of poetry of any sort. The problem is compounded by the difficulty of supplying these necessary contexts without, as one respondent put it, giving the appearance that "only dry-as-dust PhDs are authorized to have a response in the first place." This pitfall received support from another respondent, whose main obstacle in the classroom was students' "previous exposure to Milton in survey classes," where his work had seemed "boring and dry." Furthermore, in addition to being generally unfamiliar with genres in which Milton worked, today's students often have expectations not conducive to understanding the poetry. As one respondent put it, they "have the same trouble with Milton's poems that they do with most pre-Romantic poetry. That is, they have trouble with poetry that isn't primarily about feelings and are mystified by formal and public contexts."

As for the prose, the respondents also pointed to the problem of allusions and context: "students need guidance with specific historical circumstances, references, backgrounds," as one person wrote. However, the respondents unanimously agreed on the the primary impediment to teaching Milton's prose: his labyrinthine, Latinate syntax. One teacher writes, "[T]he main problems are the long syntax, the lack of short paragraphs, the length, and the density of ideas and language." Another respondent made the interesting point that as a result of these formidable obstacles, students have difficulty with Milton as a "speaker and writer and with the audience he addresses." They cannot understand, in other words, why Milton—or anyone, for that matter—would write in this style, and they cannot comprehend what sort of audience would understand Milton's prose. Another respondent pointed to how popular political culture gets in the way of reading Milton with any facility: "most of my students do not have a firm grasp of argumentation, as they take their models from television and radio talk shows (all invective, all the time) . . . and most students lack a strong historical sense, [having] only a sketchy knowledge of any history beyond American history (and that itself is limited). . . ."

Fortunately, while the respondents recognized the manifold difficulties of teaching Milton's shorter poetry and prose, they also universally agreed that the works ought to be taught, and in addition to the essays in this volume, the responses provided a wealth of suggestions for overcoming the students' problems with language and history.

The respondents situated these works in various contexts. To stimulate interest in the texts themselves and demonstrate their "relevance," one respondent suggested using *Paradise Lost* as the spine of the course, teaching the shorter poems and prose as they relate thematically to the book under discussion. For example, when reading the catalog of demons in book 2, the class also reads the Nativity Ode. The problem of free will in book 3 creates an opportunity to read *Areopagitica*, and alongside the discussion of paradisal marriage in book 4 the class reads *The Doctrine and Discipline of Divorce*. The problem of this approach is that it subordinates the shorter poetry and prose to Milton's epic, implying that these works are not worthy by themselves. One approach that works especially well for the prose is to be, as a respondent put it, "shamelessly presentist" in teaching these works, "trying to relate the questions [raised by the prose especially] to contemporary issues of freedom of the press, hereditary hierarchies, meritocracy, and sexual equity." Along these lines, one professor suggested beginning "with the sexiest prose first (*The Doctrine and Discipline of Divorce*). . . . [Students] love biography, [and the instructor should emphasize] that Milton's 'human concerns' are not all that different from our own." A third possibility, one that works for the poetry, is to keep reminding the students how important Milton's works are to the history of English poetry: "I *always* read Milton next to precursors and descendants, to suggest how innovative and fertile, provocative and formative his thinking is for all English poets."

Other respondents suggested allowing the students to, in effect, teach themselves by becoming "the 'experts for the day,' responsible for explaining all the allusions, etc." to the class. This approach has the added advantage of teaching students how to use the reference section in the library, and it can work well either with students individually or in groups. Another respondent suggested a similar strategy that involves "making use of the *OED*" and a Bible, having students look up the allusions as they occur, and then discussing their meaning or relevance. A third person asks students to purchase Isabel Rivers's *Classical and Christian Ideas in English Renaissance Poetry* as a reference for the classical allusions. The overall point of this approach is "to empower [students] enough so that they might feel able to wade through, on their own, a demanding line of verse and what appears to be an impossibly difficult sentence."

Yet for all their variety, the approaches taken by the respondents have two features in common. The first is an intense encounter with the works themselves—that is to say, teaching students to read slowly and closely, paying attention to each verbal detail. The second is the teacher's introduction of at least some of the relevant historical details and allusions. "The most successful strategy," in other words, "is still 'chalk and talk'—lecture-room classroom exposition," as one distinguished teacher puts it. Another writes that she stimulates classroom discussion through "detailed summaries and selected paraphrases; for prose, detailed timelines, and lectures." Despite the difficulties, then, in teaching Milton, many persistent teachers would probably agree with a member of the MLA Publications Committee, who wrote, "I've taught Milton in various classes over the years and find that students generally come to love him."

Theoretical Approaches

As the summary above might indicate, teachers of Milton are more concerned with getting their students to understand the literal meaning of Milton's shorter poetry and prose than with inculcating theoretical sophistication in their classrooms. When survey participants were asked, "What kind of critical approaches or methodologies have you found most helpful in teaching these texts? What approaches or methodologies do the students find helpful?" almost all answered, "Close reading." The reason is not so much theoretical conservatism as pedagogical experience. It is hard to present students a Lacanian or Derridean analysis when they cannot understand the basic sense of what Milton is saying. Yet if close reading is the main activity in the Milton classroom, it is supported by a wide range of approaches and methodologies. Given how deeply embedded Milton was in the controversies of his time, it comes as little surprise that many respondents supplemented close reading with historicism of both the new and old varieties: they supply context and then investigate in class how Milton intervenes in and becomes part of that context. Many respondents also mentioned that feminist approaches work particularly well with the divorce tracts and certain of Milton's poems (*Comus* in particular).

The responses also indicated that theoretical and methodological diversity characterize the teaching of Milton. Approaches include mythological criticism (Jung, Campbell), biblical studies, deconstruction, biographical and psychoanalytic criticism, philosophy, Fish's "affective stylistics" (this one was controversial—one respondent replied, "Most emphatically *not* Stanley Fish"), postcolonial criticism, formalist criticism, and reading aloud. Finally, notice should be taken of an event staged at some schools that does not specifically concern Milton's shorter poetry and prose but has a track record of generating considerable interest and publicity in Milton: the Milton marathon, in which the entirety of *Paradise Lost* is usually read aloud, often with different voices for the various characters (e.g., students dramatize the dialogue of Satan, Sin, and Death). *Samson Agonistes* and *Paradise Regained* could be similarly performed.

Approaches to Teaching Milton's Shorter Poetry and Prose provides a road map for teaching these works. Consequently, this anthology is divided into five parts. The first section, "Approaching Milton's Poetry and Prose," features approaches that cover both genres. "Approaching Milton's Poetry" and "Approaching Milton's Prose" cover each genre separately. The essays in the last two sections of the book, "Teaching Specific Texts: Poetry" and "Teaching Specific Texts: Prose," suggest strategies for teaching individual works.

"Approaching Milton's Poetry and Prose" begins with James Fleming's essay on how one can use biography as a way of opening up Milton's prose and "Lycidas." Andrew Escobedo suggests how contemporary nationalism can be used to understand Milton's conception of the English nation, as demonstrated by the prose works (among others, the two *Defenses* and *The History of Britain*) and such poems as "Lycidas," "Mansus," and "Damon's Epitaph," and how Milton's nationalism can help students understand nationalism in our time. Catherine Gimelli Martin turns to the especially controversial topic of gender in Milton's works, and she uses the question, "Is Milton's view of femininity more biblical, Augustinian, 'masculinist,' or early modern feminist?" as the basis for teaching Milton's sonnets, the divorce tracts, *Comus*, and *Samson Agonistes*. Jason Rosenblatt suggests the utility of looking at the Hebraism of Milton's works (usually considered as exclusively Christian), especially the prose of the 1640s and *Samson Agonistes*. Angelica Duran provides suggestions for including examples of Milton's shorter poetry and prose in the undergraduate survey course.

The next section, "Approaching Milton's Poetry," concentrates on Milton's shorter verse. Stephen Dobranski suggests that by starting a Milton course with a poem on an already familiar writer, "On Shakespeare," the instructor can ease student anxiety about an unfamiliar and probably intimidating one (Milton) while also introducing the class to some basic principles of textual studies. Wendy Furman-Adams delineates ways of using the visual arts for teaching Milton's Nativity Ode and *Samson Agonistes*. Albert C. Labriola looks at how one can use an examination of "At a Solemn Musick" (1633), sonnet 7 ("How soon hath Time" [1632]), sonnet 19 ("When I consider" [1652?]), "On the Morn-

ing of Christ's Nativity" (1629), and "Lycidas" (1637)—the poems are deliberately taught out of their order of composition—to illustrate how Milton views
the relationship of humankind and the godhead. Jennifer Lewin demonstrates
the benefits for class and instructor of teaching Milton's sonnets, in particular,
sonnet 23 ("Methought I saw"), in the context of the Petrarchan tradition. Elizabeth Sagaser shows how to take a discussion of time into a discussion of meter
to teach "How soon hath Time," "When I consider," "Methought I saw," "L'Allegro" / "Il Penseroso," and the Nativity Ode. Elizabeth Sauer explains how Milton's sonnets, in particular, the "twin-born" Trinity College Manuscript sonnets
11 and 12 (1646–47; printed in 1673), can be used to teach the young Milton's
political and religious engagements and to provide an entrée into the complex
radical politics of his time.

The third section, "Approaching Milton's Prose," provides multiple avenues
for instruction, starting with John Shawcross's detailed road map for teaching
the antiprelatical tracts. Jameela Lares confronts a fundamental problem for
the teaching of Milton: students are often unaware of the history of Bible translation and the Reformation hermeneutics so crucial to Milton and his contemporaries. Lares provides a brief overview of these issues and offers several
strategies for teaching Milton's uses of the Bible. William Kolbrener examines
how the postmodern emphasis on diversity and multiplicity can help students
examine Milton's sense of community and difference, as evidenced in *Areopagitica*. Elizabeth Skerpan-Wheeler suggests teaching the development of
Milton's political self in the late prose by asking students to keep their own
"commonplace books" as they read, while Alison Chapman uses the concept of
discipline as a theme for teaching Milton's prose (*The Reason of Church Government*) and some of the poetry (*Comus* especially). Peter C. Herman looks at
how one can use the American constitution as a way into the so-called ancient
constitution and, subsequently, *The Tenure of Kings and Magistrates*.

The next two sections focus on strategies for teaching specific pieces of poetry and prose. John Rumrich's chapter on using the Nativity Ode to introduce
students to the study of Milton is complemented by Richard Rambuss, who illuminates the Nativity Ode through an emphasis on Christ's corporeality, with
reference to other seventeenth-century poets on the Incarnation as well as the
images in Leo Steinberg's *The Sexuality of Christ*. Lynne Greenberg discusses
teaching *Comus* through the lens of early modern gender politics, especially
the legal context. Next, David Mikics looks at how teaching Milton's companion poems, "L'Allegro" and "Il Penseroso," "as a center or source of literary
history"—that is to say, not only analyzing the complexities of the poems themselves (discussing, e.g., whether they are best approached as a diptych or a sequence), but also showing how Milton draws on earlier poets and becomes the
source for later ones—opens up these works for undergraduates. Curtis Perry
suggests beginning a Milton class with "On Shakespeare," since the familiarity
of the poem's subject helps students find Milton more accessible, and he concentrates on the poem's allusion to Niobe, showing how the reference helps

students "see how intertextual allusions work as interpretive cruxes that can lead beyond the inert facts provided in the footnotes in any modern edition." Bruce Boehrer uses sonnet 19 ("When I consider") to introduce students not just to Milton but also to the techniques of close reading.

Matthew Davis and Mark K. Fulk suggest approaches for teaching Milton's most popular work, "Lycidas." Davis uses Samuel Johnson's critique of "Lycidas" as unoriginal and fundamentally insincere to help students understand Milton's use of the pastoral genre. Fulk uses genre as a way of teaching "Lycidas" in a general education classroom consisting of nonmajors, where the problem of getting students to engage with Milton is compounded by the issue of class. These students are primarily urban, working-class, and nontraditional, whereas Milton is often seen as the embodiment of elitism. The key to reaching this group, Fulk suggests, "lies in conveying to students the concept of genre and the specifics of pastoral poetry."

The next group of essays provides strategies for *Paradise Regained* and *Samson Agonistes*, poems that share the paradoxical position of being among the least taught, yet most important, of Milton's works. Barbara Lewalski highlights "the intellectual drama in the exchanges between Jesus and Satan and the ways in which Satan's temptations enable the hero, Jesus, to discover who he is and what he is to do." Lewalski also suggests a variety of teaching strategies, including pointed comparisons with *Paradise Lost* (which it inevitably follows) and situating *Paradise Regained* in its Restoration context. R. Allen Shoaf demonstrates how an emphasis on the poem's alliteration, helped along with the use of TACT (Text Analysis Computing Tools—freeware available from the University of Toronto), significantly increases the student's involvement with the poem. Jeffrey Shoulson suggests that reserving time for teaching *Paradise Regained* and *Samson Agonistes* has many advantages and that teaching these works as twin texts rather than as discrete units "not only provides the opportunity to review and consolidate many of the lessons learned in a study of the earlier poetry, it also reveals the limits and problematics of those lessons." David Loewenstein provides a map for teaching the Dalila passage in *Samson Agonistes*, an episode particularly rich in pedagogical opportunities since the critical tradition is divided on the question of how to interpret Dalila and since the passage contains echoes of Milton's earlier poetry (especially *Comus*) and prose. Teaching Dalila can thus function as a summa for both Milton and the class. Joseph Wittreich concentrates on a different issue: the problem of contemporary and, by extension, biblical terrorism: in his essay, Wittreich shows how Milton can be used to help students think about the confluence of war and religion. "Is Milton's poem a manual for killing?" Wittreich asks. "Is it a polemic in behalf of war? Is it a record of history repeating itself, grinding down and turning over again into its former self—or of history liberated, renewed, and transfigured?"

The final section concerns the prose. Gardner Campbell argues that we do students a disservice by teaching the digression in *The Reason of Church*

Government out of the context of the rest of the pamphlet. Furthermore, the connections "between Milton's poetic and political imaginations offer enticing possibilities for the classroom, as they may lead students to consider their own agency, citizenship, and identity in terms of their own growing authority as writers in a community of learning." John Leonard notes that few early modern texts can be more relevant today than Milton's *Areopagitica*, and he outlines how to bring out this text's complexities by arguing against John Illo's thesis that Milton favors the suppression of opinions different than his own. Gina Hausknecht teaches *The Tenure of Kings and Magistrates* by bringing the text into dialogue with contemporary issues about citizenship and political involvement as well as with excerpts from other seventeenth-century debates about the direction of the English commonwealth. The point, as Hausknecht writes, is to let students hear "the voices with which Milton was in conversation and [to] restore the complexity erased by posterity." Laura Lunger Knoppers suggests opening up *Eikonoklastes* by trying, through images and selections from other texts, to re-create the debate that Milton enters with this work. Shari Zimmerman offers a number of strategies for teaching Milton's divorce tracts—in particular, *The Doctrine and Discipline of Divorce*. While her students prefer to speculate about Milton's personal life (always a rich topic), Zimmerman proposes moving the class "beyond a narrowly defined preoccupation with the personal to a more broadly ranging consideration of the hermeneutical—to a consideration, that is, of what Milton is doing with biblical material he so selectively cites, elaborates, links, and deploys in his theorizing about matrimony and divorce." David V. Urban offers a method for including *De Doctrina Christiana* that focuses on teaching the debate over Milton's authorship of this text. Matthew Woodcock brings the volume to a close with an essay on teaching *The Ready and Easy Way* through the lens of utopian literature.

In sum, the essays in the volume collectively argue for the wisdom, even necessity, of teaching Milton's shorter poetry and prose—not only in courses on Milton alone but also in Renaissance survey courses and even in general education courses introducing students to literature. They demonstrate that Milton's shorter poetry and prose constitute a key background for understanding *Paradise Lost* (the centerpiece of any course on Milton) and that the works help students see the tremendous relevance the issues of Milton's era continue to have today.

NOTES

Unless indicated otherwise, all references to Milton's poetry and prose throughout this volume are to *The Riverside Milton*, edited by Roy Flannagan.

[1] However, it seems that the presence of multiple courses on Milton is driven by the presence of a distinguished Miltonist at these institutions, Stephen Dobranski at GSU, and John Shawcross at the University of Kentucky.

Biographic Milton:
Teaching the Undead Author

James Dougal Fleming

The Milton classroom is a profoundly author-centered place. In poetic passages such as the expostulations of "Lycidas" (1637), the invocations to *Paradise Lost* (1667), and the lamentations of *Samson Agonistes* (1671), students often hear echoes and allegories of an authorial personality. In the polemical prose, they repeatedly find themselves face to face with (what seems to be) a version of that same personality. Finally, if and when they turn to Milton scholarship, students find their impressions reinforced by the discipline's traditional and ongoing biographical inclination (Campbell, *Milton* and "Shakespeare"; Darbishire; Diekhoff; Evans, *Miltonic Moment*; R. Fallon; S. Fallon, *Milton* and "Spur"; French; Kerrigan, *Sacred Complex*; Labriola; Leonard, "Milton's Vow"; Lieb and Labriola; Martz, *Milton*; Orgel and Goldberg; Rumrich, "Milton's Arianism," *Milton Unbound*, and "Provenance"). In literary-theoretical terms, this is something of a problem. After all, authors are popularly supposed to have died a generation ago (S. Burke; Wittreich, " 'Reading' "). In pedagogical terms, however, the undead Milton is an opportunity, for he allows a mode of reading that teachers will find productive, because students find it both congenial and perplexing.

Let us begin with congeniality. Students are just plain interested in the biographic Milton: in his combative personality, his radical politics, and his overwhelming sense of vocation. Milton, moreover, gives them ample opportunity to pursue their interest, especially through the autobiographical digressions of his radical prose. The chief texts in this regard are the *Apology for*

Smectymnuus (1642), in which Milton is "put unwillingly to molest the publick view with the vindication of a private name" (*Complete Prose Works* 1: 870); *The Reason of Church Government* (1642), with its excited plans for writings "doctrinal and exemplary to a Nation" (*Riverside* 923); and *The Second Defense of the English People* (1654), in which the poet and polemicist narrates his life as a chapter in the story of the English revolution (1114–18).

The list need not stop there. It might go on to include the *Defense of Himself* (1655), Milton's monomaniacal follow-up to the *Second Defense*. It might also include, from an earlier polemical phase, the invective masterpiece *Colasterion* (1645), into which Milton pours all his highly personalized disappointment over the reception of his divorce tracts. Indeed, if we are willing to expand or loosen our definition of reflexive authorial statement, the autobiographical reading list might include *The Doctrine and Discipline of Divorce* (1644). Students find the story of the poet's first marriage—to a "royalist teeny-bopper," as my teacher Edward Tayler used to say—irresistible. (I often recommend that they choose Robert Graves's *Wife to Mr. Milton* as pleasure reading for the end of the semester.) Irresistible to them, too, is the literary-critical supposition that the divorce tract must in part be about that first marriage. On this reading, the "he who" of the *Doctrine and Discipline*—frustrated by his own virtues, snookered by the morality of sexual (in)experience—becomes a thinly disguised avatar for a Miltonic "I" (Patterson, " 'No Meer Amatorious Novel'?"). Since first-person avatar is, moreover, a working definition of poetic voice, the autobiographical prose thereby connects to the poetry, even as the formal difference between the two tends to fade.

At which point things begin to be perplexing. For the poet's autobiographical tendencies arise in the Milton classroom, usually, as some kind of support for the reading of his poetry. Milton appears to be answering the eternal student prayer for a poet who will explain himself, in the cool element of prose. Yet the prose is so voluminous and so much given to self-explanation that it can crowd out the poetry that students are hoping to have explained. Meanwhile, Milton's self-explanations come themselves to seem quasi-poetic, in a seventeenth-century prose style that students find (if such a thing be possible) even more difficult than the period's poetry. So in moving from Milton's reflexive poetry to his autobiographical prose, students have moved, not from a problem of reading to its solution, but from a problem of reading to a worse problem.

From the teacher's perspective, this is all to the good. Students have become involved in a hermeneutic finger puzzle of their own design. The teacher can, in good conscience, encourage students' attempts to free themselves, because their inevitable failure will involve a lot of learning. No doubt the same advice could be given about the works of almost any author. No doubt students are up against conundrums of biographical criticism—biocriticism, I like to call it—that demand, in the last analysis, theoretical illumination. Yet Milton is especially suited to this sort of dialectical process; not only because he offers the biocritical option so insistently and persuasively (S. Fallon, "Spur") but also because the biographical material he offers is so confounded and contradictory.

Miltonic ideology is the classic example of this biographical difficulty (Corns, "Milton's Quest," "Ideology," "Italianate Humanist," *Uncloistered Virtue*, and "Milton before 'Lycidas' "; Dzelzainis; C. Hill, *Milton*; Lewalski, "Milton: Political Beliefs," "How Radical," and *Life*; Loewenstein, " 'Fair Offspring' "; Norbrook, "Politics" and *Writing*; Patterson, " 'Forc'd Fingers' "). The poet who writes *Comus* for Charles I's Welsh viceroy goes on to write propaganda for Oliver Cromwell; the praiser of James I in *In Quintum Novembris* (c. 1625) becomes the burier of Charles in *Eikonoklastes* (1649). By the late 1640s, it is clear that Milton has become a committed radical. In *Eikonoklastes* and its antecedent tract *The Tenure of Kings and Magistrates*, he meticulously defends the execution of Charles and excoriates the moderate parliamentarians who deposed the king but balked at finishing the job. It is equally clear, however, that the younger Milton was not a radical. His poetry of the 1620s and 1630s, for example, is either apolitical or (what is often the same thing in the seventeenth century) complacently conservative (Corns, "Milton before 'Lycidas' "). Some critics, to be sure, have denied the validity of this evidence, insisting instead that the Anglican and royalist early poetry is really (if we look hard enough) Puritan and republican (Lewalski, "Milton: Political Beliefs," "How Radical," and *Life*; Norbrook, "Politics" and *Writing*; Wilding, *Dragon's Teeth*). But these readings are, for the most part, unpersuasive. There is a pattern of alteration in the course of Milton's career. There are major changes of politics; there are changes, apparently concomitant, of audience and genre.

This position is useful in the classroom because it provides students with interpretative gaps that they have to fill or bridge themselves. They have to determine at what biographical point Milton's poetry begins to reflect a radical agenda. They have to figure out what hermeneutic techniques will allow them to make this determination. Milton is so mercurial, moreover, that the interpretative prize tends to slip away as soon as it is grasped. Thus the biocritical turn is not stale or terminal but significantly recursive and productively interminable.

Take "Lycidas." For all biocritics, it is a crucial marker, a pivot in the tracing of Miltonic ideology. It is not, by any means, the end of the trajectory; the angry Protestant who eulogizes Edward King is not yet the Independent or even necessarily the Presbyterian of Milton's subsequent tracts. But the elegy does appear, "[b]lind mouthes" and all (104; line 119), to be a manifestly political text (Leonard, " 'Trembling Ears' "; M. Nicolson 99; Patrides). Reading politics into Milton's juvenilia is an arduous task; it gets much easier with "Lycidas." When we consider Milton before the writing of the elegy, it is possible to deny that he is aware of or concerned about the impending English crisis. When we consider Milton after he has written the elegy, we can deny his politicization no longer. This far, and no further.

I have taught, with good results, J. Martin Evans's influential version of this Tillyardian argument (" 'Lycidas' "). Evans points out that before 1638 Milton's actions and writings (insofar as we can reconstruct them) suggest poetic vocation and social reclusion. The drowning of the clergyman and minor poet Edward King, however, presents a turning point in Milton's conception of his life and work. We know that the publication of "Lycidas" in *Justa Edouardo King* coincided with the inauguration of a new phase in Milton's life. The years of postgraduate seclusion in Hammersmith and Horton came to an end in 1638. "Lycidas," it seems, both announces and enacts this change. The poem transfers Milton from *otium* to action, from pastoral retreat to the Protestant "wars of truth" (Evans, " 'Lycidas' " 52).

There is just one problem with this convincing scheme. Milton did not, in 1638, turn to any "wars of truth." The wars were certainly there, in the Laudian oppressions and the Puritan response to them. Indeed, the conflict in British society was about to be considerably magnified, and nobody who cared could fail to be concerned. In July 1637 there were riots in Edinburgh over the introduction of a Laudian prayer book. In the following March, the Scottish clergy signed a national covenant opposing Laud's reforms. Scottish defiance soon led to the (so-called) First Bishops' War; the battle for the hungry sheep, surely, was about to begin. By May 1641 Milton had joined it, with the publication of his first pro-Presbyterian and anti-episcopal pamphlet (*Of Reformation in England*). He wrote and published similar pamphlets until episcopacy was dead and buried; he then went on in this public vein, to other issues and other tracts. In short, there is a perceptible turn in Milton's life and work to a progressive, public mission—in 1641. But not in 1638. In that year, Milton did not walk out of Arcadia to put on the Protestant armor of God. He walked, instead, onto a ship at Dover and, just a month or two after the Scottish Covenant, left England for an extended tour, via France, of Catholic Italy.

The Italian tour is a perennial fascination of Milton biography (Arthos; Benet; Chaney, *Grand Tour* and "Visit"; Cinquemani; Corns, "Italianate Humanist"; Di Cesare; Liljegren). The orthodox disciplinary tendency has been to explain away or at least smooth over its ideological and confessional corners (Corns, "Italianate Humanist"; C. Hill, *Milton*; Lewalski, *Life* 87–119). As a teacher, I can only recommend the opposite tendency—whatever the scholarly truth of the matter. Students are put to sleep by authorial consistency. They are rendered alert by suggestions of inconsistency and disjunction. So one might propose that, while it is easy to understand Milton's attraction to the Italian humanist past, it is hard to ignore, in his particular biographical context, the all-too-human present. In Barberini Italy, as W. R. Parker puts it, "vice was practised openly": "courtesans were honored by all men with respectful salutations (*Milton: A Biography* 1: 181). In Rome, the English visitor attended a singing recital by the reputed mistress of two cardinals and subsequently wrote three poems to her (Campbell, *Milton* 64–65). The poet of 1638 had declined to sport "with Amaryllis in the shade" ("Lycidas," line 68). The zealot of 1641 would abhor "mixed dancing" and all the "luxurious and ribald feasts of *Baal-peor*" (*Of Reformation* [*Complete Prose* 1: 589]). Between these two positions, I usually argue, there is a prima facie moral congruity: we could attempt to draw a line between them and declare part of this biocritical territory mapped. But Italy, chronologically, is directly in the way. And to this series—"Lycidas," respected popish courtesans, *Of Reformation*—there is a prima facie moral incongruity. Confessional incongruity is also evident. The journey took Milton, as he put it, into "the very stronghold of the Pope" (*Second Defense* 1116). There the poet had a private audience with Cardinal Francesco Barberini, chief adviser to his uncle, Pope Urban VIII. Like other visiting Englishmen, Milton dined at the Jesuit College in Rome (Parker, *Milton* 1: 173, 2: 1228–29; Campbell, *Milton* 62–63). Milton's literary friends, meanwhile, seem not to have been resistant to or even ambivalent about the Roman way. As A. M. Cinquemani points out, one was "a committed and active churchman," another "a defender of the Catholic state and opponent of Protestantism," and yet another "a censor of the Roman Inquisition and author of perhaps forty religious works" (2). The problem here is not that Milton, as a Protestant intellectual, found it gainful to fraternize with his Catholic counterparts. It is not even that Milton as a godly poet found reason (research, maybe) to walk among the sons of Belial. The specifically biocritical problem (making this matter pedagogically interesting as an interconnection between Milton's texts and his life) is that the poet, as a newly awakened anti-Laudian radical—an activist, a zealot, a poet-priest-shepherd—proceeds from the turning point of "Lycidas" directly to a popish embrace.

Something of this puzzle is reflected in Milton's account of the Italian journey, to which my students and I usually turn at this point. In his *Second Defense of the English People*, Milton claims, in effect, that he was fighting for liberty in 1639—and doing so by traveling in the land of Catholic authoritarianism. This claim is clearly difficult to sustain. Yet it underwrites Milton's bizarre emphasis on how long he took on his return journey, after hearing of impending civil war at home—the very apocalypse prophesied in "Lycidas"! Eager to contribute, thinking it "base" to linger on holiday, Milton nonetheless spent "almost two more months" in the hostile fortress of Rome; "as many months as before," "by the will of God," in Florence. Milton is hastening to the fight because he is not hastening; he is already home, because he takes his time to get there. In Florence he revisits friends "who were as anxious to see me as if it were my native land to which I had returned" (1116). In short, travel is struggle. But travel is not struggle; it is base in contrast to struggle. The observation of this baseness, at the turning point of Naples, leads Milton to cut short his travels and head for England. "It was wrong to be in Italy and I therefore lingered in Italy": that would be a summary of Milton's autobiographical logic.

I am not suggesting that students are unable to square this kind of biocritical circle. I am suggesting that they can and do square it—however hard I try to emphasize the antigeometry within (Chaney, *Grand Tour* and "Visit"; Benet; Empson, "Emotion" and *Milton's God*; Liljegren; Woods). The interpretative work they do, accordingly, is both independent and significant. That alone is enough reason to bring Milton's biography into the classroom.

Past and Present:
Memorializing the English Nation

Andrew Escobedo

Milton's nationalism represents one of the hardest sells in the undergraduate classroom, since so many of our (American) students are ready to find his praise of England indicative of a narrow-minded jingoism. They are often eager to locate in his career a trajectory from mere nationalist concerns (the poetry and prose of the 1630s to the 1650s) to broader, spiritual concerns (*Paradise Lost*). Yet, without denying the painful ironies of Milton's nationalism (e.g., liberty for England but not for Ireland), we do our students a disservice by neglecting his obsession with England, an obsession that inspired so much of his early work. The issue of nationalism goes far in helping students understand Milton. Conversely, Milton can help our students understand the modern phenomenon of nationalism, especially to the degree that he and his contemporaries articulated a historical dimension of nationhood that has persisted up to our time.

To begin with, we can assist our students in exploring Milton's contradictory attitudes toward England by distinguishing between nationalism and patriotism (Kedourie 68). I find that in a classroom setting this distinction creates some useful conceptual boundaries for nationalism, which often calls forth strong feelings, positive and negative, from students. *Patriotism* refers to feelings of affection and loyalty toward one's group of origin (often a race or religion) and is sometimes coupled with xenophobia. *Nationalism*, by contrast, emerged only after the medieval period and designates the perception that the nation instills in one: an identity distinct from other nations, implicitly binding its members together in what Benedict Anderson has called a "horizontal comradeship" (16).[1] Students will see the difference if you first ask them what American patriotism is—they have little difficulty coming up with a variety of answers—and then ask them what it means to be an American as distinct from a Canadian, Spaniard, German, South Korean, and so forth. Students will have the sense that it ought to mean something, even if they find it hard to enumerate distinct characteristics. Nation is an identity more than it is pledge of allegiance; it does not mean primarily "We are better than they are" but rather "We have a communal character distinct from other communal characters."[2]

Throughout its history nationalism has overlapped with patriotism (sometimes disastrously), and it does so throughout Milton's writing. Yet the distinction shows that when Milton expresses unpatriotic sentiments, he does not therefore automatically signal an indifference to his nation. He can extol his countrymen as "the first that shall be praised" among the nations of the world and also castigate his nation for becoming "the last, and most unsettl'd in the enjoyment of that Peace, whereof she taught the way to others" (*Reason of Church Government* 919, 877). In both instances, patriotic and unpatriotic, Milton tries to articulate the special character of a national category, England. From this perspective, Milton's writing is genuinely nonnationalist when it expresses indifference to the national category, as in his 1666 letter to Peter Heimbach, where the poet speaks of feeling "expatriated" from England: "One's *Patria* [country] is wherever it is well with one" (*Works of John Milton* 12: 115). The specificity of national identity evaporates here into a general state of well-being.

There are myriad ways of approaching Milton's nationalism in the classroom. One could track the ambiguities of national membership in Milton's writing, noting the vacillations between expansive definitions of "the people"—for example, "citizens of every degree"—and limited ones: "the sound part of the parliament, in which resides the real power of the people . . . a minority" (4: 471, 457). Such ambiguities have characterized national identity since its inception. My approach in the classroom emphasizes a different kind of ambiguity, one that emerges from the memorial dimension of Milton's writing of England: remembering, lamenting, reconstructing, and criticizing the English past. Milton came to see nationhood as a community that required two senses of "memorial," remembering the past and laying the past to rest. A good way to begin this kind of exploration is to offer the students two passages, one from *The First Defense of the English People* and one from the *Second Defense*:

> [T]he English see no need for them to justify their own deeds by the example of any foreigners whatever. They have laws, and followed them; laws which they got from their fathers and which are here the most excellent, whatever may be the case in the rest of the world. They have as models their own forefathers, indomitable men, who never yielded to the unbridled sway of kings and who executed many of them when they made their rule unbearable. They were born in freedom, they live in independence, and they can make for themselves what laws they wish. . . .
>
> (*Complete Prose Works* 4: 533)

> I was born at a time in the history of my country when her citizens, with pre-eminent virtue and a nobility and steadfastness surpassing all the glory of their ancestors, invoked the Lord, followed his manifest guidance, and after accomplishing the most heroic and exemplary achievements since the founding of the world, freed the state from grievous tyranny and the church from unworthy servitude.   (4: 549)

I explain to the students that both of these passages refer to the defeat and execution of Charles I, and I ask them to talk about the language with which Milton describes the character of his nation and justifies its actions. They aptly note Milton's insistence on the uniqueness of English tradition ("their own deeds"), the emphasis on freedom, the invocation of divine authority, and other things. If I'm lucky, or if I offer a little prodding, some of the students eventually observe that the first passage justifies English identity by linking it to its past, whereas the second praises the English for breaking from and surpassing their past. English nationhood is defined by both its derivation from and its isolation from its history. These opposing views help prepare the students for Milton's nationalist rhetoric throughout much of his writing.

In the classroom I tend to first emphasize the commemorative, reminiscent dimension of Milton's nationalism. For example, I initiate an introductory discussion about "Lycidas," "Mansus," "Damon's Epitaph," and the opening to book 2 of *The History of Britain* (the first three pages of the Yale *Complete Prose Works*, in which Milton discusses the value of history). This may appear an unpromising set of texts for undergraduates, but the results are worth the effort if you give the students a little help up front. Remind them that the three poetic texts are all recollections of acquaintances separated from the narrator by distance or death and that all three texts link these recollections to national history. (I stack the deck a bit before the students read the assignment, calling their attention to the *Riverside* notes for "Lycidas" on "famous *Druids*" [line 53] and "fable of *Bellerus*" [line 160] [102n28; 106n71].) After an initial discussion, I assign students a short paper due the next class: I ask them to locate in all four texts the occurrences of memory words (*fame, memorial, recall*, etc.) and nation words (*England, Britain, native*, etc.) and to discuss what themes and contexts these occurrences appear to have in common.

The students summarize their findings during the next class, and I make an effort to quietly draw out several shared issues that nearly always arise, which include: the tension between earthly fame and heavenly reward, the association of poetic vocation with national identity, poetic history as a compensation for loss, England in competition with Italy or Rome, and British history juxtaposed with classical history. The papers usually lead to further fruitful discussion, allowing students to think about the complex analogies among national fame, poetic fame, and heavenly glory. In particular, we talk about the shared pattern in the conclusions of all three poems: a penultimate reference to British history, followed by a final appeal to divine memorial. In "Mansus," Milton speaks of his desire to write of "the kings of my native land" just before he voices his hope to dwell in "the home of the heavenly gods" (lines 234–35). In "Damon's Epitaph," he discusses his planned "tale of Britain in English" just before he describes his lost friend "among the spirits of heroes and immortal gods" (lines 242, 244). Likewise, the poet of "Lycidas" searches for his friend's body among the coasts of Britain and the "guarded Mount" of Saint Michael—the traditional guardian of Cornwall—before depicting his entertainment by "all the Saints above" (106–07; lines 161, 178).[3] Does this structure suggest an inevitable link between national memory and heavenly fame? Or does the final apotheosis replace England, revealing the superiority of divine reward to the earthly nation? I ask the class: when Milton urges the angel, in "Lycidas," to "[l]ook homeward," where is home—England or heaven (106; line 163)?

After this, I have my students consider the opposite view in several of Milton's prose tracts: English crises in the present stem from an overvaluing of national tradition and history, implying the need to leave the past behind for the sake of future progress. In class I encourage the students to think about this dimension of Milton's nationalism by asking them to read *Areopagitica* and excerpts from *Of Reformation in England* and *Animadversions*. This is a challenging reading assignment for undergraduates, and I approach it with care. The Riverside prints the complete *Of Reformation*, but, in a packed syllabus, I limit the assignment to the first book (875–87)—which focuses on the pernicious effects of antiquarians—and the apocalyptic prayer for England that concludes the treatise (900–01). *Animadversions* is absent from the Riverside, but I copy section 4 for the students (*Complete Prose Works* 1: 697–707), a manageable assignment that includes Milton's fascinating depiction of the idolatrous "Colossus" of history (699) as well as his thoroughly nationalist (but not uniformly patriotic) prayer for England in the present age (704–07).

We discuss Milton's tendency in these works to define England by condemning corrupt traditions, a tendency that contrasts, as students usually notice, with Milton's inclination elsewhere to commemorate the national past. In the antiprelatical tracts, the conversation shifts between the English nation and the English church, and the students have the opportunity to see how interwoven these two things are for Milton. I try to show the class the way Milton's critique of corrupt tradition in these texts at times shades into almost a critique of tradition per se. Milton explains that he exposes the faults of the English past "to vindicate the spotlesse *Truth* from an ignominious bondage," noting of the authority granted to earlier Protestant martyrs that "more tolerable it were for the Church of God that all these Names were utterly abolisht, like the Brazen Serpent; then that mens fond opinions should thus idolize them, and the Heavenly *Truth* be thus captivated" (879). For just a moment here, I suggest to the class, we have a scorched-earth policy toward history, a perspective that sees the corruption of the past so threatening to the present that it contemplates destroying all traditions, good and bad.[4]

Toward the end of class I ask two students to read out loud two passages. The first, from *Animadversions*, depicts history as an idol:

> [T]his unactive, and livelesse Colossus, that like a carved Gyant terribly menacing to children, and weaklings lifts up his club, but strikes not, and is subject to the muting of every Sparrow. If you let him rest upon his Basis, hee may perhaps delight the eyes of some with his huge and mountainous Bulk, and the quaint workmanship of his massie limbs; but if yee goe about to take him in pieces, yee marre him; and if you thinke like Pigmees to turne and wind him whole as hee is, besides your vaine toile and sweat, he may chance to fall upon your owne heads.
>
> (*Complete Prose Works* 1: 699–700)

The second, from *Areopagitica*, famously depicts the dismembered body of Truth:

> Truth indeed came once into the world with her divine Master, and was a perfect shape most glorious to look on: but when he ascended, and his Apostles after Him were laid asleep, then strait arose a wicked race of deceivers, who as that story goes of the Aegyptian Typhon with his conspirators, how they dealt with the good Osiris, took the virgin Truth, hewd her lovely form into a thousand peeces, and scatter'd them to the four winds. From that time ever since, the sad friends of Truth, such as durst appear, imitating the carefull search that Isis made for the mangl'd body of Osiris, went up and down gathering up limb by limb still as they could find them. We have not yet found them all, Lords and Commons, nor ever shall doe, till her Masters second comming; he shall bring together every joynt and member, and shall mould them into an immortall feature of lovelines and perfection.   (1017–18)

What, I ask, do these two passages have to do with each other, and what do they imply about Milton's attitude toward national history? This exercise usually helps crystallize our earlier discussion about Milton's critique of tradition, as well as opening up new questions. What does it mean that Milton makes the Colossus of history both massive and fragile? Does Milton want us simply to shatter the Colossus? The body of Truth, by contrast, has already been torn to pieces—how does Milton want us to feel about this state of affairs? What does the process of reconstructing truth entail? How does it differ from the construction of the Colossus? In what way does the image of Truth resonate with the later image in *Areopagitica* of the "Nation rousing herself like a strong man after sleep" (1020)? Perhaps most crucial: is the dismembering of Truth an unhappy consequence of way men "idolize" history and so harm "the Heavenly Truth" (879), as Milton complained earlier in *Of Reformation*, or does this dismembering (and subsequent re-membering) protect against such idolizing?

Finally, I try to devote at least part of a class to America. I have found students often profitably apply Milton's dual imperatives for the nation (remembering and forgetting) to their own sense of national history and national identity. If there are moments in a nation's history that appear crucial to the formulation of its future identity, many of our students feel that we live in one of those moments. This makes the discussion exciting but also potentially turbulent. Keep in mind that, even more than usual, your students will look carefully to you (the probably liberal literature professor) for cues as to how they should respond to the idea of American nationalism. I try to give them none but instead to behave as a humble questioner asking them to think about national identity and history. Do we derive our present-day American identity from a link to the past? Yes, obviously, the students answer. To all the past, such as slavery and the denial of the vote to women? Well, no, not exactly. So does our nationhood depend on overcoming the past? And how close is overcoming to forgetting? Usually, at this point, some of the students begin to see the analogy between Milton's nationalism and my questions, and, if I've set things up well, they take over the discussion to talk about the youthfulness of America, its lack of ancient traditions, the need to invent traditions that seem long-standing (e.g., the Pledge of Allegiance), and more. For me, at least, the goal of this discussion is not to make them cynical about their national identity. On the contrary, I want them to think about nationhood as a form of community that is obliged to confront its historical contingency and perhaps to think of Milton's writing, in this sense, as an early example of modern nationalism.

NOTES

[1] Yet see Lawrence Lipking's comments about nationhood, in Milton's writing, as "people bound together by bitter memories and common hatreds" (213)—comments that play provocatively in the classroom.

[2] Some scholars describe the distinction between patriotism and nationalism differently, as one between heartfelt affection and aggressive superiority (Brennan 8–11; Holderness 75). They usually do so to avoid being soft on nationalism, but for the purpose of comparing patriotism and nationalism the description is unpersuasive—the feeling of aggressive superiority was around long before modern nationalism. Although national consciousness can certainly manifest itself aggressively, so does religious consciousness, racial consciousness, class consciousness, etc.

[3] If students notice the frequent fluctuations between "British" and "English" in these poems—such as when Milton describes how "mighty Britons break Saxon battle formations" (234)—I take the opportunity to describe to them the peculiar scenario of English national history, which annexes to itself the history of the Britons, whom the English Saxons destroyed. Milton celebrates Arthur as a national hero even while acknowledging that this hero fought against earlier *English* settlers on the island. A feature of nationalist history: it tends to impose continuity over difference.

[4] Students sometimes find it interesting that whereas Milton's antiroyalist contemporaries often use their Saxon past as a historical source for parliamentary authority, Milton rarely does so except in the most inconsistent and hesitant manner—and not at all in *The History of Britain*, where we would most expect it.

Teaching Milton and Gender

Catherine Gimelli Martin

No scholarly consensus exists on Milton's treatment of gender, still one of the most hotly debated issues in Milton studies. Samuel Johnson's infamously slanted remark about the radical poet's inconsistently tyrannical or "Turkish" attitude toward women is no longer credited in many quarters, and Sandra Gilbert and Susan Gubar's misappropriation of Virginia Woolf's remark about "Milton's bogey" has become increasingly suspect (Martin, "Dalila" 53–54, 58). In fact, as the presentism of 1970s-style feminism has waned and early modern feminism has been rediscovered, the Lady of Milton's 1634 masque and the Eve of *Paradise Lost* are increasingly viewed as positive defenses of the so-called weaker sex (Shullenberger; McColley; Herman). Yet the egalitarianism of Milton's epic and his divorce tracts remains an open question, which makes teaching his prose and poetry from a gendered perspective more exciting than ever.

Recent scholarship has shown that while a tiny minority of radical seventeenth-century sects gave women greater roles in spiritual teaching and preaching than Milton's *On Christian Doctrine* allows, none actually disputed the Pauline teaching on masculine headship in marriage that Milton takes for granted. The biblical sources for this view are succinct enough to be easily included in any curriculum and, given the biblical illiteracy of so many modern students, should at least be made available in handout form for easy reference (Gen. 1.26–28, 2.18–25, 3; 1 Cor. 11.3–15, 14.34–35; 1 Tim. 2.11–14; Eph. 5.22–33). Excerpts from Augustine's *City of God* (ch. 14) provide another useful perspective on the mainline tradition drastically altered by the twentieth century. Without getting involved in bitter debates, the instructor can then turn to the primary question: is Milton's view of femininity more biblical, Augustinian, masculinist, or early modern feminist? The class will need to define each of these terms, ideally with the help of surveys of the historical development of these traditions (Bal; Pagels; Wittreich, *Feminist Milton*).

Where to go from there will depend on the instructor, the subject, and the format of the course. A literary class dealing exclusively with Milton or with seventeenth-century prose may thoroughly examine his divorce tracts and his closely related *Areopagitica* in historical context, but broader survey courses will need to use short selections from these tracts to preface readings of the Lady in *Comus*, of Eve in *Paradise Lost*, or Dalila in *Samson Agonistes*. Courses with a stronger women's studies focus may cover some of the same material in the context of seventeenth-century women's writing. However, all but the most general survey course can contrast Milton's poetic and prose representations of marriage with those of contemporary women. In advanced honors, senior level, or graduate courses, students should balance this reading with critical surveys of the marital customs and traditions that Milton inherited and transformed (Halkett; Turner; Chaplin).

A warm-up session on Milton's sonnets helps students prepare for his more difficult prose arguments on gender and sexuality. The sonnets conveniently fall into four main groups: poems offering female role models to female (but perhaps also male) subjects (9, 23); poems commending women who exhibit strong masculine qualities (10, 14); poems in which the poet takes on the role of patient feminine sufferer or comforter (7, 19, 22 ; see also "On the Death of a Fair Infant"); and poems commending heroic male attributes in men (8, 11, 12, 15, 16, 17, 21; on this classical republican rhetoric, see Hausknecht). This introductory exercise allows the class to chart the full range of gendered subject positions offered by Milton and thus better to assess how far the most progressive women writers of the period maintained, expanded, or otherwise altered them.

Unfortunately, few texts (none easily affordable) contain all the pertinent material on the early modern *querelle des femmes*, and even fewer include the men who engaged in the debate. Moira Ferguson's *First Feminists* (1–50) provides a good general background of the antimisogynistic campaign initiated by Christine de Pisan in the late Middle Ages and continued in early modern England by Margaret Tyler (fl. 1578), Jane Anger (fl. 1589), Ester Sowernam (fl. 1617), Joane Sharp (fl. 1617), Constancia Mundia (fl. 1617), Rachel Speght (fl. 1617–21), Katherine Chidley (fl. 1641–45), Margaret Cavendish (1623–73), Katherine Phillips (1631–1664), Margaret Fell Fox (1614–1702), Bathsua Makin (c. 1608–1675), Aphra Behn (1640–89), Sarah Fyge Egerton (1669/72–1722/23), Jane Barker (fl. 1688 and 1723), Mary Astell (1666–1731), and Judith Drake (fl. 1696). Since Ferguson covers the entire period from 1578 to 1799, she can include selections from less than half of the seventeenth-century feminists. Another problem is that she fails to distinguish women who argued against misogyny (Tyler, Anger, Sowernam, Sharp, Mundia, and Speght) from those who simply defended close female friendships (Cavendish, Phillips, Barker, and Behn) and those who more actively sought greater educational opportunities, congregational roles, or rights for women (Fox, Makin, Astell, and Cavendish). This approach leads her to declare that all were united in fighting "patriarchy" (27), when most accepted the secondary status of women in society and particularly in marriage (only Astell—actually an eighteenth-century figure—argued against Pauline or masculine headship in marriage). Ferguson's selections also omit early feminists like Speght, Amelia Lanier, and Elizabeth Cary (1585–1639), whose *Tragedy of Mariam, the Faire Queene of Jewry* (1613) makes her the first female dramatist to broach the subject of divorce. Thus *The Broadview Anthology of Seventeenth-Century Verse and Prose* (Rudrum, Black, and Nelson) provides a better option since it includes the most teachable early feminists— Lanier, Speght, Fell, Cavendish, Makin, and Behn—side by side with their sometimes misogynistic, sometimes more enlightened male contemporaries.[1] Nicholas Breton, Thomas Browne, and John Dryden generally fall into the first category and Owen Felltham and Lord Herbert into the second, while the earl of Rochester occupies a highly dubious middle position.

Covering the bulk of this material is possible only in a seventeenth-century survey course or a class on Milton in historical context, but having it on hand is invaluable in almost any gender-based survey of the period.[2] In general, the feminist field can be succinctly surveyed through three relatively short selections: Speght's *A Muzzle for Melastomus* (and possibly also her poem *The Dream*), Fox's *Women's Speaking Justified*, and Makin's *Essay to Revive the Ancient Education of Gentlewomen*. These texts are especially pertinent since their authors share many interests with Milton—free speech, educational reform, and some measure of female empowerment. Fox makes a good starting point despite her relatively late date because her rich scriptural hermeneutic and argumentative strategies prepare students for Milton's complex prose arguments as well as the debate between the Lady and Comus in *A Mask*. While Milton does not go as far as Fox in authorizing free speech for women in church and while *Paradise Lost* preserves Eve's silence during Raphael's lectures, students will be interested to find that the Lady's public self-defense is supported by Milton's stated belief in a woman's right to speak in public forums (*Complete Prose Works* 1: 926). Since the masque is a difficult text for many undergraduates, covering its central debate may be sufficient before turning to the divorce tracts and *Areopagitica*. A good way to involve students in *A Masque* is to have them present sincere or devil's-advocate defenses of the Lady's seemingly outmoded ideal of female chastity, either in historical context or from a modern perspective or both. This approach invites some predictable college humor but also uncovers an often overlooked historical dimension of the modern issue of a woman's right to control her own body. Asking students to create defenses also introduces them to the debate aspect of most of Milton's prose and poetry, to which *The Doctrine and Discipline of Divorce* provides an important bridge.

Conveniently divided into separate chapters addressing the general argument that mutual communication and help are even more essential to marriage than sexual intimacy, *The Doctrine and Discipline of Divorce* [*Riverside* 930–76] lends itself to close analysis of Milton's imagery and argumentative strategy and helps prepare students to tackle *Areopagitica* either as a whole or in selected passages. Fox will already have shown students that most arguments for radical social change were still grounded in biblical authority, but Milton's simultaneous appeal to secular sources in attacking custom may require additional background. As well as appealing to the *sola scriptura* (by scripture alone) principle underlying all Reformed thought (the principle subordinating mere traditions of men to the plain scriptural word), Milton draws on Parliament's recent rejection of the bishops' tradition-based arguments for their "inquisitorial" ecclesiastical authority and on Francis Bacon's denunciation of custom as an enslaving idol that prevents human progress.[3] Similarly believing that unmasking or overthrowing custom will lead to the recovery of the lost wisdom of Solomon or Moses, Milton depicts custom's hollow face and its "blind and Serpentine body (*Doctrine and Discipline* 931) as a Scylla-like obstruction to the "advancement of learning" (Martin, "Sources"). His appeal to the original Mosaic sense of uncleanness should also recall the Lady's insistence that like marriage, true "chastity" is more spiritual than physical in nature, although it is obviously both. Her belief that nature is a "good cateress" (*Comus* 158; line 764) also exemplifies the rule of charity espoused throughout the divorce tracts. For Milton, this is the foundational principle guiding the interpretation of both the Old and New Testaments, but since students may observe that this idea is not strictly scriptural, they should also note his reliance on John Selden's Hebrew studies (*De Jure* and *Uxor* [*Doctrine and Discipline* 974]) and on Bacon's reinterpretation of the causes and effects of the Fall. In Bacon's optimistic analysis, Adam's curse becomes a charitable decree on the part of a God who knows that exile will teach Adam and Eve the self-reliant work ethic they needed to regain paradise (cf. *PL* 10.1013–96). The beginning of the first book of *The Doctrine and Discipline of Divorce* reprises the Baconian rationale behind this idea: "Man is the occasion of his owne miseries, in most of those evills which hee imputes to Gods inflicting" (934), which occur whenever he refuses to allow God's gifts of reason and mercy to overcome them.

Hugo Grotius's better-recognized role in providing the other secular or "natural law" pillar of this argument is developed in chapter 10 of *Doctrine and Discipline*.[4] This chapter is especially important in setting up the text's ultrahumanistic rejection of excessively literal scriptural interpretations, overly austere sexual mores, and extreme religious fanaticism. It thus usefully counters the stereotype of the radical Puritan Milton, often mistakenly associated with the severe cult of chastity or celibacy supposedly celebrated in the masque (Martin, "Non-Puritan Ethics"). Students should be encouraged to use their own understanding of his views on women, marriage, and sexual morality to interpret what kind of Christianity and Christian politics Milton defends at this point in his career. Here an oral or written debate format is useful in sorting out the positive and negative implications of his assumptions, which in turn provide a valuable framework for reading *Of Education*, *Areopagitica*, and *Paradise Lost*. The second book of Milton's first divorce tract and *Tetrachordon* are also teachable, but since they mainly answer technical scriptural and canon law objections likely to be raised by his contemporaries, they should probably remain optional (unless one is teaching biblically oriented students) to allow more time for the major prose and poetry. *Of Education* and *Areopagitica* fall into this category, because they anticipate Milton's major epic, yet since neither text discusses the education of women, they should be studied from the perspective of their underlying goal: to develop citizens capable of making well-informed, individual choices regardless of gender.

In nodding both to the Hartlib circle's reformist ideals and to the more masculinist assumptions of the classical humanists and republicans (Hausknecht), *Of Education* does not, however, offer a thoroughly modern or enlightened— much less a coeducational—program. It simply rejects the linguistic or pictorial shortcuts to classical learning favored by Samuel Hartlib and followers of

Comenius—Milton refers somewhat sarcastically to the pragmatic, encyclope-dic *"Janua's* and *Didactics"* of Comenius (*Of Education* 980)—in favor of a more classical, humanistic approach that traditionally excluded women. Thus, while it shares Hartlib's ideal of making the teaching of rhetoric and grammar easier and more natural, it recommends a broad survey of the classical (and in most cases, then authoritative) treatments of science, ethics, and philosophy. This approach is designed to form gentlemanly citizen-soldiers, yet as in the education of Adam and Eve in *Paradise Lost*, the instructor uses a quasi-Ramist, even proto-Piagetian ladder of learning as he guides his students' as-cent from concrete subjects like natural philosophy, geography, astronomy, agriculture, medicine, arithmetic, and geometry—subjects that can be easily learned by rule, map, experiment, or demonstration—to more abstract, theo-retical subjects, which, like ethics, politics, and literature, require imaginative synthesis and application. Again like Adam and Eve, the instructor's students are asked to focus on practical and domestic ethics and politics before turning to the most abstruse liberal arts—philosophy, history, and poetry. In *Of Educa-tion*, this curriculum is supplemented with instruction by practical men experi-enced in the modern arts of hunting, gardening, fishing, sailing, architecture, engineering, fortification, anatomy, and medicine (982–84). Such training ad-dresses the double Baconian project of "learning . . . to repair the ruins of our first parents" and learning to "know God aright," not just through his word but through his works, the "sensible things" that instruct us in "things invisible . . . by orderly conning over the visible and inferior creature" (980). The breadth of this program anticipates the holistic method Raphael outlines in *Paradise Lost*, which radically departs from the more narrowly gender-based education en-dorsed by Comenius. Before or after turning to Raphael's lessons, students may thus profit from examining Makin's similarly progressive proposal for training young women in abstract as well as practical subjects, especially since Makin echoes *Areopagitica's* insistence that all learning must be permitted since it is inevitably open to both benign and malign uses by anyone, male or female.

At this point students will be fully prepared to turn to Milton's famous de-fense of speech and printing against censorship, whose intrinsic structure re-veals many logical and tactical similarities to *Doctrine and Discipline* and *Par-adise Lost*. Like Milton's first divorce tract, *Areopagitica* begins by praising Parliament as a defender of liberty and appealing to Reformed precedent for further expanding it. Although this freedom is now attributed to Athens rather than to Moses, Milton shows that it was also granted by the wisest church fa-thers before the onset of church corruption. In returning to this pure or uncor-rupted tradition of Christian liberty, he again summons Bacon to show why truly viable or "living" ideas possess a native life force. Closely paraphrasing his argument that "kill[ing]" these ideas does a grave injustice to the spirit of ra-tional freedom God originally implanted in all humankind (999), Milton insists that this spirit should always be nurtured, not stunted. This plea, along with his sifting and winnowing metaphors, lends a strong maternal cast to the harvest work Milton similarly envisions both in terms of feminine crafts and in terms of classical republican virtue (Martin, "Feminine Birth"). From either perspective, censorship is not only impossible but also completely undesirable; it produces sloth, irresponsibility, and servility, not good character, conscience, or nurture. The third and final part of the argument famously describes the bright future England will enjoy by embracing free speech, free will, and a common dedication to the Isis-like rebuilding of the Solomonic temple of truth. Although the rhetoric and imagery of all three sections afford enormous insight into Milton's value system, a gender-based course will particularly want to explore the explicitly female role models of truth—not just Isis but also Psyche and the unnamed yet clearly defined figure of Atalanta, who at last wins her race against her slow but domineering pursuer, that combination of fallen nature and corrupt custom that Bacon embodies in Hippomenes (Martin, "Feminine Birth").

Whether or not the instructor or class shares this positive evaluation of Milton's value system, exploring its imagery fully prepares students to analyze the feminine figures of unfallen nature summed up in Milton's Eden and his Eve. However, before the class takes up Eve, a short detour into Speght's defense of our "Grand Mother" (398–99) permits specific comparison between Milton's views and those of a seminal first feminist. In courses not specifically focused on Milton, students can do this simply by considering the epic debates between God, Adam, and Raphael on sexuality (*PL* 8.357–653; cf. 4.268–775) and between Adam and Eve on the purposes of work, marriage (9.205–411), and the possibility of recuperation (10.719–1104). In Milton courses, the treatment of Dalila in *Samson Agonistes* and of Mary in *Paradise Regained* (1.58–108) should provide a final review of Milton's gendered subjects, not least because the debate structure of these works is actually more prominent than in *Paradise Lost*. Dalila is the more challenging character with which to conclude, since Samson's Danite chorus is steeped in the misogynistic tradition discussed by Diane McColley and other modern feminists (Walker), and since the final confrontation and divorce between Samson and his wife reengages Milton's lifelong interest in domestic, political, and religious liberty (*The Second Defense of the English People* 1117) at an exceptionally deep level (Martin, "Dalila"). Their family quarrel usually generates particularly sensitive and close readings from the class, even if little or no time remains to compare it to Cary's *Tragedy of Mariam*, a good idea wherever feasible.

NOTES

[1] See also Henderson and McManus's *Half Humankind*. This text does not, however, treat the period after the reception of Milton's divorce tracts, which includes Makin's groundbreaking proposal for the formal education of women.

[2] Rudrum, Black, and Nelson also include an exceptionally fine selection of the general political and philosophical thought of the period.

[3] For a short introduction, see the *Broadview Anthology* selection on Bacon's idols and some of his applications of his critique (Bacon, "Aphorisms" 49–61).

[4] Grotius's scriptural commentaries (*Annotationes*) are noted in the introduction to *The Doctrine and Discipline of Divorce* (935), but his basic approach to natural law is summarized in chapter 10. Grotius's most famous work was *De Jure Belli ac Pacis* (1625), which Thomas Hobbes used in developing his own natural law theory.

Milton and Hebraism

Jason P. Rosenblatt

As Gabriel Josipovici has noted, regarding the Bible, "[i]t is a fact of interpretation that once something is presented to us in one way it becomes difficult to see it in any other way" (270). The principal justification for spending at least some classroom time discussing Milton's Hebraism is that it makes us view his poetry and prose in another way. It has been the fate of the most Hebraic of the great English poets to have been interpreted by critics and scholars, some of them great ones, who have been conspicuously inhospitable to what Ezra Pound called his "beastly hebraism" ("Notes" 109). A. S. P. Woodhouse (*Heavenly Muse* 111, "Argument") and Arthur Barker (*Milton* 105, 107, 111–12, 236) established the interpretative model still followed by most readers, examining from a Pauline perspective the relations between law and gospel and thus regarding the Hebraic factor in Milton's thought with either indifference or antipathy. By discovering the importance to Milton's oeuvre not only of the Hebrew Bible but also of postbiblical rabbinica, in creative tension with the Pauline influence already recognized by critics and scholars, students may find that specific works are ideologically fissured rather than monolithic.

Although most discussions of the topic have understandably focused on *Paradise Lost*, Milton's Hebraism can be found in some of the shorter poems and in some of his most important prose, most notably *The Doctrine and Discipline of Divorce* and the *Areopagitica*. Milton's most Hebraic prose flashes forth from those tracts of the 1640s that present England with a vision of itself as a second Israel, a holy community capable of shaping and improving its destiny. Against the argument that a partner in an inconvenient marriage display Christian patience and submit to God's will as expressed in Christ's uncompromising sentences of indissolubility in the gospels, Milton in *Doctrine and Discipline* bases his radical appeal to freedom on the Deuteronomic law of divorce (Deut. 24.1–4). In this treatise, the Mosaic law rather than the Son incarnates deity:

> The hidden ways of [God's] providence we adore & search not; but the law is his revealed will, his complete, his evident, and certain will; herein he appears to us as it were in human shape, enters into cov'nant with us, swears to keep it, binds himself like a just lawgiver to his own prescriptions, gives himself to be understood by men, *judges and is judg'd*, measures and is commensurat to right reason.
>
> (*Complete Prose Works* 2: 292; my emphasis)

If even the heavenly king submits to human judgment, how dare King Charles refuse? (Incidentally, this excerpt suggests another way of looking at the famous last line of the great epic's opening invocation, to "justifie the wayes of God to men" [*PL* 1.26 (*Riverside*)], which is generally read, however implausibly, in an evangelical context and in terms of justification by faith, when it should be read in a legal context.) Although typology is the symbolic mode most often applied to Milton's poetry, *Doctrine and Discipline* reverses the direction of typology from the New Testament to the Hebrew Bible. Of the relation between Christ's words and the Mosaic law, Milton insists, "If we examine over all [Christ's] sayings, we shall find him not so much interpreting the law with his words, as referring his owne words to be interpreted by the Law" (*Complete Prose Works* 2: 301). Milton's positive portrayal of Edenic-Mosaic law in books 5 to 8 of *Paradise Lost* owes much to his divorce tracts. There Milton presents in a favorable light the Mosaic law that will become the source of Edenic polity, and there he provides a model of that law as easy, charitable, and permissive—more charitable, in fact, than the contemporary Christian interpretation of the law of divorce.

One of the best points of entry into the divorce tracts is to ask students to find the biblical verses that are at their heart and to see how Milton deconstructs them. If they don't own a Bible, they can log on to www.holybible.com and locate the relevant texts: for example, Deut. 24.1–2, the Hebrew Bible's law of divorce; Matt. 19.3–9, Mark 10.11–12, and Luke 16.18, Jesus's explicit and categorical rejection of the Deuteronomic right; 1 Cor. 7.9, Paul's "better to marry than to burn" in lust and then in hell, which Milton reinterprets as a burning in blameless loneliness; Eph. 2.3, Paul's "children of wrath," a reference to those under a law of wrath, applied instead by Milton to the children of an unhappy marriage; Matt. 19.9, the gospel's allowing the dissolution of a marriage on grounds of "fornication," which, under Miltonic pressure, can mean almost anything, including spiritual or emotional faults or even blameless incompatibility; Mal. 2.16, "For the LORD, the God of Israel, saith that he hateth putting away," which Milton reads as "he who hates let him divorce" (*Doctrine and Discipline* [*Complete Prose Works* 2: 257]) and numerous other examples—for example, Milton's strong misreading of "What therefore God hath joined together, let not man put asunder" (Matt. 19.6). (This last—arguing that if a couple is unhappy, God must never have joined them—can provoke passionate classroom counterarguments. What about two people who have been married for many years? Does their present unhappiness mean that they were never meant to be together? Does it cancel all meaning from their past?) Discussing the difference between these verses in their biblical context and in Milton's prose should reveal that the ostensible enemies in the divorce tracts, canon law and the Pharisees, pose no real challenge. Milton's actual enemies are the pronouncements of Christ and Paul against divorce and Paul's message of death to the law.

Students who want to pursue the matter further can read texts available through *Early English Books Online* to see how works of the common expositors of scripture—Luther, Calvin, Perkins, and so forth—were read in Protestant England.

In *Doctrine and Discipline of Divorce* and the *Areopagitica*, Milton praises *De Jure Naturali et Gentium, juxta Disciplinam Ebraeorum* (1640) and its author: "that noble volume written by our learned [John] *Selden, of the law of nature & of Nations*"; "the chief of learned men reputed in this Land, Mr. *Selden*" (*Complete Prose Works* 2: 513, 350). Milton never pretended to be a Hebrew or an Aramaic scholar, but he drew on some of the immensely erudite Latin rabbinic works by Selden, including, most important, *De Jure Naturali, Uxor Ebraica, De Synedriis*, and *De Diis Syris. De Jure*, a study of the rabbinic seven Noachide laws, argues that these moral imperatives were promulgated by God at a moment in history and are of perpetual obligation to all of humankind. These laws are Judaism's version of natural law. It is impossible to summarize briefly the influence on Milton of this book of 847 folio pages, but one might note that it implicitly reduces the importance of Christian revelation and of Christ's redemptive mission. If the universal Noachide laws can redeem a virtuous gentile such as Job and if even the most minimal of Christian dogmatic beliefs are not a precondition for salvation, then the question Selden poses about salvation in his *Table Talk* is unanswerable: "why should not that portion of happiness still remain to them who do not believe in Christ, so they be morally good?" (Reynolds 171).

Although *De Jure* isn't available in English, many of its most important and provocative Hebraic ideas can be found in *Table Talk* under headings both expected and unexpected (Bible, Christians, Jews, Law of Nature, Marriage, Religion, Salvation, Zealots, and many others). This witty, worldly, and sometimes outrageous text presents students with Selden at his most entertaining.

Milton also refers favorably to Selden's *Uxor Ebraica* (it may well be the only work by a contemporary Englishman to be mentioned in Milton's *On Christian Doctrine*), which contains similar arguments regarding divorce on grounds of incompatibility. It is from that work (and from book 5 of *De Jure*, published earlier) that Milton borrows and develops the idea that fornication as grounds for divorce bears multiple meanings—indeed, can mean almost anything. Unlike Selden's other rabbinic works, the *Uxor* is available in a modern translation (*John Selden on Jewish Marriage Law*). Students choosing to write on the divorce tracts might compare the Protestant expositors on the subject with Selden's Hebraic perspective in the *Uxor. De Synedriis et Praefecturis Juridicis Veterum Ebraeorum*, which occupies 1,132 huge folio columns in his *Opera Omnia*, is a work of stupendous erudition, dealing primarily with the constitution of Jewish courts, including the Sanhedrin, which, as Selden notes pointedly, was not priestly in composition. This work almost certainly accounts for Milton's positive reference to "the supreme councel of seaventie, call'd the *Sanhedrim*, founded by *Moses*," as a model for Parliament in *The Ready and Easy Way* (*Complete Prose Works* 7: 436).

In the tripartite crescendo movement in Milton's poetry—from pagan natural law through the Hebrew Mosaic law to the Gospel—the middle term is usually elided. The instructor can correct this imbalance by noting, for example, the development of the idea of *katharos* in the successive quatrains of the twenty-third sonnet (which begin with Euripides's *Alcestis*, extend to the Levitical laws of purification after childbirth, and conclude with a vision of absolute purity in a Christian heaven) and the continuous but developing sense of the pastoral in "Lycidas" (*Riverside* 100–07), narrated by a shepherd whose consolation is measured at least in part by the progression from classical aesthetics (lines 64–84) through Hebraic prophetic ethics (113–31) to the limitless reward of a Christian heaven purged of evil. The Hebraic prophetic ethics is generally overlooked, despite the motif of the shepherd in the Psalms, Isaiah, and Jeremiah, among numerous other biblical texts.

There is almost too much to say about Milton's attempt at Judaic self-understanding in *Samson Agonistes* (*Riverside* 783–844), a work about which almost everything is contested. It's easier to say what a teacher might avoid than to prescribe an approach. A Hebraic reading would not compare Samson invidiously with the Christ of *Paradise Regained*. It would not find in the chorus or Manoa or Samson easy objects of belittlement. It would not be a totally ironic reading, such as is in vogue. And it would not degrade the Torah that Samson defends with his last unmediated words (lines 1381–86, 1408–09, 1423–25). The most direct way to reinforce a Hebraic perspective on *Samson* in the classroom is to have the students read Judges 13–16. They will note Milton's adaptations of the text but also his determination to retain as much of the original as possible. Milton's virtual obsession with the Bible—he refers to it nine thousand times in *On Christian Doctrine* alone—suggests that the primitive ruffian who so appalls some present-day readers might not have appalled Milton.

A Hebraic reading of *Samson Agonistes* would acknowledge the humanity of the chorus, its capacity for fellow feeling, and its considerable spiritual and intellectual development, instead of rejecting it in a spirit of Pauline dualism as a narrow, obsolete, erroneous "chorus of enslaved Hebrews," representing "the whole Hebrew people, bound by the law of Moses in its service to Jehovah" (Barker, "Calm" 39; Bennett 120). The dominant ironic Christian dualist reading of *Samson* presumes that "Samson lived and died in vain" (Parker, *Milton* 2: 909), because he only "beg[a]n to deliver Israel out of the hand of the Philistines" (Judg. 13.5) and neither he nor his surviving countrymen completed the act. But from an ampler biblical perspective, "he shall begin to deliver Israel . . . and the deliverance shall be carried on and perfected by others, as it was in part by *Eli*, and *Samuel*, and *Saul*, but especially by *David*" (M. Poole Bbb3).[1] Instead of merely disparaging Manoa for his parental inadequacies and for a crude ethnocentrism associated incorrectly with Judaism, a Hebraic reading compatible with Christianity would understand the love expressed by laying out money for one's child instead of laying it up for oneself and by preparing to devote the rest of one's life to nursing that child (lines 1485–89). And since devaluing the chorus and Manoa devalues their ethnicity, a corrective reading compatible with a charitable rather than a triumphalist Christianity would recognize Milton's use of a positive typology (congruity rather than disparity) and his transfer of terms from the Hebrew Bible to the New Testament in order to emphasize God's continuous ways with all his creatures.

The topic of Milton's Hebraism has not been exhausted, and Selden's influence complicates matters. For example, it is clear that Selden's *De Diis Syris* (1617; Milton used the second edition, printed in 1629), a study of the pagan gods mentioned in the Hebrew Bible, shaped the account of the cessation of the pagan oracles in "On the Morning of Christ's Nativity" (Dec. 1629 [*Riverside* 38–52]) and the catalog of pagan deities in book 1 of *Paradise Lost*. Instructors might ask students to compare the flight of the pagan gods in "On the Morning of Christ's Nativity" (lines 173–220), written when Milton turned twenty-one, with the catalog of demon-idols in book 1 of *Paradise Lost* (lines 376–505), composed thirty years later. Students might find that the same deities who inspire a feeling almost nostalgic in the ode provoke the bard's fierce denunciation in the catalog. Or they might observe an unexpected interruption of the catalog's shrillness in the extraordinary passage, filled with longing, on the sexual fluidity of the gods (lines 419–31). Although ultimately disapproving, the plangent opening lines of the ode's stanza 20 register an awareness of pagan loveliness: "The lonely mountains o'er, / And the resounding shore, / A voice of weeping heard, and loud lament" (lines 181–83). Editors invariably cite as its source the account of the slaughter of the innocents (Matt. 2.18), which echoes word for word the passage in the Hebrew Bible where Rachel weeps for her children (Jer. 31.15). But since the poem is describing the waning powers of the pagan gods, it may be more likely that Milton's true source is to be found in *De Diis*. There, speaking of the Venus of the Ascalonites, Selden quotes Macrobius, who says that "the image of this goddess was made on Mount Lebanon, her head veiled, her countenance sorrowful, her face resting in one hand and the other hand within her gown. Tears are believed to flow from her eyes at the sight of spectators" (my trans.).[2] Here, seeing things differently—namely, discovering a potential source in Selden—means breaking free from the entire Judeo-Christian paradigm, just as looking at Milton's Hebraism means breaking free, even if only provisionally, from the Pauline paradigm that governs the interpretation of Milton's work.

NOTES

[1] For Matthew Poole's reliance on *Paradise Lost* in his commentary on Genesis 3, see B3r.

[2] "Simulachrum hujus Deae in monte Libano fingitur capite obnupto, specie tristi, faciem manu laeva intra amictum sustinens, lachrimae visione conspicientium manare creduntur" (N6).

Milton and the Undergraduate British Literature Survey Course: Who, Where, When, How, and, by All Means, Why?

Angelica Duran

Undergraduate English literature survey courses can be mind-numbing experiences that drain students of any appreciation of literature and rob instructors of their belief in humanity—or exhilarating engagements that wholly inspire students and instructors alike. Instructors can create the latter type of survey course through the careful inclusion of Milton's shorter poetry and prose: selecting and situating the appropriate texts enable students to engage intelligently with those texts and to gain the critical skills, literary appreciation, and vocabulary needed for the remainder of the course and applicable to their academic careers and their professions. Because student populations, institutional resources, and instructors' concerns vary, I offer examples not only from my experiences at a large public university (University of California, Berkeley), an elite private university (Stanford), and a large land-grant university (Purdue) but also from instructors in diverse, predominantly anglophone countries and institutions (Australia, Canada, England, New Zealand, and the United States).

So, Tell Me . . . Why Teach Milton?

I have often heard versions of this question, from curious students and from skeptical colleagues. Instructors of English literature survey courses should ask it of themselves every term and with every author and text they include on their syllabi, even their favorites, as their answers will translate into new treatment of the material and renewed enthusiasm in the classroom. Those, in turn, will translate into student interest. Let me offer two especially important reasons why Milton should be included in survey courses whenever possible.

The first is the simple, honest aesthetic and intellectual pleasure Milton's works can provide. While a claim on behalf of aesthetics is fraught, even sophisticated critics like Marjorie Perloff, the 2006 MLA president, recognize the "special status" of certain texts: "sooner or later readers discover for themselves that Melville's *Moby-Dick* is, after all, a more interesting novel than *Wide, Wide World*" (qtd. in Showalter 65). This is not to say that all readers will prefer Herman Melville or Milton to Susan Warner. Indeed, when I took Perloff's Introduction to Graduate Studies course at Stanford in the fall of 1994, Perloff readily admitted that Milton's works were not among her favorites, although she quickly added that her disinclination might have to do with a poor literature course she took as a student. She did, however, articulate with refreshing honesty the visceral and intellectual pleasure that lucky readers worldwide and in different eras have discovered for themselves, including English Romantic poets, Victorian novelists, and United States writers (including Warner), politicians, and civil rights activists. Certain works generate interest year after year, era after era—or, as the American poet, critic, and translator Ezra Pound famously states, great literature is "news that stays news" (*ABC* 29). The Americanist Jay Fliegelman quips that he wishes Milton had been exiled to the American colonies along with the other regicides at the Restoration so that the poet's works would be taught more regularly in American literature courses, and the Argentine fiction writer Jorge Luis Borges goes so far as to dismiss national and historical boundaries in calling Milton "one of *our* most famous poets" (Borges 105; trans. and emphasis mine).

I have already touched on the second reason: in ways that few works can, Milton's texts enable readers to enter into a transhistoric conversation that extends forward and backward and that is at once global and intensely personal. Milton synthesized the literature of many languages—among them English, Greek, Hebrew, and Latin—and nations—African, French, Italian, Spanish, and others. No less remarkably, he greatly influenced subsequent literatures. He is intimately involved in the work of the Romantic writer Mary Shelley, whose *Frankenstein* is a good choice for survey courses that focus on epistemology, ontology, psychology, or science and that might also include Christopher Marlowe's *Dr. Faustus*; selections from Margery Kempe; Milton's "On the Death of a Fair Infant," "On Time," and "When I consider"; John Locke's *Essay concerning Human Understanding*; and William Cowper's *The Task*. Instructors might also consider assigning Philip Pullman's popular fantasy-fiction *His Dark Materials* (2001), which Margaret Kean finds particularly helpful at Oxford in providing "a sense of immediate relevance and personal resonance to classroom discussions of the psychological, social and emotional aspects" of Milton's texts. While Shelley's and Pullman's texts quote *Paradise Lost*, as prefatory epigram and series title, the epic's themes are present in concentrated form in the shorter poems.

Paradoxically, the feminism, multiculturalism, and globalism that have contributed to the growth in the canon that has squeezed out Milton from some survey courses also have increased the benefits of his inclusion. One of the reasons I was attracted to Milton's works as a first-generation United States citizen was that they clarified some of the vagaries of United States–anglophone culture and academic discourse that subsequent years of scholarship have done little to help me label but that years as a university teacher have done much to dispel. While many nonnative speakers of English turn to TV to understand anglophone popular culture and acquire spoken English, a large number of college-bound high schoolers, college students, and autodidacts turn to what used to be unabashedly called great English literature to understand academic culture, learn professional discourse, and define anglophone culture against and within their heritage culture. Indeed, Milton is used regularly for intercultural as well as intracultural comprehension. I was surprised on the first day of classes one semester to find my room filled with a much higher percentage of immigrant and international students, primarily Indian and Korean, than other sections of the course. In informal discussions, students said they had signed up for my section because they believed their exposure to Milton would help them understand not simply anglophone but also Western culture. Whether or not we include Milton on our syllabi, he is entrenched in the invisible Western high cultural reading list and arguably even its popular cultural reading list, as the collected essays of *Milton in Popular Culture* well document (Knoppers and Semenza). Omitting him is a disservice to all students and to international students and nonnative English speakers in particular.

Milton can prove invaluable on a syllabus that explores the role of literary works in the development of nationalism and internationalism. The concerns he articulates help instructors take advantage of increased classroom diversity and prepare students to meet the challenges of their global world. Students can explore nationalism and internationalism in a wide array of genres, reading Wace's *Le roman de Brut*, *Sir Gawain and the Green Knight*, Milton's religiopolitical sonnets and *Areopagitica*, John Dryden's drama *The Conquest of Granada* or historical poem *Annus Mirabilis*, and Oliver Goldsmith's elegy *The Deserted Village*; or they can trace encounters with the other in "The Wanderer" or "The Battle of Maldon," Thomas More's *Utopia*, Milton's *Samson Agonistes*, Margaret Cavendish's *Blazing World*, and Samuel Johnson's *Rasselas* or Aphra Behn's *Oroonoko*. When Miltonic texts are taught in such contexts, the outcomes can be illuminating. David Gay writes that at the University of Alberta,

> I once had an Iranian student who felt he could identify strongly with Milton because of his experience of the Iranian revolution and the resulting theocracy, and amalgam of religion and politics, and austere puritanical qualities of the new regime. He felt that he had somehow experienced an Islamic version of Milton's England. ("Re: Teaching")

The student's identification of some aspects of revolutionary Iran with revolutionary England demands careful qualification, the kind that can occur in high-level discussions instigated by challenging syllabi and invested teachers.

Our text selections and course assignments can have wide-ranging effects at local levels as well. My survey courses have a number of English education majors who often go on to teach in midwestern high schools. In large part because we discuss Milton's works in class and because they have the option of designing "Teaching Units" that include his shorter poetry and prose as their final course projects, many include Milton in their high school classes, and they do so with intelligence and care.

Who and Where

The best instructors know that the who (instructors, students, and colleagues) and where (educational institutions and nearby resources) of a course are as important as its what (texts). So they regularly consult their department and university course offerings and consider their ever-changing research interests when they sit down to construct their syllabi. Depending on whether instructors are more interested in covering a range of material or in multiple treatments of a text, they can intentionally avoid or duplicate texts included in their institution's introductory humanities course. If they know a colleague will be including Marlowe's "Come live with me" in a course, they might include Walter Raleigh's response, "The Nymph's Reply"; Milton's playful, cerebral versions of the seduction poem, "L'Allegro" and "Il Penseroso"; and William Carlos Williams's "Raleigh Was Right" (Leishman).

Course readings and themes can also respond to guest speakers, university conferences, and area events. Sometimes the primary authors will remain the same but texts and course reader supplements will change. Incorporating guest speakers from disciplines you want to learn more about can prove exciting to you and to your students. For example, when I scheduled a professor of civil engineering to deliver a lecture in my survey course, I selected Geoffrey Chaucer's Miller's Tale, More's *Utopia*, Francis Bacon's *New Atlantis*, Shakespeare's *The Tempest*, Milton's *Of Education*, Cavendish's *Blazing World*, Abraham Cowley's "To the Royal Society," and a short article by our guest speaker to emphasize the role of scholars from all disciplines in their larger communities. The engineering professor's multinational experiences informed students' understanding of the patriotism, social networks, and financing demanded by the national school system proposed in Milton's prose tract. In another semester, when a professor from computer science came in to share his experiences of the competitive spirit, foibles, and surprising successes in the early days of designing the Internet, we read the Exeter Book's "God's Gifts to Humankind," the *Canterbury Tales*'s General Prologue, Bacon's *Great Instauration*, Ben Jonson's *The Alchemist*, Milton's "Lycidas," Alexander Pope's *Essay on Man*, Jonathan Swift's *Gulliver's Travels*, and the short introductory chapter of the professor's computer textbook. Focusing on the importance of building learning communities and of the transmission of knowledge enabled students to engage seriously with the redefinitions of the pastoral community in Milton's pastoral elegy.

At times, campus events can govern text selection. As its introduction states, John Hale's *Sonnets of Four Centuries* was designed at the University of Otago, New Zealand, specifically for undergraduates. Using it as the primary compilation in an introductory literature course leaves ample time for training in scansion, concentration on literary history, in-depth research assignments, or a heavy dose of theory. A course on sonnets reveals the pivotal nature of Milton in the anglophone lyric tradition and can give instructors the opportunity and students the confidence to organize a sonnet reading at the campus library or a local bookstore.

If a community or campus theater produces a play relevant to the survey course, instructors might consider allowing drama to dominate a syllabus. Transformations of drama can be chronicled with the morality play *Everyman*, any one of Jonson's city comedies, Milton's masque *A Mask (Comus)*, one of Shakespeare's history plays, and Aphra Behn's *The Rover*. Students greatly enhance their appreciation of dramatic texts and authors as polysemous rather than monolithic when they attend to music and politics in the genre of drama in general and Milton's masque in particular; class discussion can be directed there quickly with an overhead of the title page of the first publication of *A Mask* (published not by Milton but by the royalist musician Henry Lawes, who composed the music for and played the role of the Attendant Spirit in the original production of 1634), and with an overhead of an older Milton's deprecation of masques in his defense of republicanism in *The Ready and Easy Way* (1660): "a king must be ador'd like a Demigod, with a dissolute and haughtie court about him, of vast expence and luxurie, masks and revels" (*Complete Prose Works* 7: 425). Instructors focusing on drama might also consider interlacing three tragedies—Shakespeare's *King Lear*, Milton's *Samson Agonistes*, and Dryden's *All for Love*—with short comic works: Chaucer's Wife of Bath's Tale; Milton's "On the University Carrier," "Another on the Same," and "Captain or colonel"; Swift's "A Modest Proposal" and "Verses on the Death of Dr. Swift"; and Mary Wortley Montagu's "The Reasons That Induced Dr. Swift." The combination of a particularly classical and somber Miltonic text with a set of colloquial and comedic ones is especially useful in demonstrating the variety of Milton's personas.

As Elaine Showalter does in *Teaching Literature*, I encourage instructors to take advantage of the collaborative aspects of the teaching profession. Incorporating campus and community events reduces the sense of isolation that sometimes comes with college and university teaching. Chaucer's Miller's Tale, Milton's "Ad Patrem," and William Congreve's *The Way of the World* can complement a talk on multigenerational issues sponsored by your institution's psychology, sociology, or economics department. All these pedagogical practices can contribute to one's own publications. (I was among the lucky students at the University of California, Berkeley, to hear Paul Alpers's early arguments on the pastoral, articulated years later in *What Is Pastoral?*) Class discussions give instructors a sense of their publications' future audience and students a sense of their active participation in the development of our discipline.

When and How

I have organized the above examples thematically and chronologically because doing so gives students a sense of literary history and maintains their interest. Organizing by genre (i.e., poetry, drama, and prose) works well, as does building flexibility into the syllabus. Students may be assigned to bring in short stories or newspaper articles so that they can participate more fully as cocreators of the course. There are always (and unfortunately) atrocities that illuminate the relevance today of Milton's violent poetic swan song *Samson Agonistes* or what Roy Flannagan calls his "scream of anger" (Milton, *Riverside* 254), Sonnet 18 ("On the Late Massacher in Piemont"). For example, shortly after the Twin Towers disaster of September 11, 2001, students had their choice of articles that implicitly and explicitly came to terms with the violent event through reference to Milton's dramatic poem (Engel; Guttenplan; Shea). Milton and his texts regularly make less shocking but no less provocative appearances: in the 1997 film *The Devil's Advocate*, Al Pacino's role of devil is named John Milton; and *A Mask* has been adapted and illustrated for children (Hodges).

I offer just two more examples of ways to incorporate Milton into English literature survey courses. A sequence emphasizing literature's relation to spirituality and religion might include *The Dream of the Rood*; Robert Southwell's "The Burning Babe" and "New Prince, New Pomp"; Anne Askew's "First Examination"; John Donne's Holy Sonnets or selections from George Herbert's *The Temple*; Thomas Browne's *Religio Medici*; Milton's "On the Morning of Christ's Nativity," unfinished "The Passion," and *Paradise Regained*; John Bunyan's *Pilgrim's Progress*, parts 1 and 2; and Thomas Gray's "Elegy Written in a Country Churchyard." The combination of the three Milton texts enables students to compare and contrast his representations of God, Christian believers, religion, and spirituality. Finally, students can track the development of books, literature, and the idea of "the author" with "Chaucers Wordes unto Adam, His Owne Scriveyn" and the poet's Retraction to *The Canterbury Tales*; Aemilia Lanyer's short poems; Philip Sidney's *Defence of Poesie*; Milton's *Areopagitica*, *Of Education*, and the prefaces to *Paradise Lost* and *Samson Agonistes*; Dryden's *Essay on Dramatic Poesy*; Alexander Pope's *Essay on Criticism* or *The Dunciad*; Mary Leapor's "An Essay on Woman"; Johnson's "Preface to Shakespeare" and "Milton" from *Lives of the Poets*; and John Keats's "On First Looking into Chapman's Homer" and "On the Sonnet," leading to a flourishing finish with William Wordsworth's "The Sonnet" and "London, 1802: Milton! thou should'st be living at this hour."

Milton is sometimes taught as if his texts are appreciable by only a small number of readers—the audience "fit . . . , though few." I suspect that the challenges of Milton's language, cultural assumptions, and vast learning are exacerbated when either the entirety of *Paradise Lost* remains on ever-packed syllabi (which leaves little time for in-depth discussions) or selections from the epic are assigned—usually books 1, 3, 7, and 9—leaving students feeling decidedly and unparadisically lost. Instructors can cede to "envious *Time*" and human capacity by using instead Milton's shorter poetry and prose, whose careful selection and treatment yield the intentional as well as unanticipated, the global as well as local benefits that the best survey courses provide. If instructors create well-wrought syllabi and teach with clear, manageable goals that actively engage students, students will read *Paradise Lost* and other Miltonic texts eventually, either in upper-division courses or on their own as leisure readers; and their experience of those readings will be no doubt much more meaningful because of their early and good exposure to his shorter works.

In *Of Education*, Milton characterizes a good teacher's job as requiring "sinews almost equal to those which Homer gave Ulysses." The metaphor occasionally springs to mind when I see instructors lugging around weighty anthologies, in contrast to the shorter collections and individual texts I prefer. (My hope is that my assigned books will not make their way back to the college bookstore's used-books section at the end of the term.) In all seriousness, I leave you with the image because it is an apt one for your important role in the educational odysseys with which this volume's contributors wish you all success.

NOTE

I dedicate this essay to Paul Alpers, *maestro magnifico.*

Milton and Textual Studies:
Teaching "On Shakespeare" as a Work in Progress

Stephen B. Dobranski

The strict measure and soft airs of John Milton's early poems sometimes belie the labor of their composition. Students can feel daunted by works that seem to have sprung from the poet's head like Sin in *Paradise Lost*, "shining Heav'nly fair" and fully developed (2.757). This essay addresses one strategy for demystifying Milton's authorship while respecting his poetry's complexity. Introducing students to some basic principles of textual studies helps them understand that a poem does not represent the sudden inspiration of a divine creator but instead consists of choices made by a human being in conversation with members of a printing house and in response to changing historical situations.

Devoted to the production, transmission, and reception of texts, the field of textual studies is especially relevant for Milton's poetry and prose because so many of these works survive in multiple seventeenth-century versions. Not only did Milton meticulously revise his shorter poems, as the Trinity College Manuscript shows, but he also continued polishing his works even after they were printed. Thus Milton altered the fifteenth stanza of "On the Morning of Christ's Nativity" between 1645 and 1673, made extensive changes to *A Mask Presented at Ludlow Castle* after it was first performed in 1634, and thoroughly revised and expanded *The Doctrine and Discipline of Divorce* between its first and second editions (1643, 1644).

Milton's "On Shakespeare" (*Riverside* 61–62) also underwent a series of sometimes subtle revisions during the poet's lifetime, some of which, we will see, Milton himself may not have initiated. This particular poem works well for helping students think about Milton's practice of authorship in part because it addresses the nature of a poet's lasting achievement. Although a few of Milton's longer poetic works contain more dramatic revisions—most notably, *Paradise Lost*, which was published first in ten books and later restructured into a twelve-book epic—the eight couplets that compose "On Shakespeare" provide a more manageable form for examining the provenance of Milton's writings.

Beginning with a discussion of the poem's diction and imagery emphasizes Milton's vision of a reciprocal relationship between a writer and readers. Shakespeare will achieve immortality through his verse, Milton asserts, because his writing makes such a "deep impression" on his audience's imagination. Teachers should specifically note the pun of *a*-stone-*ishment*, as Shakespeare's works have a Medusa-like effect on his audience. Transfixed by the playwright's "Delphick lines," we are figuratively transformed into a stony monument: "thou . . . / Dost make us Marble with too much conceaving."[1] In contrast to a traditional memorial built of "piled Stones"—where *piled* evokes a large building or a funeral pyre but also hints pejoratively at a disorderly mass of material—Shakespeare has "built thy self a live-long Monument." The emphasis in this latter phrase falls on the author's agency and his monument's liveliness: while "thy self" indicates that Shakespeare has personally ensured he will be remembered, "live-long" fits with other details in the poem that suggest his monument will long endure because his readers keep it alive. In contrast to the playwright's physical death—we read, for example, about Shakespeare's "honour'd Bones," "hallow'd reliques," and "Sepulcher'd" body—Milton describes how "each heart" actively helps to "conceave" Shakespeare's writings. The specific choice of "conceave" refers both to readers' imaginative faculties as well as to our generative function; we are imaginatively preserving Shakespeare's memory and simultaneously helping to create his poetic authority.

Teachers should also bring to students' attention what Milton does not say in this poem: missing from "On Shakespeare" is any mention of the theater. Instead, Milton addresses Shakespeare's accomplishments exclusively in terms of his poetry and publishing—the poet's "easie numbers," "Delphick lines," and "unvalu'd Book." This more narrow focus may be attributed to the poem's original bibliographical context: "On Shakespeare" was first printed in 1632, one of seven encomiastic poems at the start of Shakespeare's second folio, *Mr. William Shakespeare's Comedies, Histories, and Tragedies* (A5r). In this context, Milton's poem was meant to commemorate not only Shakespeare's artistry but also, it seems, the publication of such a prestigious volume.

At this point in the class discussion, as students continue to examine Milton's description of the playwright's living monument, I distribute a handout with two different copies of "On Shakespeare." This poem, I announce, was published five times during Milton's lifetime—in 1632, 1640, 1645, 1664, and 1673—on each occasion in a slightly different version. The handout only reproduces two of the poem's printings, I also explain, so as to reduce the quantity of bibliographic evidence and focus our attention on some of the poem's most revealing textual issues. At the top of the page is copied the poem's earliest surviving version, as it was published in Shakespeare's second folio (1632); the second version reproduced on the handout appeared in Milton's own first collection, *Poems of Mr. John Milton, Both English and Latin, Compos'd at Several Times* (1645):

An Epitaph on the admirable Dramaticke Poet W. SHAKESPEARE.

What neede my Shakespeare *for his honour'd bones,*	
The labour of an Age, in piled stones	
Or that his hallow'd Reliques should be hid	
Under a starre-ypointed Pyramid?	
Dear Sonne of Memory, great Heire of Fame,	5
What needst thou such dull witnesse of thy Name?	
Thou in our wonder and astonishment	
Hast built thy selfe a lasting Monument:	
For whil'st, to th' shame of slow-endevouring Art,	
Thy easie numbers flow, and that each part,	10
Hath from the leaves of thy unvalued Booke,	
Those Delphicke Lines with deepe Impression tooke:	
Then thou our fancy of her selfe bereaving,	
Dost make us Marble with too much conceiving,	
And so Sepulcher'd in such pompe dost lie,	15
That Kings for such a Tombe would wish to die.	

On *Shakespear*. 1630.

What needs my *Shakespear* for his honour'd Bones,	
The labour of an age in piled Stones,	
Or that his hallow'd reliques should be hid	
Under a Star-ypointing *Pyramid?*	
Dear son of memory, great heir of Fame,	5
What need'st thou such weak witness of thy name?	
Thou in our wonder and astonishment	
Hast built thy self a live-long Monument.	
For whilst to th' shame of slow-endeavoring art,	
Thy easie numbers flow, and that each heart	10
Hath from the leaves of thy unvalu'd Book,	
Those Delphick lines with deep impression took,	
Then thou our fancy of it self bereaving,	
Dost make us Marble with too much conceaving;	
And so Sepulcher'd in such pomp dost lie,	15
That Kings for such a Tomb would wish to die.	

Students will quickly discover significant differences between these two versions by reading either the top or bottom text silently while the teacher reads the other text aloud. I ask students to mark on the handout any discrepancies they hear, beginning most noticeably with the two versions' different titles. Except for the inclusion of line numbers, as I remind students, all aspects of these poems—capitalization, case, punctuation, and spelling—are reproduced exactly as they were published during the seventeenth century.

Then, working either in small groups or as a class, students are asked to list all the differences between the two versions that they were able to discern by ear—"*neede*"/"needs" (1), "*starre-ypointed*"/"Star-ypointing" (4), "*dull*"/"weak" (6), "*lasting*"/"live-long" (8), "*part*"/"heart" (10), and "*her selfe*"/"it self " (13)—as well as the many other differences detectable only by sight—"Shakespeare"/ "*Shakespear*" (1), "*bones*"/"Bones" (1), "*Age*"/"age" (2), "*stones*"/"Stones" (2), and so on. Variants that can be heard, I explain, have traditionally been called "substantive readings" because they alter a text's meaning, while those variants that textual critics can only see (with the exception of homonyms) are traditionally labeled "surface features" or "accidentals" because they less obviously affect meaning.

With this bibliographical evidence at hand, students are ready to discuss three questions:

> Which version of Milton's tribute to Shakespeare is generally preferable, "On *Shakespear. 1630.*" or "An Epitaph on the admirable Dramaticke Poet W. SHAKESPEARE."?
>
> Are any of the poems' individual word choices preferable—"dull" versus "weak" (6), for example, or "lasting" versus "live-long" (8)?
>
> If a new edition of Milton's poetry were being published today, which version(s) of this poem should be included?

By asking students to justify their answers to these questions, teachers help them to discover inductively competing theories of textual authority and the various criteria that modern editors use when confronted with different versions of the same work. Students may first require prompting to define "preferable" in the above questions and to decide which criteria of selection they deem most significant—order of publication, say, or their own aesthetic judgment. Critics have long noted, for example, that "starre-ypointed" probably means a pyramid with a star on top, whereas "Star-ypointing" refers to a pyramid that points to the starry sky (R. Smith 40).[2] But which type of pyramid works best in Milton's poem? And how do we decide? Having begun this exercise with a close reading, students should realize how much is at stake: which version or individual passage they select may change the poem's meaning.

Often students will resist this responsibility and appeal instead to Milton's authority; they wish to know the poet's preferences so that they have a starting point for analyzing specific passages. But "On Shakespeare" helps to illustrate the difficulty of determining an author's intentions, since we cannot know for certain which of the poem's changes between 1632 and 1645 were made by Milton and which may have been incorporated—intentionally or unintentionally— by a member of the printing house. Students must establish on their own the relative significance of the two versions by scrutinizing the available bibliographic evidence. Does the fact that "An Epitaph" was published anonymously diminish its authority, for example? Does "On *Shakespear*" better capture the author's final plans for the poem, or is it more likely to have been corrupted over time by outside agents? And which version should be treated as the older poem, given that "On *Shakespear*" was printed thirteen years after "An Epitaph" but with the earlier date of 1630?

To help students discuss these and other related questions, teachers should explain that authors during the early modern period traditionally had little legal, economic, or practical control over the publication of their works (Dobranski 20–26). While names such as "Milton" or "Shakespeare" today convey considerable cultural authority, a seventeenth-century printer or bookseller belonging to the royally chartered Company of Stationers could secure legal ownership of a text by publishing it in print or having its title recorded in the Stationers' *Register*—with or without the author's approval. Prior to England's first copyright act in 1709, authors had little recourse: they could provide the printer with a good copy so as to prevent the circulation of a poorly made edition, or they could compensate the unscrupulous stationer so that a corrected version could be later printed. Only gradually, as patronage declined and a market system arose, did authorial rights become more widely respected. In practical terms, printers and booksellers continued to make the essential decisions for transforming authors' ideas into their printed, public forms, but some authors began to assert limited control of their works by, for example, attending at the printing house or negotiating terms with specific stationers.

In the case of Milton's "On Shakespeare," the poet seems not to have participated in its 1632 printing. We do not even know how a work by the twenty-four-year-old Milton came to be anonymously included in such a distinguished volume—perhaps through his father's intervention, according to one theory, or through the influence of one of Milton's friends, such as the court musician Henry Lawes. Or perhaps some of Milton's other shorter poems had circulated in manuscript and caught the attention of members of the book trade (C. Hill, *Milton* 62). Teachers may note that "An Epitaph" in 1632 was Milton's second printed poem; his only other printed work was a copy of the commencement verses, now lost, that he was asked to write in 1628 while still a student at Cambridge.

But if Milton by the time of his 1645 *Poems* had considerably more experience with printing—in addition to his five antiprelatical tracts (1641–42), he had published *A Mask* (1637), "Lycidas" (1638), "Epitaphium Damonis" (1640), *The Doctrine and Discipline of Divorce* (1643), *The Judgment of Martin Bucer* (1644), *Of Education* (1644), and *Areopagitica* (1644)—students should not assume that this experience translated into practical control over his works' production. Milton certainly had a hand in his *Poems's* creation, supplying, for example, the information for the terse, biographical tags such as "1630" that are appended to seventeen of the collection's texts. But the bookseller Humphrey Moseley undertook the financial risk of producing the volume and thus would have had final say over its design and arrangement. A major figure in the seventeenth-century book trade, Moseley throughout the 1645 *Poems* seems to cast Milton in his own image: responding to the recent outbreak of civil war, the bookseller presents Milton as a royalist gentleman by emphasizing the poet's aristocratic connections and continental acquaintances (Dobranski 82–103).

Part of the point of comparing the 1632 and 1645 versions of "On Shakespeare" is for teachers to show students that Milton, like Shakespeare, may have "built . . . a live-long Monument," but neither author worked alone, and neither author's writings were set in stone. By continuing to revise his poems and pamphlets even after they were published, by working with printers and publishers who inserted their own changes, Milton, again like Shakespeare, created a dynamic, living monument. Students can accordingly argue that the 1645 "On Shakespear" more closely captures Milton's intentions (because the 1645 collection as a whole emphasizes his authorial presence) or that the 1632 "Epitaph" is more authoritative (because it remains the earliest printed version) or that both versions deserve to be read (because we have no bibliographic evidence suggesting either version is absolutely definitive). As with the poem itself, the textual context supports multiple interpretations, and to choose among the work's versions requires a delicate balance of imagination and discretion.

Teachers can drive home the exercise's practical value by returning to the question of a modern edition of Milton's poetry and asking students which version of "On Shakespeare" was used in the class's assigned text. How did their editor resolve the inconsistencies between the poem's surviving versions? The class may be surprised to learn that most modern editions are "eclectic": editors piece together features from all a work's versions so as to remove variance and fulfill what the editors believe the author would have ideally wanted. The resulting texts, however, never actually existed during the author's lifetime. If time permits, I then ask students to create their own eclectic text of "On Shakespeare" from the 1632 and 1645 printings so that they can experience firsthand the authority that modern readers regularly and unknowingly cede to editors. More ambitious students can also take copies of the poem's other versions into account.[3]

Inevitably, one or two students, frustrated by the absence of a definitive text for "On Shakespeare" and bothered by the intrusiveness of eclectic editing, will suggest that the best choice a modern editor can make is not to choose. According to this way of thinking, editors should include multiple versions of a work in a modern edition and allow readers to experience each separately. Such a proposal provides an opportunity for teachers then to discuss with students some of the practical considerations of modern editing, such as cost, audience, and print versus electronic format. Would high school or college students be willing to read multiple versions of Milton's works? And how can modern editors best accommodate multiple versions that have only slight variants? Teachers could also inform the class that scholars have actually identified three versions of the 1632 "An Epitaph," each containing minor differences in punctuation ("tooke:" versus "tooke" [12]), spelling ("slow-endevouring" versus "slow-endeavouring" [9]), and capitalization ("Impression" versus "impression" [12]). I ask the class whether modern readers need to know about variations that do not affect the work's meaning. Do modern readers even need to read Milton's texts in an old-spelling format with the original punctuation? And can students think of "surface features" that are actually "substantive," such as the hungry-sounding "endevouring" versus the more standard "endeavoring"?

Ultimately, by introducing textual studies into a discussion of Milton's shorter poetry and prose, I encourage students to discover how Milton's works continued to evolve over time and how seemingly minor changes in his diction, punctuation, and layout affect a reader's experience. Teachers can determine for themselves how far to take this exercise, perhaps stopping after students discuss the two versions of "On Shakespeare" or perhaps returning occasionally to this subject throughout the semester, examining, for example, the implications of Milton's publishing *Paradise Regained* and *Samson Agonistes* in the same volume and in that order.

If we wish students to study Milton's works by analyzing their subtle details, students should at least realize that such details are sometimes less stable than modern editions imply. Milton's works consist of choices that he made—and later remade—in conversation with printers and booksellers. Often I have found that students try to build their readings of individual passages on the use of capitals or italics—without taking into account that Milton, like most Renaissance writers, almost certainly did not dictate the printing of these elements. In class, I use cinema as a metaphor: just as viewers acknowledge that several agents must cooperate to make a movie, readers need to appreciate that writing similarly represents a social process requiring the contributions of various people.

In the context of Milton's tribute to Shakespeare, the multiple surviving versions of "On Shakespeare" reinforce such a collaboration, specifically the reciprocal relationship that Milton envisions in the poem between a writer and readers. Shakespeare and Milton may not "need . . . / The labour of an age in piled Stones," but they continue to depend on generations of readers who must labor to compile all of an author's copies before these works can be understood fully and memorialized.

NOTES

[1] For a possible, additional allusion to the story of Niobe, see Curtis Perry's close reading of "On Shakespeare" in this volume.

[2] Teachers also might wish to explain that the *y-* prefix in the past participle was a Middle English convention. Milton may have specifically had in mind the sixteenth-century author Edmund Spenser, who retained this archaic verb form in, for example, *The Faerie Queene.*

[3] These versions are included in *John Milton's Complete Poetical Works Reproduced in Photographic Facsimile,* vol. 1.

"That Glorious Form":
Teaching the Nativity Ode and
Samson Agonistes through Visual Images

Wendy Furman-Adams

For my *teacher Virginia James Tufte*

Twenty-first-century college students often are thoroughly daunted by the manifold complexities of Milton's conceptual universe—political, theological, ethical, and linguistic. But, in compensation for their lack of confidence in these largely verbal areas, they are quick and sophisticated visual learners—a learning style especially easy to accommodate in the Milton classroom. Milton himself, not blind until midlife, was a remarkably visual poet. Even his most studious and abstruse passages are rendered in richly visual terms. He also continually thematizes the concept of accommodation—the mediation of the nonsensory to the senses; the invisible world of Ideas (in the platonic sense) to human sight—from the cinematic fantasies of "L'Allegro" and "Il Penseroso" to Raphael's "lik'ning [of] spiritual to corporal forms" in *Paradise Lost* (5.573 [*Riverside*]). Indeed, as Raphael remarks to Adam and Eve, such accommodation may be more natural than we think, for "what if Earth / Be but the shaddow of Heav'n, and things therein / Each to other like, more then on earth is thought?" (*PL* 5.574–76).

As Roland M. Frye argued nearly three decades ago, Milton responded more deeply to his extensive, firsthand experience of the visual arts than we might expect of a radical seventeenth-century Protestant, creating his own immense universe—infernal, heavenly, and terrestrial—in conversation (sometimes appreciative, sometimes adversarial) with a vast repository of traditional visual images (9–39). Conversely, more than two hundred artists since 1688 have offered visual interpretations of Milton's works, making them—along with the Bible and Shakespeare's plays—among the most copiously illustrated texts in the Western world. In teaching Milton, I regularly use both kinds of images— images Milton might have known (or others like them) and images his texts have inspired—showing my students over a hundred works produced between the fourth and the twentieth centuries.

My pedagogy in the use of these visual materials is simple and flexible. Sometimes (particularly when teaching *Paradise Lost*), I show a few images at the beginning of each class as a way of launching our discussion of the verbal text. At other times (as in teaching the Nativity Ode and *Samson* [*Riverside* 38–52, 783–844]), I show all the visual works together—juxtaposing them with brief verbal texts or using them as an introduction to, or recap of, longer ones. I use a more or less Socratic approach to help my students "see" the questions appropriate to analyzing visual material in a literary context—that is, the questions of iconography, as opposed to primarily stylistic or historical questions.[1]

On showing an image, I generally ask them first to identify the scene the artist has chosen to represent. (These choices—what an artist represents, leaves out, or perhaps adds to Milton's work—are often significant in themselves.) Then I ask them to describe, as fully and objectively as possible, what they see, literally, in the image. What figures are represented—and how? What "moment" of the poem's action has the artist taken as exemplary, as somehow embodying the essence of the narrative?[2] What has the artist chosen to play up, play down, add, or perhaps change in response to Milton's text? What, finally, seems to be this artist's interpretation of the scene (the Nativity of Christ, Samson's final agon, etc.)? How attentive to Milton's text is this interpretation? To what extent does it illuminate or distort the event or poem as *you* read it? At this point in our analysis—without much coaxing or prodding—my students begin to own the Miltonic text in question, and they find themselves talking about its nuances with more insight and conviction than most of them would have thought possible.

Even given the limitations imposed by a thirteen-week semester, I recommend taking the time to discuss Milton's shorter poems and prose. I find that students approach *Paradise Lost* with less trepidation having first encountered similar themes and aesthetic maneuvers in the poet's earlier work. Thus, after a week introducing Milton's biography and working through selected sonnets, I spend three days on the Nativity Ode—emphasizing its role in Milton's self-consecration as inspired poet-prophet (at about my students' age!) and its place near the end of a long and varied tradition of art, poetry, and music inspired by the biblical account of the Incarnation.[3]

We spend the first day looking at several medieval and early modern poems in that tradition—including three poems by Robert Southwell ("New Prince, New Pomp," "The Nativitie of Christ," and "The Burning Babe" [16–17, 7–8, 15–16]), John Donne's "Annunciation" and "Nativity" (*Complete Poetry* 334–35), and Richard Crashaw's "A Hymn of the Nativity"—the poem perhaps most often compared with Milton's. These poems, while shorter than the Nativity Ode, are still often far from accessible apart from visual analogues, which fortunately abound. As we read them in class, I show slides of paintings that embody some of the sacramental paradoxes they express—paradoxes that introduce the idea of cyclic, liturgical time.[4] In Mantegna's *Madonna of the Stonecutters* (1488–90, Uffizi Gallery, Florence), for instance, the Virgin Mary sits in front of a craggy mountain holding the Christ child. Behind them to the left rises not Bethlehem but a city that appears, oddly, to be Jerusalem; to the right, stonecutters carve sarcophagi out of the tormented-looking mountain. I ask the students if anything else seems strange about the scene. They begin to notice that the child appears dead, that the mother appears to be grieving, even that the child's halo looks remarkably like a eucharistic wafer—that the scene superimposes a pietà on a lullaby and foreshadows, as virtually all Nativity poems do, the cross at the cradle. The Nativity scene in Mathias Grünewald's *Isenheim Altar* (1505–16, Unterlinden Museum, Colmar) also underscores the theme that "The Babe . . . on the bitter cross / Must redeem our loss" (*Riverside* 43; lines 152–53)—by wrapping the babe in swaddling clothes that my students soon recognize as a torn and slightly bloody shroud.

One way of talking about Protestant poetics is to talk about the way in which it alters this cyclic, liturgical view of time—the distinctly Catholic view in which the Eucharist is not only weekly (or even daily) sacrifice but weekly (or daily) Incarnation. Milton's Protestant aesthetic follows earlier Reformers in replacing sacrifice with memorial—and, in so doing, replacing the cycle with a linear, narrative, above all prophetic, view of time. My students see, as we move on to the Nativity Ode, that Milton's Christ child "lies yet in smiling Infancy" (151), framing the rest of the poem; the meaning of the kerygma cannot for Milton be embodied (as it can for the Catholics Southwell, Crashaw, and Mantegna—or even for the more High Church Anglican Donne) in a single, timeless image of sublimity and pathos. Rather, it must be envisioned in a series of vividly contrasting temporal images, in which sacrament gives way to prophecy. Today, Milton says, we remember "[t]hat glorious Form" of the Godhead who "[f]orsook the Courts of everlasting Day" (8–13); we remember that shepherds sat on a lawn and suddenly beheld "a Globe of circular light" (110). At that moment they experienced the momentary reign of "meek-eyed Peace" (46) and heard music not heard since the creation—music so melodious and holy that if it were to "Enwrap our fancy long, / Time *will* run back, and fetch the age of gold" (134–35). But "wisest Fate says no" (149). Still ahead for the child (and for humanity) are "the bitter cross," "the wakefull trump of doom," and "the worlds last session"—"And *then* at last our bliss / Full and perfect is" (152–66; italics mine). Thus, like virtually all Milton's poems (including sonnets 7 and 19), the Nativity Ode proves to be less about adoration than about deferred millennial hope—"till one greater Man / Restore us" (*PL* 1.4–5).

I close our class discussion of the Nativity Ode by having the students "read" William Blake's six gorgeous watercolors illustrating the poem (1809, Whitworth Art Gallery, Manchester; see Butlin)—an exercise through which they are able to see, in every sense, both what is traditional and what is radical in Milton's reinterpretation of the Nativity and, in turn, in Blake's re-vision of Milton. Faithful to Milton's vision, Blake begins and ends his series with "the Heav'n-born-childe"—at, and then in, "the rude manger" (30–31). As at home with the invisible as the visible realm—and, even more than Milton, allowing no separation between them—Blake takes Miltonic abstractions that would otherwise simply elude many of my students and renders them unforgettably visual. As I project his first design, for instance, *The Descent of Peace*, I ask the students to identify the figure flying upside-down over the "darksome" stable (meek-eyed Peace, with her myrtle wand) and the nearly naked figure lying prayerfully in the snow before it (Nature—in awe). I also ask them to identify figures not in Milton's poem (the pair of oxen), which they are by now able to tie back to earlier traditions reintroduced by Blake. In the final scene, *The Night of Peace*, they can identify "bright-harnest Angels"; they also delight in discovering "Heav'n's youngest teemed Star" in her "polisht Car" (240–44)—as well as a detail, again, which Blake has added: the stern gaze of prophecy in the eyes of the wakeful Joseph.

In *The Angels Appearing to the Shepherds* (*Annunciation to the Shepherds*), Blake equally illuminates the middle of the poem—with his stunningly realized insight, for instance, that the "Globe of circular light" seen by the astonished shepherds is in fact made up of "helmed Cherubim" and "Seraphim," although he characteristically sheathes their swords (110–13). Perhaps most remarkable is Blake's representation of *The Flight of Moloch*—leaving his "burning Idol" with the last of the children destined to satanic sacrifice (207). Here Blake, as revisionary as his master, goes beyond Milton and moves closer, for the moment, to the earlier visionary spirit of Southwell's "Burning Babe" (which my students have read and can connect to the visual image before them). For out of Moloch's fiery furnace steps a triumphant resurrected baby—dazzling the two women who witness his emergence, redeeming all contraries of time and eternity through his infant sacrifice. In adding this enigmatic figure, Blake both embraces the prophetic Milton and corrects what he views as the older poet's illusory sense of deferral and temporality, restoring the bond between time and eternity. In so doing, he teaches my students how many responses even a brief Miltonic poem can evoke—radical re-visions of a vision already radical. Through this insight—and through the further looking glass of *A Mask*—they are able to move easily to Milton's radical reworking of gender, politics, and theology in *Paradise Lost* and *Samson Agonistes*.

The terrorist nightmare of recent years has given *Samson Agonistes* new relevance, if not urgency, in the Milton classroom.[5] As with the Nativity Ode and *Paradise Lost*, moreover, visual materials can help place Milton's representation of this biblical story in a long history of interpretation—a history as ambiguous and inconclusive as his tragedy. Hundreds of artists have represented the biblical account of Samson in Judges 13–16. After my students have read both the biblical account and Milton's poem, I use some of these images to lead them to consider which aspects of a long, contradictory tradition Milton has adopted and which he has rejected or at least downplayed. Fifteen of Milton's two hundred illustrators have in turn represented *Samson Agonistes*. These images, especially when compared with images representing the biblical Samson, go on to demonstrate the profound difficulty, if not impossibility, of arriving at definitive readings of literary texts (including biblical ones)—ideally leading my students to take more responsibility for the things they "know."

I show a number of images of Samson after we have completed our still-tentative discussion of the poem—organizing them in two large categories and tracing the historical development of each: images of the biblical Samson, then visual interpretations of Milton's poem. I begin with early works that illustrate the point that until the late fifteenth century, artists and their patrons were interested in the Hebrew Bible not primarily as narrative but rather as a set of signs prefiguring the Gospel. Thus Samson, like other Old Testament heroes, was represented typologically, as one of a "great . . . cloud of witnesses" prefiguring "Jesus, the author and finisher of [Christian] faith" (Heb. 11.32, 12.1–2). By the sixteenth and seventeenth centuries, however—and especially during Milton's lifetime—Samson had become, for most artists and patrons, less a type than an individual; and his human tragedy became a favorite subject of Northern Baroque painters such as Peter Paul Rubens, Anthony Van Dyck, and especially Rembrandt. These works generally focus on the Nazarite, chosen of God, as a lover—and, above all else, as victim. Rembrandt's fascination with character and with moments of deep psychological drama seems to have drawn him especially to the characters of the Samson story, and he produced a virtual narrative cycle of Samson's agon—a group of works that I spend considerable time discussing with my students.

No one who has seen it can forget Rembrandt's heartbreaking *Samson Betrayed by Delilah* (1629–30, Gemäldegalerie, Berlin), a scene in which every figure seems to participate equally in Samson's anguish. Asked to identify the scene represented, my students can easily identify the moment in which Delilah, having at last learned Samson's secret, lets him "sleep upon her knees," as she calls a man to "shave off the seven locks of his head." Two men creep into the room from behind a curtain, faces registering—as my students describe them— something like apprehension and pity. Samson lies, childlike in his trust and "vexed unto death" (as the text tells us), in the arms of the woman he loves, his satin robe catching the strange light that seems to have entered the chamber with the invading men (Judg. 16.16–19). Asked about characters and their motives, the students note that Delilah looks up at the reluctant barber as if regretting too late her decision to betray this foolishly trusting lover. Her hands move in almost protective agitation over his hair. No one in the image appears pleased or even content with the role he or she must play in this miserable moment of sacred history. Yet, central as this scene is for Rembrandt, it is present in Milton's tragedy only as the protagonist stages and restages it on the screen of his agonized mind—and as he overcomes it in an encounter with "Dalila" (no longer the biblical courtesan but his wife) nowhere mentioned in the Judges account.

The next moment in Rembrandt's virtual cycle is *The Blinding of Samson* (1636, Städel Museum, Frankfurt am Main). Ignoring Samson's failings and the possible ambivalence of his enemies, this work clearly emphasizes their unspeakable cruelty. As a flailing Samson is pulled down onto his back into the darkness, he is held down by two intent and armored soldiers, one tightening a chain around his struggling wrist. And as a devilish-looking, turbaned assailant aims a massive spear at Samson's second eye—the other already bleeding like those of Oedipus or Gloucester—a jubilant if anguished Delilah lifts his shorn lock before her, as the fatal shears still glisten in her menacing right hand.

Christopher Brown has described *The Blinding of Samson* as "without doubt the most violent picture Rembrandt ever painted" (*Rembrandt* 72), and when I project it, it typically elicits little cries of horror. Rembrandt painted these and several others during the years before Milton became totally blind—works that show above all Samson's suffering and betrayal, themes emphasized in Milton's tragedy but not represented except as they play in the mind of his tortured protagonist. This contrast in selection can lead to fruitful discussion of what Rembrandt's and Milton's works are "about."

If for Rembrandt the exemplary moments of the Samson story are those representing his misery, other works—earlier versions of which Milton could also have known—link Samson's betrayal directly to his terrible suicide-revenge. *Delilahs Falshood to Sampson*, from a Bible published at Oxford in 1682 (fig. 1), shows the agitated gestures of soldiers and attendants, as Delilah intently wields the scissors on Samson's sleeping head—underscoring, like Rembrandt, his betrayal at her hands. An inset, however, shows the aftermath—in which a strangely childlike Samson breaks stylized pillars and Philistines tumble from the temple's collapsing roof in a horrible if primitive preplay of 9/11. Matthäus Merian's 1630 painting (fig. 2) anticipates the Oxford image, in reverse and more graphic in living color: the victim Samson is again shorn by a deliberate-looking Delilah, but in a background vignette, he furiously pulls down the temple, as his enemies struggle in midair, falling on and around him. One can even make out, as if from a child's nightmare, the round open mouths of the victims' silent cries. The contemporary resonance of this scene is not lost on my students, all of whom remember the weird silence of the falling towers and bodies that ghastly Tuesday morning. Yet they also remember that Milton's rendering of the catastrophe begins with a "noise" that "tore the Skie" (line 1472). If *Samson* has not yet seemed relevant to some, these violent images erase any remaining complacent separation of art from life.

Artists who have illustrated Milton's *Samson Agonistes* differ from those representing the biblical Samson in focusing, as the poet does, on the protagonist's inner life—which Milton largely invented for him. Seeing these works calls my students' attention to the remarkable fact that this inner life is completely absent in the Judges account; yet it is this inner life that critics since Samuel Johnson have been at pains to put forward, albeit in different ways, as the poem's "middle." Beginning in 1720, with a typical illustration by Louis Chéron (fig. 3), one artist after another represents the Judge of Israel blinded and in the hands of his enemies, reflecting on his painful plight and shameful past. Like seventeenth-century artists working just before Milton, these artists generally represent Samson less as a type than as a human being, but of a different kind: one who is above all thoughtful and contemplative, whether alone or with others. What he does is sit, brood, and, apparently, think—a radical re-vision of the nearly frenetic action of the biblical text.

Even in their representations of Samson's final violent act, artists have continued to focus on the interiority of Samson's agon, despite the long tradition of

Fig. 1.   *Delilahs Falshood to Sampson* (*The Holy Bible Containing the Old and New Testaments* [Oxford, 1682]).

extroverted violence in representations of the biblical Samson. In an engraving from 1904 (fig. 4), for instance, William Hyde represents not falling bodies but the moment of stillness and meditation in the temple of Dagon before Samson pulls down the pillars. Appearing more like an ascetic desert saint or biblical prophet than a strongman bent on avenging the loss of his eyes, "with head a while enclin'd, / And eyes fast fixt he stood, as one who pray'd, / Or some great matter in his mind revolv'd" (1636–38). Yet my students can make out that to

Fig. 2.   Matthäus Merian, *Delilah's Betrayal and the Destruction of the Temple* (*The Bible: In Word and Art* [Amsterdam, 1630]).

Fig. 3.   Louis Chéron, *Samson Sitting in Prison in Chains* (John Milton, *The Poetical Works of Mr. John Milton* [London, 1720]).

Fig. 4.   William Hyde, *Samson Contemplating the Destruction of Dagon's Temple* (John Milton, *The Poetical Works of John Milton* [London, 1904]).

his right, in a building that looks more souk than temple, stand four veiled fig-ures and an armed guard whose seconds are numbered. To the students' eyes—whatever the opinion of the Hebrew semichorus—these figures do not appear drunk, either with idolatry or with wine (1670). In this engraving, the construc-tion of the other is a political matter—as is the reading of a text about two groups of human beings still locked in deadly contention as we consider the image on the screen. If we feel for this Samson—and my students often do—he nonetheless conveys in his intent asceticism an ambiguity we have come to know too well: pure in motive, without a doubt, but about to produce an action that cannot but polarize our reactions.

Of all Samson's illustrators, Robert Medley challenges my students perhaps the most fully, by offering them a reading of Milton's poem that is finally more Rorschach than interpretation (Milton, *Samson Agonistes, a Dramatic Poem*). In his designs for a rare and sumptuous 1979 folio edition, Medley used what he has called organic abstraction, to represent scenes from Milton's tragedy. Having tried literal representation of the poem's action, he changed direction in an attempt to face the poem's difficult questions: Samson's motivation, his relation to his people and his enemies, his view of Dalila—the questions my students find most interesting in the text. Among the vivid images I show my students are one of Dalila as a ship in full rig (fig. 5). Two more of Medley's im-

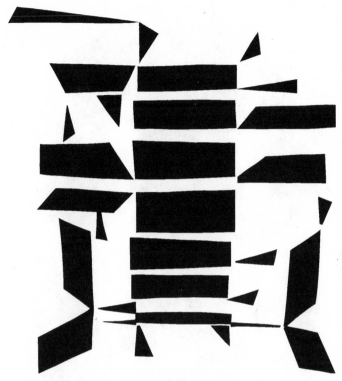

Fig. 5.   Robert Medley, *Dalila: A Ship in Full Rig* (John Milton, *Samson Agonistes: A Dramatic Poem* [Norwich: Mell Clark, 1979] illus. 12).

ages focus on harsh attitudes toward Dalila expressed in Milton's *Samson*: one equating her to a serpent in the company of Dagon; and one comparing her to "Fame," "double-mouthed" if not "double-fac't" (971). But Medley, unlike other artists we have viewed together, makes no evaluation of these views; they remain entirely relative to their speakers. And his final illustration, *Tablet for the God of Israel* (fig. 6), carries the mystery, the conundrum, of the tragedy to the end. I ask my students, Does this altar assert, with Milton's chorus, that Samson's death has fulfilled his appointed role to begin to deliver Israel out of the hands of the Philistines? Does it, conversely, lay the violence of the poem— and of our world—at Yahweh's feet? Or does it simply challenge us to continue the discussion?

By this point in the course, my students know that they can never "cover" or "master" Milton's works—or any other great literary or visual text. Yet, paradoxically, they also find themselves empowered as interpreters, by their discovery of the special and glorious form of intertextuality hovering between the sister arts. They learn that analysis of one medium can exponentially deepen analysis

Fig. 6.   Robert Medley, *Tablet for the God of Israel* (John Milton, *Samson Agonistes: A Dramatic Poem* [Norwich: Mell Clark, 1979] illus. 23).

in another. And finally, through this vast and remarkable set of visual lenses, they come to read Milton almost without trepidation—wisdom at one entrance illuminating all the rest.

NOTES

My debt to Virginia James Tufte cannot be overstated. This essay reflects her collaboration throughout—especially in the section on Samson.

[1] Erwin Panofsky defined *iconography* as "that branch of the history of art which concerns itself with the subject matter or meaning of works of art, as opposed to their form,"

and involves the analysis of images, stories, allegories, and symbols in the light of the themes particular to European (or any other) culture (3, 14–15).

[2] In 1766, G. E. Lessing famously wrote, "The [visual] artist can never seize from ever-changing nature more than a single moment." Whereas the poet can lead the reader "through a whole gallery of pictures, as it were, up to the last one," only that last and somehow exemplary moment can be represented visually (20, 83, 89). For a contemporary analysis of Lessing's historic "space-time" distinction in the "sister arts," see Mitchell 95–115.

[3] Although I address only the visual arts in this essay, I also find it helpful to play a CD of Ralph Vaughan Williams's *Hodie*, in which the composer used the Nativity Ode to create his own narrative frame. Playing parts of the oratorio that are based on Milton's poem, I ask students to reflect on how Vaughan Williams has selected and reordered pieces of Milton's narrative to create his own—one, they see, significantly different from Milton's in its prophetic stance and in its view of human time.

[4] The first eight artworks discussed—those by Mantegna, Grünewald, Blake, and Rembrandt—are readily available in color on the Internet, where they may be downloaded and projected in the classroom or viewed independently by teachers and students. All eight may be accessed, for example, through the useful Web site *Biblical Art on the WWW* (www.biblical-art.com); the four Blake illustrations are also available on the site for the Whitworth Art Gallery of the University of Manchester (www.whitworth.manchester.ac.uk).

[5] The debate about Milton's Samson as "terrorist" began in the *Times Literary Supplement*, in the 6 September 2002 issue, with an essay by John Carey, "A Work in Praise of Terrorism?" In the article, Carey challenged a view advanced by Stanley Fish in *How Milton Works*. For a review of the controversy, see D. D. Guttenplan's "Is Reading Milton Unsafe at Any Speed?" Also see Joseph Wittreich's essay in this volume.

Teaching Theology in Milton's Shorter Poetry

Albert C. Labriola

In teaching Milton to undergraduates, I stress the self-sufficiency and the interrelation of certain shorter poems to communicate Milton's theology. Instead of relying on secondary resources, on works by other seventeenth-century theologians, or on Milton's *On Christian Doctrine*, I indicate that we may infer humankind's relationship with the Godhead from an intensive scrutiny of the literature itself. In teaching undergraduates, my assumptions are that a poem is not a theological treatise; that the theological content of a poem is integrated into, and expressed through, the literary medium in which it appears; that a poem conveys the author's views of the relationship of humankind and the Godhead; and that the author's role as a poet informs and influences the text's presentation of theology. To demonstrate how theology issues from the study of Milton's shorter poems, I will recount the pedagogy by which I engaged students in a recent undergraduate survey of Milton, when, among other examples, we studied "At a Solemn Musick" (1633), sonnet 7 ("How soon hath Time" [1632]), sonnet 19 ("When I consider" [1652?]), "On the Morning of Christ's Nativity" (1629), and "Lycidas" (1637).

The sequence of poems that I outline above deliberately does not follow chronology of composition because my larger aim, which is more compatible with a synchronic, not a diachronic, perspective, emphasizes their theology. Accordingly, I begin with the twenty-eight-line poem "At a Solemn Musick," as a distillation of Milton's theology and a preamble to the unit of instruction. Then, I introduce two autobiographical sonnets, separated by approximately twenty years, in which Milton judges himself by two sets of norms: human and divine. Integrated into these two sonnets, theology provides the basis of self-examination. The remaining two works, "On the Morning of Christ's Nativity" and "Lycidas," are occasional poems. The first, composed in the predawn darkness of Christmas Day in 1629, celebrates the coming of the Christ child; the second commemorates the death of Edward King, a colleague of Milton's at Cambridge. Despite the vastly different occasions and circumstances that surround the composition of these two poems, they incorporate theology in the manner of "At a Solemn Music," sonnet 7, and sonnet 19.

From "At a Solemn Musick" (*Riverside* 56–57) students inferred that Milton's theology is ingrained in the imagery of music, the means by which humankind's relationship with the Godhead is recounted. Inviting the students to perceive how the poem presents this relationship, I elicited comments that focused on Milton's use of the language of opposites. When urged to formulate these opposites in their own language, students mentioned concord and discord, holiness and sinfulness, heaven and earth, angels and humankind. I requested that they substantiate their views by citing the language of opposites in the poem, a question that elicited the following examples: first, "fair musick" (line 21) and "harsh din" (20); then, "perfect Diapason" (23) and "dispropor-tion'd sin" that "[j]arr'd against natures chime" (19–20). I urged the students to express how Milton's theology issues from such imagery of music. They as-serted that in a state of holiness humankind is harmonized or aligned with Prov-idence, whereas in a state of sinfulness a discordant relationship disrupts this harmony and results in humankind's alienation from the Godhead. Building on their observations, I urged the students to focus on two words in the poem: "concent" (6) and "consort" (27). For each of the words, I proposed that they identify homonymic wordplay: they glossed *concent* as "harmony" and *consent* as "approval." Then, they perceived "consort" and "concert" as homonyms, the former meaning "spouse," the latter "musical performance." When I prompted them to interpret how such homonymic wordplay bears on the theology in "At a Solemn Musick," they commented that the collaboration between earth and heaven may be likened to a harmonious spousal union and that aligning one's will with Providence is an exercise in consent or approval.

At this point, I sought to promote further discussion of the theology that we inferred from "At a Solemn Musick," largely to prepare students for what we would encounter in the other short poems. I asked whether consenting to, and approving of, providential intent was an exercise of free will or a forfeiture of it. This inquiry sparked intense reaction, from which a general view emerged: paramount in Milton's theology is an exercise of faith in the higher wisdom of Providence. Conforming one's will to providential intent becomes, in other words, a faithful choice, and the image of harmony or concord signifies affinity between humankind and the Godhead.

To advance our understanding of Milton's theology, I proceeded with dis-cussion of the two autobiographical sonnets to stress how Milton prepared himself to receive the intimations of Providence in his own life. He composed sonnet 7, "How soon hath Time" (85) at the onset of his twenty-third birthday. My first question focused on the contrast between the octave and the sestet— how and why the speaker, presumably Milton himself, radically adjusts his tone. Students readily identified the tone of the octave, in which the speaker sadly recounts that others are disappointed that he has not (yet) charted a purposeful direction in life. Their disappointment is magnified because of his seeming preparation for a vocation, including a university education through the master's degree and his advancing years, which he dramatizes by saying that his "hasting dayes flie on with full career" (line 3). This observation de-rives rich significance from the word *career*, which in Milton's era meant the course over which a race is run or the fast pace of a galloping horse; the word did not yet signify a vocation and one's pursuit of it through life. Nevertheless, students will cite this more modern meaning of *career* to highlight the ironic distance between the speaker's "semblance" of "manhood" and his lack of a definite vocation (5–6). Their observation may be rectified, rather than re-jected, by suggesting that there is ironic distance between the rapidly moving years, "full career," of the speaker's life and his slowly developing "inward ripenes," a mature readiness to accept and enact a duty entrusted to him by the Godhead (3, 7).

To contrast the sestet with the octave, the students note that after the volta, or turn, which occurs at the onset of the ninth line, the speaker perceives inward ripeness as the culmination of a process, still unfolding, through which he is being led by "Time" and "the will of Heav'n" (12). The speaker affirms that his maturation and keen awareness of his assigned duty will converge at an auspicious moment under his "great task Masters eye" (14). Exercising faith, the speaker continues to manifest his willingness to serve the Lord by accepting the "grace" from above that will identify his assigned "lot" in life and that will enable him to perform it effectively (13, 11). By the end of the sonnet, the speaker achieves a psychological state of stability and equanimity, having purged himself of sadness and self-doubt, having resisted the reproach of others whose perspective typifies that of humankind, and having entrusted himself to Providence. Anticipating harmonious interaction with Providence, the speaker is prepared to accept the "lot, however mean, or high" that may be revealed to him (11).

Composed twenty years later, when Milton was totally blind, sonnet 19, "When I consider" (255), further develops Milton's theology. In line with the preceding analysis, students contrasted the octave and the sestet. In the octave, they sensed that the speaker, presumably Milton, appraises his life after the onset of blindness. Because the "[t]alent" of sight is now "useless" (lines 3–4), the speaker questions whether the Lord's expectations concerning his output should be lessened. At this point, I intervened to recount the parable of the talents from Matthew 25.14–30, in which the master having distributed talents—five, two, and one, respectively—to each of three servants summons them to accountability. Whereas the first two servants doubled what the master had initially given them, the third servant buried his one talent. The angry master rebukes the third servant, confiscates the one talent, and gives it to the more productive (first) servant. Judged "unprofitable," the third servant is cast "into outer darkness: there shall be wailing and gnashing of teeth." By this scriptural allusion, the students understood more clearly the anxiety of the speaker in Milton's sonnet. They intuited, moreover, that the speaker's anxiety subtly impugns God's justice. By the standards of the speaker, or, more broadly framed, by human standards, the master should modify his expectations concerning the output of a servant whose talents (whether construed as abilities or resources) are lesser rather than greater or of a servant whose talents initially were greater but whose disability or blindness diminished them.

In this sonnet, Milton by expostulation and reply dramatizes the anxiety of the speaker. Wondering, "Doth God exact day labour, light deny'd" (7), the speaker then judges the folly of the complaint or grievance that his question implies. By directing the students to self-characterization of the speaker, in which he uses "fondly" (or foolishly) to describe the tenor and tone of his expostulation (8), I elicited from them the observation that a debate may be unfolding. Then, I focused their attention on the speaker's use of the term "murmur" and its significance (9), largely by reading aloud certain biblical passages in which the Israelites murmured against the Lord while they sojourned in the wilderness and experienced certain privations. To engage his own question and to deter himself from impugning God's justice—or from murmuring against the Lord—the speaker cites "patience" as the virtue that informs his reply (8), which encompasses the entire sestet. Patience like fortitude is a virtue that enables one to endure increasing adversity. In this virtuous state, the speaker acknowledges that the Lord does not need the output of humankind, nor does he require the eventual return of the gifts that he granted humankind. Rather, the Lord's expectations are twofold, and both fall within the talents of humankind to meet: to "bear" one's "milde yoak" and to "serve" while one "only stand[s] and waite[s]" (11, 14). If one is never chosen for service, then the patience, fortitude, and faith exercised in the state of readiness—namely, standing and waiting—elicit divine approval. Accordingly, a servant's readiness and willingness to serve the Lord testify to a mind, heart, and soul concordant with and informed by providential intent. From such reasoning, the students concluded that a ready and willing servant is the output or outcome that the Lord expects. To phrase the observation differently, one may contend that a Christian servant of the Lord is himself the good work that will elicit divine approval on Judgment Day.

If Milton uses the two sonnets cited above for self-examination and for reconciliation with providential intent, his poems "On the Morning of Christ's Nativity," *Comus*, and "Lycidas," in the decades between the two sonnets, develop the same emphasis in their theology. My first question for the class centered on the resemblance between "On the Morning of Christ's Nativity" and "At a Solemn Musick." At once, the students cited the imagery of music in the Nativity Ode: "Divinely-warbled voice," "stringed noise" (I explained that the word *noise* meant music in the early modern era), "such harmony alone / Could hold all Heav'n and Earth in happier union" (lines 96–108). They also identified the angelic choir as the source of such heavenly music:

> glittering ranks with wings displaid,
> Harping in loud and solemn quire,
> With unexpressive notes to Heav'ns new-born Heir.
> (114–16)

From the angelic choir, the students directed their attention to the cosmos and focused on the music of the spheres, which harmonizes with the angelic choir:

> Ring out ye Chrystall sphears,
> Once bless our human ears,
>   (If ye have power to touch our senses so)
> And let your silver chime

Move in melodious time;
  And let the Base of Heav'ns deep Organ blow,
And with your ninefold harmony
Make up full consort to th' Angelike symphony.
                                        (125–32)

Recognizing the wordplay on "consort" and "concert" (from our previous discussion of "At a Solemn Musick"), the students focused on the speaker or narrator of the Nativity Ode, who becomes a singer of praise and thanksgiving for the advent of the Christ child. The singer maintains a state of readiness and holiness to be receptive to the music of the heavenly choir and of the spheres, which resonates downward to the earth. Informed by such harmonies, the singer frames his ode or hymn as a verbal artifact or "good work." Using his talents and dedicating his will to accord with the inspiration that he receives from above, the singer accepts the "lot, however mean or high" (sonnet 7), to which he is impelled and for which he executes the task of composition. Indeed, the students contended that as the singer consorts with the harmonies from above, he participates in a concert that resonates praise and thanksgiving. In so doing, the singer exemplifies the theology of ready, willing, and active service on behalf of the Lord.

Virtually the same theology undergirds "Lycidas" (100–07), the students noted, because the pastoral elegy whose ostensible purpose is to mourn the death of a friend manifests a deeper motive: to educate the narrator. Despite its use of conventions distinctive to the pastoral elegy, a hallmark that has caused commentators to perceive the poem as artificial, "Lycidas" presents a narrator whose outlook on his friend's death is earnest and heartfelt. At first, the speaker laments the premature death of Lycidas, the allegorical name of the poet Edward King, Milton's fellow student at Christ's College, Cambridge. King was preparing for the ministry in the Church of England and drowned in the Irish Sea while traveling to his first pastoral assignment in Ireland. He appears in "Lycidas" as the victim of "hard mishap" (line 92) or unduly harsh fate. To the students, the narrator perceives the fate of King as an example of justice gone awry. They cited passages in the poem in which the corrupt clergy and bishops of the Church of England are thriving, whereas King, a model of integrity, drowns even before he can begin what would almost surely have been an ideal, even Christlike, ministry. The students cited particular verses—"Comes the blind *Fury* with th' abhorred shears, / And slits the thin-spun life" (75–76)—that indict God's justice, an indictment couched in and thereby mitigated by classical allusion and allegory. Such oblique questioning of the ways of the Godhead enables Milton, I contended, to escape allegations of blasphemy. I explained, moreover, how Milton may be conflating the Fates and the Furies of classical antiquity in these verses. The Fates collaborate in spinning the thread of one's life, casting lots to determine how long one will live, then snipping the thread. The Furies, who in classical mythology are not blind but clear-sighted, enact retributive justice on behalf of the gods and goddesses. I pointed out that Milton likens the Fate who is equipped with shears to snip the thread of life to a sharp-sighted Fury personifying divine retribution.

At this point, I posed two questions: Why would Milton interrelate two myths in such an unusual and eye-catching way? Most surprising, why would Milton use *blind* to describe a sharp-sighted Fury? The students burrowed into these questions earnestly. They were insightful in explaining the paradox of "blind Fury," suggesting that Milton means to emphasize the blindness of the all-seeing eye of the Godhead in cutting short the thread of King's life. Some students argued that the narrator of "Lycidas" perceives the deity as callous, if not unjust, in permitting the death of King while other ministers in the Church of England prosper on earth. But the students discerned that the narrator changes his perception of King's demise: "Weep no more, woful Shepherds weep no more, / For *Lycidas* your sorrow is not dead" (165–66). At this point, the tone of the narrator changes from sorrow to joy because he comes to realize and affirm that in dying prematurely King was taken much sooner to his heavenly reward. The students acknowledged that the narrator at this point, having relinquished his human perspective, achieves a providential view of death, the means by which the blessed on earth enter eternal life. But at their death, the venal prelates and clergy will be eternally damned. In sum, the narrator in accord with Providence becomes a foremost expositor of the theology that informs Milton's shorter poems and that is even more fully developed in the later ones.

Milton's Sonnets and the Sonnet Tradition

Jennifer Lewin

Milton's sonnets offer instructors in undergraduate and graduate classrooms alike a range of wonderful opportunities to discuss, debate, and appreciate the poet's unique and memorable contributions to a major literary genre. Such opportunities arise in both single-author and survey courses. The task of introducing students to the sonnets is facilitated by the popularity of the genre: most students already will have encountered other sonnets from one period or another, be they by Shakespeare or Seamus Heaney, and the instructor can immediately begin to build on this prior knowledge. In a survey of English literature where Milton appears near or at the end of the syllabus, one can place the sonnets in a historically specific context, such as the post-Petrarchan lyric tradition. An extended discussion of sonnet 23 below ("Methought I saw my late-espoused Saint") reveals how the sonnet can serve as a culmination of and peculiarly poignant commentary on this tradition. If the course focuses largely on *Paradise Lost*, then the sonnets can be used in other ways, such as creating an awareness of the frequently subtle interplay between autobiographical and fictional elements in Milton's poetry. Finally, an understanding of the sonnets' shared, intense preoccupation with temporality helps students to think about the role of time in other genres and aspects of Milton's work and especially in his anxieties about the development of his poetic career. All these qualities give the sonnets an anticipatory effect and enable them to act as touchstones in the course: put simply, one can use the sonnets to introduce strategies for reading Milton's longer work.

My knowledge about teaching Milton's sonnets mainly derives from my experiences as an instructor of a single-author undergraduate lecture course and a graduate seminar; I pay more attention to the sonnets in the undergraduate course and therefore my essay focuses on that context. In my graduate course, time's winged chariot often transports us to other issues centering on *Paradise Lost*, and in the past we have not engaged the shorter poems as much as we should; at the end of this essay, however, I mention some themes that have arisen in relation to the sonnets.

In the undergraduate classroom, initially one can rely on students' familiarity with the sonnet and quickly review its basic formal features (length, typical rhyme schemes, its tendency to divide into the two halves of octave and sestet, with a volta, or turn—a resolution, challenge, questioning, affirming, or answering of the poem's central argument or problem usually found at the ninth line), recalling that the subject with which we most associate the form is erotic love. This overview can be accomplished by reminding students of the sonnet's origins in Italy and France and of the vogue for translating and "Englishing" Petrarch during the sixteenth century, famously in the works of Spenser, Sidney, and Shakespeare. Bringing in handouts with examples of these poets' sonnets is a great help. It is easy to proceed from here to speculations about the ambivalence that poets (especially after the 1590s) felt about their abilities to make the sonnet new once again, given the virtuosic formal innovations it demands from its best practitioners. These speculations are relevant to, even indispensable in, fostering an appreciation for how Milton distinguishes himself as an inventive formalist capable of transforming a tradition largely preoccupied with erotic love into a vehicle for exploring political, religious, and vocational topics. Such an appreciation is helpful at the start of a course, when it is important to provoke interest in Milton's originality and his daring as a poet and as a thinker.

The matter of Milton and sonnets arises on the first day of instruction in the single-author course I teach (in the survey of English poetry that ends with *Paradise Lost*, I introduce Milton after metaphysical lyric poetry with "On Shakespeare" and its not being a sonnet, "How soon hath Time," and "When I consider" [*Riverside* 61, 85, 256]). I start by lecturing on Milton's decisive effect on a wide variety of readers, stressing his attractiveness to revolutionary thinkers by offering examples of his influence on later poets and novelists, including feminists and other political activists. Then I distribute Wordsworth's sonnet "London, 1802," attending to the national as well as the personal vitality Milton symbolizes for the Romantic poet:

> Milton! thou shouldst be living at this hour:
> England hath need of thee: she is a fen
> Of stagnant waters: altar, sword, and pen,
> Fireside, the heroic wealth of hall and bower,
> Have forfeited their ancient English dower
> Of inward happiness. We are selfish men;
> O raise us up, return to us again,
> And give us manners, virtue, freedom, power!
> Thy soul was like a Star, and dwelt apart;
> Thou hadst a voice whose sound was like the sea:
> Pure as the naked heavens, majestic, free,
> So didst thou travel on life's common way,
> In cheerful godliness; and yet thy heart
> The lowliest duties on herself did lay.   (286)

It does not take long for students to observe that Wordsworth wishes that Milton were alive because of the precarious state of matters in England on fronts political, domestic, religious, and literary. By tying these matters to the concept of inward happiness, Wordsworth binds the personal nature of the sonnet form with Milton's significance as a literary precursor. The kinds of visionary renewal Wordsworth seeks for his fellow countrymen at a time of revolution on the Continent and in England seem possible through an understanding of Milton— the unique inspirational qualities of his unfettered "soul," "voice," and "heart"—as a highly solitary, directed, and disciplined guide. Milton was free to pursue and intensely concentrated on his lowliest duties and his highest aspirations.

After glancing at this sonnet, I remark that it would not be surprising if in addition to *Paradise Lost* it was the sonnets that offered Wordsworth clues about how to fashion this compact and powerful version of Milton's achievement. As one of the twentieth century's best explicators of the sonnets writes, some of them are Milton's "most self-evidently occasional poems of political import," and they also serve as a record of the "public and private evolution of the poet as a teacher of his nation" (Radzinowicz 128, 129). Even Milton's love sonnets (2 through 6)—the more traditional theme associated with the form—while closely modeled on various Italian sonnets, are highly original efforts in a genre that tends toward conformity to certain standards and expectations, as Barbara Lewalski trenchantly notices:

> His sonnet lady is not coy or reserved or forbidding, but gentle and gracious; she is no silent object of adoration, but charms her lover with bilingual speech and enthralling songs. Also, this lover-poet carefully avoids Petrarchan subjection to the bonds of Cupid and the lady's power, retaining his autonomy and insisting on his own virtue and worth . . . and the last sonnet in the sequence is a curious self-blazon, praising the speaker's own moral virtues and poetic aspirations rather than the physical beauties of the lady.   (*Life* 11)

Another mark of strong originality is Milton's keen obsession, as early as the first sonnet, with time's passing and his ability to live up to his expectations for his writing career, a preoccupation that will persist throughout his work. (The Miltonic associations with this theme we've just seen in Wordsworth's sonnet.) In a handout containing sonnets 1 and 7 (*Riverside* 78, 85), we examine how Milton's speaker implores the nightingale to "timely sing" (line 9) before the cuckoo does, even though he has no reason to expect that it will: "As thou from yeer to yeer hast sung too late / For my relief;" (11–12). Still, he considers himself part of the "train" of both the "Muse" and "Love," despite finding himself time and time again dismayed at his inability to find "relief" in this poetic identity. He wants the nightingale to perform a task that it never before has performed for the speaker. In a reading of the poem that differs from this one mainly in its increased optimism about the relation between poetic symbol and speaker, Anna K. Nardo writes:

> "O Nightingale" does more than lament the woes of the forlorn lover; the poem turns outward, away from self-pity toward hope for another spring, another chance at fulfilled service to love and the muse. Out of the darkness comes the nightingale's promise of love, and out of isolation and frustration comes the young lover's song of hope.   (31)

The song is one of identification as well as hope; the last line ("Both them I serve, and of their train am I") indicates at once a deep commitment to his searching and a recognition of the lack of reciprocity in the search. It will continue for a long time, and no respite is visible.

If the idea of the nightingale being "too late / For my relief" shows an acute self-consciousness about the relation among the speaker's state of mind, his productivity, and the passage of time, I explain, then perhaps it should come as no surprise that this frustrating subject of time is again thematized in the octet of sonnet 7, "How soon hath Time":

> How soon hath Time the suttle theef of youth,
>> Stoln on his wing my three and twentieth yeer!
>> My hasting dayes flie on with full career,
> But my late spring no bud or blossom shew'th.
> Perhaps my semblance might deceive the truth,
>> That I to manhood am arriv'd so near,
>> And inward ripenes doth much less appear,
> That som more timely-happy spirits indu'th.   (lines 1–8)

At this point in our discussion, students pay attention to the inextricability of the sonnet's formal properties—especially rhythm—and its content. The experience of reading the poem aloud can dramatize how rapid time has been for the speaker, as the rhythm pushes the reader toward the ends of lines with heavy iambic stress placed on words like "soon," "Time," and "yeer" and on phrases like "My hasting days" (made more prominent by the internal rhyme) and "deceive the truth." Milton even breaks the normal pattern of the octet (one quatrain followed by another) by introducing a turn in thought not in the poem's fifth line but in the fourth, which opens with "But," a word that commonly starts either a new quatrain or the sestet. Milton characteristically also anticipates the readerly response to his complaint with "Perhaps my semblance might deceive the truth" in the following line, imagining that a well-meaning auditor might try to reassure the speaker or deny his concern. No room for such consolation here: the speaker is too hard on himself to contemplate such deception. Instead, the trochaic "semblance" contrasts with the trochaic phrase "inward ripeness" to indicate the poet's anxiety about the arrival of his "manhood." He is set apart from others and is not one of those "timely-happy spirits" whose inwardness is in sync with their age. Yet because he is doing something else—namely, waiting for the appearance of ripeness rather than actively doing anything specific or noteworthy to cultivate it—Milton's speaker is in a somewhat passive position. In other words, he is waiting more than he is acting; only in a much later sonnet will standing and waiting be tantamount to serving God. Here, until the sestet, what bothers the speaker is the gap between his age and his accomplishments and his inability to do anything about it. He is anxious and anticipatory. His career hasn't yet gotten started, and one can sense in the verse that he worries that this does not bode well for his future.

The sestet takes us in another direction, toward a resolution that the speaker of the octave seems incapable of fathoming. In *Milton's Burden of Interpretation*, Dayton Haskin reminds readers that in the original edition, the ordering of the sonnets (in which this one appears right after five sonnets to a [semi-] Petrarchan beloved) "conspicuously alters the object of the poet's service from the beautiful mistress to a God who compels his obedience" and that "he reconciles himself to a Judge who will finally take a true account." Haskin too, perhaps, finds passivity in the poem, for he notes the oddity of Milton's including a phrase like "task Master" in the final line, by which the poet "seems so casually to accept the image of a God who assigns particular tasks, perhaps ones such as the writing of a sonnet" (111, 112). After having been provoked to analysis of self (and others) by the gap between his outer appearance and inner feeling, he waits for directions (knowing they will come) rather than seeking them. He calms himself down with a reminder of God's responsiveness and his confidence in God's communication of his "will."

By the end of this first session, during which we will have spent more time on sonnet 7 than on any other, students are ready to answer the questions I leave them with: After reading this sonnet and Wordsworth's sonnet, what qualities do you expect to find in Milton's poetry? Are there writers who have had this powerful an effect on you as readers, and if so, who? If not, why do you think that is? The point is to get students thinking about what qualities make for literary power and about its importance for the study of Milton.

Spatial limitations prevent me from going into detail about the four topics around which one might examine how innovations in Miltonic form relate to the political and the poetic selves fashioned by the sonnets, but readers can imagine how the discussion I've outlined above easily can lead to interesting explorations of "When I consider," "To Cyriack Skinner," and "Methought I saw." These all can be read in relation to the invocation to book 3 of *Paradise Lost* and reviewed when approaching *Samson Agonistes*. The themes of political and religious freedom that reemerge in the Wordsworth sonnet appear in "To the Lord General Cromwell," "To Sir Henry Vane the Younger," and "On the Late Massacre."[1] Finally, a return to the sonnet's origins and Petrarchan themes can illuminate "Lady that in the prime" and "Methought I saw."

An instructor can make two compelling contexts, the biography—specifically, Milton's marriages—and the Petrarchan sonnet tradition, relevant to an in-depth classroom examination of sonnet 23, "Methought I saw" (259) This discussion can stand alone or alongside the other blindness sonnets and books 7 and 8 of *Paradise Lost* so that it relates to Milton's blindness as well as to Adam's account of Eve's creation. Likewise, one can distribute English post-Petrarchan sonnets about dreaming of the beloved and awakening to the disappointment of her loss, from Sidney's *Astrophil and Stella* (sonnet 38 [181]) and

Spenser's *Amoretti* (sonnet 77 [*Yale Edition* 646–47]) to selections from the sequences of Mary Wroth (85) and Shakespeare.

I emphasize to students the intense allusiveness of Milton's sonnet and ask them to consider before and during class what differences are created by this feature as well as by the unique presence of the death of the beloved and the speaker's blindness in both the poem and Milton's life; cruel literalizations of tropes that remain figurative in the work of previous poets, these facts return the class to the question of the sonnet as the vehicle for the powerful transformation of personal experience. Milton's sonnet achieves with the intricate evasions of *as*—a word used five times—a highly charged and vivid account of a love dream:

> Methought I saw my late espoused Saint
>   Brought to me like *Alcestis* from the grave,
>   Whom *Joves* great Son to her glad Husband gave,
>   Rescu'd from death by force though pale and faint.
> Mine as whom washt from spot of child-bed taint,
>   Purification in the old Law did save,
>   And such, as yet once more I trust to have
>   Full sight of her in Heaven without restraint,
> Came vested all in white, pure as her mind:
>   Her face was val'd, yet to my fancied sight,
>   Love, sweetness, goodness, in her person shin'd
> So clear, as in no face with more delight.
>   But O as to embrace me she enclin'd,
>   I wak'd, she fled, and day brought back my night.

The most perplexing aspect of this poem for readers of the last sixty years seems to have been the identity of the saint, and critics have used their claims of identity to build cases that the sonnet encapsulates Milton's entire view on Christianity, marriage, and literary form.[2] Milton's opening phrase, "Methought I saw," recalls "a complex layered effect" implying that "what one perceived may be so, or not so, or it may be in the realm of figuration where something is and is not so at once."[3] So the beloved may be an amalgamation of Mary Powell, Katherine Woodcock, and a traditional love dream beloved whose flight typically marks the end of the vision. In the undergraduate classroom, it tends not to be useful to spend a great deal of time on this conundrum. The idea that the poem exclusively "refers to" anyone at all may be doubtful, I remark: the poem insists on an alienation between the speaker and the dead beloved that sense experience, mediated through literary and biblical allusion, provides a language for.

One possible avenue of exploration is to show how Milton imagines the beloved's visual externalization of inward virtue in a way that is consistent with his anxieties about bodily and mental purity in other contexts, such as *Comus*.

The speaker goes to such great lengths to focus on the purity of the physical body of his dead beloved that one can identify an acute worry about the relationship of that body to his own. It is strange that he chooses to emphasize this detail in so many places. The speaker seems so careful to protest her having been "washt from spot of child-bed taint" that she already seems tainted, the spot a residual and irrevocable part of her being even as she also "[c]ame vested all in white, pure as her mind."[4] The speaker has a dual vision of the beloved as pure but also as bearing traces of a former, spotted, state. He is so concerned to specify the beloved's presence and gesture—she "enclin'd" to "embrace" him, not he, her—that it is difficult to see the poem as anything but interested in maintaining, painfully, the isolation of the speaker from the beloved, an isolation about which we cannot discern his true stance, and an isolation that actually begins not in the moment of waking but in the lack of an embrace. It is as though the embrace or touch would prove to be damaging.

Milton's deep ambivalence toward being entangled by the beloved can be measured by the extent to which he distances himself from her as well as how he dwells on her physical manifestation of inward virtues.[5] This aspect of the poem can be related to *Comus*, in which a strain is placed on the Lady by herself—and by Comus on the Lady—that aims at such an estimation of her virtue, but the dynamic in the masque is more subtle because we witness the Lady's descriptions of her thoughts and her experiences form her belief. Still, as Michael Lieb notes, "Even after the Lady is liberated, the unsettling sense of her vulnerability persists" (*Milton* 109). This vulnerability makes her more like Eve in book 5 in relation to Satan and possibly aligns the dreamer-Milton with these female figures rather than male rescuers such as Hercules and Orpheus, present by implication in sonnet 23. Milton resists the disparate roles of those classical figures in favor of a depiction of himself as more permanently bereft of his beloved. But perhaps, as Gerald Hammond subtly suggests, he also seeks to avoid her grasp, a position the Petrarchan lover rarely achieves. These complicated gender-role reversals can generate much fruitful discussion.

Twentieth- and twenty-first-century readers have considered Milton's sonnets some of his most exciting and most problematic poetic works. They combine innovative prosody and complex ideas with a faithfulness to traditional forms that is never superficial. Perhaps the most epigrammatic of all his poems, their intense allusiveness contributes to the tantalizing ambiguity of their language. Topics including the identity of addressees or central subjects; dates of composition; punctuation and spelling; uses of biblical, classical, and contemporary sources; the relevance of contemporaneous contexts; as well as wildly divergent opinions on tone and meaning have kept readers engaged with the poems and proved that the length of a poem bears no relation to the critical energy expended on it. Still, as I emphasize in my graduate course, a peculiar situation has arisen: many major Miltonists do not integrate discussions of either the sonnets or the odes in their book-length studies, and the recent collections of essays on Milton contain few if any essays on them. In venues such as *Milton Quarterly* or *Milton Studies*, one usually finds at least an article or two a year on any given sonnet, but no more than that, and rarely are the sonnets incorporated into discussions of other works or topics. William Kerrigan is alone in considering them as consistently important as the invocations in *Paradise Lost* and the autobiographical sections of the prose: his extended arguments in *The Prophetic Milton* and *The Sacred Complex* frequently rely on and make references to the sonnets. The more general critical silence about them provokes this essay's central questions: What are these poems' potential roles in rethinking the relation between Milton's work and his life? What unique problems or issues might they pose? The urgency, the successes, and the pleasures of these poems largely reflect and center on the poet's acute obsession with two major subjects: the distinctive interconnections among his literary, political, and religious vocations; and the changing nature of his views on time and erotic love. As one quickly discovers in the classroom, the study of all the sonnets is amply rewarded.

NOTES

[1] In addition, John T. Shawcross's recent and suggestive discussion of the allusiveness of sonnet 20 ("Lawrence of vertuous Father vertuous Son") and of the poem's representation of time can relate usefully to the approach to sonnet 23 that I outline below.

[2] William Riley Parker's position that it refers to Mary Powell opposes Elijah Fenton's (1725) claim that it refers to Katherine Woodcock (Parker, "Milton's Last Sonnet" and "Milton's Last Sonnet Again"). For a revival of the Woodcock theory, see Honigmann's summary in his edition of the sonnets (Milton, *Milton's Sonnets* 190–92). For the view that the sonnet "teaches Christ's love for both the living and the dead," see McLoone 18; that Milton sought to show how "sexual love within the context of marriage was a good and beautiful thing," see Gregory 266. For a rhetorical perspective indebted to the work of Thomas Sloane, see Wallerstein. See also Spitzer; Williamson; Sokol; Cheney 72–73; and Jones 114–25.

[3] Cook 36, 39. See also E. Hill; and Hollander 86. Hollander proposes that the condensation of dream-work might make a composite of Mary and Katherine, as dreams often do.

[4] For more on the words *taint* and *spot* in Milton, see Boesky.

[5] Gerald Hammond notes that part of the sonnet's "power" is "that while he gives full expression to the hold the past has upon him, he refuses to be trapped by or in it" (215).

Pursuing the Subtle Thief:
Teaching Meter in Milton's Short Poems

Elizabeth Harris Sagaser

How do you measure time? How does time measure you?

These provocative questions serve me well at the beginning of a Milton course or unit as I introduce "How soon hath Time," "When I consider," "Methought I saw," "L'Allegro," "Il Penseroso," and the Nativity Ode. I ask the easy question first, and students note we measure time by clocks, calendars, the sun and moon, the seasons, and holidays. I add syllabi and due dates. What do you do when you listen to music, I ask, or when you learn a new dance step or guitar song? Students note they tap their feet or count beats.

The next question, how does time measure you, creates a little palpable stress in the classroom. What did you accomplish by the time you graduated from high school? Since you started college? I inquire gently, do you seniors have jobs lined up for next year? I hurry to the next question. What do you expect to have accomplished by the time you are thirty? forty? fifty? sixty? What do you expect of yourselves in a lifetime? Where do these pressures, values, and expectations come from? I give students time to sketch out some responses.

By the time we read together sonnet 7, "How soon hath Time" (about fifteen minutes into class), students are ready to discover how Milton's young speaker represents his anxieties about time and achievement and how he coaches himself in patience and humility. I have usually begun the class speaking the poem by heart, as I always prefer to present poems in as live and present a way as possible. Now I have a student read the poem, and I ask the student to inhabit the speaker's anxiety about his limited achievements so far in his life, his unrealized promise, his sense of urgency, and at the turn, his self-soothing reminders and deferral to a greater power.

If this is not a course in which we have already studied sonnets, I map on the board Petrarchan sonnet structure, demonstrating with zigzags and half circles how the first eight lines of the poem—the octave—are entwined through rhyme and how the last six lines—the sestet—are also entwined, though a little less intensely (three rhymes for six lines versus two rhymes for eight). I also talk about the turn—the shift from octave to sestet that usually represents or coincides with a shift in the speaker's mood, direction of thought, energy or attitude.

A live demonstration like this is more engaging than a handout or *PowerPoint* presentation because meter and form are things to experience with one's whole body, not merely one's brain. Students have known this about patterned language since their nursery rhyme days, and a college English class is no place to forget it. Prepackaged lessons or definitions in literary dictionaries can sap the blood right out of a poem and out of a class.

I do, however, hand out a version of the poem in which I have changed all the present tense verbs to past tense—a surprisingly efficient and enlightening exercise. A student reads this version aloud. I ask how the poem has changed; students notice how much less tension there is now in the poem, how reading the poem we don't feel we are in the middle of building anxiety but are speaking instead from a place of resolution. The speaker seems older, one student noted recently; "It's as if he's giving advice to younger people." The sonnet form suits the story told in retrospect, but it is not as powerful as when it helps construct the speaker's anxiety and then his self-initiated quelling of that anxiety.

If I am teaching Milton's short poems in a poetry course, I would have already taken a couple of class periods early in the semester to introduce meter using the hands-on, creative methods I've described in detail elsewhere (Sagaser). If you do not have time for such an introduction, I recommend at least incorporating an abbreviated version of these strategies into your teaching of Milton's sonnets. First, demonstrate that English is an accentual language by pronouncing student names and multisyllabic words with the wrong accents: marGARitt, niKULLiss, IMposSIBil. (This would also be a good time to tell students who do not already know that the suffix *ed* is pronounced as its own syllable, but the suffix *'d* is not.) Second, explain how meter is a pattern of accents (for poetry always seeks to explore and exploit the innate features of the language in which it is written). Third, together with the class, create and observe naturally occurring iambic pentameter to demonstrate how we sometimes speak iambically without any intent to do so: "If only I could still be home in bed"; "I promise I will finish it tonight"; "A double cappuccino, please, to go." Iambic pentameter, then, is one of many natural ways to speak. It is not natural in everyday speech to speak *only* iambically without mixing in prose rhythms, but in and of itself, iambic pentameter is not unusual, difficult, or esoteric. Remind the class that trying too hard to identify meter in a poem can inhibit anyone's most sensitive awareness, just as thinking too much about your baseball swing or tennis serve can scramble your natural concentration and physical intuition.

Finally, begin to write a sonnet together on the board, brainstorming and composing lines that meet the demands of the sonnet form, however goofily they do so. Aim for four lines, at least, before the bell rings, maybe four or five. Students can finish the sonnet later, each in his or her own way (though still meeting the demands of the form), and the following week you can read (anonymously) the best ones aloud to the class.

To help along our discussion of meter in "How soon hath Time," I hand out an adaptation of the poem in which I maintain at least the general sense of each line but replace the iambic pentameter and rhyme with sentences in ordinary prose rhythms.

Wow, Time has really been a sneaky thief of my youth!
Now it has stolen and flown off with my twenty-third year.

My days are rushing along at top speed,
But I am a late bloomer; my spring just isn't happening.
Maybe my boyish appearance fools people
Into not knowing I'm nearly a grown man.
And it's plain my inner ripeness or genius isn't evident
To others—as genius *is* evident in my luckier, more productive peers.
However, whether it happens quite soon or much later,
The maturing of my genius will take place appropriately,
And my minimal or high achievements will be
Exactly what Heaven intends for them to be.
So stop obsessing: all is well if I have the grace to use my talents
As I always should, with God's will and vision, not my own.

As I hand this adaptation out, I emphasize its purpose: these prose rhythms throw into relief the iambic meter of the original. The adaptation might also help students get a handle on the poem, but I remind them the adaptation does not in any way substitute for the precise language of the poem.

After listening to this nonmetrical version, we focus on the octave of the true poem to see which version more persuasively represents mounting anxiety and holds its own as a coherent, authoritative tension. Sometimes students discuss the differences readily. If they are hesitant, we look at line three: "My hasting days fly on with full career" (*Complete Poems and Major Prose* 76). This line has the power and momentum of repetition, all the more so because it is preceded and followed by lines with the same meter. I even propose the iambic pentameter in this context embodies the abstract, unrelenting progression of time as it happens. Although my prose version of the line, "My days are rushing along at top speed," can be spoken with persuasive worry and even panic, it does not stir in readers a deep-seated awareness of time.

We focus next on the transition from octave to sestet:

Yet be it less or more, or soon or slow,
It shall be still in strictest measure ev'n
To that same lot, however mean or high,
Toward which Time leads me, and the will of Heav'n.
                                        (77; lines 9–12)

I read line 9 aloud, then read lines 5 through 9, and then have a student read those lines. I point out how the lines before line 9 contain fancy, intellectual, multisyllabic terms. Speaking these lines works the tongue and brain more than speaking line 9 does, so a reader easily registers the pleasing simplicity of line 9, which is made up of short, simple words. Because we sometimes associate elaborate talk with evasion or falsity (thus our phrase "beating around the bush" and the maxim still popular all these centuries later, "More matter, less art"), we might experience the speaker in line 9 as particularly sincere and capable of grasping truth. Further, in this case, the monosyllabic words of the line create a regular, calming iambic pentameter. It *feels* good (rather than merely *is* good) to reject urgency and remember patience with these words:

> Yet be it less or more, or soon or slow,
> It shall be still in strictest measure ev'n
> To that same lot, however mean or high,
> Toward which Time leads me, and the will of Heav'n;
> All is, if I have grace to use it so,
> As ever in my great task-Master's eye.   (lines 9–14)

We might read "shall be still" with stresses on every syllable of the phrase, and then fall back to the even, unflappable iambs and attitudes of the speaker's new reliance on a power beyond his mortal self. The statement "All is" (13), even in the present tense, sounds prophetic, particularly in its parallelism with "As ever" (14). You might also demonstrate how these last lines are rich in internal rhyme, a technique used in poetry and rhetoric through ages to give lines an aural integrity that might suggest a broader one.

My students and I now fly two decades beyond "How soon hath Time" to "When I consider." Though written about twenty years apart, the poems are kin: anxiety and ambition would run unchecked in both poems without the intervention of patience and the recourse to God's will. In the later poem, however, the speaker does not interrupt his anxiety with a calm, steady reminder of humility and faith. Something much more dramatic happens: Patience itself speaks. I do not want a single student to miss the strangeness and intensity of this intervention, so after presenting the poem myself and having a student or two read it aloud, I have my students go through the poem slowly, tracking the restless enjambments, unconventional caesuras, and edgy shifts of verb tense until they discover that Patience not only interrupts the speaker's anxiety but also interrupts that anxiety retrospectively, preventing a murmur that has already happened. Does the speaker suggest divine patience is *that* mighty in the mortal world? The speech Patience gives on ways men serve God has an epic sweep—fascinating, considering it is only a few lines long. But they are unusual lines, muscular and independent, inspired and irreverent, clearly superior to regular old end-stopped lines . . . or are they? Patience delivers its final comforting message in a line that fits without struggle into one sentence and vice-versa, a line of monosyllabic words and easy iambs, a line that emerges from the rush with calm wisdom: "They also serve who only stand and wait" (*Complete Poems and Major Prose* 168).

Time is an explicit subject (as well as an implicit subject) of many sonnets from the Renaissance into the twentieth century, and some of these compare fruitfully with Milton's time sonnets. Setting up comparisons—whether for class discussions, essay exams, or analytical paper assignments—prompts students to make finer distinctions than they usually make studying a poem alone. "How soon hath Time" and "When I consider" compare well with a number of Shakespeare's sonnets, including 18, 19, 55, 64, and 65. Where Milton's speakers interrupt their obsessive thoughts to defer to "the will of Heaven," a "great task-Master," or to Patience itself, the speakers of Shakespeare's poems interrupt their obsessive thoughts to defer to another potentially transcendent power, poetry. Or, in the case of Shakespeare's sonnet 64, the speaker seems poised to defer to poetry but cannot muster sufficient faith in it; his own vivid, overwhelming argument for time's cruelty leaves him stunned and bankrupt. Suffering from the thought of losing his beloved—a thought that "is as a death," he can defer only to inarticulate tears, a move shocking to readers familiar with the eternizing conceit of early modern sonnets (*Shakespeare's Sonnets* 56; line 13).

John Keats's "When I have fears" compares powerfully with Milton's "How soon hath Time." Because Milton's and Keats's speakers write as young men striving to control obsessive worries about their mortality and ambition, students should be curious—and maybe even feel suspense—as they turn from Milton's poem to Keats's: how does *this* speaker quell an intense episode of fear and self-doubt? As Milton's speaker does, Keats's speaker interrupts his fervent, complex thoughts with an entirely different attitude and insight, this one simple, straightforward, and quietly nonnegotiable. This intervention unfolds, as Milton's does, in mostly monosyllabic words, producing a particularly even, calming iambic pentameter. When in a state of painful yearning and fear, he explains, "on the shore / Of the wide world I stand alone and think / Till love and fame to nothingness do sink" (Ferguson, Salter, and Stallworthy 906; lines 12–14). The intervention might be effective, but it is radical: Keats's speaker defers neither to God nor poetry nor virtue, nor even to grief and tears, but instead he defers to apathy. Or one may argue (an engaged student, perhaps), that this speaker doesn't so much defer to apathy as find peace in mortality, and maybe pleasure as well in his solitary thought.

Milton's sonnet 23, "Methought I saw," compares richly with both "How soon hath Time" and "When I consider." All three poems represent a solitary mind wrestling with conflicting experiences of, and attitudes toward, time. Verb tenses shift before our eyes, and we may find ourselves anxiously engaged in the daunting work of meaningfully relating the present to the future, the present to the past, the past to the future, and so forth.

"Methought" is particularly fraught with tension between these realms of time. The speaker only begins to tell readers—and himself—the story of his dream; then he deflects their attention and his own to other times, places, and personas. However, his indirect, restless telling of his story (through the octave) helps him conjure—step by step—the profound vision of his dream. In fact, the octave—or at least the second half of it—*delivers* the sestet: the subject presented in line 5, "Mine," finally catches up with its predicate in line 9: "Mine" . . . "came vested all in white, pure as her mind" (*Complete Poems and Major Prose* 170–71). In between the subject and predicate, the speaker's description of his "late espoused saint" ricochets from ancient ritual to a fantasy of future perfection—seeing his beloved "in Heaven without restraint" (line 8). As you discuss the poem's last line, again draw students' attention to the power of plain diction, monosyllabic words, easy iambs, and the way these features give readers a subliminal sense of a speaker's sincerity and honesty, particularly when plain speech follows more complex diction and rhythms. The heart-wrenching syntax of the last line is all the more heart-wrenching for being plainly spoken: "I wak'd, she fled, and day brought back my night" (line 14).

Once students have grasped the structure and dynamics of the poem, they may not only like "Methought I saw" but love it. I therefore frequently include among paper topics a comparison between "Methought I saw" and another early modern sonnet in the dream poem subgenre, such as Shakespeare's sonnet 27, "Weary with toil," or 43, "When most I wink." If I have students who study Italian, who have just come back from a semester in Florence or Rome, or who love lyric poetry, I also suggest comparing Milton's sonnet with one or more dream poems from Petrarch's *Rime sparse*. These poems are rife with longing and specific memory-fantasies that students find accessible and moving even if they also find them bizarrely extreme.

In poem 341, Laura is an "angel"; the speaker feels her "return, with that sweet, chaste bearing of hers . . . to quiet my wretched heart." In poem 342, he asserts that she "comes to the bed where I lie sick, so lovely that I hardly dare to look at her, and full of pity sits on the edge" (538). In poem 343, he says he would not still be alive "if she . . . were not so quick to help me there near the dawn" (540), and with this claim, he zooms in on her presence, her voice and her actions, and then her departure:

> Oh what sweet and chaste and kind greetings! and how intently she listens to, and takes note of, the long history of my sufferings!

> When bright day seems to strike her she returns to Heaven, for she knows all the ways, her eyes and both her cheeks wet. (540; poem 343)

Incorporating Petrarch in your teaching of Milton's short poems is particularly warranted because Milton not only read widely in Italian (including the *Rime*), he also composed sonnets in Italian. And his masterful Miltonic sonnets owe more to the Italian sonnet tradition than to any other.

When I teach Milton's early, energetic poems of mood, "L'Allegro" and "Il Penseroso" (*Complete Poems and Major Prose* 68–72, 72–76), I help students experience the expressive possibilities of a different form and meter: rhyming couplets in iambic tetrameter. First we read aloud the poems, each on a separate class day. I usually read the invocations, observing with the students how the alternating line lengths plus the forceful meter contribute to a sense of spell or incantation: "Hence loathed Melancholy / Of *Cerberus* and blackest midnight born" ("L'Allegro," lines 1–2).

Then we read around the class, a couplet per person. I hope you discover as I have that few poems are easier and more delightful to read as a group than "L'Allegro." How can one keep a straight face or a monotone voice while pronouncing "Quips and Cranks, and wanton Wiles / Nods, and Becks, and wreathed smiles"? (27–28). Those lines are almost as much fun as these: "Come, and trip it as ye go / On the light fantastic toe"! (33–34). I challenge any student to read these lines without feeling some pleasure.

I also have students search through the poems on their own for their favorite couplet or two. They e-mail their chosen lines to the class and to me in the subject line of the e-mail so we each will have a fresh encounter with the lines—an encounter in a time and context we do not know about ahead of time. A couple of students also posted their lines on their dorm doors, they told me. Often I have students memorize their favorite couplets to present in class, and I have them write eight or so lines of iambic tetrameter couplets experimenting with ways short lines can aid joyful momentum but can also, in a different poem, help represent intense ideas or driven states of mind. I also offer a pentameter adaptation of some of the lines, or I have the students write their own adaptations—to further put them in touch with the energy and momentum tetrameter can convey. For example, I ask students to compare this pentameter adaptation of lines 11 through 16 of "L'Allegro" with the original lines:

> But come thou Goddess, cheerful, fair and free
> In Heav'n yclep'd the sweet *Euphrosyne*
> And by men, proclaimed heart-easing Mirth
> Whom lovely *Venus* at a joyful birth
> With two pretty sister Graces more
> To Ivy-crowned *Bacchus* proudly bore. . . .

What sorts of words—parts of speech—have I added here? Do these terms enhance the imagery or dilute it? Do they construct a different state of mind for the speaker? Do they alter his seeming purpose in speaking the poem? Do we feel more invited or less invited to participate in the poem ourselves? Why do you think Milton chose the shorter lines for this poem? After students have discussed some of these questions, I might add my own observations: reading the tetrameter lines in "L'Allegro" offers me easy, immediate pleasure. Along with the constant and clever full rhymes, the tetrameter suggests galloping toward social and sensual highs, possibly aided by "Spicy Nut-brown ale" (70;

line 100). (No one in the poem drinks so much, however, that he or she cannot dance or tell stories, go to the theater or enjoy the company of others, I emphasize.)

In "Il Penseroso," the determined pursuit is all about creative power—a Petrarchan melancholia of rich despair and uncommon inspiration. The melancholy man milks his profound sorrows and solitude for out-of-body awareness, insight, and linguistic fluency, if not creative genius. The tetrameter in "Il Penseroso" is a runway down which solitary thoughts speed and take flight. A powerful contrast to this poem of elated sorrow is the invocation to book 3 of *Paradise Lost* (3.40–50), in which the narrator speaks in rhymeless iambic pentameter of true darkness and irreparable loss.

Once students have explored questions of time and meter in the sonnets and mood poems, "On the Morning of Christ's Nativity" is more likely to intrigue and engage them. As you read the poem aloud with them in class, coach students to apply the skills they've learned reading the shorter poems. Remind them to listen for and map out tensions created and resolved by the varying line lengths and rhyme schemes. Encourage them to better tune their ears to the meter of the original by imitating it in a poem of their own or by lengthening or shortening Milton's lines. Perhaps most important in reading the Nativity Ode, urge students to track through the poem every shift in verb tense. The shifts are dramatic, and the stakes are high: Milton here tests his powers as a prophetic poet, a poet who masters time before it masters him, who can speak authoritatively of immortality.

The present tense radiates through the rhyme royal introductory stanzas, becoming particularly powerful in the third stanza when the speaker addresses his "Heav'nly Muse" (*Complete Poems and Major Prose* 43; line 15), an address made even more urgent by imperatives and the sudden "Now" (line 19). But then the speaker shifts to the past tense and a new stanza form for "The Hymn," and within the hymn, he continually shifts verb tense to dismantle and empower various representations of time. In stanza 9, for example, the air (by way of echoes) "still prolongs each heav'nly close" (45; line 100). In stanza 13, the speaker suddenly cries, "Ring out ye Crystal spheres" in the midst of music he has just described as being in the past (46; line 125); and in stanza 16, the speaker intervenes in his own rushing ahead, striving for the patience necessary to tell the story. To help students analyze these shifts for themselves, I ask as we read: What is strange about this stanza? What is strange about this line? Does this shift seem illogical or persuasive to you, or both?

Explorations of time, form, and meter in these short poems are valuable in any Renaissance or seventeenth-century literature course and indeed in any number of general poetry courses. In a Milton course, such explorations are doubly useful: when students read the short poems skillfully, they not only learn about Milton's lyric poetry, but they also discover paradoxes and tensions that are everywhere in Milton's great epic, *Paradise Lost*. Specifically, they observe

Milton's attempts to accommodate or reconcile seemingly contradictory states of mind or philosophies: fearing time's speed versus trusting patience; being personally ambitious versus standing and waiting; exercising free will versus being controlled by forces beyond the self; accepting mortality and loss versus seeking transcendence. Above all, they open their eyes and ears to Milton's radical, exhilarating challenges to conventional representations of time.

Radical Politics and Milton's Civil War Verse: "Licence" and "Libertie"

Elizabeth Sauer

Milton's sonnets offer rewarding insights into the young poet's political and religious engagements and into the complex radical politics of his time. This essay demonstrates how the textual pairing and the formal and historical contextualization of Milton's "twin-born" Trinity Manuscript sonnets 11 and 12 (1646–47; printed 1673 [*Riverside* 250, 251–52]) present suggestive pedagogical opportunities. Under consideration as well is the question of how poetry performs cultural and political work and whether "political poetry [can] be justified as poetry" (Mueller 475). Investigations of these poems allow instructors to bridge the gap between research and pedagogy. Topical, satirical, elliptical, these modified Petrarchan sonnets respond to the critical reception of various controversialist treatises Milton wrote, including *The Doctrine and Discipline of Divorce* (1643, 2nd ed. 1644), *The Judgment of Martin Bucer* (1644), and the nonidentical twin-born, Greek-titled *Tetrachordon* and *Colasterion* (4 Mar. 1645)—the unnamed printer of which may have been Matthew Simmons. The sonnets also anticipate the anatomization of civil, religious, and particularly domestic liberty in *The Second Defense of the English People* (1654). Analyses of select passages from these pamphlets and from the diatribes on Milton's 1640s radical views help illuminate the poems while involving students in conversations about the interconnections of verse and prose and about literary, religious, and political writings and issues.

This case study is designed for courses on Milton and his contemporaries or senior seminars on political and literary culture in the seventeenth century. I have found the subject ideal for three courses I teach: Milton and the Literature of His Time; Literature of the English Revolution (a cross-listed senior history and English course); and Early Modern Popular Culture, a graduate course. In history courses particularly, the sonnets illuminate the multivalent concepts of liberty and moral responsibility; licensing and censorship; manuscript and print culture; the wars of truth; political and religious toleration; sectaries; heresy; popular culture and readerships; the (fluctuating) representation of the English people; Presbyterianism; and radicalism.

Recognizing the different goals and methodologies of discipline-specific courses, I propose here a variety of topics and points of entry into the sonnets. Regardless of the course in which the poems are taught, the instructor should use well-annotated, well-edited versions of the sonnets to increase students' confidence in their ability to interpret them.[1] At the same time, students must be cautioned about not restricting their readings to annotations and editorial notes and comments. Ideally, formal considerations, textual analysis, and historical contextualization should be mutually reinforcing. The following recommended approaches to teaching Milton's sonnets might begin as seminar presentations or short assignments, which can then be developed into essay-length arguments. All the topics invite textual pairings and manageable comparative investigations.

Textual History

The textual and editorial histories of the sonnets encourage discussions about manuscript and print, the malleability of texts, textual variants and their effect on diction and meaning, and, notably, the order of their composition. Three versions of each sonnet are extant: one autograph (in Milton's hand) and one scribal copy of each are contained in the Cambridge Trinity Manuscript, and both sonnets are printed in Milton's 1673 poetry edition. In the Trinity Manuscript, sonnet 11 ("A Book was writ") was numbered 12 in the autograph and appears on the recto following that containing sonnet 13 and "I did but prompt." Inserted between the leaves is another leaf with scribal copies of sonnets 11 and 12 (1673 ed.) on a single sheet and numbered 12. The scribal versions of the poems featured the caption: "these sonnets follow ye 10. in ye printed booke / On the detraccon which followed upon my writeng certaine treatises" (*Riverside* 250). A slight variation on the second half of the caption headed the autograph version of "I did but prompt." The printed 1673 edition identifies "I did but prompt" as sonnet 12 and the poem on *Tetrachordon*, sonnet 11. In the volume, then, the poem on "A Book was writ" precedes the more general defense of the divorce tracts in "I did but prompt," subtitled "*On the same*" (*Variorum Commentary* 2: 387-88). Students should be encouraged to consider how headings, placement, and numbering affect their reading of the thematic relation and pairing of the sonnets, as well as the poems' significance in Milton's sonnet sequence and in his mid-1640s corpus. Examinations of textual variants and changes in wording among the different versions of the poems (the alteration from "barbarous names" to "rough-hewn" and finally "rugged" in the autograph of "A Book was writ," for example) challenge assumptions about the fixity of textual meaning, invite evaluations of source texts, and prompt discussions about editorial decisions made by Milton critics and anthology compilers.

Poetic Form

Regardless of the disciplinary approach, some consideration of form is essential for any analysis. Students should be directed to Anna K. Nardo's study of Milton's indebtedness to and deviation from the Renaissance Italian and Elizabethan sonnet traditions (chs. 1 and 8). Milton's innovations of the Petrarchan sonnet form resist the octave-sestet division. While adhering to a Petrarchan rhyme scheme in sonnet 11 (abbaabba cdcdcd), Milton uses enjambment to carry the grating, uncivil street talk and barbaric Scottish names—a slur on

Scottish Stuart monarchy—into the sestet. Allusions in the first and last lines of the sonnet to the Greek tradition of piety and learning—upheld by the concordant, decorous *Tetrachordon* (line 1) and by John Cheke, professor of Greek at Cambridge and tutor of King Edward VI (14)—frame and contain the language of dissonance in the poem.

Sonnet 12 also bleeds the octave to sestet through the brawling of the misguided rabble who, by ignorantly renouncing "the known rules of antient libertie" outlined in Deuteronomy 24.1–2 (and Milton's divorce tracts), produce "this wast of wealth, and loss of blood" (lines 2, 14). "Wealth" refers here not only to the riches lost during the civil war but also to Milton's "Pearl" (8) of wisdom—the key to a commonwealth that might have enjoyed true liberty and the end of bloodshed. But the truth is compromised by the railing at Milton's *Tetrachordon* and *Colasterion*, which is likened to the contempt of the rustics in Ovid's *Metamorphoses* 6.331–81 for Apollo and Diana ("Sun" and "Moon")—Latona's "twin-born progenie" (lines 6–7). Both Latona's and Milton's pearls are cast to the Lycian boors who mistake "[l]icence" for "libertie" (line 11) and are thereupon metamorphosed into "Froggs" (line 5) and compared to "Hoggs; / That bawle for freedom in their senceless mood" (lines 8–9), an enjambed line that transfers the din into the sestet. Students respond well to questions about the function of the animal imagery and the language of depravity and degeneration used to malign Milton's detractors. Analyses of the semantic relation of rhymed words and of the hissing sibilants demonstrate how effectively the confusion is managed by the poetic diction, verse form, and the persona's sober and satirical voice (Mueller 485; Lewalski, *Life* 203).

Poetic Voice and Readerships

The sonnets betray the disjunction between Milton's implied or intended readers and his actual audiences, a disjunction that becomes increasingly more pronounced. A comparison of the poetic voices and of the addresses in the two sonnets is essential for understanding the sonnets and Milton's fraught relationship with and characterization of the English people. The personas of both poems are cast as classical orators, Puritan scholars, humanists, freeborn citizens, and defenders of liberty. The change in tone from wry humor, disaffection, and satire in sonnet 11 to vituperation in sonnet 12 is hardly straightforward and is further complicated by the chronology of the poems' original composition ("I did but prompt" was probably written first). The readers of Milton's divorce tracts appear in the sonnets as foolish calumniators. They represent the Presbyterians, with whom Milton originally sided, and the pamphleteers who now vilify the author as a licentious heretic. The respondents are also portrayed as vulgar, barbarous "stall-reader[s]," ironically and frustratingly privileging "licence" over "libertie." For courses devoted largely to a study of

Milton, the sonnets mark a pivotal moment in the poet's literary, religious, and political careers, which, as outlined by Joan S. Bennett, otherwise

> followed a typical Puritan radical's development in their progression from an unexamined Calvinism that had been inspired by the courage of the reforming Presbyterians, to an Independency based initially on a reaction against Presbyterian intolerance, and finally to individually posited heretical views. (106)

Prose Contexts

Arrange for the relevant volumes of the Yale prose editions to be put on reserve (*Complete Prose Works*), and ask students to explain how these treatises complement the poems: *The Doctrine and Discipline of Divorce* (1643, 1644); *The Judgment of Martin Bucer* (1644); *Areopagitica* (1644); *Tetrachordon* (1645); and *Colasterion* (1645). The widespread disapproval of Milton's position on divorce is evidenced not only in Milton's tracts, which answer the critics of *The Doctrine and Discipline of Divorce*, but also in readily available texts that students might consult to establish a fuller context for analyzing the sonnets and mid-1640s tracts. All the non-Miltonic texts cited below are reproduced in their original form and in some of their later seventeenth-century editions in *Early English Books Online*. Relevant texts include John Ward's *God Judging among the Gods. Opened in a Sermon before the Honourable House of Commons* (1645), Ephraim Pagitt's 1645 *Heresiography; or, A Discription of the Hereticks and Sectaries of These Latter Times*, Thomas Edward's *Gangraena* and *The Second Part of Gangraena* (1646), Nathaniel Hardy's printed indictment of heterodoxy in *The Arraignment of Licentious Libertie, and Oppressing Tyrannie . . . Preached before the Right Honourable House of Peeres* (1647). Herbert Palmer's 13 August 1644 *The Glasse of Gods Providence towards His Faithfull Ones. Held Forth in a Sermon Preached . . . against the Ungodly Toleration* (against which Milton inveighs in *Tetrachordon*); William Prynne's *Twelve Considerable Serious Questions Touching Church Government* (1645), which Milton refutes in the opening of *Colasterion*; and Daniel Featley's *The Dippers Dipt; or, The Anabaptists Duck'd and Plung'd* (1645) also discredited Milton's radical views and company the poet purportedly kept and generated the "barbarous noise" (sonnet 12, line 3) of which Milton's speaker complains. The clamor is produced, furthermore, by those, like Justices Reeves and Bacon (read: "Hoggs"; Parker, *Milton* 1: 264),[2] who enforced licensing regulations and examined Milton in 1644 for the unauthorized publication of *The Doctrine and Discipline of Divorce*. Milton's counterresponse is *Areopagitica*, his speech "For the Liberty of unlicenc'd Printing." Interpretations of the sonnets in terms of the prose enable students to reconstruct the literary, cultural, and political milieu in which the poems were composed and in which they take on added meaning.

Libertas *and* Licentia

The sonnets serve as valuable vehicles for discussing Milton's definitions of Christian liberty or the *libertas-licentia* antithesis in such texts as *The Doctrine and Discipline of Divorce, Areopagitica, Tetrachordon, The Tenure of Kings and Magistrates* (1649), *The History of Britain* (begun 1640s; publ. 1670), and the *Second Defense*. Liberty, the responsible exercise of free will, contrasts with license as abusive, licentious behavior, which gives free rein to "unbridl'd and vagabond lust" (*Complete Prose Works* 2: 227, 235). In *God Judging among the Gods*, John Ward announces that the conditions for the enjoyment of true liberty have been established by the expulsion of the "tyrannie of Prelacy," but "libertie is abused to loosenesse, profanenesse, insolencie," with the result that "all manner Sectaries creepe forth, and multiplie, as frogs, and flies, and vermine in the Spring." (31; sig. E4r). Milton reworks such distinctions in *The Doctrine and Discipline of Divorce*: "honest liberty is the greatest foe to dishonest licence" (*Complete Prose Works* 2: 225). Word searches facilitated by prose concordances and online editions of the prose present exciting opportunities for investigating the *libertas-licentia* antithesis.

Milton's "Licence" refers to "abused libertie" and "unmercifull restraint" (2: 235), "unbounded licence" (2: 227, 262), and "inordinate licence" (2: 236), including press censorship, which chokes self-expression, as Milton insists in *Areopagitica*:

> But lest I should be condemn'd of introducing licence, while I oppose Licencing, I refuse not the paines to be so much Historicall, as will serve to shew what hath been done by ancient and famous Commonwealths, against this disorder, till the very time that this project of licencing crept out of the Inquisition. (2: 493)

The worthiness of the people, then, is determined by their adherence to the "rules of antient libertie" (sonnet 12, line 2). *Tetrachordon* declares:

> If we consider that just and naturall privileges men neither can rightly see, nor dare full claime, unless they be ally'd to inward goodnesse, and stedfast knowledge, and that the want of this quells them to a servile sense of their own conscious unworthinesse, it may save the wondering why in this age many are so opposite to human and to Christian liberty.

This liberty alone can "restore us in some competent measure to a right in every good thing both of this life and the other" (*Complete Prose Works* 2: 587, 601). At the close of the decade, when his confidence in the English people wanes dramatically, Milton protests in *Tenure* that "none can love freedom heartily, but good men; the rest love not freedom, but licence" and in the *History of Britain* that "libertie hath a sharp and double edge fitt onelie to be handl'd by just and virtuous men" (*Complete Prose Works* 3: 190, 5: 449). These views form the basis of his designation in *Paradise Lost* of a meritorious audience consisting of the "fit . . . though few" (7.31).

Though often situated in his "lonely eminence" by methodologically prudent Miltonists, Milton in fact registered an acute awareness of the reception of his writings, aggravation over the critical responses of his audiences, and a desire to address like-minded, "good intellects" differentiated from vulgar (sonnet 11, line 4). Analyses of sonnets 11 and 12 enable students to discover for themselves the populist and elitist networks in response to which Milton composed his works. Instructors will find that these approaches—ranging from formalist to historicist—offer provocative strategies for teaching Milton's short poems in ways that invigorate the pedagogical experience not only of Milton as poet but also as a polemicist intimately engaged with radical politics and poetics.

NOTES

[1] Recommended editions include Honigmann's *Milton's Sonnets*, Hughes's *A Variorum Commentary* and *Complete Poems and Major Prose*, Carey and Fowler's *The Poems of Milton*, and Flannagan's *Riverside Milton*. Honigmann uses the manuscript versions of sonnets 11 and 12 while Hughes, Flannagan, and Carey and Fowler feature the 1673 editions. Unless indicated otherwise, all references to Milton's poetry will be to the *Riverside*. References to Milton's prose are to Wolfe's *Complete Prose Works*.

[2] Also see Honigmann's generous annotations in *Milton's Sonnets*, and Christopher Hill's "Milton's Reputation" (ch. 17 of *Milton and the English Revolution*).

Approaching the Antiprelatical Tracts

John T. Shawcross

John Milton's five (or six) antiprelatical tracts of 1641–42 are not included in undergraduate or usually in graduate courses except, infrequently, for excerpts of autobiographical sections. The tracts may, however, prove significant in theme or period courses (such as The Foundations of Liberty or Political Conflicts during the Seventeenth Century) in addition to those directly concerned with Milton. The tracts are *Of Reformation* (*Riverside* 875–901), *Of Prelatical Episcopacy* (*Complete Prose Works* 1: 623–52), *Animadversions upon the Remonstrants Defence against Smectymnuus* (*Complete Prose Works* 1: 661–735), *The Reason of Church-Government* (*Riverside* 903–25), *An Apology against a Pamphlet Call'd A Modest Confutation* (*Complete Prose Works* 1: 867–953), and the ascribed "A Postscript" in Smectymnuus's *An Answer to a Booke Entituled,* An Humble Remonstrance (*Complete Prose Works* 1: 966–75). Three strategies that aid in reading many of Milton's works, both prose and poetry, are recognition of intentionality; of genre, rhetoric, and style; and of humor. Examination of the antiprelatical tracts can set up more informed reading of Milton's other writings. The introductory section of an undergraduate course in Milton that I describe here can be adapted to fit other courses, other antiprelatical works, and available class time. These approaches can be expanded if one or more of the tracts are read in full and if time allows for discussion of their relation to additional prose or poetic works. The instructor may wish to pursue these approaches at separate times rather than together at the beginning of a course.

The following presupposes a class that meets three times a week. One that meets only two times a week might, in the first meeting devoted to this program, combine session 1 and the discussion described in session 2; the second meeting would start with the first student report, followed by discussion and then the second student report. This program should begin in the second, or at most third, meeting of the class. In the usual fifteen-week class, twelve weeks would be left for coverage of the stated content of the course (e.g., most of Milton's poetry and selected prose).

Session 1

1. Eliciting definitions from the class starts a discussion of what a "prelate" is and what "prelacy" and "prelatical" and thus "antiprelatical" mean, which establishes what a so-called antiprelatical author would be concerned with. Why is he or she writing something that opposes some church or its administration by prelates? To what churches does this apply, and how do one's religious beliefs enter or not enter into that opposition? Raised is the issue of intentionality—why a writer writes what he or she does—and what the reader takes from the text. (The so-called intentionality fallacy may arise, and that raises the significance of the reader's response to the work.)
2. Students recognize that the specific church and its discipline when Milton wrote must be considered, and a little prompting will bring forth those who can offer differences between the Roman Catholic Church and such Protestant groups as Presbyterians or Baptists; there should also be those who will speak of High or Low Episcopalian churches. (The following session about the State Church of the 1640s will supply information primarily through a student oral report and identify who "Smectymnuus" was [the five State Church ministers who denounced prelacy as a remnant of Roman Catholicism and whose initials compose the pseudonym: Stephen Marshall, Edmund Calamy, Thomas Young, Matthew Newcomen, and William Spurstow].)
3. The discussion then shifts to qualities of a written work: its genre (what is meant by that and why it may be important; what might be the genre of an antiprelatical tract), its rhetorical bases (what is meant by *rhetoric* and how it may be used differently in different circumstances—students will offer examples of writing for different audiences with different educational backgrounds, for example, or of the satirist exploiting rhetoric to poke fun), and its style (a difficult concept that student examples from advertising or movies may, at least, broadly define). What might be the genre or genres, the rhetorical principles, and the style that an antiprelatical tract will exhibit to achieve its "intentionality"?
4. What is humor? Is it only the "funny," or may it also include satire, ridicule, such name-calling as to be invective? What are the reasons for using humor—both funny humor and abusive humor? What is the effect on the reader?
5. The schedule for the ensuing weeks is then presented: discussion of three of Milton's antiprelatical works that provide attention to intentionaliy; genre, rhetoric, and style; and humor in order, with student oral presentations.

Assignments cite three popular Milton texts that offer selected prose and two of which provide all the poetry: C. A. Patrides's edition, *John Milton: Selected Prose*; Merritt Y. Hughes's edition, *Complete Poems and Major Prose*; and Roy C. Flannagan's edition, *The Riverside Milton*. Hughes does not include *Of Reformation*; excerpts from *The Reason of Church Government* in Patrides and Flannagan are inadequate; and Flannagan does not include *Apology*.

Sessions 2 and 3

Class assignment: *Of Reformation* (*John Milton: Selected Prose* 77–83, 89–90, 94–97; *Riverside* 875–78, 886–87, 889, 891–92). The two sessions each include general discussion of the reading and what can be discerned as Milton's "intentionality" in the tract. (Milton's aim is to lay forth the causes for the hindrance of complete reformation of the Church and to argue that the continuance of prelacy in the State Church is a remnant of Catholicism.)

Questions to be pursued by the class:

What is Milton's "intentionality" in this tract?

How does your understanding of that intentionality influence how you read the tract? That is, does this alter what you thought or previously read about Milton's political and religious position?

What is Milton's attitude toward the king and toward monarchy? Is this different from what you previously thought?

What are Milton's strategies for trying to get his ideas across to his readers? (One is satiric or abusive humor; another is a résumé of the history of the church and of religious authorities.)

One session will have a student oral presentation of about fifteen minutes that will provide the class with a few more facts about the tract and about the religious and political period in which it appeared. Two students (perhaps three) should be assigned to make this report, and some references should be suggested to help them with historical and rhetorical matters. (These references are included in the materials section in this volume.) The report might pursue the following questions:

When was the tract written, and did it get any reactions?

What were the circumstances out of which it came? That is, tell us something about some of the other books that provoked *Of Reformation*— Bishop Joseph Hall's *An Humble Remonstrance to the High Court of Parliament* and his *A Defence of the Humble Remonstrance, against the Frivolous and False Exceptions of Smectymnuus* and Smectymnuus's *An Answer to a Booke Entituled*, An Humble Remonstrance, which includes "A Postscript," ascribed to Milton.

Why is the tract divided into two books?

The other session should have a student oral presentation of about fifteen minutes that suggests how the discussion of intentionality may relate to other work written by Milton: for example, the tailed sonnet "On the New Forcers of Conscience" (*Complete Poems and Major Prose* 144–45; *Riverside* 265–66), *The Tenure of Kings and Magistrates* (*John Milton: Selected Prose* 249–59; *Complete Poems and Major Prose* 750–57; *Riverside* 1057–61), or *Paradise Lost* 1.1–26, 9.1–47 (*Complete Poems and Major Prose* 211–12, 378–79; *Riverside* 354–55, 583–85). In what way does paying attention to intentionality in these works lead to an interpretation of them and of what they present? Does that interpretation differ from what you have thought Milton was arguing—what you thought his political position concerning monarchy was or what the thesis of his epic is? (It is best to have the student report concentrate on one or two examples, which the full class will also have read. The examples should be works to be covered later in the course, at which time this preliminary discussion will be reprised.)

Sessions 4 and 5

Class assignment: *The Reason of Church Government* (*John Milton: Selected Prose* 49–60; *Complete Poems and Major Prose* 640–42, ending of ch. 7 on 663–64, 665–71, 683–89; *Riverside* 903–04, ending of ch. 7 on 919–20, 920–25). Two sessions of discussion and student presentations examine genre, rhetoric, and style and their significance for interpretation.

Questions to be pursued by the class:

> How does presentation of this tract in two books suggest differences in genre from a monograph not divided into books or chapters?
>
> Is "intentionality" defined by this separation?
>
> How does the preface to book 2, a long autobiographical section, set up certain reactions to the content of the full tract that you might not expect in a polemical work rejecting prelacy in the Church?
>
> Is this preface a digression? If so, why is it there? If not, how is it part of the argument that Milton is making?
>
> Classical writers such as Aristotle said that the aim of rhetoric (writing) is persuasion, which implies that the author takes a positive or a negative position on a given topic. Have you engaged in a formal debate? What can we conclude from a debater and his or her "sincerity" who argues a proposition affirmatively one day and negatively the next day?
>
> Classical rhetoric was taught to students in Cambridge (as well as in European universities during the Renaissance and afterward) when Milton was at Christ's College; they prepared orations (much like arguments presented in formal debate) that had specific parts and that were most successful if built on invention (that is, original material or strategy and new research into the subject). In the sections of *Reason*

that you have read, what would you classify as Milton's invention? You might consider his unexpected content and his strategies (such as his language, his autobiographical statement, and his assigning of his words to God).

Style involves the language used and the tone that emerges from a piece of writing. What are your feelings about the appropriateness of the specific words or allusions in the text? What would you say is the tone of this tract?

The first student report on *Reason* should consider these questions:

What is the usual structure of an oration? How does this tract divide into the five divisions of an oration? (The structure will be important if the class later reads *Areopagitica*, as many do.)

What is the classical employment of a digression, and how do you view Milton's use of it here in the second preface (that to the second book)?

What do we learn in the autobiographical section about Milton and his plans for future writing?

In comparison with *Of Reformation*, what would you say the tone of this tract is? What does that tone say about Milton and the controversy about prelacy in which he was enmeshed? (Class discussion in session 5 will pursue this further.)

The second student report might look first at the autobiographical section and discuss how it foreshadows *Paradise Lost* and *Paradise Regain'd*. Comparisons of genre, rhetoric, and style might be made with *On Christian Doctrine* in terms of its genre and division into two books of thirty-three and seventeen chapters (*John Milton: Selected Prose* 360–97; *Complete Poems and Major Prose* 903–1020; *Riverside* 1158–201), with "L'Allegro" and "Il Penseroso" in terms of a debate between contrastive lifestyles (*Complete Poems and Major Prose* 68–76; *Riverside* 66–71; 71–77), or with sonnet 18, "Avenge O Lord thy slaughter'd Saints," in terms of the intentionality implied by the Petrarchan sonnet construction and of what is being persuaded (*Complete Poems and Major Prose* 167–68; *Riverside* 255). (Structure and debate elements should be recalled when *Paradise Regain'd* is read. Genre, rhetoric, and style will also be significant.)

Sessions 6 and 7

Class assignment: *An Apology against a Pamphlet Call'd* A Modest Confutation. Two sessions of discussion and two student reports will examine the role of humor in this tract. (The insulting and name-calling invective, as well as sarcasm, that emerges in Milton's texts is not pervasive or analytic of the thesis proffered, yet it represents an aspect of his writing that is frequently unexamined. Comparison with similar invective in diatribes from other authors will suggest the mildness of Milton's satiric language. A discussion sheet with excerpts from *A Dialogue of Sir Thomas More*—more commonly known as Thomas More's *A Dialogue concerning Heresies*—and William Tyndale's *An Answer to Sir Thomas More's Dialogue*, for example, substantiates this point.)

Questions to be pursued by the class:

> What kind of humor do you find in this tract?
>
> What effect does each of the examples you observe have on your reading of the text? Does that humor tell you significant things about the author of *A Modest Confutation*? Does that humor influence your attitude toward Milton as a person and toward his ideas?
>
> Why do you think Milton used humor in this serious tract arguing against prelacy in the State Church?
>
> Contrast the autobiographical section here with that which you read in *Reason*. Why does Milton use autobiography in this tract? What is its effect on you, the reader?

The first student report should pursue the following questions, and class discussion should be encouraged:

> What are the rhetorical concepts of dianoia (thought) and ethos (personal character)?
>
> How do these concepts relate to the use of autobiography in a text?
>
> Does the humor tell you something about the author's character? Does it enhance or reduce your evaluation of the author?
>
> The author's humor attacks and attempts to disparage the antagonist's thought or argument. What is your attitude toward this means of refuting an argument?
>
> Do you find the thought (dianoia) exhibited by the author significant in determining the character (ethos) of the author? Is the thought necessarily, therefore, complete or to be fully accepted as the author's unmodified belief?

The second student report may look at any or all of the following passages and comment on the humor in them, the attitude that a reader might have toward the work in which they appear and toward Milton as author, and what they suggest about the intentionality of the work or that part of the work in which they appear:

> In *Of Reformation*, the reader is immediately plunged into considering "the new-vomited Paganisme" that has drawn "downe all the Divine intercourse, betwixt *God*, and the Soule," decking it out "not in robes of

pure innocency, but of pure Linnen, with other deformed, and fanta-stick dresses in Palls, and Miters, gold, and guegaw's fetcht from *Arons* old wardrope, or the *Flamins vestry*" (876).

In *Animadversions upon the Remonstrants against Smectymnuus*, the Remonstrant's "If yet you can blush" (but none of the rest of the sentence) is quoted and brings forth the comment, "[Y]ou thus persecute ingenuous men over all your booke, with this one over-tir'd rubricall conceit still of blushing; but if you have no mercy upon them, yet spare your selfe, lest you bejade the good galloway, your owne opiniaster wit, and make the very conceit it selfe blush with spur-galling" (*Complete Prose Works* 1: 725).

In *Colasterion*, Milton calls the confuter of his position on divorce "this hoyd'n," "this Pork," and asks, "But what should a man say more to a snout in this pickle, what language can be low and degenerat anough?" (*Complete Prose Works* 2: 742, 737, 747).

In *Comus: A Mask*, the younger brother exclaims, after the elder brother has expounded on the hidden strength of chastity, "How charming is divine Philosophy!" (145; line 476).

In *Samson Agonistes*, the giant Harapha shuns Samson: "To combat with a blind man I disdain, / And thou hast need much washing to be toucht" (lines 1106–07).

Also in *Samson Agonistes*, the Chorus speaks as Dalila turns her back and walks away: "She's gone, a manifest Serpent by her sting / Discover'd in the end, till now conceal'd" (lines 997–98).

The full class should be encouraged to discuss these excerpts with the students as they present their remarks.

These approaches have proved salient and purposively successful in courses on Milton that cover much of the poetry, or much of the poetry and selected prose, or courses with concentration on only specific works. Syllabi most frequently include reading "On the Morning of Christ's Nativity," *Comus*, "Lycidas," some of the sonnets, *Areopagitica*, *Paradise Lost*, *Samson Agonistes*, and sometimes *Of Education* and *Paradise Regain'd*. All these works may be introduced, with success, through one or all of these avenues into understanding Milton's writing.

Milton and the Bible

Jameela Lares

One of the great divides between Milton and the modern student is the Bible, a text fundamental to Milton's thought and expression. He cites it as proof, alludes to its phrasings or episodes as a discursive shorthand, and borrows its narrative and argumentative structures. So pervasive is biblical reference in Milton's work—and in the literature of his age—that modern editors can hardly gloss it thoroughly, even if they recognize its presence. Indeed, James H. Sims notes that even though editors of Milton's epics from Patrick Hume (1695) to Merritt Hughes (1957) had among them identified a composite sum of 1,364 individual citations of Scripture, Sims himself found an additional 816 Bible citations (2–3). Because Bible references are markedly underglossed and because modern students typically have little knowledge of the Bible—few have read it even once—most of them have little idea of the rich biblical presence in Milton's texts or how that presence can help them understand those texts.

Most instructors will lack the time to direct a thorough investigation of Milton's biblicism, but students will benefit from whatever amount can be included. They can better understand what modern critics mean by "intertextuality" by watching it being constructed. By seeing the effect of the Bible on one author, they can also begin to recognize its effect on most authors writing in English, perhaps with a little help from Robert Atwan and Laurence Wieder's *Chapters into Verse*. Students should begin to understand the extent to which the Bible explicitly or implicitly informs all other seventeenth-century authors, not only poets such as John Donne, George Herbert, Abraham Cowley, and John Dryden but authors in every genre and on every subject. A student of mine once set herself the task of searching our seventeenth-century microfilm collection for a text that "did *not* mention God"—and hence implicitly the Bible. She searched long and without success. As the professor advises his student in the beginning of Christopher Hill's *The English Bible and the Seventeenth-Century Revolution*, "If you really want to understand the period, go away and read the Bible" (4). In this chapter, I provide specific suggestions for teaching—in passing or at length—Milton's use of the Bible. I find it helpful to think of that use on levels of specificity. Milton uses the Bible locally as argumentative proof, usually by citing specific biblical verses ("proof texts") as authority for his position, a common practice at the time. In addition, Milton often engages in discursive shorthand, referring briefly to much longer sections of the Bible that were known more or less intimately by his original audience. Finally, Milton borrows larger narrative and argumentative structures from the Scripture. I discuss these three Miltonic uses of the Bible below, but first let me provide some background information on early modern Bible translation and hermeneutics, information that should help students understand the context of Milton's biblicism.

Students will probably not know that the Authorized or King James Bible (1611), a notable presence in Milton's work as well as in English literature in general, was the culmination of nearly a century of Protestant Bible translation, beginning with William Tyndale's New Testament of 1525 and including such landmark versions as Myles Coverdale's (1535), the Great Bible (1539), the Geneva Bible (1560), the Bishop's Bible (1568), and also a rival Roman Catholic translation, the Rheims-Douai (New Testament, 1582; complete Bible, 1609-10). Numerous scholarly resources on this process of translation are available. An excellent pictorial overview of the translation history is provided by Craig R. Thompson's illustrated booklet *The Bible in English, 1525–1611*, which although unfortunately out of print, is still widely available in university libraries. Another pictorial overview (sixteen plates) can be found in David Norton's *A History of the English Bible as Literature*, along with the translation history detailed at more length, as it is in F. F. Bruce's landmark *History of the Bible in English* and in the equally authoritative study by Bruce M. Metzger, *The Bible in Translation: Ancient and English Versions*. Other recent studies of English Bible translation include Alister McGrath's *In the Beginning: The Story of the King James Bible and How It Changed a Nation, a Language, and a Culture*, David Daniell's *The Bible in English: Its History and Influence*, and Adam Nicolson's *God's Secretaries: The Making of the King James Bible*. I find it helpful to have copies on hand to pass around, so that students have often weighty proof—Daniell's six-hundred-page book is particularly hefty—of scholarly interest in the topic. Two films might also be considered for classroom use. "A Muse of Fire," from the PBS series *The Story of English*, examines the effect on the English language of Shakespeare and the King James Bible. "Paradise Lost," from the BBC series *Testament: The Bible and History*, looks at Bible translation and authority since the Renaissance and glances at the work of Milton at least in its title. Milton increasingly favored the King James Bible for English citation; there is, oddly enough, no evidence that he was influenced by the more "Puritan" Geneva Bible with its heavy marginalia (Sims 4–5). Milton also knew the biblical texts in their original Hebrew and Greek. In *Of Education*, Milton even suggests that the students at his ideal academy could learn Chaldean and Syriac (*Complete Prose Works* 2: 400)—that is, versions of what we now call Aramaic, which though spoken widely in the ancient Near East are only minor Old Testament languages (Emerton). I preserve the terms "Old Testament" and "New Testament" in my teaching, incidentally, since they were the terms, derived from Jeremiah 31.31–34, known to Milton and his contemporaries, but I also explain how the Hebrew scriptures are viewed in Judaism as the Tanakh (an acronym made up of the initial letters of the Hebrew words for law, prophets, and writings).

Behind Milton's biblicism is the driving force of Reformation hermeneutics, and especially the principle of *sola scriptura*, or the singular authority of Scripture. Protestants believed that man's reconciliation to God was guided by scriptural revelation alone, aided by God's Spirit without the additional glosses of later tradition. This revelation was typically given to the individual believer who puzzled out scriptural meaning. Reliance on the Bible thus became a mark of the committed Protestant; Milton's father was disinherited by his "Romanist" father for reading or at least owning a Bible (Aubrey 1; J. Phillips 18).[1] In practice, all interpreters depend on additional aids, and Milton's list in *On Christian Doctrine* comprises:

> linguistic ability, knowledge of the original sources, consideration of the overall intent, distinction between literal and figurative language, examination of the causes and circumstances, and of what comes before and after the passage in question, and comparison of one text with another.
>
> (*Complete Prose Works* 6: 582)

As Isabel Rivers notes in *Classical and Christian Ideas in English Renaissance Poetry*, Protestant interpretation of the Bible stressed two meanings: the literal and the typological (140–49). One handy example she cites as proof is Michael's lecture to Adam on typology at *Paradise Lost* 12.227–44 and 300–14. Longer passages of Milton that specifically discuss the Bible include his comparison of tangled tradition with clear Scripture in *Of Reformation* (*Complete Prose Works* 1: 563–70), his discussion of Scripture in *On Christian Doctrine*, book 1, chapter 30 (*Complete Prose Works* 6: 574–92), and the Son's claim in *Paradise Regained* that biblical literature far excels that of Greece and Rome, not only in content but also in style (4.286–364). This passage, it should be noted, has occasioned much critical disagreement, and students might want to compare Milton's statements in the prose with those of the Son in the short epic to see if Milton intends the Son to echo his own sentiments.

If time permits, students can also look at how scriptural interpretation is treated in the Thirty-Nine Articles of the Church of England and in its rival, the Presbyterians' Westminster Confession. To the extent students can access earlier material by microfilm, database, or interlibrary loan, they can also look at any of the many theological summaries published during the period, especially those by William Ames and Jean Wolleb, which furnished the main material for Milton's *On Christian Doctrine*. There are already several studies of Milton's hermeneutics, including Georgia B. Christopher's *Milton and the Science of the Saints*, Dayton Haskin's *Milton's Burden of Interpretation*, and David Gay's *The Endless Kingdom: Milton's Scriptural Society*. Students who want to pursue the matter even further can look at relevant selections from such classic works as A. G. Dickens's *The English Reformation*, Patrick Collinson's *The Religion of Protestants*, and William Haller's *The Rise of Puritanism* and *Liberty and Reformation in the Puritan Revolution*, or more recently published church historians such as Nicholas Tyacke, Peter Lake, Kenneth Fincham, and Peter McCullough. I have had good success teaching an advanced Milton seminar using Nigel Smith's *Literature and Revolution in England, 1640–1660*.

Students might be assigned the task of looking up the proof texts, or Bible verses cited as proof, in one or more paragraphs. They can then see how Milton puts biblical citation to work as proof in any of several prose works, including his divorce tracts, his antimonarchical pamphlets, and his later arguments about effective church administration—for example, *The Likeliest Means to Remove Hirelings* (*Complete Prose Works* 7: 273–321). The divorce tracts can be an especially rich field of inquiry for students, since Milton must argue against seemingly clear individual proof texts forbidding divorce—spoken by Christ himself—and must do so by means of a single principle derived from Scripture: the New Testament Gospel is always easier than the Old Testament Law.

Even as students are examining Milton's use of proof texts, they can see another major use to which he put Scripture: discursive shorthand. Because Milton's original audience was more or less versed in Scripture, Milton can cite mere tags of Scripture to represent larger commonplaces, such as the texts and meanings of various parables.

Students should also be able to see how Milton adopted larger discursive structures from the biblical originals, perhaps with some help from a student report on Barbara Lewalski's *Protestant Poetics and the Seventeenth-Century Religious Lyric*, which traces various genres and stylistic effects, or from Donald Davie's *Psalms in English*, which shows that Milton's youthful translation of Psalm 114 was part of a wider cultural practice. I also mention to the class how Milton's controversial practice is consonant with the Protestant "redargutive" sermon, with its explicitly biblicist rationale, and how Milton joined his contemporaries in claiming that Scripture was not only the superior doctrinal statement but also the superior communicative model. Modern students might find this little-known claim arresting—it astonished no less than C. A. Patrides—and they may well want to engage the issue by looking, for example, at the extent to which the Protestant sermon was structured according to the classical oration and by asking whether discursive success depends more on the perceived source of its inspiration than on the nature of language itself.

NOTE

[1] I have cited the standard edition of this text, edited by Darbishire, who attributes authorship of this anonymous biography of Milton to the poet's nephew John Phillips, though modern critics tend to identify the biographer as Milton's amanuensis Cyriack Skinner.

Elaborating Differences:
Milton's *Areopagitica*
in the Postmodern Classroom

William Kolbrener

One might think that teaching Milton in the postmodern classroom entails special preparation for a special audience—to address students immersed, for example, in the languages of postmodernism or poststructuralist literary theory. The postmodern classroom, however, in my experience—whether in New York, Los Angeles, or Tel Aviv—is not a special pedagogical context but rather the normative context in the contemporary university. Indeed, the postmodernist emphasis on what Derridean deconstructionists refer to as *différance* has given rise, in social and political frameworks, to a parallel emphasis on diversity and multiplicity (undermining traditional conceptions of community) to which most students assent—either consciously or not. This is to say that students don't need to be schooled in the languages of Derridean philosophy to understand a postmodern sensibility. Most of the students I have encountered, coming from widely different educational and cultural backgrounds, evidence (if not embrace) conceptions of truth, individualism, and difference that, whether they know it or not, have much in common with postmodern theoretical discourses.

To make Milton accessible to the postmodern classroom, I turn to Milton's own metaphors of difference—to show the means by which he accommodates, with his conception of Christian commonwealth, the seemingly opposing tendencies of the individual and the community. Before addressing the conceptions of community implicit in Milton's works, I ask my students to identify those contemporary metaphors used to embody conceptions of community and individual difference. Such an exercise not only provides a standard against which they can compare Milton's metaphors of difference, it also has the effect of allowing students to articulate and foreground their conceptions of community and the role of difference in it. In the American context, students are generally enthusiastic about tracing the relation between the individual and community as it developed in the American imagination through the older metaphor of the melting pot to the more contemporary metaphor of the salad bowl. Asking students to evaluate the ideological work achieved by the vehicle of the two metaphors provides an excellent preparation for evaluating Milton's metaphors of difference. Students will usually volunteer that the melting pot (which alloys a variety of metals into one homogenous substance) corresponds to a culture in which immigrants of the twenties and thirties desired assimilation and were thus willing to compromise their cultural difference. The salad bowl, by contrast, attests to a reality of a multicultural society in which individuals are not so ready to give up those differences.

The introductory exercise leads to a more general discussion of the ways in which individual differences are alternately accommodated or repressed in larger cultural contexts or communities. There are inevitably reference points in twenty-first-century events—like the debates in France about the display of religious symbols. From the question of individual differences and community, I ask how, in the various models that we have discussed, conceptions of value and truth are likely to emerge. More specifically, in a multicultural society represented in the image of the salad bowl, does truth emerge collectively or as a function of the individual? A quotation (much out of context) from *Paradise Lost* provides a good means of sharpening the issue: "The Mind is its own Place, and in itself / Can make a Heaven of Hell, a Hell of Heaven" (the Satanic utterance is actually attributed to Milton—without qualification—on a Web page devoted to him [www.brainyquote.com/quotes/authors/j/john_milton.html]). With encouragement, students are able to identify the ways in which the passage seems to advocate conceptions of value—and difference—linked to contemporary models where value is inevitably subjective. In any classroom of diversity, students almost always assent to the subjectivist criterion established in the quotation from Milton's epic. I like to end the introductory discussion with a question: based on the passage from *Paradise Lost*, is Milton perhaps a postmodernist like us?

The more theoretical discussion of difference yields to the elaboration of another set of frameworks: the specific contexts—technological and theological—for Milton's writing of *Areopagitica* in 1644. Depending on the class, some brief recapitulation of the history of the period is necessary, emphasizing that when the king retreated from London in 1642, the Parliament assumed power and then requested an ordinance to license printing. A couple of questions naturally emerge: If the parliamentary forces embraced the print revolution as a means of furthering their cause, why would they embrace a practice of licensing? Further, and more pointedly, why would the Parliament, itself espousing principles of Protestant liberty and individualism, negate those principles in their ordinance? The answers help illustrate that not all opponents to the king were alike: Independents and Congregationalists, like Milton, advocated a radical form of Protestant individualism; in contrast, Presbyterians, who represented a majority in Parliament, may have turned against the king as well as Catholic rituals and theology but nonetheless wanted to maintain church hierarchy. What usually results from the discussion is that parliamentarians were not merely selling out radical principles but were cognizant and worried about the centrifugal forces of the unbridled individualism advocated by some of the more radical Protestant sects. If Puritanism rose into ascendancy on a wave of individualism, then there were many, even in the parliamentary party, who were wary of this new wave of individual and interpretive freedom.[1] Thus, parliamentarians attempted to limit the technology (printing) in which this danger was expressing itself most powerfully. If sectarians and schismatics were using the mechanisms of print to spread their views in the unprecedented publication (in Britain) of political and theological tracts, then Presbyters would advocate a clampdown on the technology that had helped bring them to power and that, further, seemed to embody the ideals they cherished.[2]

Before foregrounding Milton's conceptions of difference, I introduce one of Milton's Presbyterian contemporaries, Thomas Edwards, and his massive compilation of heresies, *Gangraena*. By turning to that tract, one can easily convey what was at stake between the Independency that Milton advocated and Edwards's Presbyterian agenda. To be sure, the title of Edwards's tract implies its conception of differences—that they are to be cut off from the commonwealth, like an infected limb. Edwards's lengthy catalog of blasphemies, heresies, and schisms to be repressed reads, and can be presented, like a David Letterman top-ten list:

> 58: There is no originall sin in us. . . .
> 71: That the doctrine of repentance is a soul-destroying doctrine.
> 91: There is no hell but in this life. . . .
> 114: That the Church of England is anti-Christian. . . .
> 140: That love-feasts, or feasts of love . . . is a perpetual ordinance of Christ. . . .
> 160: 'Tis unlawfull to fight at all, or to kill any man, yea to kill any of the creatures for our use, as a chicken, or on any other occasion.   (20–29)

Edward not only provides a catalog of heresies, he also stands as spokesman for the culture of the Presbyterians against whom Milton would have to make his case for difference. Edwards, though rejecting (in good Protestant fashion) "Popery," "tyranny," and "superstitions," emerges as a kind of seventeenth-century afternoon talk-radio host, lamenting that "every day" things "grow worse and worse," affirming that one could "hardly conceive and imagine them so bad as they are." For Edwards, the proliferation of sects and schisms—the manifestation of difference in the 1640s—produces only "*Horrid Blasphemies, Libertinisme, and fearfull Anarchy.*" As Edwards writes, the proposed "[t]oleration" of such difference (was he thinking of Milton?) is "the grand designe of the Devil" (A4r–B1v). Prompting students to evaluate Edwards's arguments (and the responses usually range from grudging approval of his realism to adamant rejection of his paternalism) is another useful way for students to foreground their assumptions and prepare for the engagement with Milton's conception of difference.

Taking account of the political and theological contexts of the 1640s, I provide a first reading through *Areopagitica* (*Riverside* 987–1024) in which Milton figures as a Puritan hero fighting the repressive forces evidenced in Edwards's work. When working through the tract, I focus on Milton's conception of truth as multiple and changeable and on a subjectivist epistemology that emphasizes the individual conscience as the origin of value. To be sure, Milton's metaphors of truth throughout *Areopagitica* are associated with flux and change: "Truth," Milton writes, "is compar'd in Scripture to a streaming fountain; if her waters flow not in a perpetuall progression, they sick'n into a muddy pool of conformity and tradition" (1015). For Milton, in this reading, truth is associated with a dynamic and perpetual process of scriptural interpretation, while falsehood is associated with static singularity—"obedient unanimity" and "a fine conformity" (1016).

From this Miltonic perspective, truth is associated not only with progress but also with multiplicity. As elaborated in *Areopagitica*, "Truth" may have once come into the world in the figure of Jesus, but after his death, "a wicked race of deceivers" took the "virgin Truth," in Milton's metaphoric treatment of the Christian story, and "hewd her lovely form into a thousand peeces, and scatter'd them to the four winds." "From that time ever since," Milton continues, "the sad friends of Truth . . . went up and down gathering up limb by limb, still as they could find them." Truth may have once manifested itself in the world in its "lovelines and perfection," but in the world of history before the "second comming," the location of truth in one place—or one perspective—is impossible (1017–18). Given the multiplicity of truth—that the limbs of Milton's God have been figuratively scattered—the claim that one can possess the truth is an assertion of bad faith: "he who thinks we are to pitch our tent here, and have attain'd the utmost prospect of reformation . . . by this very opinion declares, that he is yet farre short of truth" (1017). One who avows that he possesses the truth, Milton argues, by this very assertion, shows himself to lack the truth.

From Milton's affirmation of the ineradicable multiplicity of truth, I turn to *Areopagitica*'s assertion of a subjectivist epistemology focused in the individual conscience. The priority of liberty of conscience is present throughout the tract but distilled in Milton's representation of the apostle Peter's rebellion against law. Against the Old Testament rules about forbidden foods, Milton represents God enjoining the apostle, "Rise, *Peter*, kill and eat," thus "leaving the choice to each mans discretion" (1005). Seeming to dovetail with the perspective elaborated in the citation from *Paradise Lost*, *Areopagitica* foregrounds a conception of value that emerges not from the object (or from law) but rather through the powers of the individual conscience. On the basis of these readings, I lead the class toward an apparent conclusion—arguing that Milton, with his emphases on subjectivity, liberty, and truth conceived of as multiple, anticipates postmodern conceptions of individuality and difference. *Areopagitica*, in this reading, a postmodern text *avant la lettre*, idealizes a conception of community where differences, indeed multiple truths, are celebrated.

In my experience, the number of students who, having dutifully recorded this summation, pack up their books to leave class is usually offset by an equal number who evidence discomfort with the (bogus) conclusion offered. Almost inevitably someone will call attention to Milton's conclusion of the tract where he significantly qualifies his call for toleration: "I mean not tolerated Popery, and open superstition" (1022). The foregoing approach to *Areopagitica* now bears its pedagogical fruits. For how is it that Milton could articulate principles of liberal individualism, establishing him on a continuum of thinkers that would lead to postmodernism, yet at the same time exclude Catholics from his commonwealth? One can further ask, to raise the stakes of the discussion, what Milton might have thought about the differences represented by Muslims, Jews, or atheists. How do Miltonic principles of subjectivity, multiplicity, and process resolve with the exclusions at the end of the tract?[23]

Why did Milton tolerate sectarians? Was he in favor of democracy? Was he a pluralist? a multiculturalist in disguise? If so, what could possibly be the basis for Milton's exclusions? If students have been provided with basic background to Catholicism and the Protestant Reformation, they are likely to realize that by Milton's lights, Catholics could never be tolerated. For their principles committed them to a belief in tradition and conformity that was in opposition to Reformed Protestant theology—which distinguished itself from its predecessors in its embrace of process. Catholics believed the truth could be embodied, could find a physical or doctrinal manifestation; such a belief, for Milton, disqualified Catholics from the interpretive processes of finding truth (for by their own admissions they have already pitched their tent). For Milton, believers in other religions and certainly atheists, having committed themselves to a perspective entrenched in falsehood, could find no place in a Protestant community. Protestant sectarians, however, no matter how "heretical" their perspectives, are part of that search that would lead, inevitably, to the "closing up truth to truth" (1018).[4] In Milton's trope of Solomon's temple at the end of the tract, differences not only emerge but are also maintained through a precedent agreement on Reformed Protestant principles. All the passages examined previously can be reexamined in this light, showing that Milton's advocacy of subjectivity, multiplicity, and process is always circumscribed by his precedent commitment to Protestant truth. For example, though Milton argues that truth is like a fountain and at a certain level unattainable, he also argues that truth in all her body will one day appear "*homogeneal*" (1018).

The Miltonic conception of difference is represented in the temple trope as Milton defends those "schismaticks and sectaries," participating in the building of "the Temple of the Lord," against "a sort of irrationall men who could not consider there must be many schisms and many dissections made in the quarry and in the timber, ere the house of God can be built." Milton continues by imagining the completion of the temple:

> And when every stone is laid artfully together, it cannot be united into a continuity, it can but be contiguous in this world; neither can every peece of the building be of one form; nay rather the perfection consists in this, that out of many moderat varieties and brotherly dissimilitudes that are not vastly disproportionall arises the goodly and the gracefull symmetry that commends the whole pile and structure.   (1019)

To be sure, the salad bowl and the melting pot are straightforward metaphors compared with Milton's metaphysical conceit. Here, I focus the discussion by attending to the Miltonic distinction between "continuity," which implies a singular nondiversified truth (not available in this world, as Milton insists), and what Milton defines as the "contigu[ity]" of difference. (One can ask at this point: who might Milton have had in mind—if not Presbyters like Edwards—when he identifies "irrationall men" objecting to sects and schisms?) If the temple conceit rejects continuity and posits a "contiguity" of differences, does it not contradict the exclusions made explicit at the end of the tract? For if Milton celebrates differences for their own sake, then there should be no possible place for any exclusion. As a way of dramatizing Milton's commitments, I ask students whether, in the last main clause of the passage, Milton emphasizes similarity or difference. That is, does the "perfection" of the commonwealth to which Milton refers emerge simply as a function of multiplicity of differences, or rather does it come from the resemblance among the constituent parts?

The whole clause bears close reading, but I concentrate on the term "brotherly dissimilitudes." Breaking down the oxymoronic phrase helps further dramatize Miltonic conceptions of difference: if the embedded term "similitudes" emphasizes similarity and the prefix "dis" emphasizes difference, how does the adjective "brotherly" work? How does Milton's advocacy of "moderate varieties" that are not "vastly disproportionall" figure in his representation of the temple? Like any metaphysical conceit, Milton's trope resists simplistic rendering, but it has the effect of asserting differences maintained in agreement. Milton's reformed England, therefore, establishes its "goodly and gracefull symmetry" through "brotherly dissimilitudes," at once mediating and preserving the differences it acknowledges and circumscribes.

The ensuing class discussion can foreground the way in which Milton's conceptions of community emerge as distinct from those in postmodern models, which tend to celebrate difference and multiplicity for their own sake. Miltonic difference, as Milton's temple trope demonstrates, is always framed by relations of similarity: differences are permitted, provided they are elaborated within the framework of Reformed Protestant theology. From this perspective the reading offered earlier, which emphasized (without qualification) the Miltonic celebration of multiplicity and difference, shows itself a species of bad or partial reading—a projection of contemporary paradigms and concerns onto Milton's work (at this point, one can inform or remind students that the citation from *Paradise Lost* celebrating value as subjective is voiced by none other than Satan).

Pedagogically, the current reading serves as a way not only of understanding the difference of Milton but also, equally important, of establishing a postmodern principle in interpretive practice where acknowledging the other necessarily entails a partial suspension of one's own presuppositions and assumptions. That is, students can be encouraged to use the engagement with Milton's text as a means of meditating on the processes by which their precedent assumptions helped to reveal and at the same time obscure aspects of Milton's work.[5] This discussion can help students understand how Milton's conceptions of community and difference have their own integrity and specificity—themselves radically different and distinct from our postmodern concerns. The experience of the dissonance between the reader's interpretive expectations and the text can help foreground other, more general questions: if Milton's conceptions of difference are autonomous and different from contemporary postmodern conceptions, are his commitments only a cause for condemnation or disappointment (that for example, he did not go far enough)? Could one entertain the possibility that Milton's formal principles of exclusion (not the actual exclusions he recommends) permit a conception of community not present in contemporary multicultural models? Lest Milton, from a postmodern perspective, seem to some students a hypocrite, I try to end by pushing the class to think in Milton's own terms, where the elaboration of circumscribed differences yields an ideal of community very different from that of contemporary models. The encounters with Milton's text thus not only reveal his distinct conceptions of difference but also help us articulate—perhaps even interrogate—our postmodern assumptions.

NOTES

[1] Students might be reminded that though the schematic historiographical narrative of emergent Protestant individualism serves a heuristic function, conceptions of selfhood, interiority, and individuality were present much earlier. Just as Frank Kermode questions T. S. Eliot's formulations about the "dissociation of sensibility" in the seventeenth century (Kermode gamely pushes it back to the thirteenth century [141]), so students should be encouraged to be wary about a hard-and-fast date for a fluid historical phenomenon.

[2] This can be a good opportunity to introduce Milton's poem "On the New Forcers of Conscience under the Long Parliament," which ends with the famous line, "*New Presbyter* is but *Old Priest* writ Large" (266).

[3] There are more ways to bring out the force of the contradiction: for one, the class can turn to Milton's *A Treatise of Civil Power*, in which Milton uses the term "heresie" with approval. Though he starts by affirming that *heresy* is "no word of evil note" (1124), he concludes that "a true heresie, or rather an impietie; wherein a right conscience can have naught to do; . . . a magistrate can hardly err in prohibiting" (1127).

[4] Milton may provide a figure of Edwards (or an Edwards-like figure, since *Gangraena* was published after *Areopagitica*). While Milton envisions "an Eagle muing her mighty youth, and kindling her undazl'd eyes at the full midday beam; purging and unscaling her long abused sight at the fountain it self of heav'nly radiance," he also imagines a "whole noise of timorous and flocking birds, with those also that love the twilight, flutter about, amaz'd at what she means, and in their envious gabble would prognosticat a year of sects and schisms" (1020).

[5] Advanced students might pursue work on Milton's political languages or on the historiographical assumptions that frame historical inquiry. For a broader contextualization of the republican languages Milton uses, see Armitage, Himy, and Skinner; Nigel Smith; Norbrook, *Writing*. For the historiographical issues, see my *Milton's Warring Angels*, especially chapter 1. For a more general inquiry into the problems of "anachronistic" and "proleptic" histories, see Skinner 57–89.

Teaching Milton's Late Political Tracts in a Public, Comprehensive University

Elizabeth Skerpan-Wheeler

Thanks to decades of vigorous research, teachers fully accept the importance of Milton's prose works to our understanding of Milton and to the development of Anglo-American political expression. The political prose of Milton and others has been central to my own scholarly career. Yet, when I work on my syllabi, I find myself continually confronting the same broad and ultimately practical question: how do these works fit—in the course and in the context of my students' larger university education? Our learning and teaching increasingly take place in universities that emphasize professional training at the expense of traditional liberal arts. These trends are manifest in such phenomena as increasing class sizes and decreasing support for research materials in the humanities: more subscriptions for business and scientific publications, but no money for *Early English Books Online*. My enthusiasm for the prose and for contextual, historical scholarship runs headlong into the challenge of keeping the syllabus and assignments manageable in the limits of our resources.

I have found that the most effective way of approaching Milton's late prose works is to consider seriously the lessons of my own research in Milton and the history of rhetoric: to pay attention to my audience and the rhetorical situation in which we find ourselves. By acknowledging our contexts as well as Milton's, I can pursue the suitably Miltonic ends of promoting students' engagement with the ideas in the texts they read and of emphasizing the connections among art, education, and citizenship: why it all *matters*. These goals are well suited to our upper-division Milton course, although I consider them and the methods I use to advance them equally applicable to lower-division classes.

I teach *The Tenure of Kings and Magistrates* (1649), *The Second Defense of the English People* (1654), and *The Ready and Easy Way to Establish a Free Commonwealth* (1660) (all appearing in the three most widely available editions—*Riverside Milton* [ed. Flannagan], *John Milton: The Major Works* [ed. Orgel and Goldberg], and *Complete Poems and Major Prose* [ed. Hughes]) as part of a focus on the relation of Milton's life and works. My methodology is shaped by university curricular requirements and the character of our typical students. Thanks to a requirement that English majors take a single-author course before graduation, our senior-level Milton course, offered every fall, is always full. It therefore is not an entirely self-selecting group. Some students have not studied early modern literature since their sophomore survey course. Further, because of state laws regarding transfer credits, research skills vary wildly. Most of our students are traditional college age, and most are underprepared in historical and literary knowledge, as well as language skills. Still, as a group, our undergraduate majors are intelligent and curious. They come to the course toward the end of their college careers, and they are urgently concerned with making their way in the world. Moreover, they think about the problem of balancing those practical considerations with their individual ideals. Milton thus becomes for them a study example of finding one's way in difficult times. Milton's life and his wide-ranging interests also allow students to draw on their own previous coursework (all are required to take courses in American history, American national government, and critical thinking), so the course functions as a kind of capstone, encouraging students to tie together the various strands of their educations.

Reflecting my own research in Milton's prose and poetics, I teach the later prose works as explorations of Milton's paradoxical conception of the political self: a self that must exist and be realized in public exercise but that also possesses an internal essence that may be compromised or irreparably damaged through conflict with others. We study how that tension informs the prose and how Milton's efforts to resolve it vary over time. This approach allows us to consider broad questions of political philosophy and then to see how one person understood them and applied them to himself and his times. We also examine Milton's historical contexts, so that students may see where his ideas came from, why they appealed to the poet, and what happened to them. I connect these questions to our ultimate focus: reading *Paradise Lost* and writing individual term projects.

Students begin their engagement with the texts with an exercise inspired by early modern commonplace books. I first explain what commonplace books were, using examples from Milton (supported by the scholarship of Mary Thomas Crane), and show that the technique encouraged careful reading as well as organizing with an eye to eventual writing. Then I provide each student with a six-page packet, which they are to complete. The packet includes description and instructions; a page each devoted to the *Tenure*, *Second Defense*, and *Ready and Easy Way*; a flowchart; and a summary. The description reads:

> The guiding idea of this assignment is that Milton's complex prose works are more easily followed and appreciated when students have certain specific themes to look for, both as guideposts within particular works and as points of connection between works. So I have provided forms for tracking three themes common to Milton's work as a whole (themes we've been studying throughout the semester, but especially in *Areopagitica*), a blank chart for making connections among the three works we'll be studying, and a comment page, on which you may sum up your findings. I hope that the visual representations you'll create will help you *see* how some of Milton's ideas (and the ways he presents them) change from work to work, and in what ways they remain the same.

The instructions read:

1. As you read each assignment, track each of the given topics by writing down illustrating quotations and phrases (with page references) in the appropriate columns. Use just enough of the quotation to enable you to find it quickly when you refer back to the text.
2. When you have completed all three forms, transfer your chief discoveries to the tracking chart. The chart should help you make comparisons among the three works.
3. When you have finished the chart, write some conclusions on the summary page. Your guiding question should be, Now that I have made these comparisons, what do I notice about Milton's ideas on these three topics? *The process should prepare you to answer a required essay question on the final exam.*

Each page for a single work has three columns, with the headings Public Character, Self-Representation, and Risk or Danger to Self. The chart (see illustration) allows students to organize the three topics and three texts on one page. The unstructured summary page encourages writers to expand their own thoughts on what they've been reading.

After receiving some coaching in how to read a periodic sentence, students complete the assignment out of class and bring their packets with them for ready reference as we discuss each work in turn. The topics I've provided are designed to provide clues for reading: the threads that help them find their way through the labyrinths of the texts. The writing requirement encourages students to digest what they are reading. Filling in the tables lets them know whether they're being thorough. Moreover, I provide a powerful incentive to be meticulous: students may use their completed packets during the final examination (the packets are turned in with the exam).

I have never seen completely empty pages, and many students leave no blank spaces, with both columns and margins covered with quotations and comments. Their packets reveal that they notice the different kinds of evidence used in the

TRACKING CHART

TENURE (1649)	SECOND DEFENSE (1654)	READY AND EASY WAY (1660)
Public Character	Public Character	Public Character
Self-Representation	Self-Representation	Self-Representation
Risk or Danger to Self	Risk or Danger to Self	Risk or Danger to Self

tracts: the use of proof texts, classical political theory, and the works of Protestant divines in *Tenure*; the ethical proofs of *Second Defense*; the sustained characterization of the political public in the *Ready and Easy Way*. They are alert to changes of tone and emphasis and clearly see how Milton's historical moments affect his argumentative strategy.

Aside from providing guided reading, the exercise builds students' confidence in their ability to read difficult prose. The process of selecting quotations helps readers avoid being overwhelmed by Milton's language, as it forces close reading. Further, it helps students be specific as they search for evidence. This specificity translates into class discussions as well. All come to class with notes they themselves have prepared; thus, they have some investment in the accuracy and quality of the notes and their commentary on them. Since I inaugurated the assignment, I've gone from directing to refereeing discussions. Armed with their charts, students respond readily and directly to each other, challenging readings, pointing out what others may have overlooked. The need to provide specific evidence keeps exchanges civil, as participants notice the possibility of divergent readings of the same passages.

The critical spirit prompted by the primary-text assignment carries over into a short, secondary-source exercise that prepares students for their final projects. This exercise has students write short papers on topics raised by current criticism. I provide the topics, which I choose by reviewing the most recent *MLA Bibliography*; I try to provide at least as many topics as there are students, so that the class may appreciate the wide variety of ways of thinking about and interpreting Milton's prose. Recent topics include Milton and classical republicanism, prophetic language, Milton's readers, and the relation of religion and politics in Milton's works. The papers are short—two to three pages—and are to be reports that apply what scholars are currently saying to specific prose works. In addition to the topics, I provide suggestions for proceeding, including guidance on using the library and online databases and on distinguishing good Internet sources from questionable ones. I conclude with this advice: "your note should be analytic and evaluative, not just a report on what someone else has written: use your new knowledge to interpret *one tract* in a new way (new to you)."

Students share and discuss their papers as they apply those topics to specific prose works. The sharing may be done electronically (through a class Web site) or through hard copies, either multiple or placed on reserve. Students thus complete a graded writing assignment and actively provide classroom materials that otherwise would need to be supplied by the instructor. They also receive some instruction in basic, literary research skills, as it is not unusual to encounter transfer students with little or no experience with writing documented essays, and even otherwise sophisticated students sometimes have trouble understanding the varying quality of Web-based sources. Finally, it helps them use scholarship to formulate and shape their arguments.

These two exercises have the additional benefit of being portable. I have modified both for use in advanced courses in Restoration and late-eighteenth-century literature and in our undergraduate course in literary theory. The exercise for reading primary texts, Miltonic or otherwise, works well in large, undergraduate survey courses, especially when teaching assistants use it to guide small-group discussions. It may also be effective in any situation that requires reading difficult texts. I use a short version when students begin their encounter with the first-year reader required in our composition classes. Both exercises work best when students clearly see them as means to particular ends (graded assignments, aids for exams) and understand that they are meant to generate ideas rather than to produce packaged explanations of meaning.

That final point—of the exercises and of the life-and-works approach that governs my design of the Milton course—is ultimately the most important. Our students today enter the university after passing through primary and secondary schools structured around relentless objective testing and necessarily formulaic writing. Their experience often leaves them fearful of open-ended inquiries and any texts that do not immediately proclaim their meanings. They are uneasy with ambiguity and complexity. Studying Milton, especially his prose, can build students' confidence in their ability to read, think, and understand. Following the development of his ideas about the relations between public and private spheres, the connections between self and society, and the whole notion of the public citizen raises exactly the kinds of questions that students need and want to examine, especially as most of them conclude their formal education. My promise to students at the beginning of the semester is that they will leave feeling truly educated. It is a promise easy to keep.

Discipline in the Classroom

Alison A. Chapman

The first chapter of *The Reason of Church Government* (excerpted in *Riverside* 903–25) is a panegyric to discipline. Given the pamphlet's larger goal of ecclesiastical reform, Milton seems to play on the early modern meaning of "discipline" as a synonym for church structure, as he does in the full title of his treatise *Of Reformation: Touching Church-Discipline in England* (873–901). When considered further, however, Milton's understanding of discipline has implications beyond the more limited question of the "Presbyteriall, or Prelaticall" form of government (904). Indeed, my argument to my annual undergraduate Milton class is that Milton here probes a fundamental question of how Christians are to behave in the world. Near the beginning of the semester, I take a full class period to explore Milton's understanding of discipline as articulated in both *Reason* and *Of Reformation*. The understanding of discipline that emerges through our collective discussion provides an important foundation for subsequent encounters with other texts. I find that if students can fully grasp what Milton sees as so vital about discipline, they are better prepared to discuss works like *Areopagitica*, *Comus*, and the sonnets.

This pedagogical focus on discipline works well primarily because of the kinds of students I teach. Almost all are southern; many come from underprivileged urban areas with marginal high school training; a large percentage are older, returning students with family commitments; and virtually all of them work at least part time. Single parenting, all-night work shifts, major chronic illnesses, and one-hour commutes to school are fairly common. I had a seventy-year-old student who wheeled her oxygen tank to class every day and who could not handwrite any work because of tremors induced by her massive medications. Halfway through the semester, she told me that her goal was simply to get a college degree before she died. Because of these demographics, my students can be remarkably disciplined. While I do not want to idealize a student body that has its share of slackers, I am regularly struck by the tenacity that most students bring to Milton's work. Even when confronted with political treatises like *Reason* and *Of Reformation* that are difficult and unfamiliar, they doggedly plow their way through Milton's prose, sentence by sentence. Although Milton's concepts of self-restraint and hard work can speak to all students at all colleges and universities, I find they have a personal resonance for students with little experience of educational privilege.

In one sense, the theme of discipline differs only slightly from the obedience that Stanley Fish argues is crucial to understanding "how Milton works": obedience is not possible without discipline, and, for Milton, discipline must be obediently directed toward a religious, ethical end (Fish, *How*). I have found, however, that my students have more to say about discipline than about obedience. They tell me of getting up at 3:00 a.m. to work on papers before their kids awake and of reading *Paradise Lost* in the dialysis clinic. The usually difficult and protracted business of getting a degree on top of work and family commitments gives them a deep personal experience to draw on when grappling with Milton's notion of discipline. Obedience is less personally urgent for them. Many of our students enroll as freshman after several years of work experience and so owe obedience to no one, and even the religious students who profess obedience to God do not typically think of God as a master in the same sense that Milton did. Because they know well enough the rigors and rewards of a disciplined approach to schoolwork, my students tend to be more keenly sensitive to the ways in which Milton's notion of discipline differs from their own. For example, most of them have not previously considered discipline itself in relation to some overarching philosophical principle. It is simply what they do to get through the day, the week, the semester. For Milton, in contrast, discipline is central to religion and a visible manifestation of theology. By beginning with a topic that makes Milton seem familiar and accessible, I have more luck in then showing students the ways in which his assumptions differ fundamentally from their own.

Before we can work on Milton's concept of discipline, I have to tackle first the issue of his prose style. Because most of my students have not had a demanding high school curriculum, Milton's prose can be rough going. I find that if I don't talk about the difficulty factor up front, students are more apt to lapse into anger and frustration at what they consider Milton's unnecessarily convoluted style. I try to preempt this response by explaining that their notions of enjoyable prose style are very different from those of the English Renaissance. In other words, Milton is not just trying to be obscure and difficult. I also spend time reading Milton's prose aloud, and students who have trouble with Milton's style on the page often comprehend better when they hear it read. This phenomenon itself can become a topic of discussion, for it allows me to bring up the classical tradition of oral delivery that informs Milton's prose and the early modern conviction that writing should serve a public, civic function. Sometimes when students seem especially determined to dislike Milton's prose, I have resorted to translating a key passage into "modern English," reading it aloud, and asking students which version they prefer. Once we get past joking requests that I summarize all of Milton for their benefit, the class typically admits that Milton's version works much better, and we discuss why and identify what gets lost in the translation.

Early in the semester, I assign the preface and chapter 1 of *Reason*. Before class, students have to investigate *discipline* in the *Oxford English Dictionary* and come to class with a list of the early modern meanings of the word and its etymological roots. This assignment has three purposes. First, this deliberately short bit of reading allows me to ease them into Milton's prose, and it gets them warmed up for the coming *Areopagitica*. Second, it introduces them to the online version of the *OED*. Later in the semester, they will write an "*OED* paper" in which they use seventeenth-century word meanings to make an argument about a single passage. For many of my students, the idea that word meanings change over time, sometimes dramatically, is a new idea, and they find investigating lexical shifts in the OED an exciting and gratifying business. Finally, this reading assignment gives me a logical way to introduce Milton's concept of discipline, one that we will return to often during the semester. Having read *Reason* and consulted the OED, students come to class understanding that *discipline*, in the seventeenth century, had several now-obsolete meanings relating to church governance.

The disappearance of these meanings from modern usage serves as the starting point for class discussion. Most of my students have grown up attending church and Sunday school, and while there are a few Episcopalians and Catholics, many of them were raised in evangelical or fundamentalist congregations. Accordingly, when I raise the question of ecclesiastical hierarchy, their responses range from indifferent shrugs to uncomprehending stares. As one student tentatively put it, "Isn't that something church elders are supposed to worry about?" As we talk about Milton's emphasis on church discipline, I direct them back to the biographical excerpt from *The Second Defense of the English People* (1096–118), a section assigned the first week to let students hear Milton talking about his life's work. I draw their attention to Milton's assertions there that rejecting bishops constitutes "the true path to liberty" and "the liberation of all human life from slavery" (1117). At best, these statements can strike students as hyperbolic, and, at worst, they can confirm negative stereotypes of Milton as an obsessive, overserious Puritan. My job as a teacher is to help them understand the degree to which questions of church discipline informed early modern English political and cultural discourse. I find that this issue provides an important conceptual bridge between our secular world and an early modern one in which religion more deeply saturated contemporary culture.

This background helps students make sense of statements in *Reason of Church Government* such as "there is not that thing in the world of more grave and urgent importance throughout the whole life of man, then is discipline" and "Nor is there any sociable perfection in this life civill or sacred that can be above discipline." I spend time trying to help students understand both what Milton means by "discipline" (and here students refer again to their OED notes) and why he sees "the axle of discipline" as the hinge for "all the moments and turnings of humane occasions" (905). We discuss the etymological roots of *discipline*. It comes from *disciple*, or student, as opposed to *doctor*, or teacher. Doctors formulate doctrine, which they give to their disciples as disciplines. Discipline, then, is merely the practical application of doctrine in any given situation. This discussion opens up the title of *The Doctrine and Discipline of Divorce*—which we read in excerpt later in the semester—in new ways. Students are more prepared to consider how Milton presents divorce both as a set of abstract theological precepts (a doctrine grounded in biblical texts) and as a pragmatic code of behavior (a discipline to be applied).

The link between doctrine and discipline lets students see how, for Milton, discipline is inherently ethical. As he says in *Reason*, discipline is "not only the removall of disorder" but "the very visible shape and image of vertue" (905). This issue crystallizes when I ask the class, "Can one be disciplined at doing a bad thing?" In a post-9/11 world, students may mention terrorists who show remarkable discipline in the service of a violent, hate-filled cause. What we hammer out in class, however, is that given Milton's definition of discipline as the practical application of right doctrine, discipline inherently involves virtuous action. Milton would argue that terrorists are not really being disciplined, since "true," "inner" discipline would mean renouncing evil in favor of good. Students usually figure out the problem with Milton's underlying premise or warrant, one in which opponents are always already wrong. Some students get understandably exasperated with Milton's basic assumptions: one student protested the injustice of a view that condemns all Catholics as irrational and undisciplined because they are not Protestants. But most students seem gratified to talk about the problems in Milton's thinking. It renders him less intimidating and makes them more confident as readers and critics.

This discussion of discipline provides an important foundation for later encounters with Milton's villains. For example, students easily identify Comus's lack of discipline, and they can see how his unregulated laxity makes him relatively easy for the Lady to defeat. Satan and the fallen angels in *Paradise Lost* and Dalila in *Samson Agonistes*, however, are more formidable opponents in part because they appear more disciplined, more willing to sacrifice self in service of seeming principles. When we read Milton's description of the fallen angels in perfect military order in book 1, I ask whether, for Milton, they are displaying discipline. Responses can range from "No, they are merely showing an external, debased version of true, inner discipline" to "Yes, they are practicing a form of obedience that, even in hell, is a kind of right doctrine." We can also talk effectively about how the discipline displayed early on in hell steadily erodes over the course of the epic. Toward the end of the semester, students have equally animated discussions about the motives for Dalila's actions. Playing devil's advocate, I ask, "Why shouldn't we admire the discipline she displays in service of her nation?" Students sometimes refer to the etymological discussion from earlier in the semester and remark that as a wife, Dalila is the disciple, and her husband, according to early modern views of marriage, is the doctor. In thus betraying her husband, she is acting in an inherently undisciplined way. Feminist students will sometimes remark that Milton's logical warrant is unfair: if the wife is assumed to be the disciple, she can never have a good reason for disagreeing with her husband. This realization, and the discussions that ensue, can help the class come to terms with a more hierarchical culture than our own. We also talk about Samson's discipline. Students seem to enjoy discussing his initial moral slackness, and they mull over the hard question of what doctrine his final act of destruction serves.

The discussion of how Milton understands discipline and its relation to doctrine informs other texts. For example, I ask if they regard their professors as doctors in the Miltonic sense, as those who hand down precepts for right living. Not surprisingly, the answer is no. This discussion helps them understand the difference between their view of education for employment's sake and Milton's view of education for righteousness's sake. At this point, we turn to "Of Education," in which Milton defines the goal of education as "regaining to know God aright" (980). Many of my students would agree that the point of life is knowing God but see church as the primary educational forum: one goes to church or Bible study to learn about God and attends the University of Alabama, Birmingham, to learn about argumentative writing, molecular biology, and the history of Western Europe. I often direct their attention to the apparent lack of religious instruction in Milton's ideal academy. The question arises, "Given that most of the students' time is spent in studying languages and classical texts and in physical activity, what aspects of this curriculum teach students to 'know God aright'?" This question can generate fruitful discussion about Milton's understanding of true religion as inseparable from true reason so that disciplined training in all rational pursuits advances doctrine and righteousness.

Students also read the sonnets as studies of how to live rigorously disciplined lives in the face of adversity and evil. The concluding line of sonnet 7 ("How soon hath Time the suttle theef of youth") refers to God as the "great task Master" (85), a view of God that religious students often resist as too adversarial and that can remind the nonreligious students why they don't go to church. If I ask, however, "Why does God require tasks?" then students can begin to talk about God's demands as emerging out of his pastoral care, allowing humans to practice doctrine in dynamic and redemptive ways. If challenged to find other examples of discipline in the sonnets, students easily identify both sonnet 9 ("Lady that in the prime"), where the Lady labors "up the Hill of heav'nly Truth" and zealously fills her lamp "with deeds of light" (87), and sonnet 19 ("When I consider"), where the speaker makes the disciplined decision to "stand and waite" (256). Alert students may even point to sonnet 12 ("I did but prompt the age") as Milton's proclamation of his own disciplined behavior. Given that Milton thinks of divorce as a doctrine, it follows that by advocating it in the face of hostile opposition, he acts as a true and faithful disciple. The recurrence of discipline in Milton's sonnets makes an interesting contrast with Petrarchan conventions. When prompted, students figure out quickly that the sonnet tradition as a whole does not place a high premium on disciplined (i.e., doctrinally coherent and consistent) behavior. Indeed, in most sonnets, the male speaker is only disciplined in writing sonnet after sonnet and in conforming to a fourteen-line, iambic pentameter format. By this point, students understand that this is not how Milton would define true discipline, and we can talk about how Milton's sonnets stand in relation to a larger lyric tradition.

Finally, my teaching of *Comus* and *Paradise Regained* crystallizes around the question of disciplined human action. If I were to subtitle my teaching of *Comus*, I would call it "The Doctrine and Discipline of Chastity." The Lady herself refers to the "serious doctrine of Virginity" (158). When presented with this line, students sometimes remark that they had not thought of virginity as a doctrine but as a physical condition. Our previous reading of *Reason of Church Government* helps them work through how Milton's view of chastity differs from Comus's understanding of mere "Abstinence" (155). Abstinence, as Comus presents it, is discipline without any theological underpinnings, restraint for restraint's sake. The Lady's chastity, however, is a disciplined expression of theology and doctrine. Students puzzle, too, over to what degree the two brothers show disciplined behavior and whether or not Milton depicts them serving a clearly defined doctrine in the way that the Lady does. This discussion can sometimes range into how Milton positions himself as the doctor or teacher who provides instruction in proper doctrine, a view that positions the masque's aristocratic audience as the disciples in need of practical moral discipline. With a semester-long grounding in Milton's emphasis on self-restraint and the need for obedient adherence to doctrinal truth, students are well-equipped to read *Paradise Regained*, a text that alternates every other year with *Samson Agonistes* on my syllabus. Jesus is clearly the human embodiment of disciplined behavior, and students are attuned to the ways his discipline emerges straight out of his doctrinal commitments. They quickly pick up on his use of scripture to refute Satan's arguments, and they can see how his rigorous yet imaginative understanding of the Bible is enacted in his disciplined responses to temptation.

My use of discipline as an overarching theme is, in one sense, a purely semantic choice. Discipline, for Milton, is so linked to other religious issues that I could readily replace discipline with other rubrics like sin, obedience, restraining desire, knowing God, the right use of human reason, and so on. Each of these strands provides access to an interconnected network of ideas about the nature of God and how human beings are to live in the world, questions that inform all Milton's writings at a fundamental level. This semantic choice, however, is a strategic one that works for this particular student population. While my students know that they possess no more obedience or moral reason than students elsewhere, they tend to believe, with some justification, that they have a more highly developed practice of academic discipline. Because they feel a sense of mastery in this area of human endeavor, they respond to Milton's depictions of discipline with vigor and volubility.

Milton and the Constitution, Ancient and American

Peter C. Herman

Many students find Milton's prose a tough sell, partly because of the often thorny style, partly because of the seemingly recondite subject matter (the distinctions between episcopal and prelatical forms of church government not being a topic of immediate relevance to most of today's students). America's constitution, however, is a different story. The vast majority of my students claim to be patriotic, and almost all assert a passionate familiarity with the general principles underlying the Declaration of Independence, the Constitution, and the Bill of Rights. Their familiarity with America's founding texts offers a way of understanding—and creating further enthusiasm for—John Milton. While I generally teach Milton's prose tracts as a prolegomenon to *Paradise Lost*, I begin this section of the class by very precisely emphasizing the ideological continuity between Milton and the American polity, between the American and English Revolutions, and between the American Constitution and the ancient constitution. In other words, I stress how the roots of America's political structure run through Milton and that therefore Milton's political writing is of considerably more than merely antiquarian interest.

I start by placing before the class the familiar preamble to the Constitution:

> We the People of the United States, in Order to form a more perfect Union, establish Justice, insure domestic Tranquility, provide for the common defense, promote the general Welfare, and secure the Blessings of Liberty to ourselves and our Posterity, do ordain and establish this Constitution for the United States of America.

We then parse this statement for the assumptions underlying it. Who, I ask, is doing the constituting here? After receiving the obvious response ("the People"), I then ask, Who or what is missing from this statement—"the People" as opposed to what other entity? To make the point, I reach for the opening sentence of the sixteenth-century *Homily on Obedience*—"Almighty God hath created and appointed all things in heaven, earth, and waters, in a most excellent and perfect order"—and ask the class to compare the two. After realizing that the American Constitution has a human, rather than a divine, origin, I then ask the class what the purpose of this "more perfect Union" is. To what end do "the People" establish this constitution? (I reserve the important question of who exactly makes up "the People" for a discussion of *The Ready and Easy Way*). Again, comparing the preamble with another statement from the *Homily* brings out the point:

Take away Kings, Princes, Rulers, Magistrates, Judges, and such estates of GODS order, no man shall ride or goe by the highway unrobbed, no man shall sleep in his owne house or bedde unkilled, no man shall keepe his wife, children, and possessions in quietnesse, all things shall bee common, and there must needes follow all mischiefe, and utter destruction both of soules, bodies, goodes, and common wealthes.

Whereas the *Homily* regards the hierarchy of God's order as the bulwark against social chaos and the theft of private property (including, alas, wives and children), students almost immediately note that the preamble is much more idealistic and abstract. I then ask what key term in the Constitution's preamble is missing in the *Homily*, and almost instantly, students will give the answer: "Liberty."

At this point, we turn to Milton. The best text to illustrate Milton's adherence to constitutional principles, I have found, is the *Tenure of Kings and Magistrates*, and I begin by asking the class to compare Milton with the American Constitution. The first similarity, they quickly note, concerns the common belief that liberty is at the center of humankind's political nature (although Milton uses considerably harsher, more elitist language than the framers do): "No man," Milton thunders at the start of his tract, "who knows ought, can be so stupid to deny that all men naturally were borne free, being the image and resemblance of God himself " (1060). After noting that the United States' founders and Milton agree on liberty as an inalienable right, I then ask the class to discuss their theories of government's origin and where power ultimately likes.

The Declaration of Independence states:

> Governments are instituted among Men, deriving their just powers from the consent of the governed, —That whenever any Form of Government becomes destructive of these ends, it is the Right of the People to alter or to abolish it, and to institute new Government, laying its foundation on such principles and organizing its powers in such form, as to them shall seem most likely to effect their Safety and Happiness.

The same assumption underlies the preamble: "We the people . . . do ordain and establish this Constitution," as well as the Bill of Rights:

> The Conventions of a number of the States having, at the time of their adopting the Constitution, expressed a desire, in order to prevent misconstruction or abuse of its powers, that further declaratory and restrictive clauses should be added. . . .

The key here, as students quickly realize, is that government is not created or maintained from the top down. Government, very much unlike the theory presented in the *Homily*, begins with the people, and it can be ended by the people if they so desire.

While students are familiar with these concepts as they pertain to contemporary America, they are often surprised to discover that Milton adheres to exactly these positions throughout the *Tenure*. According to Milton, governments are instituted by people, not by God. Faced with the political chaos resulting from the Fall, "foreseeing that such courses must needs tend to the destruction of them all, they agreed by common league to bind each other from mutual injury, and joyntly to defend themselves against any that gave disturbance or opposition to such agreement." And to maintain order, "they saw it needfull to ordaine som authoritie, that might restrain by force and punishment what was violated against peace and common right." But because human beings are fallen creatures and therefore liable to corruption and tyranny, the first rulers soon started to abuse their power. Therefore, Milton writes, the people came up with various means of restraining their rulers:

> Then did they who now by tryal had found the danger and inconveniences of committing arbitrary power to any, invent Laws either fram'd, or consented to by all, that should confine and limit the autority of whom they chose to govern them.   (1060)

Furthermore, the nation's founders and Milton believed in the people's right to change the government if they so desired. Since power and authority emanate from the people, the people have the inalienable right to withdraw it:

> [S]ince the King or Magistrate holds his autoritie of the people, both originaly and naturally for their good in the first place, and not his own, then may the people as oft as they shall judge it for the best, either choose him or reject him, retaine him or depose him though no Tyrant, merely by the Liberty and right of free born Men, to be govern'd as seems to them best.   (1061)

In sum, Milton, like the founders, believed that England was a nation of laws, not men: "While as the Magistrate was set above the people, so the Law was set above the Magistrate" (1060). The law not only governed what the monarch could and could not do but also specifically allowed for the monarch to be judged. Just as article 2, section 4 of the Constitution states, "The President, Vice President and all civil Officers of the United States, shall be removed from Office on Impeachment for, and Conviction of, Treason, Bribery, or other high Crimes and Misdemeanors," Milton also finds that "the Peers and Barons of England had a legal right to judge the King" (1065). In fact, English liberties and the right to enforce them against encroaching monarchs have been in place so long that they might as well be a property of the natural world:

Whence doubtless our Ancestors who were not ignorant with what rights either Nature or ancient Constitution had endowd them, when Oaths both at Coronation, and renewd in Parlament would not serve, thought it no way illegal to depose and put to death thir tyrannous Kings. Insomuch that the Parlament drew up a charge against *Richard the second,* and the Commons requested to have judgement decree'd against him, that the realme might not be endangerd. And *Peter Martyr* a Divine of formost rank, on the third of *Judges* approves thir doings. Sir *Thomas Smith* also a Protestant and a Statesman, in his Common-welth of *England,* putting the question whether it be lawfull to rise against a Tyrant, answers that the vulgar judge of it according to the event, and the lerned according to the purpose of them that do it.   (1065)

Even further, the framers of the Constitution and Milton believed that it was not only a right but also a moral obligation to take up arms against tyranny. As the Declaration puts it:

But when a long train of abuses and usurpations, pursuing invariably the same Object evinces a design to reduce [the people] under absolute Despotism, it is their right, it is their duty, to throw off such Government, and to provide new Guards for their future security.

For Milton, overthrowing Charles I will constitute a shining "precedent to others," who "will look up with honour, and aspire toward these exemplary, and matchless deeds of thir Ancestors, as to the highest top of thir civil glory and emulation" (1070).

By now, students understand that there are significant commonalities between America's constitutional documents and Milton's positions in *The Tenure of Kings and Magistrates,* and at this point—not before, because I do not want to distract them from discovering on their own the parallels between the two— I alert students to the work of George F. Sensabaugh and Bernard Bailyn, both of whom provide copious evidence of Milton's influence in the pamphlet literature of the American Revolution. Sometimes the debt is overt. For example, in *The Snare Broken* (1766), Jonathan Mayhew writes that he was "initiated, in youth, in the doctrines of civil liberty, as they were taught by such men . . . as [Algernon] Sidney and Milton" (qtd. in Bailyn, "Transforming Radicalism" 34).

But at other times, the debt is subtler. Milton, for example, is never mentioned by name in Mayhew's *A Discourse Concerning Unlimited Submission and Non-resistance to the Higher Powers* (1750), yet if students read it (I always put it on reserve, and I include among the various essay questions a request for a comparison-contrast between the two documents), they realize that the assumptions underlying Mayhew's sermon and *Tenure* are almost identical. For example, Mayhew justifies the people's rising "unanimously even against the sovereign himself in order to redress their grievances, to vindicate their natural and legal rights, to break the yoke of tyranny, and free themselves and posterity from inglorious servitude and ruin" through historical examples: the Roman king, Tarquin; King Charles I; and King James, who "was made to fly that country which he aimed at enslaving" (222). Milton uses the same method, giving examples from biblical and recent history (e.g., Mary, Queen of Scots; Richard II) to prove that "the people of Britain have depos'd and put to death" tyrants (1065). The documents define "tyrant" similarly. A tyrant, according to Milton, is "he who regarding neither Law nor the common good, reigns onely for himself and his faction" (1063), and Mayhew writes that the good ruler rules "for the good of society, which is the only end of their institution" (231). Finally, both Milton and Mayhew agree that the monarch's power "is *limited by law*," as Mayhew puts it (242), and that the unforgivable crime Charles committed, the act that made it completely lawful to depose him, was his assumption that he was not bound by the law: "King Charles sat himself up above all these as much as he did the written laws of the realm, and made mere humor and caprice, which are no rule at all, the only rule and measure of his administration" (242). Charles ignored the fact, as Milton puts it, that "[w]hile as the Magistrate was set above the people, so the Law was set above the Magistrate" (1060).

At this point in the class discussion, I broaden the context by showing how both Milton and Mayhew owe their positions to the English common law traditions known generally as the ancient constitution.[1] This term (which achieved currency during the 1640s) refers to four overlapping principles enshrined in English common law and political practice: monarchy's human, rather than divine, origin; the necessity of the monarch's ruling in concert with Parliament (also known as "mixed monarchy"); the monarch's inability to alter the nation's laws without Parliament's explicit consent; and the monarch's being subject to the law. That is, a monarch who defies these principles can be deposed.

While one can find expressions of the ancient constitution in England from the tenth century onward, the underlying principles received their fullest articulation in John Fortescue's highly influential late-fifteenth-century treatise, *In Praise of the Laws of England* (*De Laudibus Legum Anglie* [Fortescue 1–80]; a dialogue between the Prince of Wales and the Lord Chancellor), and his translation of the relevant chapters into English, "Of the Difference between an Absolute and Limited Monarchy" (Fortescue 81–125), passages from which I circulate in a class handout. Fortescue's point in both texts is that in England, the king is subject to the law, not vice versa. The statutes of England, Fortescue writes, "are made not only by the prince's will, but also by the assent of the whole realm, so they cannot be injurious to the people nor fail to secure their advantage" (27). Even further, just as the American president swears an oath to uphold the constitution, so is the English monarch "bound by oath at his coronation to the observance of his law" (48).

The fundamental concern, however, that connects Fortescue with the founders and with the pamphleteers of the American Revolution is his concern for the sanctity of private property and for the principle of no taxation without representation:

> For the king of England is not able to change the laws of his kingdom at pleasure, for he rules his people with a government not only royal but also political. If he were to rule over them with a power only royal, he could be able to change the laws of the realm, and also impose on them tallages [taxes] and other burdens without consulting them; this is the sort of dominion which the civil laws indicate when they state that "what pleased the prince has the force of law." But it is far otherwise with the king ruling his people politically, because he himself is not able to change the laws without the assent of his subjects nor to burden an unwilling people with strange impositions, so that, ruled by laws that they themselves desire, they freely enjoy their goods, and are despoiled neither by their own king nor any other. (17)

In the English version, Fortescue boils this passage down to its essential point:

> There are two kinds of kingdoms, one of which is a lordship called in Latin *dominium regale*, and the other is called *dominium politicum et regale*. And they differ in that the first king may rule his people by such laws as he makes himself and therefore he may set upon them taxes and other impositions, such as he will himself, without their assent. The second king may not rule his people by other laws than such as they assent to and therefore he may set upon them no impositions without their own assent. (83)

Fortescue does not say what should happen if the monarchs regress and start ruling by will and not by law, but other authors were not shy about recommending deposition. As John Selden puts it in his *Table Talk*, "Though there bee no written law for it [deposition], yet there is Custome which is the best Law of the Kingdome; for in England they have allwayes done it" (Pollock 137).

By bringing America's constitution and the ancient constitution to bear on Milton's political prose, students can see that Milton stands in the middle of a long tradition that bequeaths to America its own constitutional principles. They see that rights assumed to characterize the American polity have their origin— and at the time of the American Revolution were understood as having their origin—in the English Revolution, which Milton defended, and that those rights in turn have their origin in England's constitutional history. Far from a monument to dead ideas, Milton stands as a conduit for the traditions of liberty and rule of law informing the theory and practice of the American experiment. Ultimately, for students reading Milton in American classrooms, the study of Milton is the study of ourselves.

NOTE

[1] Milton was also influenced by the mid-sixteenth-century "monarchomach" pamphlets by François Hotman, Theodore Beza, and Philippe du Plessis–Mornay, conveniently collected in *Constitutionalism and Resistance in the Sixteenth Century* (Franklin). However, for Milton, continental republican theory was important because it provided further support for the ancient constitution.

Introducing John Milton:
Why, When, and How to Teach
"On the Morning of Christ's Nativity"

John Rumrich

My assumption is that approaches to teaching "On the Morning of Christ's Nativity" are best reckoned from the perspective of both teacher and student (*Riverside* 38–47).[1] Teachers seek to augment their students' competency and knowledge in specific fields. Many of us expect that successful communication in the classroom will also change students' minds in ways that are more far-reaching and unpredictable. This subtle and indefinite effect inevitably includes the teacher as well as the student, for it is the nature of communication to increase the mutuality of conscious understanding (Sperber and Wilson 39). Teachers initiate the process, and their success depends on an informed sense of audience—that is, on reasonably accurate assumptions about the students: about what they know already, explicitly or implicitly; about what is of concern to them.

Given this general theory of how teaching works, I make the case that beginning students of Milton should not only be taught the Nativity Ode; they should be taught it first. As Richard Rambuss demonstrates in this volume, the ode bears thematically on other of Milton's works. Excellent biographical, bibliographical, and aesthetic reasons also justify its use as a college student's introduction to Milton. Biographically, it is the composition of a twenty-one-year-old home for the holidays, which introduces students to Milton not as a preachy old man but as a college student like themselves, if a remarkably gifted, ambitious, and disciplined one. Bibliographically, the Nativity Ode appears as the first piece in both the 1645 and 1673 editions of his poems, and editors have since recognized the justice of its prime location. Aesthetically, Milton chooses to represent the birth of Christ not by dwelling on the emotionally compelling details of the familiar stable scene but by setting forth in a distinctively unsentimental, historical-philosophical manner a panoramic vision of Christ's impact on the world. The chosen generic vehicle is the ode, the most exalted lyric form. The application of a high classical genre to a moment that does not seem amenable to heroic treatment—a baby's birth in a barn, to poor folks— anticipates the aesthetic-ethical revisionism of Milton's late masterpieces and does so more fully than any other of his early poems.

While Milton's yoking of humble Christian matter and noble classical form indicates the direction his poetic career will follow, specific formal features of the Nativity Ode suggest his artistic origins. Taking the time to elaborate these origins serves both to situate Milton among early modern British poets and to stress the oft-neglected significance of prosody in literary analysis. The meter and rhyme scheme of the ode's four prefatory stanzas, for example, are nearly rhyme royal, the stanza form of Chaucer's *Troilus*, several of the *Canterbury Tales*, and Spenser's *Four Hymns* (*Yale Edition* 681–752). The induction's lone variation from Chaucer's ur-stanza lies in the last line's extra foot. This modified version of the exclusively pentameter rhyme royal also bears comparison with the nine-line stanza of Spenser's *Faerie Queene*, with its signature concluding alexandrine: *Faerie Queene*—ababbcbcc; Nativity Ode induction—ababbcc. It is as if Milton strips down the stanza of Spenser's masterpiece, filtering out the allegorical elaboration that typically occurs in verses 6 and 7 but retaining the sonorous concluding hexameter with which Spenser bridged the gap between stanzas. Although for the body of the poem Milton invents a new and intricate stanza, even there he retains the hexameter concluding line. The octosyllabic penultimate line of that more complex stanza, furthermore, accentuates by its comparative brevity the unhurried confidence and deliberate calm of the Spenserian conclusion.

Thus with each closing hexameter Milton makes a graceful metrical bow to his original. His use of Spenser's metrical trademark in a representation of the Nativity, however, where faerie and reality may be said to intersect, simultaneously suggests that as Christ is to the pagan oracles, so Milton's aspiring prophetic poetry is to Spenser's never-ending romance (Gross). Milton's rage for historical verity perhaps precludes indulgence of Spenser's narrative inconclusiveness and allegorical slipperiness.

Both "On the Death of a Fair Infant" (c. 1626–28) and the unfinished "The Passion" (1630) are written entirely in the stanzaic form that the induction to the Nativity Ode reprises, and for thematic as well as formal reasons, both can be profitably assigned in conjunction with it. They are similar to each other in the artifice of their poetic diction and imaginative use of mythic conceits, which to some have seemed strained, extravagant, or even inappropriate to their sad occasions. Like the Nativity Ode, "Death of a Fair Infant" takes a broad, cross-cultural perspective, but it does so to assess the death, not the birth, of a child, who per Edward Phillips's claim is usually identified as Milton's niece (62). In this poem of consolation for the baby's mother, winter brings death figured as sexual violence, instead of providing, as in the Nativity Ode, a cover for corruption and the promise of salvation. "Death of a Fair Infant" opens with the reverse-Ovidian metamorphosis of a flower into a corpse, not the Christian metamorphosis of the deity into a baby. Yet as "The Passion" makes clear, the Christian metamorphosis occurs so that the child can ultimately die and ransom humanity. Similarly, "Death of a Fair Infant" in the end exalts the violated baby to a Christlike station as intercessor against the plague.

Most American college students cannot help being familiar with Christmas celebrations and with the Christmas-card principals of the Nativity scene and story: virgin, baby, singing angels, lowing oxen, sheep, shepherds, manger, snow, star, magi. Other Nativity poems of the seventeenth century meditate on the paradox of eternal God incarnate as a baby; Milton merely glances at that paradox in the second stanza of his introduction. Other poets of the period linger over the tender love between Mary and the newborn Savior; Milton nods at this theme in his final stanza. Instead of the customary matters that preoccupy other lyrics on this topic, Milton spends most of his stanzas elaborating the significance of the Nativity in Christian history and indicates his interest in Christianity's relation with various cultures, religions, and artistic traditions at the time of Christ's birth. In the Nativity Ode, Milton's Christian art tends to be relatively unsentimental and impersonal, as it could not be, Milton seems later to have realized, in a poem on the Crucifixion. The truth Milton presents is philosophical-historical, or, if the term can be used neutrally, ideological rather than emotional. He does not organize his ode according to the sensuous diligence of the meditative tradition (Martz, *Poetry* 164–67). Mel Gibson, the director of the 2004 film *The Passion of the Christ*, and the author of "On the Morning of Christ's Nativity" are religious artists of distinct houses. What concerns Milton in the Nativity Ode (as in his most memorable masterpieces) is a strategic vision of the conflict between heaven and hell and between the Son and Satan as their champions, not what a sweet baby or thoroughly tortured victim the incarnate redeemer makes.

Milton's artistic turning away from the emotionally provocative details of the God-man's humble birth permits the class to move discussion from aesthetic strategy to biographical character. An account of the author at twenty is, in comparison with analysis of the prosody and generic form of the ode, a ready and easy way with engage student attention. Most undergraduates beginning a course in which Milton figures prominently have read few or none of his works and are largely uninformed about seventeenth-century English history. The more candid of them will concede this unfamiliarity yet also acknowledge a vague impression of Milton as an old, blind man, who was hostile to women and wrote long, demanding, religious poetry. "Stuffy" is, in my informal survey, the most common adjective used of Milton among undergraduates who admit not knowing much about him. Introducing Milton through the Nativity Ode presents an opportunity to confirm and challenge this opinion, in a manner that motivates students and points the way to deeper inquiry.

As to the challenge, it helps to show students studying the ode a portrait of the artist at about the time he wrote it. The well-known painting in the collection of the National Portrait Gallery (NPG 4222) was done shortly after Milton had left his teens behind, circa 1629, the year of the ode's composition. Of all the likenesses of Milton taken from his lifetime, it comes closest to his actual appearance as an adult, at least according to the testimony of his youngest daughter, Deborah, when in 1721 she was shown various portraits of her father. At twenty or twenty-one, he appears to have been a brightly handsome, well-dressed boy whose eyes, along with the turn of his mouth, suggest both sensitivity and ironic intelligence. I say boy instead of man because the primary impression that students take from the portrait is that Milton, at their age, looked considerably younger than they do. As he later concedes in sonnet 7, at age twenty-three he continues to look younger than his years. The image of the tedious old man thus gives way to a goodwill-hunting college student, a sublimely precocious twenty-one-year-old who wakes up Christmas morning to write a hymn for the baby Jesus. This passionate, aspiring youth with talent, discipline, and accomplishment beyond his years is for uninitiated twenty-somethings a more captivating figure than the gouty old blind man bellowing at his daughters. I am not recommending students be given the impression that the already intellectually accomplished Milton was just like one of them, a college kid home for Christmas break. Indeed, the adjective "stuffy" may represent a defensive reaction to a life of unabashed commitment that can seem like a reproach to anyone less accomplished, zealous, and gifted than Milton—that is, to nearly everyone who has lived in North America since the time of Thomas Jefferson.

"At a Vacation Exercise" can also be cited to combat the image of Milton the smug prig. During summer festivities at Christ's College, Cambridge, little more than a year before writing the hymn, the young poet defected from his role as master of ceremonies to tell the crowd of fellow students what he'd rather be doing, if he were to choose. In the midst of the revelry, he broke from a light-hearted Latin prolusion and used his native tongue to announce he would prefer to use English "in some graver subject," writing poetry of a different tone than their celebration occasioned. His chosen theme would instead elevate the reader's "deep transported mind" to the door of heaven itself and bring the past to life, permitting mythic history to unfold as the enraptured audiences sat "[i]n willing chains and sweet captivity" (262). The slight, prim, intense-looking young man of the portrait stood before a throng of his peers and unequivocally predicted his own poetic greatness with a startling command of English pentameters that perhaps made some in the audience believe him. No, young Milton was not a typical twenty-year-old. Though he looks like them in the portrait, he was unlike anyone today's college students are likely to have met.

If students need more reason to find Milton extraordinary, they may look to elegy 6, which, like "On the Death of a Fair Infant," "The Passion," "At a Vacation Exercise," and sonnet 7, is a short work that can profitably be assigned with the ode. Composed almost immediately after the ode and addressed to the beloved friend of Milton's youth, Charles Diodati, the elegy offers telling context for the hymn:

> At tu si quid agam, scitabere (si modò saltem
>   Esse putas tanti noscere siquid agam)
> Paciferum canimus cælesti semine regem,
>   Faustaque sacratis sæcula pacta libris,
> Vagitumque Dei, & stabulantem paupere tecto
>   Qui suprema suo cum patre regna colit.
> Stelliparumque polum, modulantesque æthere turmas,
>   Et subitò elisos ad sua fana Deos.
> Dona quidem dedimus Christi natalibus illa,
>   Illa sub auroram lux mihi prima tulit.   (198)

> If you would know what I am doing (if indeed you think it worthwhile to know what I am doing), we are singing the peace-bringing king of heavenly seed, and the happy ages promised in the sacred books, and the baby cries of God, and the stabling under a poor roof of him who inhabits the highest kingdom with his father, and the star-spawning sky, and the hosts making music in the air, and the gods suddenly shattered in their own shrines. These gifts indeed we have given for Christ's birthday; these the first light brought me at dawn.   (Braden)

Diodati, the confidant to whom Milton often expressed his poetic ambitions, had written Milton during that same December to excuse himself for celebrating Christmas in the more familiar way—by drinking wine and neglecting his studies. In a classically pure Latin elegy, Milton replies that he spent Christmas writing a poem on the Nativity. But the elegy's tone is far from austere—Milton loved and respected his dear Diodati too much to scorn the man's lifestyle. On the contrary, Milton insists that wine suits some poets perfectly well. Milton, however, felt called instead to the poetic priesthood, a vocation that required an exalted asceticism. He sought "somthing like Prophetic strain" ("Il Penseroso" [77]), and that led him to devote most of the Nativity Ode not to the human appeal of Christ's birth but to the oracular ramifications of the event.

In teaching the Nativity Ode, I believe it is vital to evoke an image of the poet that students can get excited about—a man about their age with uncanny drive and prodigious gifts, ready to embark on a poetic career of epic proportions. The poem that Milton describes for Diodati aims to deposit readers at the precise historical instant for them to experience firsthand the earth-shattering effects of Christ's Incarnation, at the strategic point J. Martin Evans has called the "moment of revolution" (*Miltonic Moment* 9). While it is tempting to overstate the extent to which Milton uses Christ's birth to announce the author's own nativity as a mature poet, one can at least, with James Holly Hanford, assume that "the coincidence of his birthday and the Christmas season explains the mood in which he took up the subject of the Nativity" (*John Milton* 123).

NOTE

[1] In writing this essay, I had the benefit of conversation with Mary Maddox, an undergraduate English major at the University of Texas. My characterizations of student attitudes toward Milton often depend on Maddox's insights.

Milton and the Incarnation:
Embodiment, Gender, and Eroticism in
"On the Morning of Christ's Nativity"

Richard Rambuss

> And corporeal to incorporeal turn.
>
> —*Paradise Lost* 5.413

My Milton course begins with "On the Morning of Christ's Nativity," the poem that commences the 1645 *Poems*, Milton's first volume of verse. That work, as Richard Halpern has taught us, stages twin advents: Christ's advent, of course, but also the Christianized pastoral advent of Milton's career as Christ's poet (6). I find that the Nativity Ode—a poem whose subject is the Incarnation of the Son of God and the radically transformative effects of this signal event, not only on the natural world and its supernatural superstructure but also on the religio-literary landscape—is a productive way to raise many of the questions about figuration in Milton that I want to hold in view as course-long concerns. One set of questions (and the subject of this brief essay) has to do with Milton and materialism: more specifically here, the relation his writings present between spirituality and embodiment. That relation, I want my students to come to understand over the semester, hardly remains static or stable.

At one pole, we could schematically set *A Mask*, which renders a starkly dualistic world where the Lady can vanquish the tempter who has designs on her body by simply declaring, "Thou canst not touch the freedom of my *minde*" (153; line 663; my emphasis). Adherence to virtue here transumes the "unpolluted" "outward shape," turning it "by degrees to the souls essence" (144; lines 460–62): a deincarnative process whereby (unsullied) flesh is made spirit. Milton's masque also envisions the reverse of this operation. A devotion to carnality engineers the degeneration of spiritual essence into base materiality: "The soul grows clotted by contagion, / Imbodies, and imbrutes, till she quite loose / The divine property of her first being" (144; lines 467–69). To another pole—a materialist or vitalist one[1]—we could assign the corporeal figurations of *Areopagitica*, where texts are animated as "armed men" and books viscerally valued as "the life-blood of a master-spirit" (999). Perhaps at the same pole we should plot Milton's unabashed insistence in book 4 of *Paradise Lost* that Adam and Eve had sex before the Fall; indeed, the poem gives the impression that love-making was a practice as customary for them as daily devotions. Alongside Milton's famous hymn to "wedded Love" (4.750) we might also set Raphael's sensuous evocation, at Adam's prompting, of angelic homosexual intercourse in book 8.[2] Milton's astonishing angels—who eat, drink, and interpenetratively make love with relish—are eminently materialist in their spiritual substance:

"Whatever pure thou in the body enjoy'st / (And pure thou wert created) we enjoy," Raphael instructs Adam, "In eminence" (8.622–24).

The Nativity Ode seems to verge between these poles. The prologue's first stanza announces that the poem was written to commemorate "the happy morn" on which Christ was born into the material world in human form, an event that sets in motion the workings of "Our great redemption" (lines 1, 4) Yet the poem's terms for rendering the Incarnation, as I look to draw out by guiding my students through a close reading of the prologue's second stanza (more on that in a moment), signal what John Guillory has described in another context as Milton's anti-incarnative poetics (83).

With a maximum enrollment of twenty-five students, my Milton class is small enough to be conducted as directed discussion rather than lecture. But I know from experience not to presume how much knowledge of the Bible or Christian doctrine my students will bring to that discussion. Since I think that a grasp of the significance—literary, as well as theological—of the Incarnation is essential for understanding seventeenth-century religious poetry, I devote some time to spelling out its meaning.[3] Indeed, I present the Incarnation—which conceives Christ to be at once fully divine and fully human, like us in all respects, save for sin—as the doctrinal core of Christianity. I then inform the class that one of our endeavors will be to construe from his poetry what the Incarnation means to Milton.

The Nativity Ode is our central text, but I also typically direct my students to a glancing consideration (there is seldom time for more) of the two other works in the 1645 *Poems*—"Upon the Circumcision" and "The Passion"—that render incidences in the life of Jesus of what I call "deep Incarnationalism" (Rambuss, "Sacred Subjects" 516). What kind of corporeality do these poems accord—allow—the Son of God? That is, what kind of body does Milton's Christ possess? How does that body perform, and what kinds of meaning (figural, typological, theological, devotional, aesthetic) does Milton's poetry ascribe to its performances? In "Upon the Circumcision," the infant Savior "bleeds to give us ease" (55; line 11). That palpably startling image rivets attention on the exposed and vulnerable sacred body. But what, I ponder with my students, are we to make of the fact that Milton's only Passion poem (an immensely popular seventeenth-century devotional topic) abruptly stops dead in its tracks before it has to come to terms with the greater exhibition of Jesus's body on the cross, with what even John Donne envisions in "Good Friday, 1613. Riding Westward" as "That spectacle of too much weight for me" (line 16)? The postscript of "The Passion" declares that its author found his subject "to be above the yeers he had, when he wrote it, and nothing satisfi'd with what was begun, left it unfinisht" (52). We don't know for sure how old Milton was when he wrote "The Passion," but he was thirty-seven—hardly a youth—when he published it as a fragment.[4] This self-purported piece of devotional juvenilia retains its unfinished form in Milton's revised and expanded 1673 *Poems*. What does it mean, I ask the class further to consider, that Milton never returned to this great Christian subject to complete a poem about it? What does it mean that this peculiar, aborted work, which makes no mention of the Crucifixion, stands as the Miltonic version of "the Passion of the Christ"? If *Paradise Regained* is part of the course, I can return to these questions at the semester's end. How is it that *Paradise Regained* is also not about Jesus's Crucifixion and Resurrection: that is, not about the gruesome sacrifice made of his body on the cross and its eventual triumph over death and the grave? How is it that Milton's Christ can effect mankind's redemption by seemingly doing no more than retreating to the desert and there resisting all Satan's temptations—in other words, by merely being a hermit and an ascetic? Is it enough to say simply that Milton's "Protestant imagination was not stirred by the Passion" (Lewalski, *Life* 38)?

I eventually return the discussion to the Nativity Ode with another question, one that I think is central to the endeavor of understanding this poem, Milton's Christ, and the representational status of embodiment in his work more generally: how does Milton render the moment, the act in which the Son of God appears in human form, in our form? I am especially interested in what my students make of line 14, which metaphorizes the body that Jesus assumes as "a darksom House of mortal Clay." Every word of this figuration, I have found, is worth lingering over in the classroom. The class is usually quick to grasp the sharp contrast that the poem posits here between "That glorious Form, that Light unsufferable" (line 8), which the Son lays aside in heaven, and the "darksom," dingy, obscurant quality of the material form that he assumes on being born into our world. I remember one student's surprise at discovering that Milton does not figure the preincarnate Son as being utterly disembodied, that the poem envisions him as having (or as if having) a "Form," one that "sit[s]" in "the midst of Trinal Unity": an observation that led this student to wonder further how the poem means us to understand the difference between a form and a body. This is an especially interesting question, I then added, given the continued passivity of the incarnate Son in the Nativity Ode. Used to sitting in heaven, he does no more on earth with his new human body than smile and sleep. Even to put it that way may be to impute more activity to him than Milton here accords. For it isn't so much that Christ smiles and sleeps in the poem as that he is there found to be "smiling," there found to be already "sleeping," which is his state as the poem ends (lines 151, 242). I use textual details like these to suggest that Milton's Christ—who he is, what he does, how he means to "work us a perpetual peace" (line 7)—may be a less familiar figure than he seems at first glance.

Discussion in another memorable class brought us to the conclusion that in line 14's rendering of the Incarnation there is no body in the actual moment of Christ's embodiment, only metaphor, only "a darksom House of mortal Clay." My Milton classes do not always find this deconstructive register. But the crucial point of this endeavor of close reading is that the Son's human body is hardly more than a residence, an abode, and one ill-suited for him at that. Here the body—and the human nature for which it serves as the prime metonym in Incarnation theology—is never quite married to Christ's divine nature. In the

Nativity Ode, Milton's Incarnation poem, the Word is not made flesh but is instead made to be its tenant. Perhaps this seems like too big a theological claim for so small a bit of poetry. What English teacher hasn't encountered the undergraduate protestation, "You're reading too much into it"? Sometimes I heed this response as a signal that I need to make the case for the analysis in question more persuasively. More often than not, however, I sense that the charge of overreading has less to do with skepticism about the interpretation than with the student protester's inclination to delimit meaning, as though to insist that texts cannot be so dense with significance. Or with a desire that texts mean less, not more. Or with the simple wish that there were not so much interpretive work (Spenser calls it "an endlesse worke" [*Faerie Queene* 4.12.1]) to be done. But lest it seem that I am indeed making too much out of a single line, I can return the class to "The Passion," where Christ is likewise said to make his seat in a "Poor fleshly Tabernacle," a material misplacement that prompts Milton to mix his metaphors and exclaim: "O what a Mask was there, what a disguise!" (lines 17, 19). Similarly, *Paradise Regained* renders Christ "remote from Heaven, enshrin'd / In fleshly Tabernacle, and human form" (4.598–99). In his Christ poems, Milton consistently expresses the Incarnation with figures of tenancy rather than conjoinment and union.

No doubt it is clear by now that I regard the poems in Milton's corpus that are specifically devoted to Christ as slanting away from a wholly orthodox Christology, as well as from the deep Incarnational renderings one sees in other seventeenth-century English poets, however conformist they are or are not. I have found that I can most dramatically make both points in the classroom by providing Richard Crashaw's roughly contemporary "A Hymn of the Nativity" (1646) as a foil to Milton. When I ask my students to speak to the differences between these two renderings of the same event, they are usually quick to remark the stylistic dissimilarities between the Puritan Milton and the High Church Anglican Crashaw. (On occasion, some of the better students have also discerned unexpected resemblances, not so much between the two Nativity poems but between Crashaw's Nativity poem and Milton's Passion and Circumcision poems. And there begins new matter.) Fairly quickly everyone also recognizes that what serves as the affective focal point of Crashaw's Nativity tableau—and of nearly every Nativity tableau, when one comes to think about it—is all but missing in Milton. That would be the scene of the Christ child ensconced at the maternal bosom, those "Two sister-Seas of virgins Milke" (line 61) as Crashaw so lavishly blazons them in his hymn:

> The Babe no sooner 'gan to seeke,
>   Where to lay his lovely head,
> But streight his eyes advis'd his Cheeke,
>   'Twixt Mothers Brests to goe to bed.
> Sweet choise (said I) no way but so.
> Not to lye cold, yet sleepe in snow.   (lines 47–52)

I supplement Crashaw's poem with slides of Renaissance paintings of the Nativity to remind the class that Crashaw's depiction, notwithstanding (perhaps even because of) its overt sensuousness, comes closer to the Christian icono-graphic norm than does Milton's.[5] Leo Steinberg's still astonishing *The Sexual-ity of Christ* is an excellent source for such images, particularly those in which the display of Jesus's uncovered (and sexed) body is the painting's principal point, its central event.[6] How are we to read nakedness in these works? I've found that some students, when asked to think about these images in such terms, suddenly come to regard what at first seemed merely conventional as now rather disturbing. I believe that this is a pedagogically productive re-sponse, one to which I try to give further scope with another set of questions: Are these works sacrilegious? Or worse, pornographic? Or might they be (as Steinberg proposes) acts of devotion: graphic aesthetic affirmations of the truth of the Son of God's full Incarnation?[7] In pursuing this line of analysis, I try to maintain paradoxically both a recognition of the utter conventionality of such images and an appreciation of their power to disturb, especially certain modern religious sensibilities. And what, I further ask my students, might someone like Milton have to do with the formation of those sensibilities?

These paintings, coupled with the Crashaw poem, also set in relief how little Mary figures into Milton's poem. She's altogether absent from its first Nativity scene in stanza 1 of the hymn proper, which presents only the child "All meanly wrapt" in "the rude manger" (line 31). Apart from the prologue's third line, Mary's only other mention in the poem comes (and this almost in passing) in its final stanza: "But see the Virgin blest, / Hath laid her Babe to rest" (lines 237–38). Here it seems that Mary's chief role in the Nativity is to see that the "dredded" Infant gets his sleep (line 222). Can the differences (I ask my stu-dents) between Milton's Nativity and what is depicted in Crashaw and in the paintings entirely be accounted for as an expression of Milton's Puritan anti-Mariolatry? And even if they can be, what does it mean for the status of Jesus's body that Milton's poem about his Incarnation nearly writes his human mother out of the picture? For Christianity maintains that Christ's body is materially derived from the matter of his mother's body: "he became incarnate from the Virgin Mary," as the Nicene Creed recites. I tie this line of inquiry to another task of close reading, this one focused on lines 29 through 31, which proffer Christ as "the *Heav'n*-born-childe" (my emphasis). Considered from the van-tage of Incarnational theology, this startling phrase precisely inverts orthodoxy. Christ is supposed to be not heaven-born but rather earth-born, of woman born: that is, to be conceived and birthed through a real human body, Mary's body. In the Nativity Ode, however, Jesus isn't so much born into, born part of, our world as borne down from heaven to earth, where he suddenly shows up, making his abode in a body already formed and apparently in Milton's render-ing already clothed too. *Ecce deus.*

There is something of a female presence in the first stanza of the Hymn: Na-ture, who, in what could be said to be a rather unnatural gesture of natural sympathy for "her great Master," recognizes that "It was no season then for her / To wanton with the Sun her lusty Paramour" (lines 34–36). Crashaw's Nativity Hymn accords to Jesus's birth a bidirectional conjunctive force, as it "Lifts Earth to Heaven, stoops heaven to earth" (line 58). The intimate contact the Incarnation brokers between the divine and the earthly thus has a pervasive redemptive effect on the natural (and literary) world of Crashaw's poem. In Milton, by contrast, Christ's advent shames Nature and dampens her natural eroticism (Halpern 11–12, 17). A similar response is reported in stanza 20, where the virgin God's virgin nativity also drives the nymphs (more female figures of natural sensuality) into a state of tress-tearing despondency. These observations about Mary, Nature, and the nymphs initiate a course-long consideration of representations of the female in Milton. But my aim is not to have my students mark Milton from the beginning merely as a misogynist. Nor is it by any means to make him out to be an erotophobe. I always try to press class discussion as far as I can past such crude judgments, just as I want to move it beyond a simplistic counterposing of Catholic and Protestant poetics. My alignment of the marginalization of Mary (and what she represents corporeally) in the Nativity Ode with the elision of the Crucifixion in "The Passion" and *Paradise Regained* is meant to open onto a larger, more nuanced conversation about Milton and materialism, one that is subtended by a recognition of the tension between Pauline Platonism and a Christian Incarnational theology and poetics. And it is from that vantage that I ultimately want to take up questions about how Milton's various figurations of the incarnate in these and other works bear on attendant matters of embodiment, including gender, sexuality, the senses, and the passions.

The scene of instruction may inevitably be schematic, even perforce reductive. (Certainly the endeavor to render the scene of instruction is such.) My classroom positioning of *Comus* in the dualism camp of Miltonic representation is complicated by the masque's generic resolution in dance, in a rhythmic choreography of bodies and sound. Similarly, my positing of an anti-incarnative poetics to Milton's Christ poems does not fully account for Milton's Christology, just as it is too simple to say that Milton's figurations of the Incarnation are either orthodox or heterodox, especially when we have not broached his *On Christian Doctrine*, much less taken up *Paradise Lost*. In the epic, the Son is yet to be incarnate, and interestingly the theology lesson that the Father delivers about this process in book 3 bespeaks a degree of hypostatic union, an imbrication of human and divine nature in the Son that Milton's Christ poems do not exactly deliver (*PL* 3.281–85, 303–04, 313–16). The question of why the Christology of Milton's epic is different—or appears different—from that of his lyric poetry is beyond the scope of this essay, just as it is beyond the first few meetings of my undergraduate class, which are all that I am attempting to give an account of here. What those initial classes can effectively deliver is a Milton who is none too familiar.

NOTES

[1] On Milton's relation to vitalism, see John Rogers's excellent study *The Matter of Revolution: Science, Poetry, and Politics in the Age of Milton*.

[2] This is an account of Miltonic lovemaking that triggers a blush—the angel's: "To whom the Angel with a smile that glow'd / Celestial rosie red, *Loves proper hue*, / Answered" (8.618–20; my emphasis). In view of present-day political debates about the historical meaning and purpose of marriage—namely, the endeavor to exclude same-sex couples from the institution by contending that the primary purpose of marriage has always been procreation—it may also be worth pointing out to our students that the "Rites / Mysterious of connubial Love" (4.742–43) Milton's Adam and Eve enjoy do not turn reproductive until after the Fall and the pair's expulsion from Eden.

[3] In "Milton on the Incarnation," W. B. Hunter contextualizes the vexed matter of Milton's Christology in terms of various early Church doctrinal controversies.

[4] "The Passion" is customarily dated c. 1630, a year after the date Milton accords to the Nativity Ode in the 1645 *Poems*.

[5] John Rumrich, in his contribution to his volume, also notices that Milton's Nativity Ode is not especially engaged with the customary Incarnational matters of narrative, theology, and sentiment that preoccupy other Christian poets (and not only Crashaw).

[6] Two good examples are Antonio da Correggio's *The Madonna of the Basket* (*Madonna della Cesta*, c. 1524) and Sebastiano del Piombo's *Madonna and Child with Saints Joseph and John the Baptist and a Donor* (c. 1530), both at the National Gallery, London. The paintings are available in color at the museum's Web site (www.nationalgallery.org.uk), where they may be downloaded and projected in the classroom or viewed independently by teachers and students. The images may also be accessed, along with numerous other paintings discussed in Steinberg, through *Biblical Art on the WWW* (www.biblical-art.com).

[7] I discuss Steinberg's argument, as well as Caroline Walker Bynum's strident objections to it, at greater length in *Closet Devotions* (2–3, 42–49).

The "Unowned" Lady:
Teaching *Comus* and Gender

Lynne A. Greenberg

How to help students move past the hierarchical inequities of "Hee for God only, shee for God in him" (*PL* 4.299) and to appreciate Milton's more complex gender politics? I teach *Comus* (*Riverside* 121–71) at the undergraduate and master's levels at Hunter College, an urban, heterogeneous college where English students are by and large versed in feminist theory. The risk is that students, agreeing with Sandra Gilbert and Susan Gubar, will too quickly dismiss Milton as a "patriarchal bogey" (187); alternatively, I want students to grapple with the tenacity and pervasiveness of seventeenth-century patriarchy and Milton's multivalent responses to it. While my approaches to teaching *Comus* differ somewhat for my seventeenth-century survey and upper-level Milton seminars, in each course I am invested in providing sociocultural contexts that can enable students to examine gender relations in seventeenth-century England generally and in Milton's work specifically.

In the field of Milton studies, scholarship on *Comus* offers particularly rich historical analyses. *Comus: Contexts* (Flannagan), a special issue of *Milton Quarterly*, is devoted to exploring the social, political, domestic, and topical contexts of the masque; Leah Marcus ("Earl," "Milieu," and "Justice"), Nancy Weitz Miller, and Barbara Breasted each connect the masque to the life and family of the poem's patron, John Egerton, the earl of Bridgewater, and to the governmental and judicial structure of the masque's locale. I assign several of these essays to my master's students, as they offer a discrete and unique foray into contradictory critical methodologies. These readings also provide invaluable background to my class discussions.

In my seventeenth-century survey course, the masque offers an opportunity to study the normative life cycle of the early modern female: maid, wife, mother, and widow. We contextualize the masque within a variety of contemporaneous discourses that explore women's role and position in seventeenth-century England. To facilitate these discussions, I supplement our reading of the masque with excerpts from seventeenth-century legal, domestic conduct, and educational manuals.

Selections from the legal treatise *The Lawes Resolutions of Womens Rights* (1632) provide students with background on the early modern laws governing women. Students in my Milton course also read the introductory sections to the first book in the *Lawes* (3–6), a politicized biblical interpretation that uses Genesis to justify women's inferior legal status and offers an illuminating comparison with *Paradise Lost*, read later in the semester. The important legal issues emphasized in class discussions include the legal ages of majority, the duties of minors and the rights of their guardians, the legal status of the single versus that of the married woman, coverture, and primogeniture. Applying these legal principles to the masque and particularly to the main performers in the masque, I remind students that the Lady was written for the fifteen-year-old Lady Alice Egerton, the only unmarried daughter of John and Frances Egerton, the earl and countess of Bridgewater. Lady Alice had seven older, married sisters and two younger brothers: John, eleven, and Thomas, nine, both minors at the time they performed in the masque. John, the Elder Brother, is described in the masque as the father's "heir" (line 501), indicating that the system of primogeniture operated in the family. We explore how the Lady's age and unmarried, or in the Elder Brother's words, "unowned" status (407), nevertheless, gave her access to rights and freedoms denied her married sisters and younger brothers, and we discuss the extent to which the masque foregrounds this inherent potential. Students initially remark on Milton's choice of situating the Lady in a liminal space that she traverses independently and note that she appears to have no patriarchal attachments, paternal or fraternal, to guide her. Placing special attention on the Lady's debate with Comus, I ask students to analyze to what extent the Lady's assertions of personal authority and power can be attributed to her legal status.

Having mapped the legal background of relevance to the masque, students read short excerpts from Richard Brathwaite's (1631) domestic conduct manual, *The English Gentlewoman* (50–51, 82–89), and William Whateley's (1623) sermon *A Bride-Bush; or, A Direction for Married Persons* (2–13, 189–216). These texts expose students to the period's gender norms and expectations and offer a ready source for idealized constructions of women's comportment in the period—how they should speak, carry themselves, and behave toward men, particularly their husbands, and what their domestic duties entailed. Focusing on the customary triad of virtues, chastity, silence, obedience, class discussions explore the extent to which the Lady represents the ideal woman. In what ways does the Lady capitulate or alternatively rebel against these expectations? Do the brothers share in these cultural expectations? Does Comus? This discussion also permits students to appreciate the tremendous appeal as well as the gravity of Comus's temptation to wayfarers.

We then turn to the importance, even fetishism, of chastity, both in the poem and the period. Students read excerpts from *The English Gentlewoman* and John Dod and Robert Cleaver's *A Godly Forme of Household Government* (1630) that provide excellent comparisons with and contextualizations for the brothers' preoccupation with the Lady's chastity. In addition, I suggest an economic interpretation of the cultural importance of chastity to patrilineage, primogeniture, and dynastic marriage in the period, a reading that is indebted to Gayle Rubin's description of such marriage practices as a form of "traffic in women" (157). I further explain that chastity underwent substantial redefinition at the time, as the Protestant glorification of married chastity—that is, sexual fidelity in marriage—replaced the Catholic elevation of perpetual virginity. Envisioning no viable alternative to marriage, Protestant writers espoused as the ideal a state of unmarried virginity supplanted ultimately and unavoidably by marital chastity.

This background helps contextualize Comus's rhetoric, his commodification of the Lady, and his reliance on economic and proprietary metaphors to describe her sexuality. The legal and economic analysis also focuses our discussion of the 1645 additions to the text that celebrate the Lady's virginity and not merely her chastity. Helpful discussion questions include: Why does the masque substitute chastity for the Pauline virtue of charity (213–15)? How do we define chastity? Is it a physical or spiritual virtue? Does it represent perpetual sexual abstinence or virginity until and fidelity within marriage? Why does the Lady describe virginity as a "pure cause" (794)? Is it political then? Students offer several interpretations of the meaning of chastity and the Lady's privileging of virginity ranging from the psychological and sexual to the historical, legal, and economic, and they often elect to write their final papers on this topic.

We conclude our discussion of chastity by exploring the masque's several embedded allusions to the rape or abduction of women, including Callisto (341, 422), Daphne (661), Helena (676), Sabrina (826), and Philomel (234). Students have found the background on the Castlehaven scandal particularly suggestive, and we discuss whether the masque offers a "ritual purification of the entire family" (Breasted 211). In addition, students read excerpts from the fifth book of *The Lawes Resolutions* (376–77, 384–92) that provide the legal definitions of rape in the period. These excerpts clarify that while the sexual meaning of rape as forcible intercourse with a woman without her consent existed in the seventeenth century, the concept of rape as a crime of property constituted the more prevalent definition of the crime. Asking students to apply these legal definitions to Comus's threat to the Lady, I emphasize that the relevant statute operative at the time of *Comus*'s performance specifically targeted the abduction and marriage of heiresses without the consent of their fathers.

I also provide students with the Bridgewater family tree, as it situates Lady Alice in a long line of elder sisters whose marriages were expensive and complicated negotiations for the earl of Bridgewater. Demographic information indicating a dramatic increase in the number of unmarried adult women and women who never married (Bennett and Froide 237) supplements this biographical information. The fact that Lady Alice did not marry until age thirty-one, only months after her father's death, interests students greatly, and they begin to question the masque's ending. We look carefully at the epilogue's allusions to the myths of Hesperus, Venus and Adonis, and Cupid and Psyche and discuss what they reveal about the masque's stance toward marriage and motherhood. Does the masque assume that the Lady will eventually marry and bear children? If the vision of Cupid and Psyche offers a prefiguring of the Lady's future, then what kind of marriage is envisioned? Students are troubled by Psyche's lack of consent to her marriage ("Till free consent the gods among / Make her his eternal bride" [1007–08]) and suggest that Psyche bears resemblance to the Lady, entranced and silenced at the time of her rescue.

Students also debate how to interpret the Lady's rescue and return to her father's home. Is it significant that the brothers botch her rescue and that a female spirit accomplishes this deed? Is it significant that Sabrina too was saved by nymphs? Why does the Lady become silent on her rescue? Is it relevant that the brothers also become silent on their failed rescue attempt? If the masque has opened up a space for an unmarried woman's autonomy and power, then does the Lady's return to her father signal her return to patriarchal control?

Many of the foregoing contextualizations are brought to bear in my Milton courses, since we use the masque to test Milton's early radicalism. In addition, we explore the allegorical meanings of the Lady's journey into the wilderness, her temptation, and her heroic triumph. Surprised that Milton would have created a damsel in distress not in need of a male savior, students applaud his depictions of the Lady as a female Christian wayfarer and of Sabrina as a figure of grace and resurrection. The important Miltonic concepts of freedom to choose and mental liberty voiced by the Lady are given special attention, as they will resonate later in the course. I emphasize Milton's reevaluation of classical heroism and his construction of a heroine endowed with virtues that they will see again in *Paradise Lost*: spiritual faith, patience, temperance, reason, self-control, and resistance to temptation.

Students are also encouraged to explore the repressed anxieties and tensions that percolate in Milton's construction of the disciplined self. They are suspicious of the Lady's disavowals and question why she chooses to wander off rather than wait for her brothers to return. Further, why does she seek out the "Riot, and ill-manag'd Merriment" (172)? Would it not have been safer to rush in the opposite direction? They also become animated over the question of whose "gumms of glutenous heat" have immobilized her (917): her own or those of Comus? In my master's courses, students particularly enjoy selections from the debate between John Leonard ("Saying No") and William Kerrigan ("Politically Correct *Comus*") on the issues of sexual desire and consent. We further discuss whether the masque agrees with the Elder or the Second Brother as to the Lady's inviolability. If she remained mentally and physically chaste, then why does she remain immobilized on her rescue, and why does Sabrina need to purify her? Does Sabrina initiate a baptismal cleansing of the Lady or, alternatively, a sexual initiation rite?

Our discussions then turn to the personal importance of chastity to Milton. Reminded of elegy 6 and the autobiographical digression in *The Second Defense of the English People*, both read earlier in the semester, students are quick to point out that Milton stressed the virtue of chastity for the Protestant Everyperson and not only for women. They also draw parallels between the Lady and Milton, the "Lady of Christ's College," and we discuss Milton's celebration of chastity at this stage of his life.

Our analysis of *Comus* serves as an important prelude to later discussions of Milton's complicated and complicating gender politics in the divorce tracts and *Paradise Lost*. Ultimately, students leave the masque with an appreciation of Milton's creation of a female heroine whose resilience and strength do not depend on her relations with men and whose "freedom of . . . minde" liberates her (663), even if only temporarily, from the strictures of patriarchy.

Companionable Poetry:
Milton's "L'Allegro" and "Il Penseroso"

David Mikics

Why teach "L'Allegro" and "Il Penseroso" in a Milton course (*Riverside* 66–71, 71–77)? There are at least two reasons. First, the companion poems present a pair of goddesses—and a pair of moods—that will become crucial aspects of Milton's later poetic career, the poles around which *Comus* and *Paradise Lost*, especially, will circle. The field of brightly achieved, hearty desire in "L'Allegro" allures more directly and frontally than the shadowy seductions of "Il Penseroso"; but the insinuating *penseroso* powers are more intense, ambivalent, and anxious and therefore more crucial for Milton. Both moods show up in Milton's *Comus: A Mask*. Comus's false pitch to the Lady offers an *allegro* praise, seeing nature's wonder in its available pleasures; whereas the Lady's song has a sidelong, haunting *penseroso* effect on her tempter. *Paradise Lost* counters Eden's *allegro* beauty (book 4) with Eve's *penseroso* dream (book 5), in which Satan gives Eve, and us, another (he says truer or more telling) view of the same place we saw in book 4.

The second reason for teaching the companion poems has to do with Milton's role as a center or source of literary history. "L'Allegro" and "Il Penseroso" stand at the beginning of the tradition of a certain kind of poem, the kind that Roger Gilbert has called *ambulatory*: the meditative walk through the landscape associated with Wordsworth, Frost, Stevens, and others. (To be sure, an earlier poem like Spenser's "Prothalamion," not to mention medieval dream visions, might also begin with a poet walking. But Milton makes the walk the way for a poet to join with his surroundings and with his own mood, so that walking and poetic thinking are melded as never before.) In my teaching of the companion poems, I prepare my students for the destiny of these poems in Milton's later writing, but I also try to hint at their epochal significance for English and American poetic tradition in general. (The legacy of "Il Penseroso" goes all the way down to Bob Dylan's recent song "Mississippi." In class I sometimes compare "And missing thee, I walk unseen / On the dry smooth-shaven Green" [lines 65–66] to Dylan's haunting "Walking through the leaves / Falling from the trees / Feeling like a stranger / Nobody sees.") My standing assumption is that a proper emphasis of any Milton course is getting some sense of the way that Milton made so much poetry that came after him look and sound different.

Part of the difference that Milton made, specifically by means of the companion poems, has to do with his music, or atmospheric project: the tones that transform the austerity of "Penseroso" into a complete pleasure, rather than a defensive or embattled one, and the mirth of "Allegro" into a generous embrace, tinged with wholesome color. Never before in poetry, one is tempted to say, have virtues been so enjoyable. It is hard to imagine John Keats's poetry of earth without Milton's *allegro* mood; or William Wordsworth's and Wallace Stevens's transports, their love of finding a contemplative focus, without the Miltonic *penseroso*. (I illustrate this legacy by giving the class a few lines from Keats's "To Autumn" or Wordsworth's "The Solitary Reaper.")

The teaching of "L'Allegro" and "Il Penseroso" can be a defining early moment in a Milton course, because of the crucial way that these poems bring forward matters of definition, decision, and moving on. Here, Milton draws on the ancient rhetorical tradition of *in utramque partem*, arguing both sides of a question, and turns such argument from a mere exercise into a weighty event.

When I teach the companion poems, I begin with a familiar question: should the two be seen as a diptych or as a sequence? If the poems are read in sequence, leading from "L'Allegro" to "Il Penseroso," then Milton becomes a poet oriented toward a momentous goal, the greater gravity of the *penseroso* mood. There is a large element of truth in the sequential picture of the companion poems, in which the "Allegro" persona is made to yield to his more authoritative successor, Mr. Penseroso. What this sequence conveys is that Milton is, finally, an ascetic author, headed for a severe and solemn commitment. With his eyes "sad Leaden downward cast," he finds the firm basis for his authorial self-image ("Il Penseroso" 43).

At the beginning of "Il Penseroso," a somber, solid divinity dismisses the flitting fancies of the *allegro* mood, an expulsion much more resounding and assured than "L'Allegro"'s frightened waving away of his melancholy enemy. A close reading of the opening banishments of the two poems will be instructive for any Milton class. The "Penseroso" poet achieves a greater authority than the "Allegro" poet when he derides his opposite number as insubstantial (rather than merely hideous, as Mirth calls Melancholy in *her* poem). Mirth, unmasked by Melancholy, is revealed in her true instability and therefore unattractiveness: exposed as the "vain deluding joyes" and "hovering dreams" born of folly ("Il Penseroso" 1, 10).

In class, I compare Melancholy's opening victory over the opposition to that of the infant god in the Nativity Ode (the "Saviorator," as one witty student recently named him). The shrinking, affrighted pagan deities in the Nativity Ode feel the terrible radiance of the newly rising Son, who stretches out his hand to scatter and demoralize them (the same gesture used by Moses's God when he casts terror on the Egyptians). The young Son is more real and therefore more true than the lingering, shadowy gods who preceded him. This new god represents a divinity of sacrifice, demanding that his followers choose between the comforts of accustomed imagination and the hard brightness of truth.

The dynamic of the Nativity Ode resembles the expulsion of Mirth at the beginning of "Il Penseroso." Students readily notice the resemblance; the next step is for them to see the differences. "Il Penseroso," after the harsh clarity of this opening, reverts to a realm of shadows, of half-light. "Penseroso" does not stand against "Allegro" like truth against lie, like the Son against the dog Anubis and blood-smeared Moloch in the Nativity Ode. The pagan deities of the ode, like the fallen angels of *Paradise Lost*, are bold and sometimes deeply sympathetic powers, but they bear no true argument. Despite its aggressive opening lines, "Il Penseroso" does not set itself to the definitive conquest of the merely fictive that occurs so often in Milton, from the Nativity Ode to *Paradise Regained*. Instead, "Il Penseroso" knows, just as "L'Allegro" does, the partial, perspectival character of its images. The comedy of "L'Allegro" deals in pleasant fantasy, the source of endless delight (at least until exhaustion sets in with dusk). "Il Penseroso" presents a more grave and intense, but just as fantastic, scenario.

The idea for the class to grasp is that Milton's is, in Leslie Brisman's phrase, a "poetry of choice" in more subtle ways than the stark claim of truth-against-falsehood. (I rely, in my teaching of these two works, on Brisman's study of "L'Allegro" as an "and" poem, a study in *copia*, in contrast to "Il Penseroso" as a poem of "or," of choice. Students are amazed to discover the prevalence of *and* in the first poem and of *or* in the second [Brisman 9–24].) The vision of choice presented in "Il Penseroso" is not a strict one and so differs from Miltonic judgment in *Paradise Lost*, which divides good from evil, God from devil. Instead, the *ors* give a rich, chiaroscuro sense of alternatives: "Or if the Ayr will not permit, / Som still removed place will fit, / Where glowing Embers through the room / Teach light to counterfeit a gloom" (77–80).

"Il Penseroso" nevertheless presents a sacrificial poetics. The sacrifice endorsed by "Il Penseroso" is that required by the life of learning and mystical study. So, pledges the poet and visionary ephebe, "let my due feet never fail / To walk the studious Cloysters pale" (155–56). Milton, as the class knows by now, commands as proof of virtue the relinquishing of easier satisfactions. What is it, I ask them, that prevents this praise of renunciation from being boring and uninstructive, a merely dutiful moralizing? Milton knows he is divided between *allegro* and *penseroso* (and, in the Nativity Ode, between pagan and Christian-ascetic inclinations). Instead of merely, condescendingly, giving the losing side its due in these debates, he imagines what the world would look like if the loser had won. The *allegro* mood expresses, just as much as the *penseroso*, what poetry itself is and wants. "Streit mine eye hath caught new pleasures," Milton's "Allegro" poet boasts, in a state of constant, controlled (but not too controlled) delight (69): subject to the surprise of the next new thing that appears, and equally ready to place that thing, to measure it. The solid promise in "L'Allegro" of the eye that eats up the landscape yields, in "Il Penseroso," to the study of shades, both near and distant. That eager consumer of enjoyments, the speaker of Milton's "L'Allegro," keeps a natural rhythm going of wandering-satiety-dream-rest. The "Penseroso" mystic, by contrast, stays up all night.

Milton indeed becomes a *penseroso* poet of loss, whose great subject will be the fall of man. Yet the later Milton also devotes himself to the forms of happy, surprising plenitude suggested in "L'Allegro." He shows us the embowered bliss and variety of unfallen Eden, whose each twist of activity rises unexpected in its newness; and he records the glory of the creation's outward-bursting impulses in book 7 of *Paradise Lost*. Following Samuel Johnson's famous observation ("no mirth can indeed be found in [Milton's] melancholy; but I am afraid that I always meet some melancholy in his mirth" [*Selections* 81]), I like to ask my class whether Mirth and Melancholy are, at certain points in their poems, truly companionable, mingled by design together, rather than stark alternatives. (Here I mention Milton's presentation of the clash between Day and Night in his first prolusion, a much more warlike version of such a contrast.)

I ask students to try to define the form of inwardness that the goddess Melancholy figures forth, when she is told by the poet,

> Com, but keep thy wonted state,
> With eev'n step, and musing gate,
> And looks commercing with the skies,
> Thy rapt soul sitting in thine eyes:
> There held in holy passion still,
> Forget thyself to Marble, till
> With a sad Leaden downward cast,
> Thou fix them on the earth as fast.
>   ("Il Penseroso" 37–44)

Here I present to the class, as a contrast to Milton's own allegorical method, Cesare Ripa's iconographic diagram of Melancholy, who seems overliteralized, rather like a hat rack rigidly adorned with her various attributes (book, money-bag, bird of night). I then contrast Ripa's stiff emblem to Albrecht Dürer's famous *Melencolia I* (Klibansky, Panofsky, and Saxl, plates 1 and 68). Dürer's figure exhibits a feeling that departs from the categorical, or stereotypical, sort seen in the emblem books (see the discussion in Klibansky, Panofsky, and Saxl). Instead, Dürer's Melencolia demonstrates an inner mystery that adheres as well to Milton's depiction of his muse and his own poetic identity in "Il Penseroso." (So Milton in *Paradise Lost* will re-create Eve and Satan, especially, in response to a tradition that often made them tediously predictable. The poet bestows a new and unaccustomed complexity: no more cartoons.)

Part of the significance of the companion poems for later tradition hangs, I think, on their unusual (for Milton) character, their companionable rambling. Milton is a poet supremely interested in progress, in forward movement, and in the secure establishment of a proper place, one sanctified and defended by a pure will. But in "L'Allegro" and "Il Penseroso," he lets himself roam. The companion poems engage in a gentle wandering that will eventually become the casual (but sometimes severely impatient, even prophetically driven) questing of a poet like A. R. Ammons. But they are also fixated, in proper Miltonic fashion, around certain cynosures, when the well-traveled speaker, all tired out, comes to rest. Angus Fletcher notes that "L'Allegro" and "Il Penseroso," when they reach their respective centers, register a consuming debate concerning the essence of poetry, one that will have a future, most familiarly, in Keats: is the poet a daydreamer (as in "L'Allegro") or a visionary (as in "Il Penseroso")?

A catalog of further questions remains for a class on the companion poems. How does Milton make the tetrameter dancing measures of "L'Allegro," associated with Shakespeare's Puck and Ariel, so much slower and more somber in "Il Penseroso"? Why is tragedy associated with mystical study in "Il Penseroso"? How and why do the two poems bend the Orpheus-Eurydice legend in different directions, and why is the legend important as an instance of poetry's alliance with magic? How does Milton imagine or invent his relation to Chaucer and Shakespeare in the poems? Why do the festive laborers of "L'Allegro" suddenly disappear in favor of dimmer chivalric enchantments? Here, in these two small poems, lies a great landscape to be explored and measured.

"On Shakespeare," Poetic Rivalry, and the Art of the Intertext

Curtis Perry

This essay offers a lesson plan for the first week of an undergraduate Milton class. After providing an overview of Milton's career and the class's objectives, I always begin my Milton course with a discussion of "On Shakespeare" (*Riverside* 61–62), the conventional sixteen-line epitaph poem that Milton contributed to the second folio edition of Shakespeare's plays (1632). "On Shakespeare" is a valuable teaching tool because it is immediately accessible to undergraduates— it can be read aloud in the classroom and understood in a matter of minutes— and surprisingly rich in ways that are characteristically Miltonic. It opens up key interpretive issues that recur throughout the poems and so offers at once a valuable introduction to Milton and a nice inaugural close-reading exercise for students, who will be asked to interpret more-difficult texts later in the semester.[1] A practical advantage of starting with the poem is that it does not take time away from *Paradise Lost* or other major works but instead helps maximize the utility of the otherwise dead first week of the semester when students have not yet had time to read anything. Another is that it helps locate Milton historically in relation to Shakespeare, who may well be the only Renaissance writer many students have studied.

To get the ball rolling, I direct students to the Shakespeare epitaph and read it aloud. I ask them to think of it as a poem about poetry by an aspiring poet, and then I throw the floor open for discussion. There is a special energy in any class on the first day, and in my experience students in an elective Milton class are especially eager to get at big truths. There tends, therefore, to be some initial disappointment as students recognize how conventional Milton's poem really is. This conventionality is made clear by comparing the poem with its models, and for that I use the two short poems written in memory of members of the Stanley family that are self-evidently the basis for some of Milton's conceits. These epitaphs, which Milton and his contemporaries attributed to Shakespeare, are reproduced in the notes to *The Riverside Milton* (61n1). Regardless of the accuracy of this attribution (which is made in several manuscript copies of the poems), what matters is that Milton based his poem memorializing Shakespeare on what he took to be Shakespeare's own poetry (for more, see Campbell, "Shakespeare"). One could bring in other models as well—Ben Jonson's poem on Shakespeare from the first Shakespeare folio (1623) or Shakespeare's own memorializing sonnets—but here less is more: it is better at this point to let students have command over a limited referential field than to overwhelm them with too many texts. Grappling with the idea that a lyric poem might be based on inherited generic models is valuable, though, since modern students sometimes have difficulty reconciling their ideas of originality with the kind of deep engagement with convention and genre characteristic of the poetry of Milton and his contemporaries. I find that speaking about the meaning of formal convention paves the way for dealing with pastoral form in "Lycidas," for example, or for digging into the enormously complex tissue of formal borrowing that helps structure *Paradise Lost* (see Lewalski, Paradise Lost *and the Rhetoric*).

The other thing that tends to come up right away in class discussion is the relation between homage and rivalry in Milton's poem. There is something aggressive about the possessiveness of the poem's initial address to "my *Shakespear*" (line 1): the as yet unknown Milton stakes a claim to the legacy he purports to be celebrating. At the same time, though, this identification seems vexed. Shakespeare's artistic imagination is imagined in terms of a fluidity—"Thy easie numbers flow" (10)—that shames "slow-endeavouring art" (9)[2] and that seems literally to petrify his readers ("Dost make us Marble" [14]). Though it is possible, as Paul Stevens has shown ("Subversion"), to understand the "astonishment" created by Shakespeare in positive terms (line 7; with a pun on *stone*)—as a kind of ecstatic rapture, like the moment when the speaker in "Il Penseroso" forgets himself "to Marble" (73; line 42)—the poem as a whole is structured around the opposition between Shakespeare's fluency and the laboriously constructed monuments that fail to do it justice.[3] It is not hard therefore to see a kind of barely suppressed anxiety in the poem about the relationship between the speaker, who must labor to memorialize Shakespeare, and the subject memorialized, whose own works do it better. Moreover, since Milton would have thought of the Stanley epitaphs as Shakespeare's poems, he is here in the position simultaneously of praising Shakespeare and of imitating him, as if the only way to memorialize a poet whose works memorialize themselves is by simply copying them. A judiciously guided class discussion of the poem can tease out a connection between the poem's sense of belatedness and its larger sense that in attempting to memorialize Shakespeare one is oneself turned to stone and deprived of Shakespeare's easy fluency.

The key to this reading—and the point at which I most actively intervene in class discussion—is the buried allusion to the Ovidian story of Niobe in lines 12 through 14:

> For whilst to th' shame of slow-endeavouring art,
> Thy easie numbers flow, and that each heart
> Hath from the leaves of thy unvalu'd Book
> Those Delphick lines with deep impression took,
> Then thou our fancy of it self bereaving,
> Dost make us Marble with too much conceaving . . .
> (9–14)

In book 6 of Ovid's *Metamorphoses*, Niobe, the overproud mother of seven sons and seven daughters, made the mistake of boasting that she was happier and more successful than the goddess Latona, the mother of the gods Apollo and Diana only. Apollo, so the story goes, takes revenge by killing all Niobe's children, and, as the last of her daughters perishes in her arms, Niobe turns to marble. In the end, all that remains of the flesh and blood Niobe is her extreme grief, and so her tears continue to trickle out of the marble statue.

Though subtle, Milton's allusion to this story is unmistakable. For one thing, describing Shakespeare's lines as Delphic refers to the Delphic oracle—Apollo's prophetic mouthpiece—and establishes a link between Shakespeare and Apollo, the classical god of poetry. For another, the source of Niobe's overweening pride is her having conceived more children than Latona: in this way, Niobe has been made marble as a result of "much conceaving." Niobe is also an archetypal figure of bereavement, so lines 12 through 14 can be read as densely packed with gestures toward this classical legend. I have found that taking the time to address student skepticism about the allusion—Is it there? Is it intended? Are we reading too much into the lines?—anticipates the kinds of arguments likely to crop up later around Milton's more elaborately allusive poetry and prose.

Roy Flannagan's gloss in *The Riverside Milton* explains the allusion as follows: "Like Niobe, the mourner for Shakespeare becomes, by the process of grieving, a monument to his memory"—readers of Shakespeare mourn for him like Niobe mourning for her lost children (62n8). There is another way to approach the allusion: the Niobe legend is a story of rivalry, and the allusion to it can be understood in relation to Milton's rivalry with his subject, a reading all the more compelling because it was so conventional in the Renaissance to describe one's poems as offspring.[4] Perhaps, then, the allusion to Niobe works as follows: "Like Niobe, who boasted that her children surpassed Latona's, I have dared to compare my poem with Shakespeare's divine offspring, and I fear that I too will be turned to stone as a result." Given the contrast between flowing verse and stone monument elsewhere in the poem, the full Ovidian image of a marble statue with flowing tears is also suggestive.

The important thing is to give students a chance to experience the rigorous creativity involved in this kind of interpretive process—to see how intertextual allusions work as interpretive cruxes that can lead beyond the inert facts provided in the footnotes in any modern edition. This lesson for students is related to the thematic content of Milton's epitaph in that the poem's intertextual allusion invites a process of reading involving open-ended application, so that thinking about the meaning of the poem means thinking about it as containing unfixed juxtapositions rather than monumental or static meanings. This disposition toward the creation of poetic meaning is essential to Milton's poetic practice throughout his career. It is part of his profound iconoclasm, his restless distrust of anything too fixed or set in stone. And this is why (Stevens notwithstanding) I think John Guillory is right to compare the poem's imagery of stony fixity with the experience of the Lady in *Comus* and to note that "the condition of arrest or paralysis is everywhere morally suspect in Milton's poetry" (19). Pedagogically speaking, pursuing the implications of the Niobe story in this way opens the poem up and gives access to meanings that students will not have intuited even though they have at one level understood the poem at first glance. This interpretation provides a model that can be returned to throughout the semester: one of the struggles in any Milton class is to make students see that allusions can be rich resources rather than just bewildering extraneous things that have to be taken on board to decode a given poem or passage.

The next step is to compare the notion of direct and unmediated reading associated with the Shakespeare in Milton's text ("each heart" can take "deep impression" from Shakespeare's "Delphick lines") with the complex and scholarly interpretive practice that Milton's poem seems to invite. Milton imagines Shakespeare's lines having about them a greatness that is accessible to the hearts of readers and separated from the relics, monuments, and "pomp" (15) that are the markers of status and achievement. This notion, cognate with the iconoclasm articulated throughout Milton's career, derives ultimately from two closely linked and fundamental Protestant tenants: that scripture is the sole authority in doctrinal matters and that every believer can and must interpret scripture on his own. Milton imagines Shakespeare as a kind of Bible for poets—the highest aspiration imaginable for inspired human speech (see Lanier, esp. 237–39). At the same time, though, if we recognize that dialogue with texts like Ovid's *Metamorphoses* or the Stanley epitaphs forms an important part of the poem's meaning, then "On Shakespeare" turns out not to be the kind of poem with which a heart can just commune. One needs to bring outside knowledge to bear and to think about the poem not as an autonomous source of oracular or inspired meaning but rather as part of a larger intertextual conversation.

The poem, then, contains competing notions of what a poem should be, and exploring this tension offers students an opportunity to examine their own romantic notions about what poetry is and does. I find it useful to link this discussion back to the early modern period by describing the difference between Milton's complex allusiveness and the oracular simplicity that he praises in Shakespeare as a tension built into Protestant poetics: a tension between, on the one hand, the Reformation vision of the individual reading scripture through the lens of personal inspiration and, on the other, humanist scholarly practice, in which emulation and imitation are central to the process of writing and in which reading to understand requires both extensive learning and intertextual interpretive creativity.

This tension is also writ large in Milton's later writings. He is a profoundly learned and allusive writer, but he is often skeptical about the relation between learning and moral truth, as when Jesus dismisses classical philosophy in *Paradise Regained*. The idea here is to give students a comparatively simple tool with which to see Milton's mind in action and also to get them acclimated to the kinds of interpretive work that Milton's poetry demands. "On Shakespeare" allows students to grapple with several of the topics and concerns (such as Milton's ongoing project of vocational self-fashioning, the tensions between iconoclasm and art and between learning and faith) that inevitably become major preoccupations in a Milton class. Best of all, it introduces these issues in a primary text that students—who often feel intimidated by the demands placed on them by Milton's more ambitious works—will feel confident working with. As a result, these issues can be broached not as hopelessly daunting complexities but as interesting and engaging questions, and the formulations that a class arrives at by discussing them in "On Shakespeare" can be used as points of entry into Milton's more ambitious works.

NOTES

[1] Stephen B. Dobranski's essay in this volume shows how the poem can also provide a manageable introduction to the complexities of early modern textual studies.

[2] Such as Milton's? Those who wish to read the poem in terms of Milton's vocational anxieties might compare sonnet 7 ("How soon hath Time" [85]).

[3] Milton's phrase is borrowed from Jonson's epitaph on Shakespeare. Lanier argues that Milton's rivalry with Shakespeare is thus mediated through Jonson (236).

[4] As in the first lines of the dedicatory poem that begins Spenser's *Shepheardes Calender*: "Goe little booke: thy selfe present, / As child whose parent is unkent" (*Yale Edition* 12).

Reading for Detail:
Four Approaches to Sonnet 19

Bruce Boehrer

In 1977, Philip J. Gallagher began an essay on Milton pedagogy by remarking that "the category 'Problems in Teaching Milton to Undergraduates' is really a species of the genus 'Milton and the Modern Reader'" (5). This point usefully focuses the challenge of teaching undergraduates to read Milton's shorter verse, which I take to be the challenge of contextualizing the interpretive process itself. For the triumph of universal literacy in twentieth-century America has generated certain popular prejudices about the nature of reading, prejudices deriving from the attitude, expressed parodically by David Lodge, that "reading [is] a comparatively simple matter, something you learn . . . in primary school" (27). An effective response to these prejudices is to insist not on the simplicity and determinacy of the reading process but rather on its variability over the cultural *longue durée*: to demonstrate that all teachers of Milton have at one time or another been students, that past readers of Milton were once present-day readers, and that current readers, too, will eventually be less so.

Such reflections encourage a pedagogical model at once "literalist and historicist" (Gallagher 6), within whose framework the practice of close reading assumes particular significance. Milton himself was adept at close, often literal, reading. In this sense, historicism in Milton studies entails a certain literalism, and by the same token, Milton embodies the historicist principle that time-specific shifts in how we read are themselves an essential object of literary study. No such shift gives contemporary American students of Milton more trouble, or opportunity, than the historical ascendance of the plain style, which often defines their literary "horizon of expectations" so as to render Milton's work almost impenetrable (Jauss 69). (I sometimes wonder if this is the effect to which T. S. Eliot was referring when he charged that "Milton writes English like a dead language" [261].)

But if Milton can thus strike a modern reader as alien and unapproachable, he also exemplifies the importance of his literary project. As a close reader, he models the behavior he expects of his audience, and he shows how this behavior matters. For instance, when he expounds Deuteronomy 24.1 ("*When a man hath tak'n a wife and married her, and it come to passe that she find no favour in his eyes, because he hath found some uncleannesse in her, let him write her a bill of divorcement*") by declaring in *The Doctrine and Discipline of Divorce* (1644) that

> [t]he cause of divorce mention'd in the Law is translated some uncleannesse, but in the Hebrew it sounds nakedness of ought, or any reall nakednes: which by all the learned interpreters is refer'd to the mind, as

well as to the body. And what greater nakednes or unfitnes of mind then that which hinders ever the solace and peacefull society of the married couple . . . ?

(*Riverside* 937)

he engages in a traditional hermeneutics—comparing translation with original, invoking interpretive precedent, and concentrating on the semantics of a single phrase—with practical consequences for students accustomed to twenty-first-century divorce. One could multiply such examples at will; again and again, an alien idiom discloses a familiar, important model of thought and behavior.

The only way to convey this aspect of Milton to students is to slow him down and play him over, repeatedly, bit by bit. Indeed, one may come to feel that Milton envisioned his "fit audience, . . . though few" specifically as a society of trained exegetes (*PL* 7.31). But the practice that Harry Berger, Jr., has called "decelerated close reading" (45) can prove incompatible, in the classroom, with the diegetic range of Milton's epics and prose. In these works, the imperative to get on with the story interferes with the urge to slow things down, and given the time constraints of classroom teaching, it's small wonder if the forward impulse often triumphs. As a result, the poet's shorter verse, particularly his sonnets, can prove a superior vehicle for developing the interpretive skills his work as a whole demands.

My response to this situation lays little claim to novelty. I introduce my students to close reading through a series of class sessions on that most canonical of Milton's shorter poems, sonnet 19 ("When I consider how my light is spent" [256]). The sessions typically consume about four hours of class time, involve three supplementary handouts, and require students to go through the same poem, again and again, with different considerations in mind each time.

Their first time through sonnet 19, students concentrate on its formal structures of prosody and syntax. They note how its binary division into octave and sestet reinforces binary rhetorical patterns: question and answer, problem and solution, past and present, ephemerality and eternity, and so forth. I then challenge them to parse the octave's sentence structure. This exercise occasions much chagrin, for many students find that they can't successfully identify the grammatical subject and main verb of the poem's opening sentence. But frustration yields to surprise and intrigue as they discover the sentence's kernel clause right where common sense would dictate that it shouldn't be: nestled unobtrusively at the end of a sixty-word sentence. This combination of syntactical extension and inversion, I suggest, explains why Milton can be so annoying to nonprofessional modern (or postmodern) readers.

So one addresses the off-putting qualities of Milton's style in effect by confronting them head-on. The obvious question then follows: why would an author choose to express himself in such a tortured and oblique fashion? Why prefer the convoluted and opaque to the direct and transparent? This question has the effect of presenting the plain style—what many students seem to take for granted as the only sensible stylistic choice—as merely one rhetorical option among many. Classroom speculation then moves along certain predictable paths. Students note that, among other things, Milton's poem is about the process of discovering meaning and justice in events that at first seem to possess neither; about the importance, and difficulty, of relinquishing personal vanity and expectations; about embracing loss so as to convert it into a renewed sense of self. It stands to reason that Milton's stylistic choices should respond to such subject matter by imposing on the reader an initial sense of confusion and frustration. In Milton's sonnet 19, meaning is something to be earned, not given.

But lest this interpretation of the poem seem too pat, one may also note the ways sonnet 19 seemingly mocks one's efforts to achieve interpretive closure. From the shifting, entangling syntax of the sonnet's octave to the volta that occurs half a line earlier than one would anticipate to the paradoxical behavior of a personified patience who rushes to "prevent" a murmur the poem has already uttered, sonnet 19 behaves in ways that confound expectation. From this standpoint, the poem seems a monument to authorial perversity: a literary achievement whose crowning glory is its steadfast refusal to do what we want it to. Its resistance to meaning becomes, in a way, the most glorious thing about it.

Often, students who accede to this argument discover that the qualities of style they found least attractive in Milton's verse become, on riper consideration, the source of its peculiar strength. As they digest this point, I supply a copy of Matthew 25 and encourage them to read sonnet 19 again, this time in terms of its scriptural context. Here again, the instructional move is obvious, even hoary, but it raises questions regarding the poem's allusive environment that need to be considered by anyone learning basic techniques of close reading. What does it mean, for instance, to tell the parable of the talents from the viewpoint of its malefactor? What does it mean, within the logic of the parable, to punish a servant who has acted earnestly and in fear of the Lord? What does it mean to translate a tale whose original literal referent was a sum of money ("that one Talent which is death to hide") into a story about personal endowments and callings? What does it mean to revise the parable's end so that the quality on which it insists most vigorously—the necessity of working for one's salvation—is rendered superfluous? What kind of relation does this revision imply among the theological categories of works, faith, and justification? What kind of relation does it suggest between labor and capital? What does it suggest about the character of Milton's personal family romance? Such questions have the aggregate effect of presenting sonnet 19 not only as a forum for the exercise of close-reading skills but as a product of close reading itself. Moreover, the close reading in question appears to have consequences for how one might think and behave in the political and social spheres.

At this point, I then start the entire reading process again, this time giving it a bibliographical inflection. Here we read sonnet 19 against itself, or, to put things less succinctly, we read two differently edited texts of sonnet 19: the influential student editions produced by Merritt Hughes (*Complete Poems* 168) and by Roy Flannagan (*Riverside*). In this context, the contrast between

Hughes's regularized accidentals and the 1673 pointing of Flannagan's text can elicit vigorous discussion of the relation between authorship and editing, the character of editorial responsibilities, and the nature of reading itself. Following the structuralist principle that " 'meaning' . . . resides in the *total* act of communication" (Hawkes 83), one may consider the semantic potential delineated and foreclosed by such typographical minutiae as quotation marks, commas, semicolons, and alternate spellings. While in my experience students tend to favor Flannagan's text over Hughes's (there's something a tad condescending about an editorial procedure that neutralizes irregularities to produce, among other things, a text that modern readers find easily consumable), one need not privilege either editorial method. On the contrary, Friedrich Nietzsche's notion of philosophy as the "history of an error" (23) reminds one that differing textualities acquire meaning in relation to one another, functioning often in mutually corrective ways. As a result, it becomes necessary for the careful reader not only to understand the nature of a given text's syntax and semantics, prosody and accidentals, tropes and allusions but also to grasp the historical process through which the text acquires a particular form.

This point made, we then return to sonnet 19 one final time, now considering Milton's poem in relation to Shakespeare's sonnet 15 ("When I consider everything that grows" [16–17]). The focus here is on dynamics of literary competition and filiation and on how Milton's sonnet functions both as a continuation of and as a rejoinder to Shakespeare's prior achievement. This final exercise encourages students to reinforce their close-reading skills by studying Shakespeare's poem on its own and then by relating it to Milton's work via diction, theme, and poetic form. In the process, students work through the peculiar admixture of reverence and antagonism that composes the anxiety of influence in its classic, Bloomian form. Further, they begin to appreciate the tonal and thematic qualities that distinguish Milton's voice from Shakespeare's: the recurring, strangely interconnected complaints that the poet is both premature in his literary efforts and somehow belated, washed up, exhausted; the emphasis on a Christian self-abnegation that becomes, paradoxically, the vehicle of a resonant self-assertion; the fascination with standing and waiting—the term *waiting* embodying, as it does, the paranomasial interplay between expectation and obedience. Beyond this, students may glimpse, in the interaction between Milton's and Shakespeare's sonnets, something like the free play of Derridian signification, as Shakespeare's language, disengaged from the author-function, takes on a ghostly life of its own in Milton's verse.

The nineteenth sonnet's extraordinary density of reference not only makes the poem manifestly deserving of this sort of intensive scrutiny, it also requires of students the skills of recognition and response they will need to study and eventually, in some cases, teach literature. In this respect, Milton's work offers an ideal proving ground for techniques of close literary analysis. His poetry demands readers well-versed in such techniques, because it is the product of a poetics that regards the exercise of close-reading skills as second nature: fundamental not only to literary production but to spiritual discipline as well.

To approach Milton from this standpoint is to take his work on its own terms, terms that require a broad readjustment of how most contemporary students understand the nature of the reading process. In pursuing such a readjustment, I make no claims for the originality of my pedagogical procedure; on the contrary, I believe its strength lies in its conventionality. While the teaching techniques I have outlined above owe a great deal to scholars of widely divergent critical backgrounds,[1] I think they would all agree that—to adapt Foucault— "the function of knowledge [in Milton] is not seeing or demonstrating; it is interpreting" (40), and I feel certain they would agree that if Milton's poetry is to be studied at all, it needs to be studied in detail. I offer the foregoing exercise as a modest contribution to that end.

NOTE

[1] Among the scholars and teachers who have influenced my procedure as delineated here, Philip Gallagher is responsible for the generally literalist and historicist bent of my approach, while Maureen Quilligan supplied the initial model for its focus on editorial procedures. The decision to read sonnet 19 alongside Matthew's gospel, while obvious enough, nonetheless owes much in this particular case to the influence of Roland Mushat Frye. The parallel study of Milton and Shakespeare was originally suggested by chapter three of Jonathan Goldberg's *Voice Terminal Echo*.

Johnson, Genre, and "Lycidas"

Matthew Davis

When teaching "Lycidas" (*Riverside* 100–07), I begin with Bond—James Bond—and end with a visit from the doctor—Dr. Johnson. My assumption is that "Lycidas" must be understood as a work written within a particular generic tradition. However, students are unlikely to know the genre of pastoral elegy, and some may not even know the word *genre*. Therefore I begin by briefly discussing a genre most students do know: the James Bond film. I ask students to identify some elements one expects to find in a Bond film. A Bond film is sure to have an opening action sequence, an evil villain pursuing a nefarious plot, and several attractive women for Bond to bed. Bond will use various high-tech gadgets—for example, pens that emit sleeping gas and sports cars that drop oil slicks. He will visit exotic locales, wear a tuxedo, and order a martini, shaken, not stirred. There will be chase scenes and near escapes. In the end Bond will triumph.

I explain that Bond films can be thought of as constituting a genre, because we have certain expectations when we sit down to watch one, and we get pleasure from seeing these expectations met or tweaked.

Next, we discuss a genre that is more obviously relevant to "Lycidas": the funeral speech. I ask students to identify some changes people make in their dress, demeanor, and speech when speaking at a funeral. We discuss how such changes can be seen as artificial, in the sense that they are conscious departures from everyday practice, and yet also as signs of respect and affection. We discuss what kinds of people speak at funerals and what sorts of things they say.

Finally, with this background in place, I explain that, for the next class, students will be reading a pastoral elegy by Milton. I explain that an elegy is a poem for a dead person and a pastoral a poem about shepherds (from Latin, *pastor*). A pastoral elegy combines these two genres, to make a hybrid genre in which a shepherd mourns for a dead shepherd—or else the survivor merely writes as if he and his lost friend were shepherds for the sake of the generic tradition. I tell students that a pastoral elegy is like a funeral speech in that it is a response to death that is a formalized and artificial way of expressing natural emotions. At the same time, a pastoral elegy is like a Bond film in that there are certain elements one expects to find in any example of the genre.[1]

Next, I introduce seven elements found in many pastoral elegies:

> Glory days: the speaker recalls his relationship with the deceased.
> Procession of speakers: a succession of humans, spirits, or gods appear, like funeral speakers, to memorialize the deceased.
> Natural lamentation: all nature is said to lament the deceased—birds, trees, and flowers weep.

Singing shepherds: there may be some connections drawn between shepherds and poets since shepherds sing songs to pass the time.

Pious pastors: if the writer is a Christian, there may also be a connection
drawn between shepherds and religious leaders, both of whom tend a
"flock." Precedents for this connection can be found in the Old Testament (Ps. 23) and the New Testament (John 10.1–6).

Interrogation of supervisors: the speaker may interrogate the gods, the
spirits of the place, or other supernatural forces, asking, "Where were
you when this happened?"

Moral of the story: finally, there may be some attempt to answer philosophical or religious questions: Why did the person die? Was it fate?
bad luck? the cruelty of the gods? providence? Is death a horrible thing
or a reward after hard life?

For the next class, students are directed to read "Lycidas" at least twice: once
on their own and a second time while filling out a worksheet. The worksheet
lists the elements noted above, gives an example of each, and contains blanks
for students to write down line numbers where they detect an element in Milton's poem.

I begin the next class with an unbroken oral reading. This takes about ten
minutes. Although some might prefer to go directly to explication or discussion,
I find that an expressive reading is one of the best forms of explication. The
reading provides an additional exposure to the poem, models the kind of
rereading necessary to understand poetry, and helps students transition from
sociology or accounting to literature. Moreover, having completed the worksheet, students are now prepared to begin to hear the poem differently, as a
work within a generic tradition. But perhaps most important is the oral reading's potential for disambiguation. In those ten minutes it is possible to strike
many blows for comprehension: one can convey the voices of the various speakers in the poem, for example, by adopting a deeper and more sonorous tone for
Apollo's speech (lines 76–84) and for the "dread voice" of Saint Peter, so terri-
fying that it evidently leaves a river scared streamless (113–33). A reading can
also alleviate some uncertainties about pronunciation—is "tear" in "melodious
tear" pronounced "tare" or "teer"? How do you pronounce Hippotades, Panope,
Guerdon, Gessamine? Students who are not sure how to pronounce words are
more likely to keep silent during discussions, for fear of embarrassing themselves. A good reading can ease anxieties of this sort.

After the reading, we use the worksheet as a launching pad for a close reading
of the poem, within the generic framework, with brief historical, biographical,
mythological, and theological excursions as needed. My goal is to help students
appreciate the poem on its own terms, as a work written within a highly structured generic framework. I try to touch on Orpheus as a member of the dead
poets' society (58), the speaker's momentary crisis of vocation ("What boots
it . . . ?" [64–69]), the momentary contemplation of an erotic alternative to hard

study ("sport[ing] with *Amaryllis* in the shade" [67]), the revisionist interpretation of fame by Phoebus (76–84), the dire pronunciations of Saint Peter (108–31), the philosophic consolation ("Lycidas . . . is not dead" [166–85]), and the conclusion, with its unexpected framing movement ("Thus sang the uncouth swain" [186–93]).

Questions of artificiality and sincerity almost always come up: students wonder if "Lycidas" can be an expression of genuine grief given that it so elaborately structured and artistic. During this class I do everything I can to counter these objections and defend Milton, in part because I know the next reading will be Samuel Johnson's notorious attack on the poem, which raises similar objections.

Before the next class, students are asked to read "Lycidas" once more, then read Johnson's critique from the "Life of Milton" and write a brief response to Johnson—again, to prime the engines. Johnson's analysis is only five paragraphs long. It is available in many anthologies, in C. A. Patrides's *Milton's "Lycidas,"* in numerous public-domain editions, including G. B. Hill's edition of the *Lives of the Poets*, and in various online editions.

The next class is devoted to trying to understand Johnson's critique of "Lycidas" and discussing whether students think it is warranted or not. Johnson introduces at least six criticisms of the poem: (1) the diction is harsh, (2) the rhymes are uncertain, (3) the "numbers" (or metrics) are unpleasing, (4) it is not an effusion of real passion, (5) it is not original, (6) it approaches impiety in its mingling of pagan mythology with "sacred truths" (165). Generally some objections similar to 4 have surfaced in the previous class. There are usually a few students who find that Johnson gives voice to some of their own issues with the poem and who are invigorated and attracted by Johnson's attack; there are others who are dismayed to find an "approved" poem under assault or are unpersuaded by Johnson's objections.

Johnson's criticism is interesting for many reasons, but especially for its refusal to accept the poem in the way I have been trying to get students to accept it, as a work within a generic tradition. Johnson is annoyed by Milton's adoption of the generic repertoire of pastoral: "We know that they never drove a field," he grumbles. Indeed, Johnson sees the use of pastoral formulae as evidence that there is no real passion behind the poem: "Passion plucks no berries from the myrtle and ivy. . . . Where there is leisure for fiction, there is little grief" (163–64). I ask students what this might mean and how far we are meant to extend the principle. Should we also say, "Where there is leisure for metaphor, there is no grief"? "Where there is leisure for rhyme, there is no grief"? Is all artifice verboten in an elegy?

My goal is not to set Milton up only to have Johnson tear him down. If things seem to be drifting in that direction I reiterate the idea that there need not be any conflict between following forms and truly grieving. I also try to float the notion that the poem may be at least as much about the survivor as it is about the deceased—that, however deep Milton's feelings for his classmate Edward

King may have been, the poem reveals profound concern for his own future, concern that his own life, like the lives of King and Orpheus, might be cut short by "the blind fury with the abhorred shears" before the poet can realize the potential he is so confident he possesses. This interpretation addresses Johnson's objection that the poem is not a true effusion of emotion by suggesting that perhaps the poem is ultimately about the survivor, his hopes and dreams and anxieties. But what sort of person gives a funeral oration about himself? Or do we all do that?

This unit helps students understand "Lycidas" on its own terms, then introduces a challenging critical perspective on the poem. Students are offered a chance to "think like Milton" or "think like Johnson." They are allowed to make up their own minds, but in an informed, considered way.

The unit also illustrates the conflicts inherent in literary tradition. Literary tradition is not merely Pope saying amen to Dryden and Johnson saying amen to Pope. It is also a running dialogue and debate, in which Johnson blasts "Lycidas," Byron needles Coleridge—"I wish he would explain his Explanation" ("Dedication," line 16)—and Blake uses a Roman persona to tell off Johnson: "A ha To Doctor Johnson / said Scipio Africanus / Lift up my Roman Petticoatt and kiss my Roman Anus" (*Poetry* 448–49). By considering the poetry of a major author and the negative criticism of another major author, students are exposed to the great debate and invited to become participants in the tradition.

NOTE

[1] This list is based on the pastoral elegy tradition as documented in Hanford ("Pastoral Elegy") and the Milton volumes edited by Elledge (*Paradise*), Flannagan (*Riverside*), and Carey (*Complete Shorter Poems*).

Exploring Early Modern Homosociality: Milton's "Lycidas" in the General Education Classroom

Mark K. Fulk

In this essay, I explore some of the methods I have developed to convey the beauty of Milton's "Lycidas" (*Riverside* 100-07) to nonmajors in general education courses in the humanities. The problems that confront the teacher of "Lycidas" in this venue are manifold: First, the language and density of classical allusion seems deliberately and needlessly archaic to most of our students. The poem's complexity thus reinforces their fear of poetry as something they will never understand, let alone cherish and enjoy. Also, the genre of the pastoral elegy appears regimented and its gestures seem unfamiliar to modern readers. Finally, the social values that produced "Lycidas" and that it represents and sustains are viewed by many students as elitist. Add to these textual issues a classroom of primarily urban, working-class students diverse in age, lifestyle, profession, and experience, and the professor may seemingly be left without a laurel to crown his or her wearied brow.

The key to teaching this poem fully lies in conveying to students the concept of genre and the specifics of pastoral poetry. I choose the pastoral for specific interrogation in my introductory poetry classes because of the students' unfamiliarity with the genre—I find that my students develop a greater and richer analytic detachment with it than they can with the more familiar genres and gestures of other forms of poetry.

To develop their analytic abilities, I steep the students in a mix of pre- and post-Romantic pastoral poetry. I use as the basic textbook the *Norton Anthology of Poetry* (Ferguson, Salter, and Stallworthy), and from the readings in this anthology, I pair "Lycidas" with "Aprill" from Edmund Spenser's *Shepheardes Calender*, Percy Shelley's *Adonais*, and Matthew Arnold's "Thyrsis" (410–15, 159–65, 879–91, 1095–100). Occasionally, depending on time, I also provide copies of select works of Vergil (*Eclogues*) and Theocritus, Bion (J. Edwards), more from Spenser's *Shepheardes Calender* and perhaps "Astrophel," Alexander Pope's early pastorals, William Wordsworth's "Michael," and Theodore Roethke's elegies. I use Spenser's "Januarye," which I recommend handing out in class, as my prototype for pastoral poetry.[1] On the day we cover Spenser, I give my students the background of pastoral as a form of address especially associated with elite early modern culture, point out the ways that Spenser is trying to win recognition and patronage from the court and his social superiors, and show them the ornate manner in which some Renaissance pastoral poetry was published. The *Norton Anthology* reprints the woodcuts from the original edition of Spenser's "Januarye," along with the pseudo-classical glosses of

Spenser's "alter ego," E. K. I then have the students analyze "Januarye," urging them to begin to see the poem as a pattern for the genre of pastoral poetry itself. First, I introduce them to the notion of the Golden Age in Latin literature, and we discuss its roots in classical mythology using Ovid's *Metamorphoses*. Then, I point out the use of pastoral masks, noting that E. K. and the characters of Rosalind, Hobbinol, and others are most likely barely disguised acquaintances in Spenser's intimate circle. Finally, I call the students' attention to the signs of the all-male world of European higher education at the time, and especially to the figure of Hobbinol. I note the feelings that Hobbinol expresses for Colin, pointing to the strong homosocial (and even homoerotic) undertones encoded in elitist forms. This discussion makes the poem more relevant to questions of desire at the forefront of many students' lives and introduces the historical construction of what Bruce Boehrer refers to as the "element of same-sex . . . cathexis" at the heart of many Renaissance pastoral poems (231).

When we come to Milton's "Lycidas"—normally in the next class period—the students discover that the poem evokes and complicates the earlier description of pastoral. I have my students list again the template we developed for the genre of pastoral. Putting this list on the chalkboard or an overhead, I then have the students identify how "Lycidas" uses these elements of the pastoral. First, the students note that the Golden Age of the poem is situated firmly in the past—in particular, the undergraduate years of Milton and Lycidas (Milton's classmate Edward King) at Cambridge, when they and their associates were young and full of unrealized potential. This Golden Age ends with the death by drowning of Lycidas. I explore with the students the use of water imagery, pointing out that while it can be perceived in terms of a womb, the power of this womb is rather ambiguous, since it both gives and takes away life. The personifications of the fountain Arethuse (line 85) and of the river Cam (103) and the ocean god Neptune (90) all desire to save Lycidas but cannot: the womb appears barren, full of potential not realized and offering only a chimera of hope. By sorting out and elaborating these images and their mythological resonances, students become engaged in Milton's depiction of the young King, also a figure of unrealized hope, and begin to feel empowered to interpret a poem they initially thought impenetrable.

I encourage my students then to step from interpretation to critique through an examination of the elitist, homosocial world of higher education in seventeenth-century Europe. I discuss with them the book history of the poem, published as it was in a collection of Latin, Greek, and English elegies entitled *Justa Edouardo King Naufrago* (1638), written by men educated at Cambridge and published by T. Buck and R. Daniel, noted on the original 1638 title page as famous Cambridge typesetters. My use of book history is not meant to be an end in itself[2] but a way of bringing class and sexuality more firmly into our reading of the text.

The publication history of the poem proves that Milton's intended audience is male. The earlier discussion of potential womb imagery and the powerlessness of the shepherd and the gods to save Lycidas, when brought back into the context of publication and readership, starts students on the path toward a more thorough analysis of the homosocial-homosexual nexus in the poem. I turn my students at this point to the blissful vision of the shepherd poet as he observes Lycidas in heaven. Milton writes: "With *Nectar* pure his oozy Lock's he laves, / And hears the unexpressive nuptiall Song, / In the blest Kingdoms meek of joy and love" (175–77). Whom Lycidas is expected to marry in the all-male world of this poem (Christ? The other male saints?), the masturbatory imagery of his locks bathed in oozy nectar, and the overall exultation of this passage raise many issues for my students. Boehrer, building on the now lengthy tradition of analysis of the homosocial-homosexual nexus in this poem, presents a useful reading of this troubling passage. Boehrer posits that "Lycidas" undermines the "heteronormativity of Christian marriage" through the standard trope of (male) literary production and fecundity.[3] Boehrer concludes:

> ["Lycidas"] gives voice in various ways to a range of differing sexual subject positions and . . . in the process Milton's efforts to imagine the company of the elect in heaven—and the company of poets on earth—involve a substantial same-sex erotic charge.   (231)

The all-male context of the imagery of the locks of hair makes the reading of a same-sex erotic charge possible. And here again, the potential womb imagery of the water comes full circle for the students: one of the great fears of male writers in this period, who often usurp images of birthing to discuss their creation of literary works, is that their wombs will be barren, unable to realize the hope of (poetic) fruition, just like the gods, the shepherd, and Edward King.

I conclude our classroom analysis of "Lycidas" by pointing out how the poem's homosociality works on multiple levels: as noted above, the writing and publication history of pastoral and of this poem in particular participate in elitism and exclusivity in the all-male world of Cambridge academics in seventeenth-century England. Second, theologically, Milton would be comfortable with the notion of Christ's church being subjugated to the female position as the bride of Christ. This theological belief has a psychological value as well. I concur here with Julia Kristeva, who, in *The Sense and Non-sense of Revolt*, posits bisexuality as the model of psychic integration. By writing the "nuptiall song" as the conclusion of "Lycidas," Milton shows that loss is recovered and death's breach can be healed through integration with Lycidas's potential and with Christ. The fecundity of the creative (male) womb can be achieved only through this integration, which becomes gendered as both male and (potentially) female.

At the end of this general education unit on the pastoral, I often have students produce an in-class, open-book essay comparing one pre-Romantic with one Romantic (or post-Romantic) pastoral poem, isolating for them several possible avenues for comparison. Some of these avenues include desire, the consolation offered (or lack thereof), the implied reader, gender (both male and female imagery), and the use of classical myth. This in-class essay, a mixed-modes piece that calls for definition and for comparison and contrast, allows them to examine and build on their understanding of the genre. Even though they initially viewed "Lycidas" as impenetrable and impractical, many of the students produce successful essays using genre, sexuality, gender, and publication history as analytic tools.[4] Their provocative and indeed timely readings show how the literature of the past—even the pastoral—has commentary for the sexual and textual issues alive in our world today.

NOTES

[1] Because this course is not for majors, I do not distinguish herein the subgenres of pastoral poetry (e.g., elegy, song contest); rather, I give the students a sense of the general outlines of pastoral poetry and its concerns. In a course for majors, I would use "Januarye" not as a prototype for all pastoral but rather as an example of a nonelegiac form of pastoral poetry.

[2] For a critique of the ways that book history has been used to resist and obscure questions of gender, class, and power, see Ezell, ch. 1.

[3] With my nonmajors, I would not use a term such as *heteronormativity* because it would seem obscure, potentially elitist, and ultimately inapplicable for them. However, the concept behind the term is not hard to convey. I explain that we are conditioned to read people (and desires) as heterosexual unless we are directly told otherwise. In texts such as Milton's "Lycidas," Spenser's "Januarye," and with pastoral in general, we will miss other, more provocative readings (like Boehrer's) if we make that assumption without question.

[4] By the end of this unit, I am proud to note that students are no longer fearful of classical allusion but use the tools they have to find the references and interpret their usage.

Teaching *Paradise Regained*

Barbara K. Lewalski

Paradise Regained may well be the most difficult of Milton's poems to teach to undergraduates, especially following *Paradise Lost,* because the brief epic seems to lack the longer poem's drama and human interest. In the week I can give to *Paradise Regained* in a semester course on Milton, I find it most useful to highlight the intellectual drama in the exchanges between Jesus and Satan and the ways in which Satan's temptations enable the hero, Jesus, to discover who he is and what he is to do.

It is useful at the outset to ask students to compare the poem with its only major sources, the few short verses in Matthew 4.1–11, Mark 1.12–13, and Luke 4.1–13. Partly for dramatic effect Milton followed the Luke sequence (stones, kingdoms, tower) rather than the more often cited Matthew sequence. How, from this slender basis, does Milton produce a narrative in four books—2,070 blank-verse lines? And why, students should be invited to consider, did Milton choose the Temptation in the Wilderness as subject rather than the Passion-Crucifixion narrative? Why, moreover, does he portray Jesus as an austere, nay-saying figure who discounts and refuses all worldly pleasures and goods (Fisher 206)? Is or is not Milton's Jesus a pacifist or a quietist who entirely repudiates warfare and political action (Coffey)?

It might be suggested that this choice of subject allows Milton to present Jesus's moral and intellectual trials as a higher epic heroism, as a model for right knowing and choosing, and as a creative and liberating force in history. As he does in *Paradise Lost,* Milton here creates imaginative experiences to help readers gain moral and political knowledge, virtue, and inner freedom—the "paradise within" that is also the necessary precondition for gaining liberty in the public sphere (Lewalski, *Life* 510). Beyond that, *Paradise Regained* rewards attention to its immediate Restoration context: the unmoved Jesus standing firm against every temptation and trial invites association with Puritan dissidents subjected to harassment and persecution after the Restoration (Knoppers, *Historicizing* 123–41; Loewenstein, *Representing* 242–68). And the Jesus-Satan debates challenge readers of any era to think rightly about kingship, prophecy, idolatry, millenarian zeal, the proper uses of civil power, the place of secular learning, and the abuses of pleasure, glory, and power.

I also invite comparisons with *Paradise Lost* in generic terms. The epic proposition in *Paradise Regained* makes the rather startling claim that this poem treats a vastly more noble and heroic subject than *Paradise Lost,* in that this hero conquers his enemy, regains the regions lost to Satan, and establishes his own realm—in this, more like Aeneas than like Adam. The opening lines allude to the verses, then widely accepted as genuine, that introduce the *Aeneid* in most Renaissance editions and supposedly announce Vergil's movement from pastoral

and georgic to an epic subject (Vergil, *Aeneid* 1.240–41 [trans. Fairclough]).
That echo and the reference to *Paradise Lost* as a poem about a happy garden
suggest, with witty audacity, that Milton has now, like Vergil, graduated from
pastoral apprentice-work to the true epic subject, the spiritual warfare and victory of Jesus:

> I who e're while the happy Garden sung,
> By one mans disobedience lost, now sing
> Recover'd Paradise to all mankind,
> By one mans firm obedience fully tri'd
> Through all temptation, and the Tempter foil'd
> In all his wiles, defeated and repuls't,
> And *Eden* rais'd in the wast Wilderness (1.1–7)

Students might consider the several allusions to the Book of Job (Lewalski, *Milton's Brief Epic* 10–36) and refer back to Milton's poetic project imagined a
quarter of a century earlier in *The Reason of Church Government*, when he
proposed Vergil and Tasso as models for a long epic and the Book of Job as a
"brief model" of epic (*Complete Prose Works* 1: 813). They might also compare
the invocation to the Spirit in this poem with the invocations in *Paradise Lost*
and consider reasons for the striking difference in tone.

Students might go on to discuss how Milton has reworked and adapted epic
conventions and topics to this unusual subject. The central epic episode, the single combat of hero and antagonist, is transformed into a three-day verbal battle,
a poem-long intellectual and moral struggle. The poem begins in medias res with
the baptism of Jesus. There are two Satanic councils and a council in heaven; two
epic recitals (Jesus's meditation about his youthful experiences and aspirations
and Mary's reminiscences about the prophecies attending the hero's early life); a
transformed prophetic vision in which the hero, instead of viewing his own destined kingdom (as Aeneas does), sees and rejects all the kingdoms that are not
his; an epic catalog of the kingdoms of the world displayed to Jesus; a martial
pageant of Parthian warriors; and a few striking epic similes in book 4. Stylistic
comparisons with *Paradise Lost* are also rewarding. The brief epic eschews the
soaring, eloquent style of the longer epic to create a style more restrained, dialogic, and tense with the parry and thrust of intellectual exchange, as Satan's in-
flated epic rhetoric is met by Jesus's spare answers (Martz, *Milton* 183).

It is important to underscore how Milton's Antitrinitarianism allows for some
drama in the debate-duel between Jesus and Satan, even though the reader
knows that Jesus will not fall (Rumrich, "Milton's Arianism"). In *Paradise Lost*
Milton portrayed the Son in heaven as mutable and as sharing only such part of
the divine knowledge and power as God devolved upon him at certain times.
Here he portrays the incarnate Christ, in accordance with *On Christian Doctrine's* treatment of Kenosis, as a real emptying out of the divine knowledge and
power the Son exercised in heaven, so that he is "liable to sin" and subject to

death in both natures (*Complete Prose Works* 6: 438–40). Attending closely to the induction to book 1 (lines 1–293) will allow students to recognize the limited knowledge of both Jesus and Satan. God describes Jesus to the angels in almost Socinian terms: they now and men hereafter are to learn from the temptation episode, "From what consummate vertue I have chose / This perfect Man, by merit call'd my Son, / To earn Salvation for the Sons of men" (1.165–67). A puzzled Satan in his first council recognizes that Jesus shows some glimpses of the Father's glory, but he cannot imagine that this humble man is one with the Son in Heaven: "His first-begot we know, and sore have felt, / When his fierce thunder drove us to the deep; / Who this is we must learn" (1.89–91). Jesus's meditation as he enters the desert shows that he has no recollection of his former state. He has learned what he knows of himself as the promised Messiah from his mother's testimony and from reading the prophets: that his birth was miraculous; that he is "King of *Israel* born" and will sit on David's throne; and that he is to work redemption for humankind through "many a hard assay even to the death" (1.254–64). But he does not yet understand the full meaning of the prophetic metaphors or of the divine Sonship proclaimed at his baptism or just what his "God-like office now mature" will entail (1.188). He is conscious of his limited knowledge, being led "to what intent / I learn not yet, perhaps I need not know," but also of the guidance and ongoing illumination of the Spirit: "For what concerns my knowledge God reveals" (1.291–93).

These uncertainties sometimes make for moments of emotional distress, as when the hungry Jesus experiences a hunger dream in the desert and questions, "Where will this end?" (2.245). Or when Satan "inly rackt" voices his psychic desperation to have it over with, even though it means his destruction: "I would be at the worst; worst is my Port, / My harbour and my ultimate repose, / The end I would attain, my final good" (3.203, 209–11). They also make the question of Jesus's identity a primary focus of the poem. The title "Son of God" is bestowed in a special way on Jesus at his baptism, but as Satan later remarks, that title "bears no single sence." Revealing some feelings of sibling rivalry with Jesus, Satan declares, "The Son of God I also am, or was, / And if I was, I am; relation stands; / All men are Sons of God," and then indicates that one purpose of his temptations is to discover "In what degree or meaning thou art call'd / The Son of God" (4.516–20). Students may also consider how and why Satan in this poem differs from the Satan of *Paradise Lost*. Is it that centuries of evil choices have further coarsened his nature, though he is still cunning and at times brilliant? His advantage in the temptations is his direct observation of human motives and human weakness throughout history, which Jesus knows only through wide reading. But more than compensating for that is the divine illumination Jesus merits, leading him to understand the spiritual meaning of the scriptural metaphors and prophecies that the literal-minded Satan cannot fathom. Discussion of the poem's action might point up a central paradox: Satan appears to do all the acting, dancing around Jesus in a fever of motion, trying one approach and one argument after another, while Jesus remains impassive and unmoved; and yet it is in Jesus's consciousness that real change takes place. As he withstands the several temptations, Jesus gains, apparently by divine illumination, an ever-more-complete understanding of who he is and what he is to do, whereas Satan cannot resolve the puzzle about Jesus's Sonship and mission until utter defeat and a fall from the tower force realization on him.

Why, a class might discuss, do the debates between Satan and Jesus refer continually to biblical and classical personages? For one thing, Milton creates epic scope in his brief epic by making the temptation episode encapsulate past and future history through such typological references and allusions. God sets these terms, describing Jesus to the angels as an "abler" Job and a second Adam who will win "by Conquest what the first man lost / By fallacy surpriz'd" (1.151–55). God also declares that Jesus is to lay down in the wilderness the "rudiments" of his great warfare (1.157), epitomizing there the exercise of his office of prophet, priest, and king throughout history (Lewalski, *Milton's Brief Epic* 164–92). Many of the personages referred to are commonly accepted Old Testament and classical figures of Jesus and his mission—Moses, Elijah, Gideon, David, Job, Socrates. To these, Satan proposes countermodels—Balaam, Antipater, Caesar, Alexander, the schools of Greek philosophy—or else he insists that Jesus must conform himself exactly to those earlier figures and thereby limit himself by the mandate of the past. In conflict here, students might be invited to recognize, are two conceptions of history. Satan's temptations presume the classical notion of history as cyclical repetition—what has been must be again—whereas Jesus must learn to fulfill and subsume those earlier types and models so as to redefine history as process and re-creation.

The poem's complex structure might provoke comment, since the first and third temptations are treated only briefly, while the kingdoms temptation takes up books 2, 3, and most of 4. One can call attention to several interrelated paradigms that help explain how Milton elaborates on and adds to the biblical temptations. At one level Jesus is the "second Adam," withstanding the temptations to which Adam and Eve succumbed, temptations that exegetes also linked to the root sins of humankind enumerated in 1 John 2.16: sensuality (in Protestant versions, distrust), avarice or ambition, and vainglory (E. Pope). That paradigm is explored especially in the first temptation (distrust) and in the first three segments of the second, the part pertaining to kingship over the self: the sensual banquet, desire for wealth and power, and desire for glory. Some of the temptations also pertain to the three kinds of lives Plato defines in *The Republic*: the sensual life, the active life, and (in the Athens temptation) the contemplative life. Some temptations are addressed to the three functions of Christ's office: prophet or teacher (the first temptation); king—that is, ruler and defender of his church and people (the offers of Israel, Parthia, Rome, and Athens); and priest—that is, redemptive sacrifice and mediator (the storm and tower temptations).

It will not be possible to analyze each of the temptations in detail, but it helps to look at one or two of them closely, to highlight the intellectual challenges each offers. The learning temptation is perhaps the most complex. Satan presents Athens, the zenith of classical learning, poetry, and oratory, as the fount of the nonmaterial goods Jesus needs to achieve his defined goals of teaching and persuading, though, significantly, Satan does not claim that learning is something he can give. The evocative description of pastoral delights in the "Olive Grove of Academe" is perhaps the poem's most beautiful passage:

> See there the Olive Grove of *Academe*,
> *Plato's* retirement, where the *Attic* Bird
> Trills her thick-warbl'd notes the summer long,
> There flowrie hill *Hymettus* with the sound
> Of Bees industrious murmur oft invites
> To studious musing; there *Ilissus* rouls
> His whispering stream . . .   (4.244–50)

The harshness of Jesus's responses seems to reveal Milton's deep-seated anxieties around the issue of learning, for they apparently repudiate the classical learning that has been so important to Milton throughout his life. Classical philosophy is "false, or little else but dreams, / Conjectures, fancies, built on nothing firm" (4.291–92). The Hebrew poets are far superior to classical poets, who sing "The vices of thir Deities, and thir own" (4.340) and, once their "swelling Epithetes" are removed, are "Thin sown with aught of profit or delight" (4.343–45). And the Greek orators are far inferior to the Hebrew prophets in teaching "The solid rules of Civil Government" (4.358).

But Jesus recognizes that Satan's version of learning is tainted, and Milton challenges his readers to make similar discriminations. Satan is here an arch-Sophist, proposing universal knowledge not as a way to truth but as a means to power, glory, and pleasure: "Be famous . . . / By wisdom; as thy Empire must extend, / So let extend thy mind o're all the world" (4.221–23). Satan praises Plato chiefly for the highly refined sensory delights of his pastoral retirement, Aristotle as the teacher of a world conqueror, Socrates for his great influence on later schools, Homer for the envy Apollo showed for his poem, Demosthenes for his ability to promote war—degrading the learning Athens represents even judged by humanist lights. Satan also seeks to undermine Jesus's unique role as spiritual teacher by insisting on the necessity of classical learning for the contemplative life he seems to favor, the attainment of the inner kingship: "These rules will render thee a King compleat / Within thy self" (4.283–84). He also insists that Christ's prophetic and kingly offices of teaching and ruling by persuasion require him to converse with and confute the Gentiles in their own terms. Jesus, however, denies that the classical writers are sources of true wisdom. Having no knowledge of the Creation, Fall, and redemption by grace, they are "Ignorant of themselves, of God much more" (4.309)—though he acknowledges and he has quoted their moral teachings, informed by the light of nature. Since the mission of Jesus is to bring true wisdom into history, he will not accept their lower knowledge as in any way necessary, though he may possess it:

> Think not but that I know these things, or think
> I know them not; not therefore am I short
> Of knowing what I aught: he who receives
> Light from above, from the fountain of light,
> No other doctrine needs . . .   (4.286–90)

In this repudiation Milton's Jesus reinforces for his church the position Milton defended in *The Likeliest Means to Remove Hirelings*: that learning is not necessary to ministers, who require only knowledge of scripture and the Spirit's illumination (*Complete Prose Works* 7: 315–21). Jesus's answer (and Milton's) does not repudiate learning as such but denies that it is necessary to virtue, salvation, or the accomplishment of God's work in the world.

The quiet ending of this poem also invites comparison with *Paradise Lost*. Like Adam and Eve wandering forth to begin the human history whose end Adam has foreseen, Jesus returns from the angelic celebration of his divine Sonship and final victory over Satan to his human beginnings: "hee unobserv'd / Home to his Mothers house private return'd" to live out the history foreshadowed by and prepared for in the temptation episode (4.638–39).

"By Winning Words to Conquer Willing Hearts": Teaching Miltonic Strategies of Alliteration in *Paradise Regained*

R. Allen Shoaf

Among his many gifts in prosody, Milton possessed an ear finely attuned to alliteration. He uses alliteration in *Paradise Regained* to achieve various effects (*Riverside* 720–82), from sonority to theological implication. Thus, for example, early in the poem, he writes that Jesus claims he "held it more **h**umane, more **h**eavenly, first / By **w**inning **w**ords to conquer **w**illing **h**earts, / And make pers**w**asion do the **w**ork of fear" (1.220–22). Here, the insistence on initial /h/ (four) and on /w/ (five) knits Jesus's utterance into memorable sonority (notice also noninitial *r* [nine]) but also implies that the word of God unifies meaning even as the Son unites initial letters in his language. Indeed, I suggest that Milton's late understanding of the word of God incarnate is inscribed in alliteration as the knitting, weaving, or texturing of meaning and truth. This activity is opposed to Satan's dismemberment of meaning and truth by scission and fragmentation of words, as, for example, in *Paradise Lost* when he seduces Eve:

> What can your knowledge hurt him, or this Tree
> Impart against his will if all be his?
> Or is it envie, and can envie dwell
> In heav'nly brests? these, these and many more
> Causes import your need of this fair Fruit.
> Goddess humane, reach then, and freely taste.
> (9.727–32)

The double-crossing of *impart* and *import*, the demi-echo between *envie* and *Heav'nly* (and the sly doubling of Satan's with Vergil's voice—"tantaene animis caelestibus irae?" ["Can resentment so fierce dwell in heavenly breasts?"] Vergil, *Aeneid* 1.11), the perversion of *E-d-e-n* in *n-e-e-d*, and the vicious oxymoron *Goddess humane* all point to the devil's tearing and rending of language (even as the body of truth is torn, Milton recalls in *Areopagitica* [1017–18], in the same way that Typhon dismembered Osiris, forcing Isis to search for the pieces [see also *PR* 1.432–38 and Shoaf 157–58]). Throughout *Paradise Regained* Milton suggests that Jesus has a different way with words than does Satan.

For many experts, alliteration is a problematic poetic artifact. They treat it rather in the manner of the medieval dictum "Auctoritas habet nasam ceream" ("Authority has a waxen nose") and simply dismiss it. Others, like myself—trained in Germanic, Anglo-Saxon, and high Middle English alliterative poetry (I have also lived a year in Reykjavík, Iceland, where I studied sagas and skaldic verse)—find it, to the contrary, one of the most powerful devices available to poetry. In my experience, the divide between us is largely nonnegotiable, but the conversation should continue nevertheless, especially in *Paradise Regained*, where Milton's mastery of alliteration is testimony to its enduring value to poetry.

Alliteration in *Paradise Regained* functions for Milton much like generic constraint. If he aspires to transcend conventional epic poetry and write a poem "above heroic" (1.14), he also aspires to write an epic above poetic, not only eschewing the "jingling sound of like endings" (*Paradise Lost*, "The Verse" [*Riverside* 352]) but also lifting the sound of verse to a new height of inwordness with the concatenation of initial letters and the resultant knitting of meaning in the divine *verbum*. A vivid example of this effort occurs in book 1, where Jesus discovers himself in the "Desert":

> So spake our Morning Star then in his rise,
> And looking round on every side beheld
> A pathless Desert, dusk with horrid shades;
> The way he came not having mark'd, return
> Was difficult, by humane steps untrod;
> And he still on was led, but with such thoughts
> Accompanied of things past and to come
> Lodg'd in his breast, as well might recommend
> Such Solitude before choicest Society.
> Full forty days he pass'd, whether on hill
> Sometimes, anon in shady vale, each night
> Under the covert of some ancient Oak,
> Or Cedar, to defend him from the dew,
> Or harbour'd in one Cave, is not reveal'd;
> Nor tasted humane food, nor hunger felt
> Till those days ended, hunger'd then at last
> Among wild Beasts: they at his sight grew mild,
> Nor sleeping him nor waking harm'd, his walk
> The fiery Serpent fled, and noxious Worm,
> The Lion and fierce Tiger glar'd aloof.
> But now an aged man in Rural weeds,
> Following, as seem'd, the quest of some stray Ewe,
> Or wither'd sticks to gather; which might serve
> Against a Winters day when winds blow keen,
> To warm him wet return'd from field at Eve,
> He saw approach, who first with curious eye
> Perus'd him, then with words thus utt'red spake.
> (295–321)

Using *TACT* (*Text-Analysis Computing Tools*)[1] and protocols of my own, I have determined that 11.4 percent of the 903 letters in this passage are dentals (not counting /T/h°) and 7.75 percent are sibilants. Here is the passage again in a markup designed simply to show distinct graphs:

Legend = {S} /T/ /T/h° |D| |D| (weak verb ending) |c(ee)|

{S}o {S}pake our Morning {S}/T/ar /T/h°en in hi{S} ri{S}e,
An|D| looking roun|D| on every {S}i|D|e behel|D|
A pa/T/h°le{S}{S} |D|e{S}er/T/, |D|u{S}k wi/T/h° horri|D| {S}ha|D|e{S};
/T/h°e way he came no/T/ having mark'|D|, re/T/urn
Wa{S} |D|ifficul/T/, by humane {S}/T/ep{S} un/T/ro|D|;
An|D| he {S}/T/ill on wa{S} le|D|, bu/T/ wi/T/h° {S}uch /T/h°ough/T/{S}
Accompanie|D| of /T/h°ing{S} pa{S}/T/ an|D| /T/o come
Lo|D|g'|D| in hi{S} brea{S}/T/, a{S} well migh/T/ recommen|D|
{S}uch {S}oli/T/ul|D|e before choi|c(ee)|e{S}/T/ {S}ol|c(ee)|ie/T/y.
Full for/T/y |D|ay{S} he pa{S}{S}'|D|, whe/T/h°er on hill
{S}ome/T/ime{S}, anon in {S}ha|D|ly vale, each nigh/T/
Un|D|er /T/h°e cover/T/ of {S}ome ancien/T/ Oak,
Or |C(ee)|D|ar, /T/o |D|efen|D| him from /T/h°e |D|ew,
Or harbour'|D| in one Cave, i{S} no/T/ reveal'|D|;
Nor /T/a{S}/T/e|D| humane foo|D|, nor hunger fel/T/
/T/ill /T/h°o{S}e |D|ay{S} en|D|e|D|, hunger'|D| /T/h°en a/T/ la{S}/T/
Among wil|D| Bea{S}/T/{S}: /T/h°ey a/T/ hi{S} {S}igh/T/ grew mil|D|,
Nor {S}leeping him nor waking harm'|D|, hi{S} walk
/T/h°e fiery {S}erpen/T/ fle|D|, an|D| noxiou{S} Worm,
/T/h°e Lion an|D| fier|c(ee)|e /T/iger glar'|D| aloof.
Bu/T/ now an age|D| man in Rural wee|D|{S},
Following, a{S} {S}eem'|D|, /T/h°e que{S}/T/ of {S}ome {S}/T/ray Ewe,
Or wi/T/h°er'|D| {S}/T/ick{S} /T/o ga/T/h°er; which migh/T/ {S}erve
Again{S}/T/ a Win/T/er{S} |D|ay when win|D|{S} blow keen,
/T/o warm him we/T/ re/T/urn'|D| from fiel|D| a/T/ Eve,
He {S}aw approach, who fir{S}/T/ wi/T/h° curiou{S} eye
Peru{S}'|D| him, /T/h°en wi/T/h° worl|D|{S} /T/h°u{S} u/T//T/'re|D|
{S}pake.

At just the moment that Satan approaches Jesus to tempt him, Milton insists with this extraordinary texture of alliteration that the divine word in the **DeSerT** (/d/, /s/, /t/) is whole enough and, with his Father's grace, godly enough for Jesus, by no means **DeSerT**ed, to resist the rending and tearing of truth that he is about to endure from the devil disguised in "rural weeds." Even in the **DeSerT**, in the presence of his implacable enemy, Jesus un**DeSerT**ed rests in an inwordness that Satan cannot rend asunder.

My experience in the classroom has suggested to me that demonstrating Milton's care with alliteration in *Paradise Regained* increases student engagement with the poem. In particular, the class's reaction to the poem, after reading *Paradise Lost*, is typically puzzlement or even distance, so different are the two poems in form, but early introduction to the prosody of *Paradise Regained*, especially the alliteration, enables students to reduce the distance and calm the puzzlement as they begin to grasp that the theology of *Paradise Regained* is not just *in* its prosody but *is* its prosody: alliteration—an intimation of the incarnation of the word, in which Jesus, inwordly, "**h**eld it more **h**umane, more **h**eavenly, **f**irst / By **w**inning **w**ords to conquer **w**illing **h**earts, / And make perswasion do the **w**ork of fear."

NOTES

I thank my student Kelly M. Dunn for help checking my data.

[1] This software is available from the University of Toronto (www.chass.utoronto.ca/tact/), and the manual (Lancashire) is available as a PDF file from the Modern Language Association (www.mla.org/pdftact_manual).

"Passion Spent":
Teaching *Paradise Regained* and *Samson Agonistes* as Twin Texts

Jeffrey Shoulson

If they get there at all, students and teachers typically come to the study of *Paradise Regained* and *Samson Agonistes* only after the intellectually and pedagogically exhausting experience of reading *Paradise Lost* (*Riverside* 720–82; 783–844; 348–710). What's left to say? I have found that the most effective way to introduce the two poems Milton published together in 1671 (between the 1667 and 1674 editions of his longer epic) is to ask precisely this question. I dedicate the final weeks of a course on Milton to these two late poems because teaching *Paradise Regained* and *Samson Agonistes* as twin texts not only provides the opportunity to review and consolidate many of the lessons learned in a study of the earlier poetry, it also reveals the limits and problematics of those lessons. Serving as a bipartite coda to one of the most challenging and multifaceted poetic oeuvres in the English language, the pairing of *Paradise Regained* and *Samson Agonistes* gives the instructor a powerful means to end a course with invitations to further inquiries rather than pithy and (temporarily) satisfying statements of closure and completion.

As is so often true, Milton has offered his "fit audience" (*PL* 5.31)—teachers and students alike—crucial guidance for an engagement with these poems by publishing them together (and linking the brief epic to the dramatic poem with the notorious title page phrase, "To which is added *Samson Agonistes*"). It is well worth pointing out to students that the joint publication of these two texts was a deliberate choice on Milton's part and that for the first century following their initial publication they were never published separately (Wittreich " 'Strange Text!' " 166).[1] These are poems in dialogue with each other and, by extension, with all that has come before them in Milton's writings. There is a Miltonic precedent for this kind of dialectical relation between paired texts, and a gesture to the early diptych of "L'Allegro" and "Il Penseroso" will help remind students of the poet's self-conscious approach to his work in conversation with *itself*. Though they both take up many of the same issues addressed in the longer epic—questions of religious faith, political agency, and literary history (to name only some of the central themes)—when they are read individually, these texts tell only half the story. To take full advantage of this dialogic relation, I dedicate two weeks (at least) to the study of both poems. I ask half my students to read *Paradise Regained* for the first week and the other half to read *Samson Agonistes* that same week. In the second week the two groups switch their reading assignments. In this way, even during the first week I can replicate the dialogue between the texts in the conversations in the classroom.

By calling attention to the generic and stylistic differences between the two poems, I invite students to consider the implied and explicit contrasts between ways of reading and interpretation, whether the reading is of signs and portents, internal impulses, biblical texts, historical trends, or the texts themselves. The comparisons are ready-made for the classroom. The form of *Paradise Regained* occasions a look backward at the conventions of epic familiar from *Paradise Lost*, but, when contrasted with elements of *Samson Agonistes*, it also offers the opportunity to reflect on the limitations of genre. The opening invocation of the brief epic explicitly links the recognizable call for inspiration with the ensuing account of the Son in the wilderness:

> Thou Spirit who ledst this glorious Eremite
> Into the Desert . . . inspire,
> As thou are wont, my prompted Song else mute.   (1.8–12)

Yet the "strong motion" (1.290) that leads the Son to his encounters with the archfiend sits in complex relation to the "intimate impulse" to which Samson refers when he unsuccessfully tries to justify his marriage choices or the "rouzing motions" that inspire Samson's final act of bloody vengeance on the Philistines (*Samson*, lines 223, 1382). Claims to divine authority, it would seem, are not unambiguous; they can sometimes lead a biblical hero, or a poet, astray, with catastrophic results. Another fruitful comparison can be drawn between the "multitude of thoughts" that "swarm" around the Son (*Paradise Regained* 1.196–97) and the "restless thoughts, that like a deadly swarm" attack Samson in his solitary musings (19). Ask your students how these related images offer divergent perspectives on subjectivity, especially in response to external factors. These local contrasts can lead to further questions concerning the differences between an epic form that, though filled with extensive dialogue, relies on the third-person characterizations of an omniscient narrator and a dramatic form that can only offer the limited—and competing—perspectives of its dramatis personae. This comparison can be especially effective in alerting students to the problem of the chorus in *Samson Agonistes*, its function and its reliability.

As works that are based on biblical narratives in the New Testament (*Paradise Regained*) and the Hebrew Bible (*Samson Agonistes*), the poems can elicit inquiries into Milton's use of, and distinction between, Christian and Hebraic-Judaic traditions (see Rosenblatt; and Shoulson for recent discussions of the relevance of early modern Christian Hebraism to the study of Milton). I ask my students to compare the changes (omissions, additions, and alterations) Milton makes to the Gospel accounts of the temptation in the wilderness (using that occasion also to introduce the competing versions in Matthew and Luke and Milton's preference for the Lucan sequence of temptations) with the modifications he makes to Samson's story in the Book of Judges, particularly the poet's invention of a marriage between Dalila and Samson. Indeed, the obsessive concerns with marriage, sexual desire, and the role of Dalila as temptress that take up the center of the dramatic poem (710 to 1003) can provide students with an approach to analyzing Milton's insertion of the seemingly excrescent attempts by Belial to convince Satan to tempt the Son with concupiscence (*Paradise Regained* 2.153–234), a noteworthy supplement to the sparse account of the temptations in the Gospels. Milton's poetic interest in the powers and dangers of sexual desire has a history that extends as far back as *A Mask* and "Lycidas," later finding extensive expression in *Paradise Lost*. John Shawcross has argued that "the passage [in book 2 of *Paradise Regained*] provides a clever way by which Milton was able to include sexual temptation for the Son of God without actually including it" ("Genres" 243). Independent of *Samson Agonistes*, Belial's suggestion and Satan's rejection of it seem unworthy of the brief epic. When read in dialogue with the dramatic poem's consideration of Samson's fatal uxoriousness, however, the inclusion of a meditation on extramarital sexual desire takes on a much richer significance.

Discussions of the poet's uses of biblical pretexts offer a concrete way to introduce Milton's distinctive and idiosyncratic treatment of typology. I think it is important to show students how Milton's ordering of the two texts—New Testament narrative first, followed by an older story from the Hebrew Bible—offers a striking reversal of the standard typological supersession of the Old Testament by the New. Though the Letter to the Hebrews includes Samson among its list of the faithful who anticipate Christ (Heb. 11.32), Milton presents his readers with a Samson whose actions must be read, anachronistically, as commentary on those of the Son of *Paradise Regained* (Krook offers an excellent discussion of this reversal). By approaching Milton's reading of biblical texts in this way, I can complicate the schematic binaries of Judaism/Christianity, violence/pacifism, and particularism/universalism that are too often invoked as part of a developmental narrative that charts the progress from the limited and temporary liberation brought about by Samson to the universal and enduring salvation made possible by Christ. In suggestive ways, the endings of the two poems invert expectations. Whereas students might anticipate reading of the recovery of Paradise at the moment the Son sacrifices his life on the cross, it is in *Samson Agonistes* that they read of a hero who voluntarily chooses his own death, "With both his arms [spread between] two massie Pillars" (1633). The chorus speaks of "passion spent" in the last line of the dramatic poem; yet *Paradise Regained* famously eschews the Passion, privately returning its hero "Home to his Mothers house" (4.639).

That both poems express a yearning for salvation offers another means for comparison, since those yearnings seem to take radically different forms. I try to capitalize on my students' tendency to regard the dispassionate and unmovable Son and the intemperate Israelite strongman as diametrically opposed to each other. Though Samson may be all too human and the Son perhaps insufficiently so, they wrestle in their own ways with their relations to the immediate human communities with which they are identified. Through the two protagonists' embodiment of drastically different ways to suffer "for Truths sake" (*PL*

12.569), the poems interrogate the effectiveness of resistance to a conquering power and frame those interrogations in terms of ethnic or national allegiances. Satan's argument at the end of book 3 calls on the Son to assume "*David's* royal seat" so that he may bring about "Deliverance of [his] brethren" (*Paradise Regained* 3.373–74), but the Son resists his adversary's urgings by denying any ethnic imperative. Dismissively echoing Satan's characterization, "My brethren, as thou call'st them" (3.373–74, 403), he consigns such parochial loyalties to an idolatrous past:

> Should I of these the liberty regard,
> Who freed, as to their antient Patrimony,
> Unhumbl'd, unrepentant, unreform'd,
> Headlong would follow; and to thir Gods perhaps
> Of *Bethel* and of *Dan*? no, let them serve
> Thir enemies, who serve Idols with God.
>
> (3.427–32)

This casual reference to Dan is a link to Samson's intensely ambivalent identification with his fellow Danites, one that foregrounds an account of tribal allegiance that compares usefully with the Son's statements. Though, in contrast to the Son, Samson is more than willing to justify political violence—"force with force / Is well ejected when the Conquer'd can" (1206–07)–he is just as prepared to dismiss his "brethren" when they do not welcome his help:

> I was no private but a person rais'd
> With strength sufficient and command from Heav'n
> To free my Countrey; if their servile minds
> Me their Deliverer sent would not receive,
> But to thir Masters gave me up for nought,
> Th'unworthier they; whence to this day they serve.
>
> (1211–16)

The differences between the Son and Samson are striking, but so are the parallels. Only when taken together can the complementary qualities of these two poems be made evident to students. Each one fills in gaps left open by the other, and any time spent on drawing out such parallels and divergences will be rewarded. Heroic action cannot be fully explored exclusively in an examination of the absolute and unwavering confidence of the Son or in the uncertain and volatile extremes of Samson.

The marked contrasts (and parallels) between how the Son and Samson each regard their roles open up important discussions of Milton's perspective on his historical moment. Here, historical contextualization is critical and, if it hasn't already been covered with respect to *Paradise Lost*, some classroom time dedicated to the Restoration and its effects on Milton will be productive (Christopher Hill's study of "the experience of defeat" is a useful resource [*Experience*]). Moreso, perhaps, than any other early modern writer, Milton invites a discussion of his poetry in the context of his personal (domestic and political) circumstances (Lieb and Labriola). Students are often more than willing to read the personal into the poetical. Yet to interpret any poet's works autobiographically is to make assumptions about direct correspondences that deserve careful consideration. It may be true that the Son's responses to Satan about the inward nature of obedience correspond to Milton's arguments in *A Treatise on Civil Power* on the priority of individual belief over state power (see Corns [" 'With Unaltered Brow' "] for a productive discussion of the Son as an *imitatio Miltoni*); it may also be true that Samson's story offers an occasion for Milton to rehash his troubled early domestic life or to air his resentments concerning an England that had turned its back on republican government—the so-called Good Old Cause. The coupling of these two poems, however, can go a long way to challenging the use of Milton's life as the key to all mythologies. The deeply ambiguous conclusions of each poem, their unsettling depictions of victories half won and "[h]alf yet . . . unsung" (*PL* 7.21), should inspire students to recognize the limitations of readings circumscribed by the details of Milton's life. When read together, the poems demand that students consider them in the light of literary history, biblical and religious precedent, and historical context. Instructors who take advantage of the pairing will find that, as exhausted as they may be by the end of term, the results will be well worth the "passion spent."

NOTE

[1] The title pages for *Paradise Regained* and *Samson Agonistes* are reproduced in Roy Flannagan's *Riverside Milton* (720, 783). The framing of these two texts by the dual title pages, however, should not be overly emphasized, and students should be told that the practice of multiple title pages in a single volume was commonplace in the period.

Interpreting Dalila:
Samson Agonistes and the Politics of Servility

David Loewenstein

Samson Agonistes has recently been called "the major site of contestation within Milton studies" (Kelley and Wittreich 11), and perhaps no episode in the tragedy has more potential to elicit heated discussion in the classroom than Samson's bitter confrontation with his Philistine wife, Dalila. Dalila is presented in the drama as an attractive temptress who has suffered on behalf of her people, and thus I find students often inclined to respond sympathetically to her lengthy speeches in defense of her behavior. Her appearance in the drama raises questions about Milton's view of women, and Samson's harsh responses to her may prompt some readers, at least initially, to accuse Milton of misogyny. I remind students that Milton tends to give his significant "evil" characters, including Comus and Satan, attractive qualities and that, in the words of *Areopagitica* (*Riverside* 997–1024), these characters may assume "many cunning resemblances hardly to be discern'd" in this world where "Good and evil . . . grow up together almost inseparably" (1006). Students are thus aware that they need to be particularly discerning and attentive readers (the kind of strenuous, alert readers Milton admires) when they approach this episode. In addition, I find that bringing selections from Milton's controversial prose writings into our discussion of this intensely political drama can provide a valuable perspective as we consider the tense encounter between the blind, humiliated Samson and his Philistine wife.

By the time students in my Milton course get to *Samson Agonistes* (1671), they have usually read a wide range of Milton's earlier works, including some of his political ones: all of *Paradise Lost* (1667, 1674); *Comus* (1634); *Areopagitica* (1644); *The Doctrine and Discipline of Divorce* (1644); and selections from *Eikonoklastes* (1649), where Milton scrutinizes the seductive image and rhetoric of royalism that encourage political servility. Consequently, students approaching *Samson Agonistes* for the first time already have some sense of Milton's revolutionary politics and dissenting religious views, as well as the ways the poet dramatizes or analyzes the uses and abuses of potent rhetoric, especially when it issues from the mouths of his evil but alluring characters.

Interpreting *Samson Agonistes* and the character of Dalila—judging her dangers firmly—is doubly challenging because the text, as a work of drama, lacks the strong presence of the Miltonic poet, who often guides or shapes our responses. We don't have the intrusive narrator of *Paradise Lost* warning us to be wary of her seductive powers—as he does, for example, when describing the attractive but slothful devil Belial, whose words can please "the ear" as he counsels "ignoble ease" during the political debate in hell (2.108–18, 226–28). Moreover, the drama's characters—including Samson, the chorus, and

Manoa—are hardly unbiased judges. If students have also sampled selections from the diverse criticism about the question of Samson's regeneration, they can appreciate more clearly why Milton's drama has become a site of contestation in Milton studies and why it is likely to be a subject of debate in the classroom. Thus, when I teach the drama I often juxtapose skeptical perspectives on Samson's regeneration offered by Joseph Wittreich (who sees the violent Samson as a negative hero in *Interpreting* Samson Agonistes) or Stanley Fish (*How Milton Works*, chs. 12 and 13) with a notable critical voice emphasizing regeneration (e.g., Mary Ann Radzinowicz in *Toward* Samson Agonistes).

One strategy I use to initiate debate in the classroom is as follows: the week before we hold our discussion of the Dalila episode in *Samson Agonistes*, I ask each student to prepare a written response (usually a full page) either defending or making the case against Dalila. Then on the day of our discussion, I ask four or five students to read aloud their statements to the rest of the class. Since all students have had to write something, they are well prepared for debate— and they usually voice strong opinions one way or another. Moreover, I ask students to review some key passages in the prose and early poetry that we have already studied in detail earlier in the semester. These passages provide a broader political and cultural context for interpreting *Samson Agonistes* and for refining our discussion. In particular, they remind students that Milton uses the language of sorcery and seductive temptation throughout his career and that this language is closely connected to his critical scrutiny of the politics of servility and tyranny. This strategy also gives me flexibility in the classroom: I can initiate additional open debate and discussion by asking the students to respond to the critical statements written by their peers, and I can then focus our attention on passages from the prose and early poetry (notably *Comus*, Milton's reformed masque or aristocratic entertainment). As the discussion unfolds, I ask students to think more carefully about the relation of *Samson Agonistes* to the political prose and other works we have read. This helps them to sharpen their responses to the Dalila episode—and to view her alluring rhetoric and appearance more critically and skeptically.

In the late poems, Milton often echoes or recalls his earlier works and their themes, including themes of political servility and enslavement. Milton's suspicion of sorcery and its arts (echoed in Samson's verbal attack on Dalila, as we shall see) goes back to *Comus*, the Ludlow masque (*Riverside* 120–71), in which "the foul enchanter" Comus, a seductive and dangerous adversary, is the son of Circe and is a master of rhetoric (using "well plac't words of glozing courtesie") as well as illusion (lines 645, 161); his enchanted followers have become disfigured, and a stage direction describes them as appearing like "a rout of Monsters headed like sundry sorts of wilde Beasts" (*Riverside* 127). *Comus* reminds us that in the 1630s Milton hoped that Protestant England would remain vigilant and that its aristocratic leaders (since this is a family and political entertainment about an aristocratic family) would resist the temptations of the licentious Cavaliers and the dangers posed by an increasingly ceremonial church under the power of Archbishop William Laud (appointed Archbishop of Canterbury in 1633), whose policies seemed to be subverting the progress of the Protestant Reformation. Later, in 1649 and in the midst of the upheavals of the English Revolution, Milton warned his contemporaries about the dangers of slipping back into a servile—indeed, idolatrous—worship of royalty; the most popular book of the period, *Eikon Basilike*, with its tear-jerking portrait of the martyred King Charles I (tried by Parliament and executed in 1649), seemed to threaten the hard-won achievements of the revolutionary years. Recalling the language of sorcery and servility in *Comus* and anticipating its uses in *Samson*, Milton dismissed in *Eikonoklastes* the "Image-doting rabble" (compare the description in *Samson* of the Philistines as "th' Idolatrous rout" [line 443]), which had behaved "like a credulous and hapless herd, begott'n to servility, and inchanted with these popular institutes of Tyranny" (*Complete Prose Works* 3: 601). There too he had written of "men inchanted with the *Circean* cup of servitude" (3: 488) in relation to the tyranny of Charles couched in the seductive language of *Eikon Basilike*. The English were again in grave danger of being deluded by Circean arts and needed to resist such political thralldom. Like the blind and enslaved Samson, who feels bitterly betrayed by his countrymen, Milton too worried that his contemporaries preferred (to quote Samson himself) "Bondage with ease" over "strenuous liberty" (271).

Moreover, if one wishes to reinforce the point that Milton, only weeks before the restoration of the Stuart monarchy, remained anxious about servility and idolatry encouraged by kingship, then one can also refer students to passages from the second edition of *The Ready and Easy Way* (April 1660 [*Riverside* 1134–49]), where Milton warns of "the multiplying of a servile crew" of people attending to a new Stuart king and writes scornfully about "the perpetual bowings and cringings of an abject people . . . deifying and adoring" the theatrical monarch (1139). Similarly, *Samson Agonistes*, published in 1671 along with *Paradise Regained*, can be viewed as a warning to Milton's contemporaries to remain vigilant and to resist the ongoing temptations and dangers of Restoration culture and politics. In *The Reason of Church Government* (*Riverside* 903–25), Milton expressed his desire to write a dramatic work "doctrinal and exemplary to a Nation" (923); although his nationalist ideals were shattered by the failure of the English Revolution, *Samson Agonistes* is in some sense a warning to the nation about the dangers of being enticed by ease and treachery (however attractively presented) into servility. The Dalila episode is crucial in developing this interpretation.

Thus when Samson rages against Dalila—lashing out against her "wonted arts," calling her a cunning "sorceress," and referring to her "fair enchanted cup, and warbling charms" (748, 819, 934)—we need to keep in mind the ways Milton used this similar language of enchantment, servility, idolatry, and debasement in his controversial prose works and in the Ludlow masque. The language likewise appears in *The Doctrine and Discipline of Divorce* (*Riverside* 930–76), where Milton writes about an unhappy marriage (especially to an incompatible spouse with whom one cannot share happy conversation) as "an

Idolatrous match"; such an "Idolatresse" might "pervert [her husband] to superstition by her enticing sorcery" (942). Leaving aside the probability that Milton here evokes the seducing idolatry of Henrietta Maria, Charles I's Catholic
wife, such language also anticipates *Samson Agonistes* and Samson's sense of
betrayal by Dalila—"My Wife, my Traytress" are the first words the blind, enslaved Samson utters when she approaches him (725). For in Milton's drama,
the Philistine Dalila is Samson's wife—not a harlot, as she is presented in the
Bible (Judg. 16.1)—making her betrayal of Samson in the drama all the more
treacherous and embittering. Indeed, one may also point out to students (since
I give them copies of the Samson story in Judges) that Milton highlights that
treachery by having Dalila herself shave Samson's locks (535–40), whereas in
the Bible she calls for a man to perform this task that makes Samson effeminate
and servile (Judg. 16.19), fueling his feelings of bitterness.

I usually wait to introduce other points about Dalila and about Milton's religious politics until students have a chance to air their initial views of her. Depending on the direction of our class discussion, I alternate between looking
closely at passages from Milton's other texts or the Bible and looking closely at
the way Dalila is presented in the drama. For example, the opening description
of the theatrical, seductive Dalila ("so bedeckt, ornate, and gay" [712]) recalls
the brightly dressed Whore of Babylon in the King James version of the Book of
Revelation ("arrayed in purple and scarlet colour, and decked with gold and
precious stones and pearls" [Rev. 17.4]).[1] Such a connection would have reminded Milton's contemporary godly readers in the Restoration that Dalila is
enticing—she knows how to put on a good show and is described by the chorus
as "sumptuous" (1072)—but also dangerous. That Milton has the Book of Revelation in mind as a biblical model is clear from his introduction to the drama,
where he writes about the Book of Revelation being conceived "as a Tragedy"
(*Riverside* 799). In Milton's apocalyptic drama, Dalila is alluring, yet associated
with the forces of the Antichrist. In his first fiery apocalyptic tract, *Of Reformation* (1641), the poet warned his readers of "the Sorceries of the *great Whore*"
(901), as though the sorceries of Roman Catholicism had been revived by the
ceremonial religion of prelacy, which had encouraged the servility of the English people under the power of Archbishop Laud and King Charles I.

Milton the political writer and radical Puritan dissenter continued to have
similar concerns when the Church of England and the Stuart monarchy were
restored. The language of cunning sorcery and Antichristian servility are present in *Samson Agonistes*, where Dalila's "sorceries" and "snares" make Samson
a "Bond-slave" to Dalila and to the Philistines (937, 409, 411). We are, moreover, repeatedly reminded of Samson's filthy, harsh conditions as an imprisoned
slave; the blind, debased Hebrew, subjected now to the "foul indignities" and
scorn of the Philistines (371), evokes the cruel, humiliating punishments (including imprisonment in "loathsom" prison houses [922]) endured by many
nonconformists (including Quakers, Baptists, and other Puritans) who were
persecuted during the hostile political and religious climate of the Restoration.[2]

Keeping these religious and political contexts in mind can help students place the Dalila episode in *Samson Agonistes* in a broader cultural and historical perspective. It also helps them formulate a more discriminating response to Dalila's appearance in Milton's drama and to the kinds of rhetoric and arguments she uses in her exchanges with Samson, which are likewise revealing. Unlike the chorus or Manoa, she never expresses any shock or sense of lament at Samson's tragic, altered condition; she approaches Samson "[w]ith doubtful feet and wavering resolution" (732), in contrast to Samson's father, who is immediately stunned by his son's dramatic alteration: "O miserable change!" (340). Instead of acknowledging her treachery, she makes excuses for herself—telling Samson that he should not have trusted "to womans frailty" (783), that women are always worse in argument with men (903–04), and that all women are curious to know and discover secrets (774–76). Her resorting to such stereotypes about women should make readers question Dalila's strategies and motives, especially if one recalls that at least as early as the Ludlow masque Milton was interested in portraying women who could display (as the Lady in that work puts it) "the freedom of [their] minde" (line 663). Samson dismisses Dalila's claims of female weakness and holds her and himself up to the same tough moral standards ("All wickedness is weakness," he insists [834]).

One of the potentially most compelling strategies Dalila uses, as she appeals to Samson, is to recount her own difficult agon, experienced when she was pressured by political and religious authorities to betray her Hebrew husband. She tells Samson that she was embattled—enduring "assaults" and "sieges" from state and church leaders (845–46)—as she struggled with herself: "Only my love of thee held long debate; / And combated in silence all these reasons / With hard contest" (863–65). *Samson Agonistes* is a radical Protestant tragedy about internalized struggle and states of mind; here Dalila describes to her husband (and to us) her own agonized internal trial, as though the drama might be renamed *Dalila Agonistes*, Dalila its heroine. Her account of her internal agony may indeed encourage us, at this moment, to view her more sympathetically.

Yet Dalila's agon is in some sense a caricature of Samson's. Asking students to consider exactly what motivates Dalila to ensnare Samson can lead them to a more discerning critical response to her narrative. If Samson the Nazarite is prompted by the urging of the Spirit (the "rouzing motions" he feels "in [him]" [1382]), Dalila, it seems, is prompted by other impulses: her loyalty to Dagon, a pagan fish god; a desire for fame in her country (980–94); material reward; and Philistine patriotism. Godly readers in Milton's England would have thus discriminated between her impulses and Samson's. Samson, moreover, lashes out at Dalila's "feigned Religion" and "smooth hypocrisie" (872), another moment in Milton's writings when the poet seems to be alerting readers to be wary of religion's becoming a pretence or show—much as the narrator of *Paradise Lost* warns us, after Satan's first dramatic soliloquy, to be wary of all those who (like Satan or later King Charles) have "practisd falshood under saintly shew" (4.122).

In the midst of Samson's tense confrontation with his Philistine wife, Samson asserts that Dalila's "fair enchanted cup, and warbling charms" no longer have power over him—"their force is null'd" (934–35). In the context of the Restoration and of the Miltonic works we have examined above, this response can be construed as a broken yet reviving Hebrew hero's rejection of not only the Philistines' idolatry but also, as Samson is about to go off to the Philistine temple, the constraints of "civil power" and "outward force" on an individual "conscience" (1367, 1369, 1334). These words echo the language of Milton's radical religious convictions expressed in his late prose tracts of 1659–60, notably his *Treatise of Civil Power*. In this respect, Samson can be seen as a nonconformist resisting further servility and idolatrous practices, as well as the forcing of his conscience. And in the end, as he destroys the temple of Dagon after suffering bitter subjection to his enemies, he displays what Milton elsewhere called "the unresistable *might* of *Weaknesse*, shaking the *Powers* of *Darknesse*" (*Of Reformation* [*Riverside* 877]).

The sharp confrontation between Samson and Dalila is crucial in bringing out and developing these religious and political issues. As readers of the drama, we may have to struggle to interpret Dalila's alluring rhetoric and enticing appearance, as well as the temptation she presents to Samson to experience further servility under the appealing guise of "leisure and domestic ease" (917). In Milton's tragic drama, domestic, sexual, political, and religious servility are all linked (as they are in Milton's prose writings). Yet having suffered betrayal by Dalila and, consequently, terrible humiliation at the hands of the Philistines, Samson defiantly asserts that he will not allow himself to be enticed again: "Nor think me so unwary or accurst," he tells the Circean Dalila, "To bring my feet again into the snare / Where once I have been caught" (930–32). Reading the tense encounter between Samson and Dalila alertly and critically, while drawing on the contexts I have invoked here, enables us to appreciate the ways that Milton, in his darkest political moments, represents the difficult, ongoing struggle against the dangers of religious and political servility—and highlights the urgency of preserving liberty of conscience.

NOTES

[1] The Whore of Babylon has a long and rich history in English Reformation literary culture, where the dark apocalyptic image had great potency: e.g., Spenser's Duessa (*Faerie Queene* 1.7.16). See also King (*Tudor Royal Iconography* and *Spenser's Poetry*).

[2] To convey this point more concretely, one can refer students to the Conventicles Act of 1670, issued the year before *Samson Agonistes* was published: this severe act proscribed punishments for those Protestant dissenters who did not conform to the Church of England and accused "seditious sectaries" of operating "under pretence of tender consciences" (Kenyon 356). Selections from the act are conveniently printed in *The Stuart Constitution* (Kenyon 356–59).

"Ruin, Destruction at the Utmost Point": Terrorism and *Samson Agonistes*

Joseph A. Wittreich

Nearly a century ago, one question, in different articulations, was asked repeatedly in student-oriented editions of *Samson Agonistes*: "What were the circumstances which probably led Milton to take Samson for the hero of his drama?" (Onions 83). This question, however, begs others: To what extent *is* Samson a hero either in Milton's biblical source book or in his tragedy? What are the conditions and the limitations of Samson's supposed heroism? If there are grounds for identifying the Samson story with the Prometheus myth, why is there so faulty a correspondence between *Samson Agonistes* and other poems invoking the Prometheus story?[1] When *Samson Agonistes* is ranged against its tragic models or even against poems it serves as a tragic model, which poems articulate the loftiest ethical ideals?

These questions, if still emanating from the academy, are no longer restricted to it. Thus, John Carey's "A Work in Praise of Terrorism? September 11 and *Samson Agonistes*," itself a rejoinder to Stanley Fish (*How Milton Works*), engenders response not only in *PMLA* but also in the journalistic press and on the World Wide Web, in titles such as "Was [Milton's] Samson a Terrorist?" (Shea), "Is Reading Milton Unsafe at Any Speed?" (Guttenplan), "*Samson Agonistes* (Confession of a Terrorist/Martyr)" (Engel), and "Confronting Religious Violence: Milton's *Samson Agonistes*" (Mohamed). If 9/11 provokes the complaint, "I write in the wake of the terrorist attacks, which confirm in their way the full hideousness of Milton's fantasy of exterminatory hatred upon 'all who sat beneath'" (Mendle 778), it also forces reiteration of the question, Is this "what *Samson Agonistes* teaches?" (Carey 15). Or, alternatively, are the lessons the poem supposedly teaches the same ones we learn from it? What are its (and our) ethical imperatives? Which characters best embody them? How do they mesh with or militate against the ethical standards encrypted in—and advanced by—the Samson story?

In the twenty-first century, such questions have been routed into lecture halls and seminar rooms by way of the *Times Literary Supplement*, its "Letters to the Editor: 'Samson Agonistes' and September 11" (Bayley et al. 17, 15), and by way of political reporting in the *International Herald Tribune*: "It was in Gaza that Samson brought the house down. Some Israelis say with gallows humor that in killing hundreds of Philistines he was the first suicide bomber" (J. Berger). Milton told the Samson story in a version that now matters, in a version of which there have been seven announced performance readings in New York City alone (see, e.g., Scanlan) and that is fast becoming part of an international debate and inquiry. Is Milton's poem a manual for killing? Is it a polemic in behalf of war? Is it a record of history repeating itself, grinding down and turning over again into its former self—or of history liberated, renewed, and transfigured? Is Milton's Samson a great guerilla leader or a figure hopelessly compromised in his heroism? Does his life define glory or, instead, distill into the résumé of a terrorist? Not just through recent literary criticism but also through the journalistic press, performance readings, and political debates, teachers and students of Milton can begin mapping the cultural and ideological divide, as well as the competing ethical systems, that the Samson story inscribes and that Milton's rendering of it highlights.

If our impulse is to retreat from questions that bear the marks of postmodernist experience and seemingly lock us into critical anachronism, it is also an impulse checked by the realization that if one arc of criticism, inscribing a regenerate Samson, reaches from George Frideric Handel's *Samson: An Oratorio* (completed in 1742) into our own time,[2] yet another arc of criticism, with huger span, puts this heroic Samson, secured by the typologists, under the tough scrutiny of older midrashic traditions in much the same way as Milton's last poems wrap hermeneutic suspicion around the Samson whom Milton's prose works, some of the time, seem to applaud. Teachers of Milton's tragedy may prod their students into asking: what does Milton otherwise say about Samson, directly and obliquely, in his early plans for this tragedy set forth in the Trinity Manuscript (*Complete Prose Works* 8: 556), in *The Reason of Church Government* (1: 858–59), in *Areopagitica* (2: 557–58), in *Eikonoklastes* (3: 461, 545–46), in *The First Defense of the English People* (4: 402), in *On Christian Doctrine* (6: 408), and, finally, in *Paradise Lost*, where the "*Herculean Samson*" is invoked at the moment of the Fall (9.1060)—the book where Milton turns his "Notes to Tragic" (9.6)? In examining the trajectory of Milton's responses to Samson, teachers may wish to consider with their students whether those responses emerge from an unchanging or a changing mind.

Especially in *Samson Agonistes*, we gather in an enormous grief as we respond to recent tragedy with Milton's gift of tragic poetry and, simultaneously, marvel not at this poem's didactic clarity but at its moral quandaries; at what William Empson might call their "awful warning" (*Milton's God* 12). That is, *Samson Agonistes* is a poem, unconfined by the problems of its own day, that confronts the perils of ours—at a time when catastrophe humbles us by its enormities, by the smallness of our understanding of them—and, instead of ensnaring us within, would liberate us from what has been called that "dangerous dance of hate and revenge in which we are engaged" (Ghabra). Milton's hardwon insight is that all too often violence is a way of killing the future by destroying its possibilities; the actions of his great poems, as G. Wilson Knight comprehends, shape themselves prophetically "into one remarkable prefiguration of our own gigantic, and itself archetypal, world-conflict," and Milton's Samson, it would seem, himself a weapon of mass destruction, figures all those people in history who, in Knight's words, "ruthlessly override ethical objections in obedience to an all-demanding intuition, considering themselves . . . the 'scourge of God'" (83, 39). Milton's last poems, in different ways perhaps, yet none more powerfully than *Samson Agonistes*, are apt companions as, confronting global hatreds and anger, we are haunted by images of hubris flaunted only to be followed by stunning defeat. Milton's tragedy, especially, is meant to worry our humanity by exposing us repeatedly, relentlessly to what has been called the "uncertain" world of *Samson Agonistes* (Shawcross, *Uncertain World* ix). The great surprise in reading the drama, for students and teachers alike, is that what we thought we knew for sure we eventually look on with suspicion. The reception history of Milton's tragedy is enormously instructive in this regard.

The reception of *Samson Agonistes* begins with a title page that subordinates the work to *Paradise Regained*, the poem "[t]o which [it] is added" (720), only to cast doubt on the tragedy's subordinate status through a separate title page for *Samson Agonistes*: Are these companion poems, the latter one supplementing the former? Or are they rather a purposely inverted sequence? Before anyone ever thought the poems were published, John Beale announced on Christmas Eve, 1670, that "Milton is abroad againe, in Prose, & in Verse, Epic, & Dramatic" (qtd. in W. Poole 76). The reception of *Samson Agonistes* comes swifter than previously supposed and resumes again with Andrew Marvell's interrogation of Milton and his Samson, with Marvell concluding that Milton, himself no Samson, would not ruin the sacred truths by "grop[ing] the temple's posts in spight" (192)—a reception subsequently trumped by Samuel Johnson's complaining that Samson's plaudits come from "bigotry" and "ignorance" ("Rambler 139" 103).[3] This interrogation of Milton's Samson (and sometimes of Milton himself) continues in Percy Bysshe Shelley's representation of a Samson-like Prometheus as "eyeless in hate" (103); in Mary Shelley's avengers (both Frankenstein and his creature); and in George Gilfillan's lament that the hand of Milton's Samson, as he stands at the pillars, "has few flowers in it. . . . His spirit is that of Abimelech." Indeed, his actions in the poem, according to Gilfillan, bare "the wrath of Heaven, . . . threatening to crush wonder . . . rather than to awaken . . . admiration." Samson, Gilfillan concludes, "is Milton in hard Hebrew form" (xxx). Students have much to learn from an exploration of Milton's traditions—critical, literary, and scriptural—with an eye fixed on Milton's transgressions of them.

In the final quarter of the nineteenth century, in the grip of what he calls "the Puritan Samson Agonistes," Peter Bayne concludes that "[t]he spiritual depths of Christianity, the Divine power of kindness and self-sacrifice, were fully fathomed" in none of Milton's last poems, wherein dwells instead "the inspiration of Puritan battle" (345). As if in response to Bayne, in 1897 J. Howard B. Masterman, seeking to free *Samson Agonistes* from a politics of violence and religion of retaliation, finds in Milton's poem the tragedy of Puritanism, which, he says, "appears as the blind and discredited champion of Divine Vengeance," now a "brute secular force" that "might hope to strike one more blow," only to "perish in the overthrow of its enemies." The whole point of Milton's 1671 poetic volume, where each poem is a "fragment," neither complete without the other, is (as Masterman proposes) to present, through the modifying context of *Paradise Regain'd*, as "a great alternative [to revenge] . . . the victory of patience and self-repression—the Divine overcoming of evil with good." In sum, Milton's point is to choose as "the better part . . . to be patient" and, despite the penalty of disappointment, "to hope" (69, 70, 72; cf. Hexter 248).

Recent Milton criticism is busy reviving a reading of *Samson Agonistes* that went underground for much of the twentieth century, now leaving teachers of the poem and their students to wonder why. Historically, why has there been so much hermeneutic trouble enveloping the Samson story, including Milton's rendering of it, and is there anything to be gained from now reading Milton's poem with some different inflections and in some unexpected juxtapositions— for example, in relation to William Blake's shorn Samson, or Kenneth Burke's murderous Samson, or Ralph Ellison's slyly subversive Samson? An alternative Samson tradition is enabling just because it presses old questions on us, but it also allows for new solutions to them, in this way drawing *Samson Agonistes* out of relative seclusion even as it releases meanings, over time suppressed, through new, often surprising contextualizations. Misunderstandings are thus swallowed up in new understanding as, in his last poems, Milton casts his lot with those who worked not for the undoing of the human race but for its betterment and who, planting good where others had sown evil, would still build a new world on the wreckage of failed dreams.

It is the modifying context afforded by *Paradise Regained* that best explains what Thomas De Quincey describes as "a tragedy of most tumultuous catastrophe," which, in "its most exquisite form," exhibits the "fine transfiguration of moral purpose that belongs to a higher, purer, and far holier religion" (465). Milton found in the Samson story a template for tragedy, while his successors found in *Samson Agonistes* a template for tragedy reconstituted as mental theater. In more recent reflections on tragedy, Tony Kushner, rather than reinventing, vindicates tragedy, much as Milton would do, by extrapolating from its history tragedy's enduring mission of making available "the possibility of new understanding." For Kushner, one prong in the paradox of tragedy is its "creative aspect: new meaning flows to fill the emptiness hollowed out by devastation" as we determine which path to take: that of fiery anger and unremitting spite or, again in Kushner's words, that of "imagination, compassion, and courageous intelligence." In choosing among such options, all of us are engaged in shaping interpretation of *Samson Agonistes* and of history (the Civil War in England or 9/11 and its aftermath); and in the ensuing actions of history, as well as in our interpretations of them, we all become implicated as we make, and then promulgate, our decision about whether *Samson Agonistes* is an appeal to hurl down a city or, in conjunction with *Paradise Regained*, an announcement about dwelling in renewed possibility, about recovering paradise by building up a new Jerusalem of the spirit. In its continual hankering after a better self and better time, Milton's 1671 poetic volume is a provocation to mental fight and a perpetual prompting to spiritual adventure.

NOTES

[1] Lawrence Zillman reports what Charlotte Porter and Helen Clarke document, the "Grounds for Identifying the Samson with the Prometheus Story; the Lack of Correspondence of Milton's *Samson Agonistes* with the Prometheus Story" (Porter and Clarke, qtd. in Zillman 79).

[2] Not only does the librettist for Handel's oratorio, Newburgh Hamilton, through allusion to Milton's Nativity Ode, introduce Christ to a text from which, in Milton's version, Christ is a conspicuous omission (save for the prefatory mention of Gregory Nazianzen's *Christ Suffering* [Fishbone]), but the staging of *Samson* during "the Lent of 1743" (as reported by A. W. Verity [lxiv]) reinforces the typological connection between Samson and Christ and gives rise to readings of *Samson Agonistes* as a drama of regeneration. The uncertainty of *Samson Agonistes* is lost in Hamilton's adaptation where, taking vengeance for his law, Samson operates certainly by "inward motions" with "Heav'n bid[ding] him" to "strike the blow" and is then portrayed triumphantly as "bright Seraphim . . . / Ever . . . sound his Praise in endless Blaze of Light" (Handel, *Samson* 13, 16). Stella Revard reminds me that Handel's oratorio is itself inspired by an attended reading of Milton's tragedy.

[3] Of Marvell's poem, it needs to be remembered that the poet is marking not Milton's identity with but his distinction from Samson; and of Johnson's remarks, that his harsh words come on the heels of his observation that Samson "declares himself moved by a secret impulse to comply, and utters some dark presages of a great event to be brought to pass by his agency, under the direction of Providence" ("Rambler 139" 102). Later Johnson explains that his severest censure is for "the solemn introduction of the Phoenix . . . which is . . . incongruous to the personage to who it is ascribed," hence Milton's "grossest errour" ("Rambler 140" 104).

Biography, Creation, and Authority in *The Reason of Church Government*

Gardner Campbell

The Reason of Church Government, when it appears at all, typically appears on the syllabus today in the form of the long and celebrated autobiographical passage that composes the preface to book 2. We know that Milton thought the work especially important among his antiprelatical pamphlets—it is the first one to be issued under his full name—but to judge from current anthologies and most scholarship, its value derives entirely from a digression easily separated from the main work. I argue that teachers will find the digression's undeniable power both amplified and focused if it is placed in the context of key moments in Milton's larger argument. The essential connections between Milton's poetic and political imaginations offer enticing possibilities for the classroom, as they may lead students to consider their own agency, citizenship, and identity in terms of their own growing authority as writers in a community of learning.

Unfortunately, students looking for those essential connections and enticing possibilities will not easily find them in the current scholarly conversation. Charming and forceful as it is, the autobiographical digression has effectively swallowed up the work: in most critical commentary and analysis, the digression's autobiography and literary theory are considered quite apart from the work of the pamphlet as a whole. One recent editor goes so far as to argue that the digression has "[n]ot very much at all, really" to do with the rest of the pamphlet (*Riverside* 902). Likewise, the editor of *The Reason of Church Government* in the Yale edition of the complete prose works outlines three reasons

> why *The Reason of Church-Government* is of vital illumination to Milton
> scholars and to any student of the developing human spirit[:] Milton for

the first time gives us a number of interesting facts about himself . . . he gives an outline of his poetic theory, and suggests an ambitious poetic plan of life . . . [and he] gives us a picture of his mind at the outset of [his] career . . . [when he was still] a liberal unsoured by experience. . . .

(Haug 736)

Haug locates the work's "vital illumination" almost entirely in the digression. And in the only edition of Milton's selected prose currently in print, *The Reason of Church Government* is represented *only* by the digression, and that in a section entitled "Milton on Milton" (*John Milton: Selected Prose*). In a 1972 essay, John Huntley argues for a close connection between the digression and the pamphlet, and in her recent biography of Milton Barbara Lewalski asserts that the digression "functions both as an apologia and as an ethical proof of his argument," but Lewalski's analysis is fairly general, and Huntley's analysis denies the vital links between the digression, the pamphlet, and Milton's most enduring concerns (Lewalski, *Life* 135; Huntley 85, 111).

This critical neglect distorts not only the pamphlet but the digression as well, for the story of Milton's poetic maturation and ambitions is intimately connected with Milton's imagination of the ideal form of church government and with his deeper argument about the nature and purpose of authority. Neglecting the relation of the digression to the pamphlet as a whole obscures the depth and ambition of Milton's theological imagination at a crucial stage of his early maturity, where he is thinking through issues he will return to in all his major works. Such neglect also erases potent connections with students' own lives as writers and as emerging citizens in a matrix of authority they have inherited— and, like Milton, may seek to influence and change.

If attending only to the digression wastes valuable teaching opportunities, where should one begin with the greater whole? One may well ask what "digression" means in this context, given the larger argument Milton is making. (The question of what constitutes coherence in an argument arises naturally as a result.) If the digression violates the unity of Milton's larger argument, the consequences are particularly dire, for the digression would court, if not demonstrate, schism in a way that contradicts the argument Milton makes early in the pamphlet about the true nature of order and authority (what Milton calls here "discipline"). If, on the other hand, the digression is read as an implicit demonstration of that true discipline, the argument and the digression support and elucidate each other in surprising ways. These surprises, and the close, imaginative analysis required to map Milton's writerly strategies, may lead to students' delighted recognition that there are many more paradigms of well-wrought arguments than they have yet considered or followed in their own writing.

The beginning of the pamphlet boldly imagines a set of paradoxical and highly metaphorical images of discipline, the principle Milton believes should underlie any system of governing and authority. In book 1, chapter 1, Milton calls discipline a thing of such "grave and urgent importance throughout the whole life of man" that no just or good God could possibly leave it "to the discretion of men" (*Riverside* 905), as the Anglican divines had argued in *Certain Brief Treatises*, the work to which *The Reason of Church Government* responds. Given these absolute statements, one might expect Milton to provide proof text after proof text from the Bible to demonstrate God's literal prescriptions for his church. What Milton supplies instead, however, is an "Empyreall conceit" (922)—that is, a heavenly imagination, or the power to imagine heaven, that makes discipline into the guarantor and source of wandering freedom:

> The state also of the blessed in Paradise, though never so perfect [as that of the "Angels themselves, in whom no disorder is fear'd"], is not therefore left without discipline, whose golden surveying reed marks out and measures every quarter and circuit of new Jerusalem. Yet is it not to be conceiv'd that those eternall effluences of sanctity and love in the glorified Saints should by this meanes be confin'd and cloy'd with repetition of that which is prescrib'd, but that our happinesse may orbe it selfe into a thousand vagancies of glory and delight, and with a kinde of eccentricall equation be as it were an invariable Planet of joy and felicity. . . .   (905)

Ralph Haug notes that to "orbe . . . into a thousand vagancies" means "that a thousand ways of glory and delight will all move in the same sphere." He further comments that " 'Invariable planet' is an oxymoron; 'planet' means 'wanderer' " (Milton, *Complete Prose Works* 1: 752–53n18). Milton's point is that true discipline is not elasticity of purpose but purposeful and obedient elasticity, just as the planets wander "invariabl[y]" in a circuit that freely "orbe[s] it selfe." In this context, when Milton begins chapter 1 of book 2 with the words "after this digression" (*Complete Prose Works* 1: 823), the word *digression* may have more than a rhetorical meaning: it may also have reminded Milton's contemporary reader of astronomy, in which *digression* means "[d]eviation from a particular line, or from the mean position . . . e.g. of the sun from the equator, or of an inferior planet from the sun" ("Digression"). That this "Empyreall conceit" is never far from Milton's mind is evident even within the digression when, just before Milton launches into his dizzying recitation of the art he has considered making, he tells his reader that he does not have time in the pamphlet fully to reveal "what the mind at home in the spacious circuits of her musing hath liberty to propose to her self . . ." (923). Musing, liberty, spacious circuits, and proposing subjects to oneself: the similarity to Milton's description of the discipline of the blessed in heaven is striking and is a strong indication that with his digression Milton is not only announcing his literary bona fides but executing a case in point of the "invariable Planet" that travels in a glorious and divinely appointed "eccentricall equation." In short, the liberty Milton takes in the long digression is the liberty that throughout *The Reason of Church Government* he describes as both limiting and liberating. (It is also, I would argue, a liberty that enables much or all of the best education.) The digression may therefore be seen as an example of what Milton calls the "many admirable and heavenly privileges reacht out to us by the Gospell" (904).

The digression's treatment of Milton's literary qualifications becomes even more interesting when we ask why his insistence on his potential and preparation for being a great writer should assume such prominence in an argument about church government and ecclesiastical law. The answer to this question lies in Milton's assertions, early in the pamphlet, concerning the warrant for God's lawgiving authority. Theologically, Milton is no voluntarist. Might does not make right; God's authority does not derive solely from his omnipotence. Instead, Milton argues that beneficent creativity is the source of all good law and authority:

> *Moses* therefore the only Lawgiver that we can believe to have beene visibly taught of God, knowing how vaine it was to write lawes to men whose hearts were not first season'd with the knowledge of God and of his workes, began from the book of Genesis, as a prologue to his lawes; which *Josephus* right well hath noted. That the nation of the Jewes, reading therein the universall goodnesse of God to all creatures in the Creation, and his peculiar favour to them in his election of *Abraham* their ancestor, from whom they could derive so many blessings upon themselves, might be mov'd to obey sincerely by knowing so good a reason of their obedience.   (904)

Milton's remark about Genesis as a prologue to Exodus is brief but telling, for this is, after all, the poet whose greatest work was inspired by the book of Genesis, the poet who believed Genesis uniquely able to justify the ways of God—namely, his government of creation—to man. For Milton, beneficent creation must precede any claim on our obedience, for such creation works to "incite, and in a manner, charme" us "into the love of that which is really good, as to imbrace it ever after, not of custome and awe, which most men do, but of choice and purpose, with true and constant delight" (903–04). Milton freely admits that preferring persuasion over compulsion is not a new strategy—he begins *The Reason of Church Government* by citing "the judgement of *Plato*" (903)—but his argument that the Bible reflects such a strategy in placing Genesis, which he considers the book of creation, before Exodus, in which the Ten Commandments are given to Moses, makes the rhetorical principle into an ethical imperative that can be deduced from the very structure of the Pentateuch. Thus in asserting that one may freely obey only those powers that enlarge and proliferate being by means of their creative energies, with God as his prime example, Milton implicitly argues that authority in the sense of bearing rule or giving law depends on authority in the sense of "authoring" or creating. The poet's imaginative and creative power, the *poesis* or making that the writer carries out, not only links the poet to a divine inspiration but equips the poet both to understand law and to prepare the people to receive it.

Creation for Milton was also an act of begetting and gestation. Just as the spirit of God in *Paradise Lost* sat "brooding on the vast Abyss / And mad'st it pregnant" (1.21–22), so too Milton presents his own creative work in *The Reason of Church Government* as a kind of sexual generation.[1] He writes of being "led by the genial power of nature to another task," meaning away from poetry and toward prose, but the language is interesting: that genial power is both nature's power to bring forth new life out of John Milton and John Milton's power to bring forth new life out of himself. In this light, Milton's story of how his teachers first recognized his talent can be seen as the story of a successful childbirth, with Milton's literary creations as his offspring:

> I must say therefore that after I had from my first yeeres by the ceaselesse diligence and care of my father, whom God recompence, bin exercis'd to the tongues, and some sciences, as my age would suffer, by sundry masters and teachers both at home and at the schools, it was found that whether ought was impos'd me by them that had the overlooking, or betak'n to of mine own choise in English, or other tongue, prosing or versing, but chiefly this latter, the stile by certain vital signes it had, was likely to live.

One imagines the "sundry masters and teachers" gathered around the laboring student as his first compositions emerge, looking them over and judging them robust enough to survive. This obstetric image is joined later in the digression by Milton's famous wish "that by labour and intent study . . . joyn'd with the strong propensity of nature, I might leave something so written to aftertimes, as they should not willingly let it die" (922). Now the physicians are not his teachers but his readers, and the beauty of Milton's literary offspring would move them to do all in their power not to let these offspring die. (Such a conflation of teacher with reader can enlarge students' imagination of the audience for their own work: the teacher is one instance of a wider audience, not simply a gatekeeper or grader.)

A short while later, Milton will use these images of pregnancy and birth again, and again the terms will shift. As he describes the poet's power to lead his nation to greatness, the first item in his list of poetic strengths is the power "to inbreed and cherish in a great people the seeds of vertu, and publick civility" (923). The *Oxford English Dictionary* cites this passage in definition 1 of *inbreed*: "To breed, engender, or produce within" ("Inbreed"). That the metaphor continues Milton's emphasis on sexual generation is clear from his use of the words *seeds* and *cherish*, particularly *cherish*, for in this context it strongly suggests an archaic meaning of "To keep warm; 'to give warmth, ease, or comfort to,' " a usage that Milton returns to in a passage the *OED* cites from *Paradise Lost* 10.1068–69 ("Some better warmth to cherish / Our Limbs benumm'd") and one that in the same definition includes gestation and incubation, both in

John Healey's 1610 translation of Augustine's *City of God*, where a chicken cherishes "her egges with heate," and in Robert Burns's 1785 *Vision*, where "the deep green-mantled Earth / Warm-cherished every floweret's birth" (qtd. in "Cherish"). Again, Milton asserts that creativity must precede authority, and here he expands his argument to say that writers have a life-giving power whose creations are like children born into the nursery of the world. If the children have "certain vital signes," the world will work to preserve their lives, and in that action the world will be prepared through hope and delight to receive the kind of persuasive government that enables freedom to be both wandering and invariable, both obedient and free.

The digression is the climax, then, of this crucial early work, but to make that plain and compelling—and to point out the strong connections between Milton's project and the students' own work—it should not be taught alone. I recommend that it be taught in the context of the entire preface, all of book 1, chapter 1, most or all of book 1, chapters 2 and 3, all of book 1, chapter 7 (where Milton praises the "struggl of contrarieties" and advocates the "amending hand" that will minister to the "throws and pangs that go before the birth of reformation" [918]),[2] all of book 2, chapter 2 (where Milton treats the "reason and end [i.e., purpose] of the Gospel" [*Complete Prose Works* 1: 826]), and the pamphlet's conclusion. At a minimum, the digression should be taught along with the preface and book 1, chapter 1.

Once students understand Milton's fundamental theory of government as derived from the persuasive power of beneficent creation, they may find that for them the pamphlet's most urgent questions have to do not only with a seventeenth-century religious controversy or with a compulsively self-regarding young writer but also with the enduring concerns at the heart of any liberal education: What does writing have to do with authority? How does finding a persuasive and memorable prose voice enable one to take one's place in a community of discourse? What do our biographies reveal about the nature and practice of generative authority in our lives? What is the role of individual ambition in a community? In this way, teachers who place the digression in the context of the argument that informs the entire pamphlet may illuminate surprising points of connection between the work Milton does and the work they and their students do every time they write.

NOTES

[1] Milton's "[d]ove-like" brooding (*PL* 1.21) dramatically improves the image in Joshua Sylvester's translation of Guillaume Du Bartas's epic poem of creation that may have partially inspired it: Sylvester's divine Spirit is a mere "Hen" hatching a "brood" (qtd. in Taylor 59). Thus students may both learn from and outdo their teachers.

[2] My thanks to Louis Schwartz for this reminder.

Areopagitica and Free Speech

John Leonard

Why teach *Areopagitica*? Few early modern texts are more relevant to current concerns now that free speech has once again become an urgent issue. In our time, as in Milton's, opinion is divided as to whether free speech is desirable or even possible. This sets the scene for lively debate in the classroom, where Milton's arguments can be applied to such controversial topics as hate speech and pornography. I teach *Areopagitica* (*Complete Prose Works* 2: 485–570) in two kinds of class: a Renaissance survey course and an intensive Milton course. In the survey I usually devote a two-hour class to *Areopagitica*; in the Milton course I might devote four hours. In both I begin by briefly setting the historical context (the breakdown of Laudian censorship in 1640, Milton's divorce pamphlets, and Parliament's Licensing Order of June 1643). The purpose of this is not just to give a historical background. I want to raise the question of just whose freedom *Areopagitica* defends. Hostile critics sometimes contend that Milton cares about no one's liberty but his own (this too has a modern resonance). Having set the context, I then address the question of where Milton stands on free speech.

We begin by examining the term *free speech*. Milton uses it, but not in quite the modern sense. In *The Reason of Church Government* (1642), he says he had aspired to "the honest liberty of free speech from my youth" (*Complete Prose Works* 1: 804), and in *Eikonoklastes* (1649) he avers that "freedom of speech" befits "filial words" addressed to God (*Complete Prose Works* 3: 506). *Freedom* here includes "[f]rankness, openness, familiarity" as well as "[e]xemption from . . . control" ("Freedom"). Adam uses this kind of freedom in *Paradise Lost* when he dares to contradict God and insist that he really does need a companion, even though God (who is testing him) has just told him that he doesn't: "Thus I embold'nd spake, and freedom us'd / Permissive" (8.434–35). There is some tension there between "freedom" and "Permissive." Speaking to God, Adam is required to be frank, but that does not mean that he can mouth off with impunity. What, then, of free speech in a secular context? It may be doubted whether Milton ever invokes free speech as a full-fledged political right. He never uses the word *rights* in *Areopagitica*. (He does speak of "rights" in other tracts, especially *Eikonoklastes*, which contains twenty-four of his thirty-six prose instances.) *Areopagitica* extols the virtues of freedom, but it is sometimes hard to tell just what Milton means by "free." Addressing Parliament, he writes:

> If it be desir'd to know the immediat cause of all this free writing and free speaking, there cannot be assign'd a truer then your own mild, and free, and human government; it is the liberty, Lords and Commons, which

> your own valorous and happy counsels have purchast us, liberty which is
> the nurse of all great wits.   (*Complete Prose Works* 2: 559)

There is some tension here between "free speaking" and "free . . . government." Milton wants to push Parliament's "mild, and free, and human government" in the direction of "liberty," but "mild" and "human" invite "free" to set-
tle for the narrower sense "generous, magnanimous" ("Free"). This is still a
happy sense, but it opens the troubling possibility that "free speaking" is not a
right but a privilege that can, if necessary (necessity, the tyrant's plea), be taken
away.

This brings us to the central debate about *Areopagitica*. The problem is well
known: *Areopagitica* advertises itself as "A Speech . . . for the Liberty of Unlicenc'd Printing" but it gives several approving nods to censorship. In his opening pages Milton concedes (with chilling equanimity) the right of both "Church
and Commonwealth, to have a vigilant eye how Bookes demeane themselves"
(2: 492), and in his closing pages he coolly assures us that he is not advocating
tolerance for all: "I mean not tolerated Popery, and open superstition . . . that
also which is impious or evil absolutely either against faith or maners no law can
possibly permit" (2: 565). Statements like these have led critics to wonder just
what *Areopagitica* does permit. Most critics agree that the immediate occasion
is the furor over *The Doctrine and Discipline of Divorce* and that Milton's
prime intent is to preserve his own freedom. Yet most critics also think that
Milton raises issues that go beyond his immediate concerns and that he genuinely advocates Christian liberty in things indifferent. *Areopagitica*, it is
widely agreed, is tolerationist when judged by the standards and expectations of
its time.

Not everyone shares this view. John Illo has famously argued that Milton favors (even relishes) the censoring of opinions that differ from his own. Illo's argument has had great influence on Milton studies, and it would be remiss to ignore it in the classroom. I like to approach the problem by exploring some
possible distinctions between *tolerance* and *free speech*. In current parlance,
free speech signals an absolute to be valued for its own sake. Tolerance is not an
absolute, for there can be (and arguably always are) limits to what one tolerates.
I like to remind my students that tolerance implies disapproval. This comes as a
surprise to some students, who confuse tolerance with celebration. I illustrate
the distinction with the example of a Gay Pride Day, which is not merely an appeal for restraint and forbearance but is rather an expression of more positive
emotions. Other students equate tolerance with indifference. Again, I remind
students that one dislikes what one tolerates. If one did not dislike it, one would
not need to tolerate it. Discussing *Areopagitica*, I prefer the term *tolerance* to
free speech for just this reason. It reminds us that tolerance can be difficult and
even painful. There can be degrees of tolerance. It is not clear that there can be
degrees of free speech. If *Areopagitica* is an argument for tolerance, rather than

for free speech, Milton is less vulnerable to the accusations of hypocrisy that Illo and others have brought against him. Milton can write, "I mean not tolerated Popery," and still claim to be widely tolerant. But he cannot claim to be advocating free speech as an absolute.

Having clarified the terms, I then consider some specific problems and passages in *Areopagitica*. I start with the awkward detail that Milton's title echoes that of Isocrates's *Areopagiticus*. The resemblance is problematic because Milton's declared purpose is opposite to that of Isocrates. Milton calls for relaxation of censorship; Isocrates had called for its reinstatement. Wishful critics have suggested that Milton's real allusion is not to Isocrates but to Saint Paul, who had preached on the Areopagus. The difficulty with this is that Milton clearly alludes to Isocrates in his opening address to Parliament: "I could name him who from his private house wrote that discourse to the Parlament of Athens, that perswades them to change the forme of Democraty which was then establisht" (2: 489). Like it or not, *Areopagiticus* was on Milton's mind when he wrote *Areopagitica*. Illo thinks that this clinches his case. As Illo sees it, Milton aligns himself with Isocrates because Milton, like Isocrates, unblushingly advocates censorship. Illo writes, "The very title is misunderstood. . . . The Areopagus, originally a criminal court, had become, by the time of Aeschylus, the office of Big Brother" (180). Illo infers that Milton's aim is not to dissuade Parliament from acting like Big Brother but rather to woo Big Brother to his cause: "There was censorship in Athens, and censorship in Rome, and Milton approved of each" (181).

Illo's reading has not gone unchallenged. David Norbrook has recently demonstrated that the Areopagus was "firmly associated with republican forms of government," even though it was "a conservative institution" (*Writing* 131). One can make the case more strongly even than this, for Isocrates was more tolerant than Miltonists imagine. He advocated supervision of morals and daily life, but he also discouraged any attempt to legislate virtue. One passage, ignored by Miltonists, is directly relevant to and reminiscent of Milton. It should be balanced against Isocrates's more authoritarian utterances. In my classes I present this passage (sec. 40) to my students and ask them to relate it to Milton. Isocrates praises the old Areopagus for *not* imposing laws. Athenians of Isocrates's time commonly suppose that laws make virtue. The old Areopagus knew better:

> But in fact, they thought, virtue is not advanced by written laws but by the habits of every-day life; for the majority of men tend to assimilate the manners and morals amid which they have been reared. Furthermore, they held that where there is a multitude of specific laws, it is a sign that the state is badly governed; for it is in the attempt to build up dikes against the spread of crime that men in such a state feel constrained to multiply the laws. (129–31)

This thinking is close to Milton's. It anticipates Adam's statement in *Paradise Lost* that "[s]o many Laws argue so many sins" (12.283). Isocrates's image of building dikes also resonates with Milton's image in *Areopagitica* likening would-be licensers to "that gallant man who thought to pound up the crows by shutting his Parkgate" (2: 520). This excerpt does not convey the whole story about Isocrates, but it is enough to warn us that there is a complex story to tell. By juxtaposing Milton and Isocrates one can see that the true relationship between these authors is more subtle and complex than Illo's term "Big Brother" might lead us to suppose.

Careful attention to detail exposes another misreading in Illo's "The Misreading of Milton." One of the most rhetorically devastating moments in the essay occurs when Illo draws a parallel between Milton and the Council of Trent. Illo cites the following passage from the Tridentine index of 1564:

> Whereas the number of suspected and pernicious books, wherein an impure doctrine is . . . disseminated, has . . . increased beyond measure, Fathers, especially chosen for this inquiry, should carefully consider . . . the matter of censures of books . . . to the end that this holy Synod . . . may more easily separate the various and strange doctrines, as cockle from the wheat of Christian truth.   (qtd. in Illo 184–85)

Illo seizes on the simile of cockle and wheat and draws a parallel with Milton's simile of Psyche sifting her seeds. We need to attend to Illo's precise words here, for his passive verbs elide an important distinction. He writes:

> In *Areopagitica*, for cockle and wheat, Milton used the figure of Psyche and the confused seeds. He and the Catholic Synod knew that division into clean and unclean doctrines was a matter for religious decision. Only the clean, whether Catholic or Protestant, could be freely disseminated, for human freedom is moral, and the obviously or demonstrably immoral cannot morally be tolerated.   (185)

But is this what Milton says? Illo never quotes Milton's Psyche simile, perhaps because he assumes we already know it. I ask students to read the passage closely (they have the advantage of reading it with fresh eyes), looking for similarities and differences between it and the Tridentine index quoted by Illo. The crucial question is: who sifts the seeds? Here is Milton:

> Good and evill we know in the field of this World grow up together almost inseparably; and the knowledge of good is so involv'd and interwoven with the knowledge of evill, and in so many cunning resemblances hardly to be discern'd, that those confused seeds which were impos'd on Psyche as an incessant labour to cull out, and sort asunder, were not more intermixt. It was from out the rinde of one apple tasted, that the knowledge of

good and evill as two twins cleaving together leapt forth into the World. And perhaps this is that doom which Adam fell into of knowing good and evill, that is to say of knowing good by evill. As therefore the state of man now is; what wisdom can there be to choose, what continence to for- beare without the knowledge of evill? He that can apprehend and con- sider vice with all her baits and seeming pleasures, and yet abstain, and yet distinguish, and yet prefer that which is truly better, he is the true warfaring Christian. (2: 514–15)

Illo reads this as a justification of state censorship. But Milton's point is that in- dividuals must sort the "confused seeds" for themselves. The responsibility of moral choice lies with the "true warfaring Christian," not the state. If an oblig- ing censor has already chosen for us, we can claim no credit for making a virtu- ous choice that was never ours to make.

Much depends on the significance of Milton's Psyche. Does she represent the state or the individual soul? The etymology of her name suggests that she is the soul, and this conclusion is supported by the reference to Adam, our com- mon ancestor. It is also worth pointing out that in Apuleius's *The Golden Ass* (Milton's source for this story) Psyche accomplishes her task with the help of ants. Milton in *Paradise Lost* and *The Ready and Easy Way* upholds the society of ants as an example in the natural world of "a frugal and self-governing demo- cratie or Commonwealth; safer and more thriving in the joint providence and counsels of many industrious equals, then under the single domination of one imperious Lord" (*Complete Prose Works* 7: 427). There is something rough and ready about Illo's inference that Milton is like the Roman Catholic censors be- cause he uses an image that they had also used.

The image of cockle and wheat has, in any case, a more illustrious prove- nance than the Council of Trent. Illo neglects to mention that this image comes from the parable in Matthew 13.24–30. The good man in Jesus's parable tells his servants not to separate the cockle from the wheat but to "let both grow to- gether until the harvest" (13.30). (The wording of the Geneva and King James versions is here identical.) Milton's passage accords with Jesus's advice; the Tri- dentine index would turn Jesus's words on their head. Milton is most likely thinking of Matthew rather than the Tridentine index, but Illo still deserves our gratitude for drawing attention to the index, for its distortion of Matthew pro- vides a telling contrast with Milton. If Milton is indeed echoing the Council of Trent, his point is to reclaim the responsibility of ethical choice for the individ- ual, not "Fathers, especially chosen for this inquiry."

Present space does not permit me to list all of the examples of close reading I bring into the classroom when teaching *Areopagitica*. I encourage close read- ing because it fosters alertness and can help students distinguish between gen- uine and spurious ambiguities. To my mind, Illo's parallel with the Tridentine index imports a spurious ambiguity into *Areopagitica*. Like many spurious am- biguities, this one is introduced by passive verbs, particularly the claim that "the obviously or demonstrably immoral cannot morally be tolerated." It is true that Milton holds individuals accountable for the choices they make, but he also insists on the liberty and responsibility of moral choice. His point, at least in the Psyche simile, is that we must tolerate (painfully tolerate) the immoral if moral choice is to have meaning.

I do not pretend that *Areopagitica* can be completely rescued for liberal tolerance. Milton has his limits, as is clear when he says "I mean not tolerated Popery." But this exception jars with the preceding argument. It does not (as Illo claims) consist with it. My aim in the classroom is not to get Milton off the hook. I come clean about the fact that he acted as censor for the Commonwealth, and I resist the temptation to excuse him (as some have excused him) with the hollow defense that he permitted the printing of the Racovian Catechism and then (when Parliament rebuked him) defended himself by reminding his rebukers that "he had published a tract on that subject, that men should refrain from forbidding books" (French 2: 321). If Milton really believed this, he should not have taken the job as censor. The appeal to *Areopagitica* is in any case disingenuous. The Racovian Catechism chimed with Milton's own views. His act of tolerance would be more impressive if he had had something to tolerate.

Perhaps the real problem with *Areopagitica* is that it is more tolerant than Milton recognizes. According to Thomas N. Corns, "the problem with *Areopagitica* is not that it limits toleration but that it bases its case on a cluster of arguments that point to complete toleration" (*John Milton: The Prose Works* 58). If, as Milton argues, Christians need to "consider vice with all her baits and seeming pleasures," then the logical inference is that Catholicism and royalist propaganda should also be tolerated. Milton does not push his argument to that conclusion, but that is the conclusion to which his argument logically points. As Corns succinctly notes, "we look for coherence and do not find it" (60). It may be that one can never find coherence in arguments for toleration, since everybody finds something intolerable. I illustrate this in the classroom by invoking such current topics as hate speech and pornography. Is it really true that one grows in moral stature by exposing oneself to (even if only to reject) such "baits and seeming pleasures"? I like to test the students (and myself) by introducing the (hypothetical) baits gradually, so they really are baits. Some students are happy to tolerate (and not just tolerate) pornography, but few if any countenance child pornography. I have yet to meet anyone who does not have limits, so we should not be surprised if Milton has his. In this context, I introduce discussion of the Ranters—those contemporaries of Milton who chose to see and know and *not* abstain. Were they merely perverting the argument of *Areopagitica* or pushing it to its logical conclusion? This line of inquiry raises a question about *Paradise Lost* that can be pursued in later classes: does Eve need to eat the apple in order to know why she should not eat it?

I conclude my classes on *Areopagitica* with a topic that has special relevance for our own time. Milton argues that one may be a heretic in the truth. "Truth," he writes, is compar'd in Scripture to a streaming fountain; if her waters flow not in a perpetuall progression, they sick'n into a muddy pool of conformity and tradition. A man may be a heretick in the truth; and if he beleeve things only because his Pastor sayes so, or the Assembly so determins, without knowing other reason, though his belief be true, yet the very truth he holds, becomes his heresie.   (2: 543)

This part of Milton's argument has often been ridiculed. Both sides in our current debates about free speech and speech codes assume that the issue is whether or not one should be prohibited from saying things hurtful or hateful. But Milton challenges us to consider the consequences of prescription as well as proscription. He asks us to consider what virtuous speech is worth when it is "under pittance, and prescription, and compulsion" (2: 527). In recent years it has become fashionable for courts of law and university equity offices to impose compulsory apologies as a means of redress for real or imagined verbal transgressions. To my mind, compulsory apologies are a violation of the rights not only of those who are forced to utter them but also of those who are fobbed off with them, especially when a real apology is called for. A phony apology can never be a substitute. Even worse are cases when an apology is sincere but the sincerity is rendered invisible by a mechanism dictated by political or economic considerations. There is an entire legal industry of contriving apologies that pay lip service to a complainant while declining ethical or (especially) financial responsibility. Stanley Fish ignores this issue in his book *There's No Such Thing as Free Speech, and It's a Good Thing, Too.* Fish in that book often refers to Milton, but he never quotes the Milton that matters most to free speech and free silence. He never quotes the Milton who recognizes that one may be a heretic in the truth. For Milton, the worst violation is not being gagged when one wants to speak; the worst violation is to be compelled to speak truths that are false and hollow because one does not truly believe them or has not really earned them. This is the Milton we most need today: the Milton who requires us to earn our truths. This Milton is especially needed in the university classroom, where it is the teacher's task to encourage students to prove all things and hold fast that which is good. Different students will choose different truths, but so long as they earn the truths they choose, they will have done their work—and so will Milton.

Arguing about Politics in *The Tenure of Kings and Magistrates* and Contemporary Debates

Gina Hausknecht

The Tenure of Kings and Magistrates (*Riverside* 1057–75) provides a wonderfully vigorous example of Milton's argumentative style as well as his core convictions about liberty and reason, and it has the further advantage of lending itself to excerpts so that it can be easily adapted for various kinds of syllabi and readily presented as a prompt for classroom debate. I teach Milton at a small liberal arts college with modest offerings in the early modern period. My students tend to have only a rudimentary knowledge of English history and no experience with primary historical documents, and I find that gentle immersion in early modern texts can be more effective than extensive lecturing and background reading. By "gentle," I mean providing short excerpts with brief explanatory notes, directing students toward specific issues in those excerpts, and asking questions about voice, tone, and argumentation strategies. For a course that has room for only a single prose work of Milton's, I recommend *The Tenure*: it is representative of Milton's radical politics and is, with judicious excerpting, highly readable. Perhaps most important, it connects to issues and texts students generally have at least a passing knowledge of from United States history and civics classes (see Herman's essay in this volume); this helps locate Milton within a familiar and, one hopes, compelling world of political ideas. In my Milton course, *The Tenure* is a natural fit with the first two books of *Paradise Lost* and, indeed, seems to me essential preparation for grappling with the poem's concerns about autonomy and authority. In a seventeenth-century literature class focusing on religious and political change, I have found *The Tenure* pairs well with *The Putney Debates*. With minimal framing, students can engage in spirited debate about the radical thought experiment these two texts represent: if you were to dismantle and reconstruct your existing form of government, how would you do so, and why?

Staging classroom debate is particularly appropriate and effective in the teaching of Milton; I'd argue it's pivotal to entering meaningfully into Milton's world. He was a polemicist, and his readers need to appreciate that in an immediate, sensory way. One of the gifts of *The Tenure* to undergraduates is that it dismantles the familiar notion of the Great Poet as a remote, transcendently wise, barely human figure. This is not to claim that Milton was not transcendently wise, but, rather, to assert that the sound of his humanity, of his passions and prejudices, forms an essential point of entry into his oeuvre. The grittiness of Milton's voice in parts of *The Tenure*—the vigor, the anger, and certainly the grievance—impresses on my students that the daunting depth of his knowledge is matched by a depth of passion and conviction. This conviction itself elicits some awe and admiration, and it allows students to hear a wider range of inflections in the poetry; it alerts them to the degree that the poetry is animated by fiercely contested ideas about politics and theology. Enacting the debates of Milton's era helps students understand ways in which this often apparently remotest of poets was deeply, personally moved by concerns they will recognize, if not claim as their own. Getting students to take sides pays significant dividends. After that investment has been made, the stakes of later arguments are much more available to them—or the students are more available to the arguments, more likely to be affronted or assuaged.

In my Milton class, we read *The Tenure* in tandem with the first two books of *Paradise Lost*. I ask my students to devote that week's journal to questions about citizenship and forms of political engagement, as those concepts are defined by *The Tenure* and *The Ready and Easy Way* and reflected in the early books of the epic. Typical questions and tasks I pose include: Based on the excerpts from *The Tenure* and *The Ready and Easy Way*, what is Milton's view of a good citizen? What constitutes a healthy political community? Evaluate the council in hell in book 2 in terms of citizenship and political community. How, if at all, do you see ideas in the prose tracts reflected in the poem? These are questions we return to in our discussion of book 12 of the poem. In class, we read the portions of the council in hell out loud, and I ask students to decide which positions they find most compelling. Perhaps not surprisingly, an initial response is that Satan is most convincing, because he sounds most "republican"—on the face of it, most like Milton in *The Tenure*: the proud advocate of liberty against tyranny. This link then provides the occasion for a more meticulous examination of the arguments of the poem and the tract and for a probing, in both, of that essential Miltonic distinction between license and liberty. While I don't attempt to squelch Blakean readings of Satan, I do ask that students carefully assess how he fails to meet Milton's criteria for legitimate political authority.

When we turn to the text of *The Tenure*, we start with a close reading of the opening paragraph to examine how Milton uses terms key to his political philosophy: *reason, custom, tyranny, freedom*. I ask my students to identify, in the first pages of the tract, the ways Milton characterizes friends and enemies. We then sort through the characters of the fallen angels and are able to compare the texts' respective catalogs of cowardice, servility, greed, and fickleness. For my purposes, the most important section of *The Tenure* is the definition of lawful and unlawful political authority. A relatively concise statement of Milton's consent theory can be presented by excerpting from the fifth paragraph through the first sentence of the ninth paragraph (1060–61), beginning with Milton's spirited announcement, "No man who knows ought, can be so stupid to deny that all men naturally were borne free, being the image and resemblance of God himself" and concluding with the policy statement that

> since the King or Magistrate holds his autoritie of the people, both originaly and naturally for their good in the first place, and not his own, then

> may the people as oft as they shall judge it for the best, either choose him
> or reject him, retaine him or depose him though no Tyrant, meerly by the
> liberty and right of free born Men, to be govern'd as seems to them best.
> (1061)

I've gotten good results from asking students to identify those pieces of the argument they find most compelling and those they don't. For example, students used to the American electoral process have cited the passage "then may the people as oft as they shall judge it for the best, either choose him or reject him" as potentially anarchic and have had intelligent questions about the premise of state-of-nature argumentation. To ask my students whether they are persuaded or not (rather than whether they understand or not) is to treat them as real readers of Milton, an actual audience of a political argument.

For courses with sufficient syllabus space, *The Tenure* is enlivened by being placed in the context of other seventeenth-century debates that can be represented by fairly brief documents and excerpts. Introducing such debates allows students to hear the voices with which Milton was in conversation and can restore the complexity erased by posterity. In a recent class, for example, students expressed surprise over Milton's Cromwell sonnet: "But," they said, genuinely perplexed, "wasn't Cromwell the bad guy?" To teach historical outcomes and the ultimately dominant voices in isolation is to almost automatically foreclose on the experience of the sixteenth and seventeenth centuries. A helpful way to situate Milton's politics is to explore monarchical texts antecedent to the civil war period. For example, how is Charles's voice in "The King's Declaration Showing the Causes of the Late Dissolution" different from James's in his 1610 Speech to Parliament? How do their attitudes toward their political enemies in Parliament differ? How does their conviction in absolutism manifest itself differently?

An excellent companion piece to *The Tenure* is the *Putney Debates*, the record of fall 1647 meetings of the General Council of the New Model Army to discuss the radical constitutional reform proposed in the Leveller tract *An Agreement of the People*. I assign students roles and ask them to find their positions on the following questions and argue them: what a nation is, where the sovereignty of the people is located, how it should be entrusted to representative bodies, how to distinguish between righteous and unrighteous engagements, and, perhaps most important, who should be enfranchised. My students do well fretting out the details of these positions. Initially everyone wants to be a Leveller, arguing that rights inhere in the people themselves, rather than General Henry Ireton, who, arguing that the vote should only be extended to those with "a permanent fixed interest," located the nation and rights in the land (1239). But when the obvious modern corollary to "English first" laws (popular in my state) and how immigrants should qualify for citizenship comes up, the debate gets more interesting: students stake out both John Wildman's claim that "Every person in England has as clear a right to elect his representative as the greatest person in England" and Ireton's counterargument that the man who "will live in this kingdom . . . ought to subject himself to the law made by the people who have interest of this kingdom in us" (1247–48). On a practical note, *The Putney Debates* provides a great excuse for reading out loud, which helps with mastery and develops comfort with seventeenth-century prose style. Even timid students can hear and voice the passion in Thomas Rainsborough's ringing proclamation that "really I think that the poorest he that is in England has a life to live as the greatest he" (1238–39). After Putney, students are well prepared for the drama of the deposition and trial of Charles and for Milton's argument for natural birthright and against absolutism in *The Tenure*.

The great treat of teaching these texts in this way is finding students surprised by the complexity of issues that had been resolved for them in high school (and sometimes in college) narratives. The teleologies that should dominate a course in the early modern period are its own: the providential certitude brandished by Laud or the Levellers, or Milton, for that matter, in public discourse. By focusing students' attention on the argumentation rather than the outcome of a set of problems, we can engage them with the contingency rather than the inevitability of history and evoke commitment to and investment in issues recognizable to them. Listening to seventeenth-century people squabble opens up space for students to insert themselves. By focusing on the contests, we allow students latitude in arriving at—and sometimes deferring—judgments, enhancing their intellectual participation and agency.

Milton versus King Charles:
Re-Creating the Debate of *Eikonoklastes*

Laura Lunger Knoppers

On 7 January 2001, the *New York Times* Week in Review included an article, "Restoration," that featured former president George Bush, Sr., then-current president Bill Clinton, and George W. Bush, who was on the verge of entering the White House (Toner). But what made this news piece unique—and relevant for teaching Milton—was an illustration that showed the three men dressed in the costume of mid-seventeenth-century England (fig. 1). Bush, Sr., was appareled in standing ruff collar, elaborate doublet, and slashed sleeves, as

Fig. 1.   Illustration for Robin Toner, "Restoration: What It Used to Be Just Ain't What It Used to Be" (*New York Times* 7 Jan. 2001, late ed., sec. 4: 1). © 2001 the *New York Times*. Used with permission.

the deposed Stuart king, Charles I; Clinton was in full armor (rather miscast) as the Puritan revolutionary Oliver Cromwell; and George W. Bush was the avenging son, Charles II, resplendent with flowing locks, ornately jeweled crown, and richly embroidered collar.

The *New York Times* article appeared just as I was about to teach a spring semester undergraduate survey of Milton, and on the first day of class, I brought the image in as a handout, along with contemporary engravings of Charles I, Charles II, and Oliver Cromwell. The students—many of whom knew of Milton only as a "Puritan" writer or as the author of the great epic *Paradise Lost*— were surprised at the political content of this introduction and the evidence of its present-day relevance. The invocation of parallels with the English Revolution, regicide, and Restoration proved a useful entrée into the teaching of Milton in his historical and political context and a reminder that current polemics have a long pedigree in political history.

The beheading of King Charles I outside Whitehall Banqueting House on 30 January 1649 was undoubtedly the most significant moment of the seventeenth century in England. And understanding Milton's support for the regicide, along with his deep involvement in political and religious controversy from 1640 to 1660, is crucial for understanding concepts of liberty, tyranny, justice, due punishment, rights, and individual responsibility in his prose and his poetry. Yet incorporating history into the teaching of Milton is a challenge. I introduce students to Milton's political thought by using excerpts from polemical prose, including selections from *Eikon Basilike: The Portraiture of His Sacred Majesty in His Solitudes and Sufferings* and from Milton's government-commissioned response to "the royal image": *Eikonoklastes*, or "image-breaker." In teaching selections from Milton's *Eikonoklastes*, I try to capture the drama of the revolutionary moment: the escalating crises of the civil wars; the radicalization of the army; the tiny minority in late 1648 that sought not to limit the king's powers but to execute him for tyranny and treason; the dramatic scene on the scaffold; the metamorphosis of the king into martyr.

Names and dates on the board are a must (and convenient for the short-answer section of an exam). Visual images (slides or handouts) also help to re-create the drama. Along with the costumed Stuart images of the junior and senior George Bushes and of Bill Clinton as Oliver Cromwell, I have shown students Anthony Van Dyck's elegant paintings of Charles I in a variety of poses: in armor on horseback, posed with his queen and children, or in triple profile (Christopher Brown, *Van Dyck* 162–77). Characteristic Van Dyck paintings of King Charles and Queen Henrietta Maria, in which rich and lavish clothing, swirling draperies, and elongated bodies and hands produce an image of grace and majesty, help set up for students the shock caused by the unprecedented event of regicide, as depicted in the artist Weesop's painting (widely reproduced in engravings) of the crowd before Whitehall (Knoppers, *Historicizing* 16). A second set of images includes the martial Oliver Cromwell by Robert Walker and Peter Lely, derived from Van Dyck but adapted to emphasize a new plain style, as well as the "warts and all" miniature by Samuel Cooper (images reproduced in Knoppers, "Politics" 1297, 1302, 1304).

I point out to the students that Milton's only "real job" was as Latin secretary to the Cromwellian regime and that he spent nearly twenty years writing prose tracts on domestic, civil, and religious controversies. Students are invariably interested in the details of the regicide, Cromwell's rise and fall, and the grisly hanging, drawing, and quartering of the regicides after the return of the king in 1660, including the exhumation and dismemberment of Cromwell's corpse at Tyburn. That Milton himself might well have met such a fate underscores his close involvement in contemporary politics. Finally, the radically changed world in which Milton (largely) composed and published his three major poems is brought to life in visual images of Charles II, enthroned and wearing coronation robes, and in other woodcuts from the 1660s, the analogue of today's political cartoons, that show the execution of the regicides or Cromwell's exhumed corpse being hung at Tyburn (Knoppers, *Historicizing* 42–55).

The visual image we most extensively examine, however, is William Marshall's engraved frontispiece to *Eikon Basilike* (fig. 2). As with analysis of literary texts, a series of straightforward questions can guide the students in their reading of the visual image. Where is the king? What is he doing? What is the king wearing? What cultural values does the clothing convey? What other material objects appear in the engraving? Is the image symbolic, realistic, or both? What emblems are used? What characteristics are unique to Charles I? What in the engraving enables the viewer to sympathize—even identify—with the king?

Students can easily find the material objects: three crowns, including the kingly crown spurned on the ground, the crown of thorns linked with Christ's crown of thorns, and the heavenly crown promised to martyrs in the Book of Revelation. They see that the king is kneeling, focused on meditation or prayer, and that he has been reading from an open book (the word of God). The ermine-lined robes suggest wealth and royalty (although students have also wondered about what appear to be tights and patent leather shoes). Students also have questions of their own. Why is the light coming toward the king from both sides? Why is the image inside and outside? What do the Latin inscriptions mean? Are those bells hanging from the tree? What do the rock, dark clouds, and stormy water signify?

With any luck, the mutual process of question and answer leads the class to understand how a seventeenth-century audience might have reacted to the frontispiece of *Eikon Basilike*. By showing us the inner room where the king prays, the engraving visually re-creates the promise of the printed text to show us the king's innermost thoughts. The emblematic "outside" commends and universalizes patience under suffering: the palm tree prospers under weights, the rock is immovable in the storm. The image—like the printed text—shows Charles not only as king but as model Christian with whom the reader can identify. As such, the text offers what Elizabeth Skerpan-Wheeler calls "something truly new in political propaganda: a democratized image of the king" (136).

Fig. 2.   William Marshall. Engraving. Frontispiece to *Eikon Basilike: The Portraiture of His Sacred Majestie in His Solitudes and Sufferings* (London, 1649). Courtesy of Beinecke Rare Book and Manuscript Library, Yale University.

For Milton, however, Marshall's portrait of the king was a "Picture sett in Front [that] would Martyr him and Saint him to befool the people" (*Complete Prose Works* 3: 343). Milton's vehement objections to the frontispiece epitomize his fierce challenge to *Eikon Basilike* as a whole: it is a sham, a "conceited portraiture . . . drawn out to the full measure of a Masking Scene, and sett there to catch fools and silly gazers" (3: 342). In *Eikonoklastes*, Milton undertakes a combative chapter by chapter rebuttal of the king's runaway bestseller.

Hence the class now turns to a comparison of the relative merits of *Eikon Basilike* and *Eikonoklastes*. Having distributed selections from *Eikon Basilike* and *Eikonoklastes* (e.g., the preface, "To the Prince of Wales," and "Meditations upon Death"), I ask the students which text they find more persuasive. And luckily they almost always disagree. Some students find *Eikon Basilike* sentimental and emotional, while Milton's text, in contrast, strikes them as logical and polemical. Some find the sentiment in *Eikon Basilike* contrived and unconvincing; others, in contrast, find Milton strident and caustic. Some see a powerful ego behind the apparent stance of humility and martyrdom in *Eikon Basilike*. Others are taken aback by the violent imagery—bad digestion, vomiting, wormy manna—in *Eikonoklastes*.

While choosing sides is a good initial prod to discussion and debate, it is then important to examine how, despite initial seeming dissimilarities, both *Eikon Basilike* and *Eikonoklastes* are a kind of propaganda using various rhetorical techniques to make a case. How does each text construct a persona? How does each text imagine its audience? How does each draw on earlier genres? What is the stated aim of each text? How does each text use metaphor, imagery, simile, and allusion to accomplish this aim?

Further class discussion, then, can consider how the printed text of *Eikon Basilike*—like the visual image—is a character sketch, an apologia that presents the king's motives and good faith as he meditates on the various events of the civil war. *Eikon Basilike* offers a king with whom the readers can identify, who speaks, as Paul Stevens has recently noted, in soliloquy ("Milton's Janus-Faced Nationalism" 264–66). The king echoes the language of Christ himself, professing to forgive his enemies, praying that this "bitter cup" might pass, yet steeling himself for "mortality crowned with martyrdom" (179). Milton, in contrast, links himself with the Greek Orthodox rulers who "broke all superstitious Images to peeces" (*Complete Prose Works* 3: 343). In response to Charles's self-identification with David and with Christ, Milton counters with Rehoboam, Ahab, and a string of other biblical tyrants. What Charles puts forth as piety, Milton repaints as duplicity and hypocrisy, linking the king with his Catholic grandmother, Mary, Queen of Scots, and with Shakespeare's villainous Richard III. To Charles's professed willingness to wear a crown of thorns with his savior, Milton retorts that "to weare them as our Saviour wore them is not giv'n to them that suffer by thir own demerits" (3: 417–18).

Eikonoklastes and *Eikon Basilike* envision and address specific audiences. The king hopes to reclaim the people "who have either deserted or engaged against me through the artifice and hypocrisy of their leaders" (169), while Milton has considerably less faith in the "credulous and hapless herd, begott'n to servility" (3: 601). Both texts have a complex generic makeup and history. *Eikon Basilike* draws on such powerful texts as Foxe's *Book of Martyrs*, the Bible (especially the Psalms), and the Book of Common Prayer (Sandler 162, 171–72). *Eikonoklastes* is part of the realm of public debate and polemical contest, where, Milton argues, *Eikon Basilike*—despite its claims to be private meditation and prayers—actually belongs.

A final question can alert students to further rhetorical complexities. Do the texts succeed by failing? It is worth remembering that *Eikon Basilike*—at least Charles's portion—was written while Charles was in captivity at Carisbrooke Castle. The king's execution, ironically, confirmed his worst predictions about his plotting enemies and ensured the martyrdom of which he spoke. For Milton, on the other hand, the failure of his fellow countrymen to listen to his book—rather than the king's—confirmed his role as solitary prophet and his characterization of the people as "fools and silly gazers," blinded by their own idolatry. Does each text win by losing? (Knoppers, "Imagining" 164–66).

Re-creating the debate of *Eikonoklastes* helps students see the ongoing complexities and importance of politics and rhetoric for Milton's poetry. As the class then moves on to consider *Paradise Lost*, *Paradise Regained*, and *Samson Agonistes*, they are more likely to recognize continued concerns with freedom and tyranny, rhetoric and truth, appearance and true obedience. They are also more likely to see the ongoing relevance of Miltonic concerns and issues. Amid the furor and fervor of twenty-first-century American politics, the historicizing of Milton in the classroom is a pertinent reminder to our students—and to ourselves—that the political-attack advertisement and the selling of the candidate have a long and complex history.

Reading Milton Reading in
The Doctrine and Discipline of Divorce;
or, How to Make His "Wild" and "Wary"
Hermeneutics Matter in the Classroom

Shari A. Zimmerman

This essay suggests the value of teaching students about—and ways of intro-ducing them to—the biblical hermeneutics of *The Doctrine and Discipline of Divorce* (*Riverside* 926–86).[1] Increasingly, my students, who are of varying reli-gious backgrounds (including Catholic, Protestant, Jewish, and Muslim), enter my Milton course unfamiliar with the scriptural ground of meaning on which *Doctrine* and so much of Milton's poetry and prose ride. Excepting those who have taken a course in the Bible as literature, most know little about the New and Old Testaments. And few are aware of different translations of the Bible, competing assumptions about scripture, or the many interpretations of proof texts that *Doctrine* variously foregrounds and through which Milton, like many early modern writers, elaborates so many of his claims. More to the point per-haps, and as my occasionally amused but not altogether happy students insist during the two out of fifteen weeks we spend on the tract, Milton's argument is dense, laden with references they simply do not know. For obvious reasons, then (and who can blame them), they would prefer to speculate about Milton's marriage to Mary Powell (a few are always stunned to learn he takes her back) or to focus exclusively on the distinctly male bias and even hysteria that shadow this tract—a bias and hysteria, I suggest, concealing a deeper sense of despair (and which they will again encounter, I preview, in the voices of Samson and Satan). But while attention to biography is critical in any meaningful treatment of *Doctrine* and enormously useful for later discussion of the unstable gender positions and not-so-fit conjugal ties in *Samson Agonistes* and *Paradise Lost*, my goals in teaching this text include moving students beyond a narrowly defined preoccupation with the personal to a more broadly ranging consideration of the hermeneutical—to a consideration, that is, of what Milton is doing with biblical material he so selectively cites, elaborates, links, and deploys in his theorizing about matrimony and divorce.

I introduce *Doctrine* soon after "Upon the Circumcision" (*Riverside* 54–55), whose depiction of Christ's "more exceeding love" posed in relation to the "Just law" of Moses gives me an opportunity to begin teaching students, more formally than I have thus far, about registers of meaning between which Mil-ton's argument for divorce—and his entire canon—might be said to move (55). Drawing on Genesis 17.9–14 and Luke 2.21, I begin by lecturing on circumci-sion as overdetermined Hebrew signifier—here, in Milton's poem, absorbed (uneasily, my students often observe) by the Crucifixion. I briefly discuss New and Old Testament views of the covenant to which the poem alludes (and to which we return in our study of *Doctrine*); and I turn class attention to those scriptural proof texts, appearing in both testaments, that focus on circumcision of the flesh and on circumcision of the heart. (To make the biblical material more accessible, I generally order for my classes *The New Oxford Annotated Bible*, which provides valuable guidance on individual and commonly linked proof texts, but I allow other translations, chief among them the King James Version.)[2] After reviewing selections from Romans and Galatians, along with Deuteronomy 10.16 and 30.6—material my students always find illuminating— we tease out Hebrew and Pauline formulations of circumcision as well as the very concept of abrogating Old Testament law. Having initiated students into what is for some an entirely new language and set of signifiers, I invite them to note how the Crucifixion—in the last line of Milton's poem, linked provocatively to circumcision of the heart—works to cancel, abrogate, and make void for the Christian reader the ceremonial rite of carnal circumcision. In so doing, I am not only teaching this particular (and particularly dense) text or exposing students, some for the first time, to the idea of as well as relations between Hebrew and Christian systems of meaning. I am also preparing for *Doctrine*'s treatment of an Old Testament law that Milton believed perpetual: "plainly moral, and more now in force then ever" (*Doctrine* 937). With "Upon the Circumcision," then, I can bring into view large and small matters regarding not only the Anglican Church (and, say, the Feast of the Circumcision, which Milton likely would have considered popish ritualism). I can also bring into view the Old Testament nation of Israel itself, whose precedents, practices, and laws serve as positive and negative models—indeed, as overdetermined sites of meaning—for the England that the Anglo-Christian (and varyingly Hebraic) Milton everywhere imagines. And I can lay groundwork for upcoming discussion of the Mosaic law of divorce that, unlike circumcision of the flesh, is abrogated or canceled, Milton assures us, not a jot by Christ.

Before considering the more challenging hermeneutics of *Doctrine*, however, or the dramatic reconciliation of Moses with Christ, I first provide an overview of the four divorce tracts; of the early modern state of divorce in England (all the while inviting discussion of "*Harry* the eighth" [973], with whom students have some familiarity, and to whom Milton strikingly and uncritically refers in one of his attacks on the Catholic Church [see bk. 2, ch. 21]); and of the "spurre of self-concernment" that sparks Milton's writing (931)—always tricky pedagogically, as it can lock students into the very preoccupation with the personal I must then move them beyond. I also acknowledge, through several textual examples, and without much ado, the male bias—and woundedness— marking the frequently overwrought 1644 tract; and I foreground some of the gender-specific topics to be found in *Doctrine*, to which students often return in end-of-semester papers on *Paradise Lost* and *Samson Agonistes*. In the process, I begin lecturing not only on Milton's view of an ideal marriage, fit and unfit wives, or largely blameless and innocent husbands. I also begin lecturing on the radical argument he is attempting to make for divorce, on the grounds not of adultery, consanguinity, or "impediment of carnall performance" but of spiritual or intellectual incompatibility (938). Focusing on *Doctrine*'s first four chapters, as well as on some of the Old and New Testament proof texts Milton cites (Gen. 2.18 and Deut. 24.1 only chief among them), I lay out the tract's exposition of the helpmate as "ready and reviving associate" intended, Milton insists, to prevent not sexual but spiritual loneliness; to soothe not "irrational heat" (as misguided readers of Paul have imagined—or so Milton tells us) but intellectual or "rationall burning" (938–40)—burning not of the body or flesh but of the soul and mind.

As I make my way through the amusement and even laughter now palpable in the classroom (and I do want my students to have fun with the material, although there are always a few who accept Milton's reading outright), I emphasize several points to which I have just been alluding. I underscore Milton's elevation of the spiritual and intellectual over the carnal in matters pertaining to matrimony and divorce—all the while asking students, some now convinced of Milton's sexual anxieties, to reflect on the significance of conversation in their own relationships (and to which we return when studying Adam's sustained exchange with Raphael). I discuss, too, Milton's weaving together of scriptural place with place in the advancement of local and larger arguments, a well-established strategy of reading that they themselves might be said to use in the writing of their own papers. And I tease out, with extensive use of the board, the tract's early claims to be reading—against custom, canon, superstition, and tradition—for the spirit rather than "meere *element* of the Text" (935; my emphasis). Indeed, I foreground the repeated and variously articulated attacks on the "obstinate *literality*" and "alphabeticall servility" (949) of failed readers who, Milton argues, everywhere misinterpret scripture—his rejection of the literal, I note, as fierce as his rejection of the carnal.

To make more meaningful for my students this idea of reading for the spirit or "the letter of the Text" (936), especially as some are still reeling from Milton's gender bias, devaluation of the sexual, or seemingly wild interpretation of "*It is better to marry then to burn*" (939), I find it useful at this point to shift gears. Putting aside all questions about sex and gender, matrimony and divorce, I take a moment to examine Milton's passing—and scathing—critique of an "*elementally* understood" Eucharist as being "against nature and sense" (965; my emphasis). Here I note what some in my class can by now recognize as the characteristically anti-Catholic sentiment evident in Milton's gloss; however, I am most interested in leading students to reflect on their own hermeneutical sense of communion. Much could be said here about the multiple translations of relevant proof texts giving rise to varying views of the Eucharist (consider, if you will, debates about the Latin *hoc est corpus meum*). And one could usefully pause—as I increasingly do—over the Lord's Supper as it is presented in the Thirty-Nine Articles of Religion of the Anglican Church (see article 28). One might even wish to note that Protestant theologians (say John Calvin, Martin Luther, and Huldrych Zwingli) offered subtly different observations about (and readings of) the elemental presence, or absence, of Christ's body and blood in the bread and wine.[3] But in an attempt to make the problem of interpretation real for my students (who, after all, are resistant to anything biblical), I invite them to describe their own understanding of not only transubstantiation but also the long contested and still debated meaning of "those words," as Milton sharply writes, "of *Take, eat, this is my body*" (965). Reliably, students themselves, at least those who have taken communion and who are now in dialogue with one another and with Milton, bring to life—and into the classroom— hermeneutical questions and competing religious views that continue, they suddenly realize, to this day.

That contestation of meaning ideally still dancing in their heads (and also laying groundwork for later discussion of the many styles of eating and of worship depicted in *Paradise Lost*), I move next to the problem Milton faces in reconciling the apparently competing positions on divorce expressed by Moses, "an author great beyond exception," and by Christ, "one yet greater" (933): the first presumably allows for divorce on the basis of spiritual or intellectual discord, as Milton wants; the second for what seems only the carnal act of "*fornication*," a word whose "variously significant" meaning, my students soon learn, especially those who consult the *Oxford English Dictionary* as I encourage, will allow for some variety of spiritual incompatibility (968). Having by this point discussed Milton's many references to Deuteronomy 24.1, we now begin to examine Milton's analysis of Christ's strict remarks on divorce, an analysis to which *Doctrine* everywhere alludes in its first half but does not actually articulate until chapters 8 and 9 of book 2. To help prepare for that remarkable staging of dialogue and hermeneutical debate, I ask students to review relevant passages in Matthew and Mark and to consider what might be at stake for Milton in the exchange between Christ and the Pharisees. In addition, I bring to this textual moment Milton's observations, scattered throughout the tract but appearing first in the address to Parliament, about "honest liberty" and "dishonest license" (931), observations that have to do as much with politics and human conduct (Milton indicates) as with the act of reading itself. Finally, with these and other details in mind, we move systematically through those passages in which Milton is claiming not only to read the relevant proof texts correctly—or with what he would call honest liberty—and so recover from received, misguided, and too literalist views the proper meaning and spirit of Christ's words. He is claiming, I show my class, to read Christ reading and correcting the unwarily expounding Pharisees, who are not only misreading—and abusing with dishonest license— the Mosaic law of divorce but also attempting to trick and tempt a wise and knowing Christ. (And, here, *Doctrine's* anticipation of *Paradise Regained*, which I try to get to by the semester's end, is absolutely stunning.)

When students (and not only Catholic students) show understandable skepticism about Milton's elaboration of Christ's audience-specific—in some sense

even dissembling—remarks to the Pharisees (and I always note Milton is neither the first nor the last to interpret the exchange in the fashion that he does),
I offer several comments. My prompts are intended not to convince students of
Milton's position but to help keep their eyes and their ears open to what *Doctrine* is proposing and how it is making its case. To that end, I ask my class not
only to bear in mind the idea of reading for the letter versus the spirit; not only
to recall, as Milton repeatedly notes, Christ's claim to change not one jot of the
moral Law (the ceremonial rite of carnal circumcision, I remind them, not included); nor merely to recall what they have already begun to learn from Milton's "Letter to a Friend" or, say, "When I consider" (*Riverside* 1049–50;
255–56)—that Christ speaks in riddles, parables, and hyperbole, and so in
terms requiring, as *Doctrine* regularly advises, wary expounding and "heed in
glossing" (934). I also ask that they reflect on how their own—and, as they come
to realize, rarely transparent—speech acts are shaped by those they are addressing (professors, parents, partners), the interlocutors to whom they are responding (friends, classmates, enemies), the contexts in which they are speaking
(friendly, neutral, hostile). Leading into a brief lecture on the history, literary
examples, and possible purposes of dissembling—and on this topic, Perez
Zagorin's *Ways of Lying* is invaluable—my last question tends to prompt in students surprisingly useful reflection on the exchanges in which they themselves
engage and the one being staged in *Doctrine*. In fact, studying this particular
portion of Milton's 1644 divorce tract sets up for more complex—and considerably less naive—evaluation of dialogue in the major poems.

My teaching of *Doctrine* is never as neat as the above might suggest. And, in
the two weeks I devote to the tract, I cover many other points, including, for example, Milton's critique of hypocrisy, of an outwardly held but inwardly broken
marriage contract: and here, selections from *The Tenure of Kings and Magistrates* (*Riverside* 1068) and even *Paradise Regained* (4.518–19) can help bring
into view Milton's unfolding conception of covenants that are empty and false;
contracts whose conditions are not met; relations that do not stand. I also discuss Milton's astonishing amplification of argument, made often through scripture, in his move from the 1643 to 1644 edition of *Doctrine* (for this, the text
provided in the Yale edition of the collected prose [*Complete Prose Works* 2:
217–356], which I make available to my students, is essential). And I acknowledge directly Milton's occasionally wild and wary, arguably even dissembling,
use of evidence—and here one need only look to some of the footnotes in the
Complete Prose Works to see how many times Milton fudges (by reading too literally or too widely) the meaning of texts, translations, and commentaries he
claims so honestly to cite. To demonstrate this last point (and there are many
examples from which one might choose), I have once or twice brought to my
classroom multiple translations of and commentaries on the highly contested
text of Malachi (2.10–16)—materials that would have been available to Milton
and to whose details and variants he selectively refers (see bk. 1, chs. 6–7). With
Milton's text before them, but now side by side with some of his source materials,

students can see with relative ease *Doctrine*'s subtle absorption of and creative engagement with the variously translated terms and concerns of a postexilic prophet who condemns Hebrew husbands for dealing treacherously with God, nation, and wife—a prophet in whom Milton would find an unqualified sanctioning of divorce and so link seamlessly (some might say successfully) to Moses. However, and as students often remark, the prophet's letter *and* spirit do not easily advance *Doctrine*'s purposes—even, that is, when we allow for the translation by Calvin that Milton claims to prefer (see *Complete Prose Works* 2: 257n16). Finally, and depending on the strength of a given group, I try always to cover the tract's analysis (in bk. 1, chs. 7–8) of mixed conjugal ties, spousal conversion, and the "ground of divorcing an Idolatresse" (942): an analysis that leads to a more informed understanding of Milton's view of the foreign in general and his depiction of Dalila in particular; an analysis at which Milton arrives, I slowly lay out for my class, through fast-moving citation and elaboration of Old and New Testament proof texts; an analysis in which the "cov'nant of grace" (943) appears to supersede, at least at this point in the tract, "that great Cov'nant" associated with the "law" ("Upon the Circumcision" 55).

I acknowledge the challenges of my objectives: students are more than a little resistant to the material; and time constraints permit me to focus on a limited number of issues—and to do so in only an introductory fashion. Still, even the smallest consideration of *Doctrine*'s reading practices allows me to highlight a range of questions to which we, along with Milton, return, and to introduce, as gently as I can, and through the tract's storehouse of information, key concepts that will deepen class engagement with everything we go on to study. After two weeks on *Doctrine*, in which scriptural exegesis and the problem of interpretation have been brought front and center—foregrounded equally with issues of gender, matrimony, and divorce—students are simply less afraid to pick up the Bible and explore on their own (for, say, a mid-semester paper) one of the many references in *Doctrine* that went unexamined in class. Many are better able (some even eager) to consider Milton's fidelity to and creative departures from authorizing proof texts as we turn to *Paradise Lost* and *Samson Agonistes*. And a few can appreciate, at least more than they might otherwise, the complex relation this poet and polemicist is always working out between the terms and concerns of Old and New Testament materials. Most broadly, though, by exploring even *some* of the exegetical energies of *Doctrine*—a tract in which Milton cites so many biblical fragments, works so hard to negotiate Hebrew and Christian proof texts, and brings into view so many translations and interpretations he can embrace, reject, and altogether rewrite—students get to see for themselves the hotly contested and overdetermined ground of scripture itself: a ground of meaning shaping all manner of early modern literature and life; a ground of meaning on which seventeenth-century writers thought through and fought over every personal, political, and social dilemma they faced; a ground of meaning to which Milton sometimes wildly, sometimes warily, but always provocatively returns.

NOTES

[1] My teaching of *Doctrine* has been informed by the groundbreaking work of Jason Rosenblatt (*Torah*) and of Dayton Haskin (*Milton's Burden*), whose 1994 book-length studies helped open up radically new ways of thinking about Milton's reading practices.

[2] Allowing different translations of the Bible—indeed, inviting students to read aloud multiple versions of the same proof texts—has turned out to be pedagogically useful. The practice helps students see more clearly some of the subtleties of scriptural transmission and exegesis; it makes more meaningful Milton's sharp critique of corrupt translation as misguided interpretation; and it teaches students to appreciate *and* ask questions of Milton's often dazzling interpretive claims.

[3] See Anne Barbeau Gardiner's rich and lucid treatment of early modern debates on the interpretation of key Eucharistic texts; see also Timothy Rosendale, whose illuminating study of Milton and Hobbes brings into clear and exciting view the radical (and radically diverse) consequences of the Book of Common Prayer's "remaking of the Eucharist into a newly representational event" (149).

On Christian Doctrine:
Teaching the Conflict and What's at Stake

David V. Urban

The 1823 discovery of *On Christian Doctrine* (*De Doctrina Christiana*) marked a watershed in the study of John Milton. This lengthy Latin theological treatise, published in 1825 with an English translation by Bishop Charles Sumner, offered a heterodox examination of the Trinity and of a number of other subjects, shocking the many readers who had long regarded Milton as the greatest orthodox Christian poet in the English language. Most disturbingly, *On Christian Doctrine* espoused Arianism, which taught that the Son of God was not of the same essence as God the Father but rather was a uniquely exalted and worshipped created being. The profound ramifications of *Christian Doctrine's* Arianism are often not understood in our comparatively secular age. Arianism, championed by the Libyan deacon Arius in the early fourth century, was rejected by the Nicene Council of 325, which firmly established the "orthodox" Trinitarian position on the Son and explicitly condemned those who held Arian beliefs. The Nicene Creed—which describes the Son as "begotten, not made, being of one essence with the Father," over and against Arian theology, is still affirmed by the major branches of Christianity today.[1] Simply put, *Christian Doctrine* revealed the revered poet to be a teacher of a damnable heresy, for, as the Athanasian Creed states, those who do not believe in the full deity of the Son "cannot be saved," because, among other things, the orthodox position held that the created Arian Son of God would be incapable, in his incarnation as Jesus Christ, of propitiating the Father's holy wrath against sinful humanity; consequently, those who trusted their redemption to an Arian Christ would be trusting in one who could not offer genuine forgiveness of sins.[2] *On Christian Doctrine* eventually became and continues to be a frequently used tool by which to interpret Milton's other works, especially *Paradise Lost*, a practice most famously seen in Maurice Kelley's 1941 *This Great Argument: A Study of Milton's* De Doctrina Christiana *as a Gloss upon* Paradise Lost. This study contains numerous passages from *Paradise Lost* beside related passages in *Christian Doctrine*, along with Kelley's commentary on their interrelation, including a sizable emphasis on demonstrating that *Paradise Lost's* presentation of God the Son is also Arian. One of the most influential studies of Milton in the twentieth century, Kelley's work has significantly affected Milton pedagogy, for many instructors have adopted Kelley's methodology in the classroom; consequently, showing students connections between the treatise and Milton's epic has often been the prime emphasis in the teaching of *Christian Doctrine*.

Any discussion of the treatise became significantly complicated by William B. Hunter's 1992 *SEL* article, "The Provenance of the *Christian Doctrine*." In it, Hunter argues that Milton did not write *On Christian Doctrine*. Hunter's article was, in that same issue of *SEL*, directly followed by Forum responses by Barbara K. Lewalski and John T. Shawcross defending Miltonic authorship, and the authorship debate concerning the treatises continues to this day,[3] affording instructors an exciting opportunity. I have found that "teaching the conflict," to borrow Gerald Graff's phrase, is a highly profitable approach for a number of reasons: it encourages students to consider carefully the most serious controversy in Milton studies of recent years; it allows them not only to compare passages of *Christian Doctrine* with those in *Paradise Lost* and other indisputably Miltonic works but also to think more deeply about the consequences of drawing such connections; and it allows students to understand what may be professionally at stake for scholars who argue for or against Miltonic authorship.

Because *On Christian Doctrine* is generally taught in courses devoted to Milton and not in survey courses (although it could profitably be taught in a survey of seventeenth-century British literature that has a significant focus on Milton), I will gear my discussion with such a course in mind. I recommend including a day on the treatise toward the end of the class, after having completed *Paradise Lost* and *Paradise Regained*—and, I would hope, *The Doctrine and Discipline of Divorce*, *Areopagitica*, and any other assigned prose that offers passages similar to those in *Christian Doctrine*.

Roy Flannagan's offering in the *Riverside Milton* is sufficient (1156–201), although some important chapters are not present and selections from some chapters are so generous that they can be overwhelming. Scott Elledge offers a more judicious selection in the Norton Critical Edition of *Paradise Lost* (Milton, *Paradise Lost* 396–428), although it too has its shortcomings. I recommend assigning the following sections (almost all from book 1), ideally using Elledge's selections, although Flannagan's could work for my lesson plan and the selections not found in Flannagan could be omitted: Milton's preface or "epistle" ("John Milton, Englishman"); book 1, chapter 1 ("What Christian Doctrine Is"; not found in Elledge, but Flannagan has it); chapter 2 ("Of God"); chapter 3 ("Of Divine Decree"; not found in Flannagan); chapter 4 ("Of Predestination"); chapter 5 (preface and "Of the Son of God"); and chapter 30 ("Of the Holy Scripture"; not found in Flannagan). To "teach the conflict," I also assign Hunter's article and Lewalski's response, as well as Hunter's brief Forum response to Lewalski and Shawcross. Finally, in an effort to show students what's at stake for an important Milton scholar who defends Miltonic authorship of the treatise, I assign brief passages from Lewalski's outstanding biography, *The Life of John Milton*, in which her analysis of the Son in *Paradise Lost* and *Paradise Regained* is predicated on her conviction—based on *Christian Doctrine*—that Milton was an Arian and that his poetic depiction of the Son reflects his Arianism.

I accompany the assignments with the following questions for discussion:

1. What kind of a person do we see in both the highly self-referential preface and the opening chapter of *On Christian Doctrine*? How does his methodology

of using his own understanding of "the Holy Scriptures alone" to conduct his theological investigation reveal a certain kind of character? Do we see parallels in any works indisputably written by Milton?

2. Do you see specific ways in which *Christian Doctrine* offers insight into other, indisputably Miltonic texts, particularly *Paradise Lost*? (See #5 below for an especially important consideration.)

3. Do you find Hunter's arguments concerning the provenance of *Christian Doctrine* convincing? Why or why not?

4. Do you find Lewalski's response to Hunter convincing? Why or why not?

5. According to Lewalski, how does the Arian depiction of the Son of God in *Christian Doctrine*, book 1, chapter 5, give insight to our understanding of the Son in *Paradise Lost* and *Paradise Regained*? (See *Life of John Milton* 473–74 and 513–14.)

6. What do critics such as Lewalski have invested in the treatise's being authentically Miltonic? What is at stake for such critics? What would the effect be if Miltonic authorship were definitively disproved?

7. What new avenues of inquiry and scholarship are opened up by the controversy?

The remainder of my essay discusses how I have taught and how my students have responded to these questions.

Question 1   Students generally comment—with a mixture of amusement and annoyance—on the self-confident, even arrogant manner of the author of the prefatory epistle. I emphasize here that even Hunter grudgingly later acknowledges that the epistle is probably authentically Miltonic (*Visitation* 156; this work is Hunter's book-length defense of his position), an opinion shared more enthusiastically by other Miltonists who strongly question the authenticity of large portions of the treatise (Campbell, Corns, Hale, Holmes, and Tweedie 108;[4] Lieb, "*De Doctrina*" 177–79). Particularly notable are Milton's disdain for those theologians whose efforts have preceded his and his assurance that he, through his own diligent study of the Bible, can succeed in representing rightly true Christian doctrine where all others have failed. At this point I show how this same attitude is demonstrated on the frontispiece of the 1644 *Doctrine and Discipline of Divorce*, where Milton proclaims that his tract restores this doctrine "[f]rom the bondage of CANON LAW, to the true meaning of Scripture in the Law and Gospel" (*Complete Prose Works* 2: 221; this edition should be brought to class as a visual aid, as the frontispiece is not included in the *Riverside*). I also note that Milton's invocation of the parable of the householder (Matt. 13.52) on the frontispiece—and his implicit connection between himself and the scribe of that parable[5]—is echoed in *Christian Doctrine* book 1, chapter 1, where Milton again emphasizes the primacy of the Bible and quotes Matthew 13.52, implicitly comparing himself with its scribe (*Riverside* 1160; Urban). The audacious confidence of the preface and first chapter also coincides well with the epic writer who compares himself to Moses while "pursu[ing] / Things unattempted yet in Prose or Rhime" (*PL* 1.15–16), although one student noted that the speaker in *Paradise Lost*'s invocations also demonstrates a kind of awed humility before his task. The arrogance of *Christian Doctrine*'s epistle is also tempered somewhat at its end, where Milton suggests that his readers, if guided by "God's spirit" and relying on the "clear evidence of the Bible" alone, can access his findings rightly (1159).

Lewalski's response offers a convenient aid for seeing parallels between the epistle and *Areopagitica* (regarding free inquiry) and between the epistle and the Bucer divorce tract (regarding the primacy of scripture [Forum response 148]). Her connection between the preface of book 1, chapter 5, and *The Doctrine and Discipline of Divorce* (regarding scripture and reason [149]) is also valuable.[6]

Question 2   Here is where instructors may profitably make use of Kelley's book and methodology. For my purposes, comparisons between *On Christian Doctrine*'s discussions of free will (bk. 1, ch. 3) and predestination (bk. 1, ch. 4) and *Paradise Lost* 3.92–134 and 183–202 are especially helpful (cf. Maurice Kelley 77–84 and Lewalski, Forum response 150),[7] as is comparison of the treatise's discussion of the Son of God (bk. 1, ch. 5) with *Paradise Lost* 3.138–40 and 383–92 (cf. Maurice Kelley 84–106, esp. 84–86). On this last point, however, I call attention to Hunter's reminder that people read *Paradise Lost* for many years with very few accusing him of Arianism.

Questions 3 and 4   Most students find Hunter persuasive, especially before they read Lewalski's response. This exchange is a good place to start addressing the matter of what's at stake, for students' personal commitments can come out here strongly, especially if the instructor introduces this subject in a respectful manner. Students with strong Trinitarian commitments (common at my college) have discussed how quickly they sided with Hunter and wanted him to be correct. Those less sympathetic to traditional Christian orthodoxy can have the opposite response. I try to use such responses to point out how scholars' own commitments, be they influenced by their religion or their past scholarship, can make a particular position on *Christian Doctrine*'s authorship more attractive. Once students have this in mind, Hunter generally gains some credibility because his argument against Miltonic authorship (and his new recognition of the treatise as a heterodox text) contradicts his previous scholarship ("Milton's Arianism").[8] At the same time, my students have generally felt that Lewalski's response successfully answers most but not all of Hunter's concerns.[9] After reading Lewalski, students find Hunter's essay less compelling, but it continues to cast what a number of students call "reasonable doubt" on Miltonic authorship.

Question 5   In her *Life of John Milton*, Lewalski's interpretation of Milton's Son in *Paradise Lost* and *Paradise Regained* is heavily dependent on her belief, based on *Christian Doctrine*, that Milton writes from an Arian perspective. Since Milton's Son "is not omnipotent or omniscient or eternal," Milton can "portray the Son [in *Paradise Lost*] as a genuinely dramatic and heroic figure" who can act freely and have "genuine dialogue with the Father" (473). In *Paradise Regained*, Lewalski contends that "Milton's Arianism is central to this poem, allowing for some drama in the debate-duel between Jesus and Satan" (513). I ask students to consider if the aforementioned drama and heroism in *Paradise Lost* and *Paradise Regained* must be predicated on an Arian Son. Were these poems less dramatic to them before reading *Christian Doctrine* and Lewalski? Was such drama not present for Milton's readers before the discovery of the treatise? Furthermore, if one reads Luke's and Matthew's gospel accounts of Jesus's temptation in the wilderness (on which *Paradise Regained* is based) from a Trinitarian perspective, can those accounts still contain genuine drama? Is Jesus less heroic in the gospels if one reads them from a Trinitarian perspective? Indeed, what consequences does Lewalski's perspective have on any reading of the gospels as literature?

Question 6   As students become increasingly aware that a good deal of Milton scholarship—including, for example, Lewalski's *Milton's Brief Epic*—is dependent on the assumption that Milton wrote *On Christian Doctrine* in its entirety,[10] they come to recognize how much such scholars have at stake in this controversy and how personally invested they may be in defending Miltonic authorship of the treatise. In no way do I accuse such scholars of having tainted judgment. But it is valuable, especially for those students considering graduate school, to be aware of the various concerns involved in any literary controversy. I also inform students that many recent critical works that include discussion of *On Christian Doctrine* now offer a disclaimer, often acknowledging Hunter's arguments as challenging but not finally persuasive and stating that Milton will be considered the treatise's author throughout that critical work (e.g., Fish, *How Milton Works* 15–19).

Question 7   One opportunity the provenance controversy affords is, as one student observed, the chance to study *Paradise Lost* and other texts with a fresh perspective that need not be shaped by *On Christian Doctrine*, a shaping potentially stifling and pedantic. I recommend teaching the treatise after students have had the chance to read other relevant texts in their entirety and then offering it as a possible but not necessary vehicle of interpretation. Another student commented that participating in this present controversy makes the "old" texts affected by it come alive in new ways. In terms of scholarship, I discuss Michael Lieb's recent insight that the mystery surrounding *On Christian Doctrine* and its various amanuenses, its transmission, and its translation has ensured that Milton's role (or lack thereof) in the treatise will forever remain speculative ("*De Doctrina*" 172).[11] In the light of Lieb's analysis, perhaps a valuable perspective from which to view *Christian Doctrine* is now to consider which sections are more or less Miltonic and why. Finding convincing parallels between an indisputably Miltonic piece and a section of the treatise may strongly suggest that section to be Miltonic, but this does not mean the entire text is.[12] This perspective, then, only furthers opportunities in the Milton scholarly industry, for it allows the work's provenance to be discussed extensively on a micro level without necessitating a definitive judgment regarding its whole.

NOTES

I would like to thank Calvin College, whose Calvin Research Fellowships and additional pedagogical funding supported the writing of this essay. Thanks also to former Calvin students John Cooper, Jonathan Dawes, Adam Forrest, Leslie Harkema, Matthew Jensen, Nathan Sytsma, and Abram Van Engen and to former Oklahoma Baptist University students Brent Newsom and Ashley Wells for their special help with this project.

[1] For a convenient, thorough, and well-documented online summary of these matters, see Hinks.

[2] The Westminster Larger Catechism, completed in 1647, discussed the relation between Christ's deity and his atoning work on the cross as follows: "Question 38: Why was it requisite that the Mediator should be God? Answer: It was requisite that the Mediator should be God, that he might sustain and keep the human nature from sinking under the infinite wrath of God, and the power of death; give worth and efficacy to his sufferings, obedience, and intercession; and to satisfy God's justice, procure his favor, purchase a peculiar people, give his Spirit to them, conquer all their enemies, and bring them to everlasting salvation" ("Larger Catechism" 145–46). An earlier Reformed articulation of this theological matter is found in question 14 of the Heidelberg Catechism (1563): "Q. Why must he [the mediator between God and humanity] also be true God? A. So that, by the power of his divinity, he might bear the weight of God's anger in his humanity and earn for us and restore to us righteousness and life" ("Heidelberg" 18).

[3] A recent major article on the subject is Lieb, "*De Doctrina Christiana* and the Question of Authorship." Lieb's survey of the scholarship on the topic is valuable.

[4] The influential report by Campbell, Corns, Hale, Holmes, and Tweedie, which uses quantitative computer analysis to investigate *Christian Doctrine*'s provenance, expresses considerable doubt concerning Milton's authorship of the treatise. The report's methodology, however, has recently been challenged by Rumrich ("Provenance").

[5] Milton's 1644 rendition of Matthew 13.52 is, "Every Scribe instructed to the Kingdome of Heav'n, is like the Maister of a house ["householder" in the King James Version] which bringeth out of his treasury things new and old."

[6] Additional parallels may be found in Lewalski's "Milton and the *De Doctrina Christiana*: *Evidences of Authorship*." But note also Sellin's response to this article ("Further Responses").

[7] For a learned challenge to such parallels between *On Christian Doctrine* and *Paradise Lost*, see Sellin, "John Milton's *Paradise Lost*."

[8] The most thorough defense of Milton's Arianism in *On Christian Doctrine* and *Paradise Lost* is Bauman. But note Lieb, who argues that Milton's heterodox position on the Son should not be categorized as Arian (*Theological Milton* 261–78).

[9] The most thorough recent refutation of Hunter's position is Shawcross, *Rethinking* 139–51.

[10] As Hunter notes in "Provenance," other important works shaped by the assumption of Milton's Arianism include C. Hill's *Milton and the English Revolution* and Radzino-wicz's *Toward* Samson Agonistes.

[11] It is worth noting that in an even more recent work, Lieb appears to move away from such skepticism, declaring, "I am a firm believer in Miltonic authorship" of *On Christian Doctrine*. Lieb, however, continues to affirm "that Milton's exact presence in the manuscript of the theological treatise is obscured by a host of factors" (*Theological Milton* 4).

[12] Students should know that any such comparative analysis of *On Christian Doctrine* will ideally use the Latin text over the English translations. Lieb notes how the proof sheets of Sumner's 1825 translation (the translation that appears in Columbia University Press's *The Works of John Milton* [vols. 14–17], side by side with the Latin text) were tampered with by the young poet William Sidney Walker, who "not only revised and corrected the proof sheets but altered the translation (without Sumner's approval) so that the results were more nearly in keeping with the language of Milton's own writings" (*"De Doctrina"* 188–89). Lieb also expresses concern about the John Carey translation (which appears as volume 6 of the *Complete Prose Works* with no accompanying Latin text), asserting that it too is largely interpretive and significantly removed from the Latin (193–94). Lieb goes on to voice skepticism over the reliability of even the received Latin text of the treatise (195–209).

The Ready and Easy Way:
Milton's Utopia?

Matthew Woodcock

Undergraduates at Oxford University typically study Milton's prose and later poetry in a course on English literature 1642 to 1740. My teaching of the course involved leading a series of group seminars followed by individual tutorials that started with *Areopagitica* and *Of Education* before moving on to the political treatises. I used to invite students to compare and contrast attitudes to monarchy in *The Tenure of Kings and Magistrates* and *The Ready and Easy Way* within the context of interregnum politics. One frequently emphasizes the importance of response and occasion when teaching Milton's earlier poetry, and exposition of context is vital for understanding the motivation and conviction behind *The Ready and Easy Way* (*Riverside* 1134–49) and its breathless, millenarian tone. Milton wrote the treatise's first edition in February 1660, during which time General George Monck restored to the Rump Parliament the conservative and Presbyterian members excluded from it in Pride's Purge (1648), initiating the final reconfigurations of parliamentary rule that resulted a month later in the Convention Parliament that would restore Charles II on 8 May. Milton's second edition (used here) appears in early April when the "noxious humor of returning to bondage" (1136) presented an imminent threat to the declining Commonwealth. I felt, however, that the teaching of the political treatises too often inclined toward content at the cost of attention to literary form, ignoring Milton's prose style. This essay introduces the discursive model I developed for a reworked seminar on *The Ready and Easy Way* to foreground the treatise's genre and mode of argument.

The seminar takes the form of a structured debate proposing that Milton's treatise can be discussed in relation to the subgenre of utopian literature; the question to which students are directed throughout is, "To what extent is it productive to place *The Ready and Easy Way* within the tradition of utopian writings?" My overall aim is for students to examine a critical faultline in Milton studies, an argument mooted by several earlier critics but one that can be explored anew through group discussions and assessment of textual evidence to stimulate close reading and discursive skills. Many of the more recent treatments of *The Ready and Easy Way*'s style and genre read the text as a jeremiad, a "prophetic lament over the apostasy of a chosen nation" in the mode of Old Testament prophet Jeremiah (Knoppers, "Milton's *The Readie and Easie Way*" 213). Milton presents the English people's desire to return to monarchy as a moral backsliding comparable to the Israelites' desire to return to Egypt and thus servitude (1148). I find, however, that utopian writing offers students a far more familiar imaginative model to which to cling as they read Milton's treatise. Most of my students by this point have studied Thomas More's *Utopia* and

Francis Bacon's *New Atlantis*, and their expectations of the form prove a contentious stimulus for debate. Prior to the class I also set selected passages from James Harrington's 1656 *Commonwealth of Oceana* (and as supplementary reading survey studies on Renaissance utopias by J. C. Davis and James Holstun), which, although a far less playful text than More's *Utopia*, offers a utopian model that Milton in part addresses in *The Ready and Easy Way*. *Oceana* offers a further example of one of the central tropes (used in Milton's text and other utopian writings) that we examine at the outset: *topothesia*, the construction and description of an actual or contrived location, usually for didactic ends. *The Ready and Easy Way* depicts yet another feigned commonwealth among the wide variety produced by early modern writers to model and directly advocate alternative forms of political and social order.

Duly prepared, I split the class into three and ask each group to address different portions of the text in the light of the utopian thesis and then to report back. The first group considers political organization. At the heart of Milton's proposal for a free commonwealth is the Grand Council of "ablest men, chosen by the people to consult of public affairs from time to time for the common good" (1141). Students are directed (and respond) to several major points concerning election to the council ("How do you react to a proposal for a free commonwealth that offers such a limited conception of franchise?") and the importance of education in an enlightened oligarchy. With Milton's observation in mind that "[t]o make the people fittest to chuse, and the chosen fittest to govern, will be to mend our corrupt and faulty education" (1143), we also look back to *Of Education* and consider the relative consistency of his attitude to the utilitarian pedagogical framework necessary to train the ideal form of proposed leadership. Unlike most utopias, Milton's commonwealth relies on the present governmental system's continued existence in a perfected form, and students often identify a great sense of nostalgia in how the poet writes of what is required for the present and future and note the consequent lack of specifics regarding the realization of his proposals. For example, Milton emphasizes that the council would fail under a constitutional monarchy (1144–45) but says comparatively little about how it could be established in the existing conditions. Ultimately Milton's argument registers that the victory over monarchy so dearly remembered throughout *The Ready and Easy Way* did not automatically secure longevity of the English republic. As recent world politics has shown, it is often easier to remove a power structure (however corrupt) than to successfully establish another. Students also begin to question exactly how convincing they find Milton's arguments concerning the perpetual, static nature of the council and take issue with his dismissal of Harrington's "partial rotation" using little more than a simple analogy to the "wheel of fortune" (1141), since Milton concedes later that rotation of a third of the council might prevent corruption (1148).

The second seminar group considers social organization and looks to *Utopia* for constructive parallels. Students compare Milton's text with substantive features of More's feigned commonwealth, including education, local administration of justice, the role of the military, and trade. I go on to ask why Milton fails to propose dividing the community into various political roles (akin to More's tranibores or phylarchs) and prefers to concentrate on the centralized Grand Council, and we question just how far Milton's proposals realistically address politics on a national scale. Also significant to consider is Milton's commitment to religious and civil rights, and while the poet is again less clear on the structure of religion in his free commonwealth, he lauds an individual's liberty of conscience as the key to integrity in the state (1146–47); I ask students to keep this in mind when they explore the problem of free will and its consequences in book 9 of *Paradise Lost*. The third group examines the first part of *The Ready and Easy Way* (1136–40), in which Milton writes about initial hopes for the English republic, its progressive decline, the abhorrence of monarchy (one can introduce selected passages from *The Tenure* here), and the Christlike virtues of commonwealths. My principal question is, "How does this first part of the treatise relate to Milton's proposals for the Grand Council and free commonwealth?" I also ask if we can relate this section to book 1 of *Utopia*, which—while probably written after book 2—presents initial arguments for the desirability of Utopian policies before treating more specific political and social details. *The Ready and Easy Way*'s first section provides the rationale for the details to follow, evoking nostalgia for what was lost and instilling an urgency about the need to reform. It also works hard to secure an implied agreement for Milton's subsequent (far less solidly proposed) model for a free commonwealth by stressing the abhorrence of the alternative (monarchy) and drawing in the reader through judicious use of collective as well as singular first-person pronouns.

I draw attention during the seminar to techniques used in utopists' writings and how they appear in the essay. Early on Milton establishes a carnivalesque, satirical stance through asking for "a little Shroving-time" wherein to speak freely before a "Lent of Servitude" (1136), and his language throughout aggressively chides the folly of the populace for ignorantly backsliding toward monarchy and subjugation. In its density of imagery and extensive use of adjectives, *The Ready and Easy Way* stands out from the more "sober" style of Milton's other late prose (Corns, *Development* 65), and I particularly pursue the continuing image of contagion as we reread the tract. Narrative style is also a fertile area for discussion. Can we identify the alienated perspective of the outsider Raphael Hythlodaeus in Milton's lone calls for political vigilance? Who was the implied or real audience for the text's second edition? While the treatise's title sounds like that of a constitutional self-help manual, how convincing are Milton's repeated assurances that immediate political reform will be "easy"? Does the treatise offer a blueprint or a threat—a reasoned argument for reform or an exhortation devoid of detail, as Milton's immediate critics observed (Holstun 265)?

By this point in the course, students are familiar with the sustained irony of More's text. They are equally quick to point out that a utopian text seldom presents a wholly ideal social model and that overlap between perceived utopian and dystopian elements is a chief characteristic of the form. Milton's commonwealth is no exception. In his desperate attempt to forestall the imminent restoration of monarchy Milton elides the role of legislator and dictator, advocating the imposition of greater political and social control to ensure collective freedom from the monarchic yoke. *The Ready and Easy Way* thus offers a complex contrast to much of the earlier prose work on the importance of freedom in church government, divorce, and published expression. My questions here address the paradoxical nature of Milton's attitude to liberty in *The Ready and Easy Way*, and I point out the frequently denigrating language used to describe the English people (the "misguided and abus'd multitude" [1149]). Does Milton thus present a viable rather than an ideal alternative to monarchy? Can we also identify a difference between writing a utopia (according to a formal tradition and understood nomenclature) and expressing utopian ideas? The seminar demonstrates that genre study can move beyond reductive taxonomic ascription and become a useful stimulus for further questioning.

There are of course significant differences between Milton's treatise and *Utopia*, and it is as productive to identify these differences as it is to locate direct analogies. For a start, *The Ready and Easy Way* lacks the layer of commentary found in More or Harrington, where narrators respond critically to structures imposed by legislators Utopus or Lord Archon. It particularly lacks the reflexive critical dimension generated by the dialogic form of More's book 1, instead directing the satire wholly to figures and concepts outside of the text. Milton's commonwealth also lacks the exposition of specifics found in More and Harrington and is ultimately a reactive more than a constructive model. (Again students are asked to consider why this should be.) It is also vital to stress that, whereas More's Utopia was literally as well as onomastically "no-where," Milton desires to go one step beyond a text-based model of government, as he desperately petitions for the reification of his proposals for a free commonwealth. Following the seminar, students produce papers drawing on a fortnight's study responding to a choice of questions on Milton's views on liberty, political organization, literary form, or rhetorical and poetic self-fashioning.

The Ready and Easy Way provides a useful classroom bridge between the mid-century republican prose and *Paradise Lost*, not least because it begins pursuing the kind of "What went wrong?" questioning that continues at length in the epic, again using the construction of worlds deemed ideal or inviolate. The utopian dimension has been productive to explore subsequently in teaching Renaissance survey courses at institutions in London and Norwich as it links Milton's text, through other examples of *topothesia* such as Philip Sidney's Arcadia or Spenser's fairyland, to later seventeenth-century constructions of feigned commonwealths.

NOTES ON CONTRIBUTORS

Bruce Boehrer is Bertram H. Davis Professor of English Renaissance Literature at Florida State University and editor of the *Journal for Early Modern Cultural Studies*. His most recent book, *Parrot Culture*, appeared in 2004.

Gardner Campbell is professor of English at the University of Mary Washington, where he served as assistant vice president for Teaching and Learning Technologies from 2003 to 2006. He is a contributing editor of *A Variorum Edition of Milton's* Paradise Lost and has published essays on Milton in *Milton's Legacy* (2005) and in *Arenas of Conflict: Milton and the Unfettered Mind* (1997).

Alison A. Chapman is associate professor of English Renaissance literature at the University of Alabama, Birmingham. She has researched early modern conceptions of time in the wake of the Reformation, and her work appears in such journals as *SEL, Renaissance Quarterly, Modern Philology,* and *Journal for Medieval and Early Modern Studies*. She is working on a book about early modern Protestant uses of the medieval saints' lives.

Matthew Davis is senior editor at the Core Knowledge Foundation in Charlottesville, Virginia, and an independent scholar. He has taught at the University of Virginia and the College of William and Mary and published scholarly articles on Shakespeare, Samuel Johnson, and Robert Frost.

Stephen B. Dobranski, associate professor of English at Georgia State University, is the author of *Readers and Authorship in Early Modern England* (2005; winner of the South Atlantic Modern Language Association Studies Book Award) and *Milton, Authorship, and the Book Trade* (1999). He coedited *Milton and Heresy* (1998; winner of the Irene Samuel Memorial Award) and is currently completing *A Variorum Commentary on the Poems of John Milton:* Samson Agonistes.

Angelica Duran is associate professor of English and comparative literature at Purdue University. She is the author of *The Age of Milton and the Scientific Revolution* (2007) and the editor of *A Concise Companion to Milton* (2007). Her current book-length research is on Spanish-language representations of Milton.

Andrew Escobedo is associate professor of English literature at Ohio University. He has published articles on Spenser and Milton and a book on English nationalism in the Renaissance, *Nationalism and Historical Loss in Renaissance England: Foxe, Dee, Spenser, Milton* (2004).

James Dougal Fleming teaches at Simon Fraser University. He has published articles in *Exemplaria, ELH,* and *Milton Quarterly*. His current research is in early modern science, emblem studies, and hermeneutics.

Mark K. Fulk is associate professor of British literature at State University of New York, Buffalo State College, where he specializes in early modern and Enlightenment British literature. He has published articles on seventeenth-century women writers, John Dryden, and Jane Austen and is the author of *Understanding May Sarton* (2001). He was executive president of the Aphra Behn Society for Women in the Arts, 1660–1830, for four years.

Wendy Furman-Adams is professor of English and coordinator of gender and women's studies at Whittier College. Her publications—many written collaboratively with Virginia Tufte—have dealt mainly with *Paradise Lost* as an illustrated poem and have appeared in such venues as *Philological Quarterly, Huntington Library Quarterly, Milton Quarterly,* and *Milton Studies,* as well as in critical anthologies and in the forthcoming *Milton Encyclopedia.* She is coeditor of *Renaissance Rereadings: Intertext and Context* (1988) and *Riven Unities: Authority and Experience, Self and Other in Milton's Poetry* (1992). Furman-Adams and Tufte are at work on a book-length study called "Re-Visions: Four Women Artists Reading *Paradise Lost.*"

Lynne A. Greenberg is associate professor of English at Hunter College. She has published essays on Milton and is the editor the three-volume set *Essential Works for the Study of Early Modern Women: Legal Treatises* (2005).

Gina Hausknecht is associate professor of English at Coe College, Cedar Rapids, where she teaches British Renaissance literature. She has published articles on Milton and on seventeenth-century culture and currently writes the Milton section of *The Year's Work in English Studies.*

Peter C. Herman is professor of English and comparative literature at San Diego State University. He has published two books, *Destabilizing Milton:* Paradise Lost *and the Poetics of Incertitude* (2005) and *Squitter-Wits and Muse-Haters: Sidney, Spenser, Milton, and Renaissance Antipoetic Sentiment* (1996), and has edited *Historicizing Theory* (2004), *Day Late, Dollar Short: The Next Generation and the New Academy* (2000), and *Reading Monarchs Writing: The Poetry of Henry VIII, Mary, Queen of Scots, Elizabeth I, and James VI/I* (2002). His essays have appeared in such journals as *Renaissance Quarterly, SEL,* and *Criticism.*

Laura Lunger Knoppers is professor of English at Pennsylvania State University. She is author of *Historicizing Milton: Spectacle, Power, and Poetry in Restoration England* (1994) and editor, with Gregory Colón Semenza, of *Milton in Popular Culture* (2006). She is working on a scholarly edition of Milton's 1671 poems.

William Kolbrener is associate professor in the English department at Bar-Ilan University. He has written extensively on the literature and history of early modern England. His book *Milton's Warring Angels* was published in 1997. His most recent work is *Mary Astell: Reason, Gender, Faith,* coedited with Michal Michelson (2007).

Albert C. Labriola is professor of English and Distinguished University Professor at Duquesne University. He was named Honored Scholar of the Milton Society of America in 2000. He is editor of *Milton Studies,* general editor of medieval and Renaissance literary studies for Duquesne University Press, general editor of *A Variorum Commentary on the Poems of John Milton,* and volume editor for "Songs and Sonnets" in *The Variorum Edition of the Poetry of John Donne.*

Jameela Lares is associate professor of English at the University of Southern Mississippi. Her publications include *Milton and the Preaching Arts* (2001); articles in *Milton Studies, Ben Jonson Journal, Cithara, Notes and Queries, Advances in the History of Rhetoric, Dictionary of Literary Biography;* and numerous reviews. She is contributing editor for *Paradise Lost,* books 11 and 12, for *A Variorum Commentary on the Poems of John Milton* and is working on other publications on Milton, Renaissance preaching, and children's literature.

John Leonard is professor of English at the University of Western Ontario. He has published *Naming in Paradise: Milton and the Language of Adam and Eve* (1990), *Milton's Complete Poems* (1998), and an edition of *Paradise Lost* (2000), and he has a forthcoming edition of Milton's selected poems. He is completing a volume on *Paradise Lost* for the Milton Variorum Project.

Barbara K. Lewalski is William R. Kenan Professor of History and Literature and of English Literature at Harvard University. Her recent books include *The Life of John Milton: A Critical Biography* (2000; rev., 2003), *Writing Women in Jacobean England* (1993), and Paradise Lost *and the Rhetoric of Literary Forms* (1985). She is editor of the seventeenth-century section of the *Norton Anthology of English Literature* and of an original spelling and punctuation edition of *Paradise Lost* (2007).

Jennifer Lewin is assistant professor of English at the University of Kentucky, where she teaches early modern English literature including Milton. Her publications include an edited collection, *Never Again Would Birds' Song Be the Same: Essays on Early Modern and Modern Poetry in Honor of John Hollander* (2002), and articles in *Shakespeare Studies* and *Shakespeare International Yearbook*. She is finishing a manuscript, "Wild Work: Dreaming in Renaissance England."

David Loewenstein is Marjorie and Lorin Tiefenthaler Professor of English at the University of Wisconsin, Madison. His publications include *Milton and the Drama of History: Historical Vision, Iconoclasm, and the Literary Imagination* (1990), *Milton: Paradise Lost* (1993; 2nd ed., 2004), and *Representing Revolution in Milton and His Contemporaries: Religion, Politics, and Polemics in Radical Puritanism* (2001). He is the coeditor of *The Cambridge History of Early Modern English Literature* (2002), a two-time winner of the Milton Society of America's James Holly Hanford Award for Distinguished Book, and an Honored Scholar of the Milton Society of America.

Catherine Gimelli Martin is a Dunavant Professor at the University of Memphis. She is the author of *The Ruins of Allegory:* Paradise Lost *and the Metamorphosis of Epic Convention* (1998) and the editor of two anthologies, *Milton and Gender* (2004) and, with Julie Robin Solomon, *Francis Bacon and the Refiguring of Early Modern Thought: Essays to Commemorate "The Advancement of Learning" (1605–2005)* (2005).

David Mikics, professor of English at the University of Houston, is the author of essays on Shakespeare, Milton, contemporary poetry, and literary theory and of two books: *The Limits of Moralizing: Pathos and Subjectivity in Spenser and Milton* (1994) and *The Romance of Individualism in Emerson and Nietzsche* (2003). His *New Handbook of Literary Terms* is forthcoming in 2007.

Curtis Perry is professor of English at the University of Illinois, Urbana. In addition to articles on early modern literature and culture, he is the author of *The Making of Jacobean Culture: James I and the Renegotiation of Elizabethan Literary Practice* (1997) and editor of *Material Culture and Cultural Materialisms in the Middle Ages and the Renaissance* (2001). His most recent book is *Literature and Favoritism in Early Modern England* (2006).

Richard Rambuss is professor of English at Emory University. He is the author of *Spenser's Secret Career* (1993) and *Closet Devotions* (1998), as well as numerous essays on topics ranging from Renaissance literature to gender theory to film. He is at work editing a new edition of Richard Crashaw's poetry.

Jason P. Rosenblatt, professor of English at Georgetown University, is the author of *Torah and Law in* Paradise Lost (1994), *Renaissance England's Chief Rabbi: John Selden* (2006), and numerous articles on seventeenth-century England. He has coedited a book on biblical narrative and is under contract to produce a Norton Critical Edition of Milton's selected poetry and prose.

John Rumrich is A. J. and W. D. Thaman Professor of English at the University of Texas, Austin, where he teaches early modern literature and culture. He is the editor of the *Norton Critical Edition of Seventeenth-Century British Poetry, 1603–1660* (2005) and the author of *Milton Unbound: Controversy and Reinterpretation* (1996).

Elizabeth Harris Sagaser is an associate professor at Colby College, where she teaches sixteenth- and seventeenth-century poetry as well as poetry and poetics from other time periods. Her critical essays on Shakespeare, Daniel, Spenser, Mary Sidney Herbert, and teaching Renaissance poetry have appeared or are forthcoming in *ELH*, *Exemplaria*, *Spenser Studies*, the *Sidney Journal*, and *Renaissance Literature and Its Formal Engagements* (2002). Her poems have appeared in various literary magazines.

Elizabeth Sauer, professor of English, was awarded a Chancellor's Chair for Research Excellence at Brock University, Canada. Her publications include *"Paper-Contestations" and Textual Communities in England, 1640–1675* (2005) and *Barbarous Dissonance and Images of Voice in Milton's Epics* (1996). She has edited nine editions, among them *Imperialisms: Historical and Literary Investigations, 1500–1900*, with Balachandra Rajan (2004); *Reading Early Modern Women*, with Helen Ostovich (2004; winner of the Society for the Study of Early Modern Women Best Collaborative Work Award); and *Milton and the Imperial Vision*, with Balachandra Rajan (1999; winner of the Milton Society of America Irene Samuel Memorial Award). She is editor of *Milton and the Climates of Reading* (2006) and has recently completed *Milton and Toleration*, edited with Sharon Achinstein (2007).

John T. Shawcross, professor of English emeritus at the University of Kentucky, is author of *The Arms of the Family: The Significance of John Milton's Relatives and Associates* (2004) and *Rethinking Milton Studies: Time Present and Time Past* (2005).

R. Allen Shoaf, Alumni Professor of English at the University of Florida, has published eleven books, including *The Poem as Green Girdle: "Commercium" in* Sir Gawain and the Green Knight (1984); *Troilus and Criseyde: An Edition* (1989); *Milton, Poet of Duality* (1985); *Chaucer's Body: The Anxiety of Circulation in* The Canterbury Tales (2001); and *Shakespeare's Theater of Likeness* (2006). He has twice held Fellowships of the National Endowment for the Humanities, and he has won six teaching awards, including Distinguished Teacher of the Year in the South Atlantic MLA in 1996.

Jeffrey Shoulson is associate professor of English literature at the University of Miami and Fellow at the Sue and Leonard Miller Center for Contemporary Judaic Studies. His book *Milton and the Rabbis: Hebraism, Hellenism, and Christianity* (2001) was awarded the American Academy of Jewish Research's Salo Baron Prize for Best First Book in Jewish Studies. He is coeditor of *Hebraica Veritas? Christian Hebraists and the Study of Judaism in Early Modern Europe* (2004). He is completing his second book, "Fictions of Conversion: Community, Identity, and Instability in Early Modern England."

Elizabeth Skerpan-Wheeler is professor of English at Texas State University–San Marcos, where she teaches seventeenth- and eighteenth-century English literature. She is the author of *The Rhetoric of Politics in the English Revolution, 1642–1660* (1992) and editor of *Life Writings* for the Early Modern Englishwoman series. She is working on a book on Milton's logic, rhetoric, and poetics and an electronic edition of *Eikon Basilike*.

David V. Urban is assistant professor of English at Calvin College. His articles and reviews have appeared in *ANQ*, *Christianity and Literature*, *Cithara*, *Leviathan: A Journal of Melville Studies*, *Milton Quarterly*, *Milton Studies*, *Religion and Literature*, and *Seventeenth-Century News* and in collections of essays on Milton. He is completing and editing Calvin Huckabay's *John Milton: An Annotated Bibliography, 1989–1999* and working on a book-length study of Milton and his use of and identification with parabolic figures in Matthew. He is coediting a festschrift of essays on Milton in honor of Michael Lieb.

Joseph A. Wittreich is Distinguished Professor of English at the Graduate Center of the City University of New York. He is the author of numerous books on Milton, including *Interpreting "Samson Agonistes"* (1986) and *Shifting Contexts: Reinterpreting "Samson Agonistes"* (2002). His most recent book is *Why Milton Matters: A New Preface to His Writings* (2006).

Matthew Woodcock teaches at the University of East Anglia, Norwich. He has published an essay collection on Fulke Greville (2001) and a book, *Fairy in the Faerie Queene: Renaissance Elf-Fashioning and Elizabethan Myth-Making* (2004), in addition to studies on Shakespeare, Spenser, and Elizabethan pageantry. He has written a student guide to Philip Sidney and the Sidney Circle and is completing a reception history of Shakespeare's *Henry V*.

Shari A. Zimmerman is associate professor of English at Hofstra University. Her essays on Milton have appeared in such journals as *ELH*, *Essays in Literature*, and *American Imago*. She has published as well on contemporary literature, gender, and psychoanalysis in *Pacific Coast Philology*, *Review of Contemporary Fiction*, and *Critique*; and she has written for *Essays in Criticism* and the *Journal for the Psychoanalysis of Culture and Society*. Her current research focuses on Milton's reading practices and the propagandizing uses of Hebrew precedent in seventeenth-century debates on tithing.

SURVEY PARTICIPANTS

Danny Campbell, *Chowan College*
Gardner Campbell, *University of Mary Washington*
Alison A. Chapman, *University of Alabama, Birmingham*
Clare Church, *Independent Scholar*
Matthew Davis, *Independent Scholar*
Margaret J. Dean, *Eastern Kentucky University*
Stephen B. Dobranski, *Georgia State University*
Angelica Duran, *Purdue University*
Andrew Escobedo, *Ohio University*
James Dougal Fleming, *Simon Fraser University*
Wendy Furman-Adams, *Whittier College*
Daniel Gates, *Rhodes College*
Cynthia A. Gilliatt, *James Madison University*
C. Herbert Gilliland, *United States Naval Academy*
Lynne A. Greenberg, *Hunter College*
Gina Hausknecht, *Coe College*
Peter C. Herman, *San Diego State University*
William C. Johnson, *Northern Illinois University*
Gregory Kneidel, *University of Connecticut*
Laura Lunger Knoppers, *Pennsylvania State University*
Jameela Lares, *University of Southern Mississippi*
Jennifer Lewin, *University of Kentucky*
Paula Loscocco, *Sarah Lawrence College*
Elizabeth Mazzola, *City College of New York*
Kari Boyd McBride, *University of Arizona*
David Mikics, *University of Houston*
Edmund Miller, *C. W. Post Campus of Long Island University*
Anna Nardo, *Louisiana State University*
Curtis Perry, *University of Illinois, Urbana*
Richard Rambuss, *Emory University*
Allen Rice, *University of Central Oklahoma*
Elizabeth Harris Sagaser, *Colby College*
Elizabeth Sauer, *Brock University*
John Savoie, *Southern Illinois University, Edwardsville*
Michael Schoenfeldt, *University of Michigan*
Amiya Bhushan Sharma, *Indira Gandhi National Open University*
John T. Shawcross, *University of Kentucky*
Jeffrey Shoulson, *University of Miami*
Elizabeth Skerpan-Wheeler, *Texas State University, San Marcos*
Paul G. Stanwood, *University of British Columbia*
Arlene Stiebel, *California State University, Northridge*
David Summers, *Capital University*

David V. Urban, *Calvin College*
David Scott Wilson-Okamura, *East Carolina University*
Matthew Woodcock, *University of East Anglia*
Shari A. Zimmerman, *Hofstra University*

WORKS CITED

Abrams, M. H. "Five Types of Lycidas." Patrides 216–35.

Abrams, M. H., et al., eds. *The Norton Anthology of English Literature*. 6th ed. New York: Norton, 1993.

Achinstein, Sharon. E-mail to Peter C. Herman. 2005.

———. *Milton and the Revolutionary Reader*. Princeton: Princeton UP, 1994.

Aers, David, and Bob Hodge. " 'Rational Burning': Milton on Sex and Marriage." *Literature, Language, and Society in England, 1580–1680*. Ed. Aers, Hodge, Gunther Kress. Dublin: Gill, 1981. 122–51.

An Agreement of the People for a Firme and Present Peace. London, 1647.

Alciato, Andrea. *Book of Emblems*. 1531. Ed. William Barker, Mark Feltham, and Jean Guthrie, with the assistance of Allan Farrell. 26 Apr. 2005. Memorial U of Newfoundland. 7 Apr. 2006 <http://www.mun.ca/alciato/>.

Alpers, Paul. *What Is Pastoral?* Chicago: U of Chicago P, 1996.

Ames, William. *The Marrow of Sacred Divinity: Drawne out of the Holy Scriptures and the Interpreters Thereof, and Brought into Method*. London, 1643. Rpt. as *The Marrow of Theology*. Trans. and ed. John D. Eusden. Milestone Lib. Series. Boston: Pilgrim, 1968.

Anderson, Benedict. *Imagined Communities: Reflections on the Origin and Spread of Nationalism*. London: Verso, 1983.

Armitage, David, Armand Himy, and Quentin Skinner, eds. *Milton and Republicanism*. Cambridge: Cambridge UP, 1995.

Arthos, John. *Milton and the Italian Cities*. London: Bowes, 1968.

Atwan, Robert, and Laurence Wieder, eds. *Chapters into Verse: A Selection of Poetry in English Inspired by the Bible from Genesis through Revelation*. Oxford: Oxford UP, 2000.

Aubrey, John. "Mr. John Milton: Minutes by John Aubrey." Darbishire 1–15.

Augustine. *The City of God*. Trans. Marcus Dods. New York: Modern Lib., 1950.

Bacon, Francis. "Aphorisms." Rudrum, Black, and Nelson 47–62.

———. *New Atlantis*. The Advancement of Learning *and* New Atlantis. Ed. Arthur Johnston. Oxford: Clarendon, 1974. 214–47.

Bailyn, Bernard. *The Ideological Origins of the American Revolution*. Cambridge: Belknap, 1967.

———, ed. *Pamphlets of the American Revolution, 1750–1776*. Cambridge: Belknap, 1965.

———. "The Transforming Radicalism of the American Revolution." Introduction. Bailyn, *Pamphlets* 1–202.

Baker, Herschel, ed. *The Later Renaissance in England: Nondramatic Verse and Prose, 1600–1660*. Prospect Heights: Waveland, 1996.

Bal, Mieke. "Sexuality, Sin, and Sorrow: The Emergence of the Female Character." *Lethal Love: Feminist Literary Readings of Biblical Love Stories*. Bloomington: Indiana UP, 1987. 104–30.

Barker, Arthur E. "Calm Regained through Passion Spent: The Conclusion of the Miltonic Effort." *The Prison and the Pinnacle*. Ed. Balachandra Rajan. London: Routledge, 1973. 3–48.

———. *Milton and the Puritan Dilemma*. Toronto: U of Toronto P, 1942.

Bauman, Michael. *Milton's Arianism*. Frankfurt am Main: Lang, 1987.

Bayley, John, et al. "Letters to the Editor: 'Samson Agonistes' and September 11." *Times Literary Supplement* 13 Sept. 2002: 17; 20 Sept. 2002: 15.

Bayne, Peter. *The Chief Actors in the Puritan Revolution*. London: Clarke, 1878.

Bear, Risa, gen. ed. *Renascence Editions*. 7 Apr. 2006 <http://darkwing.uoregon.edu/~rbear/ren.htm>.

Belsey, Catherine. *John Milton: Language, Gender, Power*. Oxford: Blackwell, 1988.

Benet, Diana Treviño. "The Escape from Rome: Milton's *Second Defense* and a Renaissance Genre." Di Cesare 29–51.

Benet, Diana Treviño, and Michael Lieb, eds. *Literary Milton: Text, Pretext, Context*. Pittsburgh: Duquesne UP, 1994.

Bennett, Joan S. *Reviving Liberty: Radical Christian Humanism in Milton's Great Poems*. Cambridge: Harvard UP, 1989.

Bennett, Judith M., and Amy M. Froide. *Singlewomen in the European Past, 1250–1800*. Philadelphia: U of Pennsylvania P, 1999.

Berger, Harry, Jr. "The Prince's Dog: Falstaff and the Perils of Speech-Prefixity." *Shakespeare Quarterly* 49 (1998): 40–73.

Berger, Joseph. "Orthodox Jews Temper Views on Gaza Pullout." *International Herald Tribune* 16 June 2004: 4.

The Bible, King James Version. Ed. Robert A. Kraft. *Electronic Text Center*. Alderman Lib., U of Virginia. 7 Apr. 2006 <http://etext.lib.virginia.edu/kjv.browse.html>.

Blake, William. Milton a Poem *and the Final Illuminated Works*. Ed. Robert N. Essick and Joseph Viscomi. Princeton: Princeton UP, 1993. Plate 15.

———. *The Poetry and Prose of William Blake*. Ed. David V. Erdman. Garden City: Doubleday, 1970.

Boehrer, Bruce. " 'Lycidas': The Pastoral Elegy as Same-Sex Epithalamium." *PMLA* 117 (2002): 222–36.

Boesky, Amy. "Milton, Galileo, and Sunspots: Optics and Certainty in *Paradise Lost*." *Milton Studies* 34 (1996): 23–43.

Borges, Jorge Luis. *El tamaño de mi esperanza*. Barcelona: Seix Barral, 1960.

Bowra, C. M. *From Virgil to Milton*. London: Macmillan, 1945.

Braden, Gordon, trans. Elegy 6. By John Milton. *The Complete Poetry and Essential Prose of John Milton*. Ed. William Kerrigan, John Rumrich, and Stephen Fallon. New York: Random–Modern Library, forthcoming.

Bradford, Richard. *The Complete Critical Guide to Milton*. New York: Routledge, 2001.

Bradshaw, John. *A Concordance to the Poetical Works of John Milton*. London: Sonnenschein; New York: Macmillan, 1894.

Brathwaite, Richard. *The English Gentlewoman*. London, 1631.

Breasted, Barbara. "*Comus* and the Castlehaven Scandal." *Milton Studies* 3 (1971): 201–24.

Brennan, Gillian E. *Patriotism, Power, and Print: National Consciousness in Tudor England*. Pittsburgh: Duquesne, 2003.

Brisman, Leslie. *Milton's Poetry of Choice and Its Romantic Heirs*. Ithaca: Cornell UP, 1973.

Brown, Cedric. "The Legacy of the Late Jacobean Period." Corns, *Companion* 109–23.

Brown, Christopher. *Rembrandt: Every Painting*. Vol. 1. New York: Rizzoli, 1980.

———. *Van Dyck*. Oxford: Phaidon, 1982.

Bruce, F. F. *History of the Bible in English: From the Earliest Versions*. 3rd ed. New York: Oxford UP, 1978.

Bryson, Michael. *Milton Pages*. 7 Apr. 2006 <http://www.brysons.net/miltonweb/>.

Burke, Kenneth. "The Use of Milton's Samson." *A Grammar of Motives* and *A Rhetoric of Motives*. Cleveland: Meridian, 1962. 527–44.

Burke, Seán. *The Death and Return of the Author: Criticism and Subjectivity in Barthes, Foucault and Derrida*. 2nd ed. Edinburgh: Edinburgh UP, 1998.

Bush, Douglas. *English Literature in the Earlier Seventeenth Century, 1600–1660*. 2nd ed. Oxford: Clarendon, 1962.

Butlin, Martin, ed. *On the Morning of Christ's Nativity: Milton's Hymn with Illustrations by William Blake*. Andoversford: Whittington, 1981.

Bynum, Caroline Walker. "The Body of Christ in the Later Middle Ages: A Reply to Leo Steinberg." *Renaissance Quarterly* 39 (1986): 399–439. Rpt. in *Fragmentation and Redemption: Essays on Gender and the Human Body*. By Bynum. New York: Zone, 1992. 79–118.

Byron, George Gordon, Lord. "Dedication." *Byron*. Ed. Jerome J. McGann. Oxford Authors. New York: Oxford UP, 1986. 124–26.

Campbell, Gordon. *A Milton Chronology*. New York: St. Martin's, 1997.

———. "Milton, John (1608–1674)." *Oxford Dictionary of National Biography*. Ed. H. C. G. Matthew and Brian Harrison. 61 vols. Oxford: Oxford UP, 2004. May 2006 online ed. Ed. Lawrence Goldman. 31 Oct. 2006 <http://www.oxforddnb.com/view/article/18800>.

———. "Shakespeare and the Youth of Milton." *Milton Quarterly* 33 (1999): 95–105.

Campbell, Gordon, Thomas N. Corns, John K. Hale, David I. Holmes, and Fiona J. Tweedie. "The Provenance of *De Doctrina Christiana*." *Milton Quarterly* 31 (1997): 67–121.

Carey, John. "A Work in Praise of Terrorism? September 11 and *Samson Agonistes*." *Times Literary Supplement* 6 Sept. 2002: 15+.

Cary, Elizabeth. *The Tragedy of Mariam*. *English Renaissance Drama*. Ed. David Bevington, Lars Engle, Katherine Eisaman Maus, and Eric Rasmussen. New York: Norton, 2002. 615–72.

Certain Briefe Treatises Written by Diverse Learned Men, concerning the Ancient and Moderne Government of the Church: Wherein Both the Primitive Institution of Episcopacie Is Maintained, and the Lawfulnesse of the Ordination of the Protestant Ministers beyond the Seas Likewise Defended, the Particulars Whereof Are Set Downe in the Leafe Following. Oxford: Leonard Litchfield, 1641.

Chaney, Edward. *The Grand Tour and the Great Rebellion: Richard Lassels and "The*

Voyage of Italy" in the Seventeenth Century. Moncalieri: Biblioteca del Viaggio in Italia, 1985.

———. "The Visit to Vallombrosa: A Literary Tradition." Di Cesare 113–46.

Chaplin, Gregory. " 'One Flesh, One Heart, One Soul': Renaissance Friendship and Miltonic Marriage." *Modern Philology* 99 (2001): 266–92.

Chaucer, Geoffrey. *The Works of Geoffrey Chaucer*. Ed. F. N. Robinson. 2nd ed. Boston: Houghton, 1957.

Cheney, Patrick. "Alcestis and the 'Passion for Immortality': Milton's Sonnet XXIII and Plato's *Symposium*." *Milton Studies* 18 (1983): 63–76.

"Cherish." Def. 6. *Oxford English Dictionary*. 2nd ed. 1989.

Christopher, Georgia B. *Milton and the Science of the Saints*. Princeton: Princeton UP, 1982.

Cinquemani, A. M. *Glad to Go for a Feast: Milton, Buonmattei, and the Florentine Accademici*. New York: Lang, 1998.

Cleveland, Charles Dexter. *A Complete Concordance to the Poetical Works of John Milton*. London: Low, 1867.

Coffey, John. "Pacifist, Quietist, or Patient Militant? John Milton and the Restoration." *Milton Studies* 42 (2002): 149–74.

Collinson, Patrick. *The Religion of Protestants: The Church in English Society, 1559–1625*. Oxford: Clarendon, 1982.

Cook, Eleanor. " 'Methought' as Dream-Formula in Milton, Wordsworth, Keats, and Others." *English Language Notes* 32 (1995): 34–46.

Corns, Thomas N., ed. *A Companion to Milton*. Oxford: Blackwell, 2001.

———. *The Development of Milton's Prose Style*. Oxford: Clarendon, 1982.

———. E-mail to Peter C. Herman. 2005.

———. "Ideology in the *Poemata* (1645)." *Milton Studies* 19 (1984): 195–203.

———. "John Milton: Italianate Humanist, Northern European Protestant, Englishman." Di Cesare 1–8.

———. *John Milton: The Prose Works*. New York: Twayne, 1998.

———. "Milton before 'Lycidas.' " *Milton and the Terms of Liberty*. Parry and Raymond 23–36.

———, ed. *The Milton Encyclopedia*. New Haven: Yale UP, forthcoming.

———. "Milton's Prose." Danielson, *Cambridge Companion* 84–97.

———. "Milton's Quest for Respectability." *Modern Language Review* 77 (1982): 769–79.

———. *Uncloistered Virtue: English Political Literature, 1640–1660*. Oxford: Clarendon, 1992.

———. " 'With Unaltered Brow': Milton and the Son of God." *Paradise Regained in Context: Genre, Politics, Religion*. Ed. Albert Labriola and David Loewenstein. Spec. issue of *Milton Studies* 42 (2002): 106–21.

Crane, Mary Thomas. *Framing Authority: Sayings, Self, and Society in Sixteenth-Century England*. Princeton: Princeton UP, 1993.

Crashaw, Richard. "A Hymn of the Nativity." 1646 vers. *The Poems English Latin and*

Greek of Richard Crashaw. 2nd ed. Ed. L. C. Martin. Oxford: Clarendon, 1957. 106–08.

Cummings, Robert, ed. *Seventeenth-Century Poetry: The Annotated Anthology.* Oxford: Blackwell, 2000.

Daniell, David. *The Bible in English: Its History and Influence.* New Haven: Yale UP, 2003.

Danielson, Dennis, ed. *The Cambridge Companion to Milton.* 2nd ed. Cambridge: Cambridge UP, 1999.

———. *Milton's Good God: A Study in Literary Theodicy.* Cambridge: Cambridge UP, 1982.

Darbishire, Helen, ed. *The Early Lives of Milton.* London: Constable, 1932. New York: Barnes, 1965.

Davie, Donald. *The Psalms in English.* London: Penguin, 1996.

Davies, Stevie. *Milton.* New York: St. Martin's, 1991.

Davis, J. C. *Utopia and the Ideal Society: English Utopian Writing, 1576–1700.* Cambridge: Cambridge UP, 1981.

De Quincey, Thomas. "Dr. Samuel Parr." 1831. *The Romantics on Milton: Formal Essays and Critical Asides.* Ed. Joseph Wittreich. Cleveland: Western Reserve UP, 1970. 464–65.

The Devil's Advocate. Dir. Taylor Hackford. Perf. Keanu Reeves, Al Pacino, and Charlize Theron. Warner, 1997.

Di Cesare, Mario, ed. *Milton in Italy: Contexts, Images, Contradictions.* Binghamton: Medieval and Renaissance Texts and Studies, 1991.

Dickens, A. G. *The English Reformation.* 1964. New York: Schocken, 1978.

Diekhoff, John S. *Milton on Himself.* New York: Oxford UP, 1939.

Dietz, Michael. " 'Thus Sang the Uncouth Swain': Pastoral, Prophecy, and Historicism in *Lycidas.*" *Milton Studies* 35 (1997): 42–72.

"Digression." Def. 3. *Oxford English Dictionary.* 2nd ed. 1989.

Dobranski, Stephen B. *Milton, Authorship, and the Book Trade.* Cambridge: Cambridge UP, 1999.

Dobranski, Stephen B., and John P. Rumrich, eds. *Milton and Heresy.* Cambridge: Cambridge UP, 1998.

Dod, John, and Robert Cleaver. *A Godly Forme of Household Government.* London: 1630.

Donne, John. *The Complete Poetry of John Donne.* Ed. John T. Shawcross. New York: Anchor, 1967.

———. "Good Friday, 1613. Riding Westward." *The Complete English Poems.* Ed. A. J. Smith. London: Penguin, 1971. 329–31.

Duran, Angelica, ed. *A Concise Companion to Milton.* Oxford: Blackwell, 2006.

Dylan, Bob. "Mississippi." *Love and Theft.* Special Rider Music, 1997. Legacy/Sony, 2001.

Dzelzainis, Martin. "Milton's Politics." Danielson, *Cambridge Companion* 65–78.

The Early Modern English Dictionaries Database. Ed. Ian Lancashire. 15 Oct. 1999. Dept. of English, U of Toronto. 7 Apr. 2006 <http://www.chass.utoronto.ca/english/emed/emedd.html>.

Edwards, J. M., trans. *Greek Bucolic Poets: Theocritus, Bion, Moschus.* Boston: Loeb Classical Lib., 1912.

Edwards, Thomas. *Gangraena.* London, 1646.

Eikon Basilike: The Portraiture of His Sacred Majesty in His Solitudes and Sufferings. Ed. Philip A. Knachel. Ithaca: Cornell UP for the Folger Shakespeare Lib., 1966.

Eliot, T. S. "In Memoriam." *Selected Prose of T. S. Eliot.* Ed. Frank Kermode. New York: Harcourt, 1975. 258–64.

Elledge, Scott. *Milton's "Lycidas," Edited to Serve as an Introduction to Criticism.* New York: Harper, 1966.

Ellison, Ralph. *Juneteenth: A Novel.* Ed. John F. Calahan. New York: Random, 1999.

Emerton, J. A. "Aramaic." *The Oxford Companion to the Bible.* Ed. Bruce M. Metzger and Michael D. Coogan. New York: Oxford UP, 1993. 45–46.

Empson, William. "Emotion in Words Again." *Kenyon Review* 10 (1948): 579–601.

———. *Milton's God.* Rev. ed. London: Chatto, 1965.

Engel, Adam. "*Samson Agonistes* (Confession of a Terrorist/Martyr)." *Counterpunch* 2 Nov. 2002. Ed. Alexander Cockburn and Jeffrey St. Clair. 10 Oct. 2006 <http://www.counterpunch.org/engel1102.html>.

The English Emblem Book Project. 16 Feb. 1999. Penn State U Libraries' Electronic Text Center. 7 Apr. 2006 <http://emblem.libraries.psu.edu/>.

Evans, J. Martin. "The Birth of the Author: Milton's Poetic Self-Construction." *Milton Studies* 38 (2000): 47–65.

———. " 'Lycidas.' " Danielson, *Cambridge Companion* 39–53.

———. *The Miltonic Moment.* Lexington: UP of Kentucky, 1998.

Ezell, Margaret J. M. *Social Authorship and the Advent of Print.* Baltimore: Johns Hopkins UP, 2003.

Fallon, Robert. *Milton in Government.* University Park: Pennsylvania State UP, 1993.

Fallon, Stephen M. *Milton among the Philosophers: Poetry and Materialism in Seventeenth-Century England.* Ithaca: Cornell UP, 1991.

———. "The Spur of Self-Concernment." *Milton Studies* 38 (2000): 220–42.

Ferguson, Margaret, Mary Jo Salter, and Jon Stallworthy, eds. *The Norton Anthology of Poetry.* 5th ed. New York: Norton, 2005.

Ferguson, Moira, ed. *First Feminists: British Women Writers, 1578–1799.* Bloomington: Indiana UP, 1985.

Fincham, Kenneth, ed. *The Early Stuart Church: 1603–1642.* Stanford: Stanford UP, 1993.

Fish, Stanley. *How Milton Works.* Cambridge: Harvard UP, 2001.

———. *Surprised by Sin: The Reader in* Paradise Lost. 2nd ed. Cambridge: Harvard UP, 1997.

———. *There's No Such Thing as Free Speech, and It's a Good Thing, Too.* Oxford: Oxford UP, 1994.

———. "Wanting a Supplement: The Question of Interpretation in Milton's Early Prose." Loewenstein and Turner 41–68.

Fishbone, Alan, trans. *Christos Paschon* [*Christ Suffering*]. By Gregory Nazianzen. Spec. issue of *Milton Quarterly* 36.3 (2002): 129–98.

Fisher, Alan. "Why Is *Paradise Regained* So Cold?" *Milton Studies* 14 (1980): 195–217.

Fixler, Michael. *Milton and the Kingdoms of God*. Evanston: Northwestern UP, 1964.

Flannagan, Roy, ed. Comus: *Contexts*. Spec. issue of *Milton Quarterly* 21.4 (1987): iii–76.

Fletcher, Angus. *Colors of the Mind*. Cambridge: Harvard UP, 1991.

Fliegelman, Jay. "Belongings: Dramas of American Book Ownership, 1660–1860." Leonora Woodman Lecture. Purdue U, West Lafayette. 16 Oct. 2003.

Fortescue, John. *On the Laws and Governance of England*. Ed. Shelley Lockwood. Cambridge: Cambridge UP, 1997.

Foucault, Michel. *The Order of Things: An Archaeology of the Human Sciences*. New York: Random, 1970.

Fowler, Alastair. "*Paradise Regained*: Some Problems of Style." *Medieval and Pseudo-Medieval Literatures*. Ed. Piero Boitani and Anna Torti. Cambridge: Brewer, 1984. 181–89.

Franklin, Julian H., comp. *Constitutionalism and Resistance in the Sixteenth Century: Three Treatises by Hotman, Beza, and Mornay*. Indianapolis: Bobbs, 1969.

"Free, a., sb., and adv." Def. 4a. *Oxford English Dictionary*. 2nd ed. 1989.

"Freedom." Def. 2 and def. 7a. *Oxford English Dictionary*. 2nd ed. 1989.

French, J. Milton, ed. *The Life Records of John Milton*. 5 vols. New Brunswick: Rutgers UP, 1950.

Froula, Christine. "Pechter's Specter: Milton's Bogey Writ Small; or, Why Is He Afraid of Virginia Woolf?" *Critical Inquiry* 11 (1984): 171–78.

———. "When Eve Reads Milton: Undoing the Canonical Economy." *Critical Inquiry* 10 (1983): 321–47.

Frye, Roland M. *Milton's Imagery and the Visual Arts: Iconographic Tradition in the Epic Poems*. Princeton: Princeton UP, 1978.

Gallagher, Philip J. "More Theirs by Being His: Teaching Milton to Undergraduates." *Milton Quarterly* 11 (1977): 4–9.

Gardiner, Anne Barbeau. "A Witty French Preacher in the English Court, Dryden, and the Great Debate on the Real Presence, 1661–1688." *ELH* 65 (1998): 593–616.

Gay, David. *The Endless Kingdom: Milton's Scriptural Society*. Newark: U of Delaware P, 2002.

———. "Re: Teaching Milton." E-mail to Angelica Duran. 28 Jan. 2005.

Ghabra, Shafeeq. "What Catastrophe Can Reveal." *New York Times* 26 Aug. 2002: A19.

Gilbert, Roger. *Walks in the World*. Princeton: Princeton UP, 1991

Gilbert, Sandra, and Susan Gubar. *The Madwoman in the Attic: The Woman Writer and the Nineteenth-Century Literary Imagination*. New Haven: Yale UP, 1979.

Gilfillan, George. "Critical Estimate of the Genius and Poetical Works of John Milton." *The Poetical Works of John Milton*. Ed. Charles Cowan Clarke. Vol. 2 Edinburgh: Nichol, 1853. v–xxxi. 2 vols.

Goldberg, Jonathan. *Voice Terminal Echo: Postmodernism and English Renaissance Texts*. New York: Methuen, 1986.

Graff, Gerald. *Beyond the Culture Wars: How Teaching the Conflicts Can Revitalize American Education*. New York: Norton, 1992.

Graves, Robert. *Wife to Mr. Milton: The Story of Marie Powell*. New York: Farrar, 1962.

Gregerson, Linda. "Colonials Write the Nation: Spenser, Milton, and England on the Margins." Rajan and Sauer 169–90.

Gregory, E. R. "Milton's Protestant Sonnet Lady: Revisions in the Donna Angelicata Tradition." *Comparative Literature Studies* 33 (1996): 258–79.

Gross, Kenneth. " 'Each Heav'nly Close': Mythologies and Metrics in Spenser and the Early Poetry of Milton." *PMLA* 98 (1983): 21–36.

Grossman, Allen. "Milton's Sonnet 'On the Late Massacre in Piedmont': A Note on the Vulnerability of Persons in a Revolutionary Situation." *Triquarterly* 23-24 (1972): 283–301.

Grotius, Hugo. *Annotationes in Libros Evangeliorum*. Amsterdam, 1641.

———. *De Jure Belli ac Pacis / The Rights of War and Peace*. Ed. J. Barbeyrac. Trans. anon. London, 1738.

Guillory, John. *Poetic Authority: Spenser, Milton, and Literary History*. New York: Columbia UP, 1983.

Guttenplan, D. D. "Is Reading Milton Unsafe at Any Speed?" *New York Times* 28 Dec. 2002: B9.

Hale, John. Introduction. *Sonnets of Four Centuries 1500–1900*. Ed. Hale. Dunedin: Dept. of English, U of Otago, 1992.

Halkett, John. *Milton and the Idea of Matrimony: A Study in the Divorce Tracts and Paradise Lost*. New Haven: Yale UP, 1970.

Hall, Joseph. *A Defence of the Humble Remonstrance, against the Frivolous and False Exceptions of Smectymnuus*. London: Nathaniel Butter, 1641.

———. *An Humble Remonstrance to the High Court of Parliament*. London: Nathanial Butter, 1640.

Haller, William. *Liberty and Reformation in the Puritan Revolution*. New York: Columbia UP, 1955.

———. *The Rise of Puritanism; or, The Way to the New Jerusalem As Set Forth in Pulpit and Press from Thomas Cartwright to John Lilburne and John Milton, 1570–1643*. New York: Columbia UP, 1938.

Halley, Janet. "Female Autonomy in Milton's Sexual Poetics." Walker 230–54.

Halpern, Richard. "The Great Instauration: Imaginary Narratives in Milton's 'Nativity Ode.' " Nyquist and Ferguson 3–24.

Hammond, Gerald. *Fleeting Things: Poets and Their Poems*. Cambridge: Harvard UP, 1990.

Handel, George Frideric. *L'Allegro, il Penseroso, ed il Moderato*. London: Curwen, 1953.

———. *Samson: An Oratorio, As It Is Performed at the Theatre-Royal in Covent Garden, Alter'd and Adapted to the Stage from the Samson Agonistes of John Milton*. Dublin, 1748.

Hanford, J. Holly. *John Milton, Poet and Humanist: Essays by James Holly Hanford*. Cleveland: P of Case Western Reserve U, 1966.

———. *A Milton Handbook*. 4th ed. New York: Appleton, 1954.

———. "The Pastoral Elegy and Milton's *Lycidas*." *PMLA* 25 (1910): 403–47. Rpt. in Patrides 27–55.

Harrington, James. *The Commonwealth of Oceana and* A System of Politics. Ed. J. G. A. Pocock. Cambridge: Cambridge UP, 1992. 1–266.

Haskin, Dayton. *Milton's Burden of Interpretation.* Philadelphia: U of Pennsylvania P, 1994.

Haug, Ralph A. Preface to *The Reason of Church-Government.* Milton, *Complete Prose Works* 1: 736–44.

Hausknecht, Gina. "The Gender of Civic Virtue." Martin, *Milton* 19–33.

Hawkes, Terence. *Structuralism and Semiotics.* Berkeley: U of California P, 1977.

"The Heidelberg Catechism." *Ecumenical Creeds and Reformed Confessions.* Grand Rapids: CRC, 1988. 12–77.

Helgerson, Richard. *Forms of Nationhood: The Elizabethan Writing of England.* Chicago: U of Chicago P, 1992.

———. *Self-Crowned Laureates: Spenser, Jonson, and the Literary System.* Berkeley: U of California P, 1983.

Henderson, Katherine U., and Barbara K. McManus. *Half Humankind: Contexts and Texts of the Controversy about Women in England, 1540–1640.* Urbana: U of Illinois P, 1985.

Heninger, S. K., Jr. *The Cosmographical Glass: Renaissance Diagrams of the Universe.* San Marino: Huntington Lib., 1977.

Herman, Peter C. *Destabilizing Milton:* Paradise Lost *and the Poetics of Incertitude.* New York: Palgrave, 2005.

Hexter, J. H. *Reappraisals of History.* 2nd ed. Chicago: U of Chicago P, 1979.

Highet, Gilbert. *The Art of Teaching.* New York: Vintage, 1989.

Hill, Christopher. *The English Bible and the Seventeenth-Century Revolution.* London: Penguin, 1993.

———. *The Experience of Defeat: Milton and Some Contemporaries.* New York: Viking, 1984.

———. *Milton and the English Revolution.* London: Faber, 1977.

Hill, Elizabeth K. "A Dream in the Long Valley: Some Psychological Aspects of Milton's Last Sonnet." *Greyfriar* 26 (1985): 3–13.

Hinks, Dennis. "The Arian Controversy." 1999. *Journal* 33. 12 Oct. 2006 <http://users.aol.com/myjournal/arian1.htm>.

Hodges, Margaret. *Comus: Adapted from* A Masque at Ludlow Castle *by John Milton.* New York: Holiday, 1996.

Holderness, Graham. " 'What Ish My Nation?' Shakespeare and National Identities." *Textual Practice* 5 (1991): 74–93.

Hollander, John. "Dreaming Poetry." *The Work of Poetry.* New York: Columbia UP, 1997. 78–95.

Holstun, James. *A Rational Millennium: Puritan Utopias of Seventeenth-Century England and America.* New York: Oxford UP, 1987.

The Holy Bible Containing the Old and New Testaments. Oxford, 1682.

Homily on Obedience. Ed. Ian Lancashire. *Renaissance Electronic Texts* 1. 2. 1997. U of Toronto English Lib. 21 July 2006 <http://www.library.utoronto.ca/utel/ret/homilies/bk1hom10.html>.

Hone, Ralph E., ed. *John Milton's "Samson Agonistes": The Poem and Material for Analysis*. San Francisco: Chandler, 1966.

Huckabay, Calvin. *John Milton: An Annotated Bibliography, 1929–1968*. Pittsburgh: Duquesne UP, 1969.

———, comp. *John Milton: An Annotated Bibliography, 1968–1988*. Ed. Paul J. Klemp. Pittsburgh: Duquesne UP, 1996.

Hunter, William B. Forum response. Lewalski, Shawcross, and Hunter 163–66.

———. "Milton on the Incarnation." Hunter, Patrides, and Adamson 131–48.

———. "Milton's Arianism Reconsidered." *Harvard Theological Review* 52 (1959): 9–35. Rpt. in Hunter, Patrides, and Adamson 29–51.

———. "The Provenance of the *Christian Doctrine*." *SEL* 32 (1992): 129–42.

———. *Visitation Unimplor'd: Milton and the Authorship of "De Doctrina Christiana."* Pittsburgh: Duquesne UP, 1998.

Hunter, William B., et al., eds. *A Milton Encyclopedia*. 9 vols. Lewisburg: Bucknell UP, 1978–83.

Hunter, William B., C. A. Patrides, and J. H. Adamson. *Bright Essence: Studies in Milton's Theology*. Salt Lake City: U of Utah P, 1971.

Huntley, John F. "The Images of Poet and Poetry in Milton's *The Reason of Church Government*." Lieb and Shawcross 83–120.

Illo, John. "The Misreading of Milton." *Radical Perspectives in the Arts*. Ed. Lee Baxandall. Harmondsworth: Penguin, 1972. 178–92.

"Inbreed." Def. 1. *Oxford English Dictionary*. 2nd ed. 1989.

Ingram, Randall. "The Writing Poet: The Descent from Song in *The Poems of Mr. John Milton, Both English and Latin* (1645)." *Milton Studies* 34 (1996): 179–97.

Ingram, William, and Kathleen Swaim, eds. *A Concordance to Milton's English Poetry*. Oxford: Clarendon, 1972.

Isocrates. *Areopagiticus*. Vol. 2 of *Isocrates with an English Translation*. Trans. and ed. George Norlin. London: Heinemann, 1929. 3 vols.

Jauss, Hans Robert. "Literary History as a Challenge to Literary Theory." Trans. Elizabeth Benzinger. *Literature in the Modern World: Critical Essays and Documents*. Ed. Dennis Walder. 2nd ed. Oxford: Oxford UP, 2003. 67–75.

Johnson, Samuel. "Life of Milton." *Lives of the English Poets*. Ed. George Birkbeck Hill. Vol. 1. Oxford: Clarendon, 1905. 163–65. 3 vols.

———. "The Rambler No. 139. Tuesday, July 16, 1751." Hone 97–103.

———. "The Rambler No. 140. Saturday, July 20, 1751." Hone 103–08.

———. *Selections from the* Lives of the English Poets *and "Preface to Shakepeare."* New York: Avon, 1965.

Jokinen, Anniina, ed. *Luminarium*. 7 Apr. 2006 <http://www.luminarium.org>.

Jones, Edward. *Milton's Sonnets: An Annotated Bibliography 1900–1992*. Binghamton: Center for Medieval and Renaissance Texts and Studies, 1994.

Jonson, Ben. "To the Memory of My Beloved, the Author, Mr. William Shakespeare, and What He Hath Left Us." *Mr. William Shakespeares Comedies, Histories, and Tragedies*. By William Shakespeare. London: Isaac Jaggard, 1623. A4–A4v.

Jordan, Constance, and Clare Carroll, eds. *The Longman Anthology of British Literature*. Vol. 1b. New York: Longman, 2003.

Josipovici, Gabriel. *The Book of God: A Response to the Bible*. New Haven: Yale UP, 1988.

Justa Edouardo King Naufrago. Cambridge: T. Buck and R. Daniel, 1638.

Kahn, Victoria. "The Metaphorical Contract in Milton's *Tenure of Kings and Magistrates*." Armitage, Himy, and Skinner 82–105.

Kean, Margaret. "The British Student Body and the Body of Milton's Texts, Paratexts, and Contexts." Eighth International Milton Symposium. U of Grenoble, France. 9 June 2006.

Kedourie, Elie. *Nationalism*. 4th ed. Oxford: Blackwell, 1993.

Kelley, Mark R., and Joseph Wittreich. Introduction. *Altering Eyes: New Perspectives on "Samson Agonistes."* Ed. Kelley and Wittreich. Newark: U of Delaware P, 2002. 11–29.

Kelley, Maurice. *This Great Argument: A Study of Milton's* De Doctrina Christiana *as a Gloss upon* Paradise Lost. Princeton: Princeton UP, 1941.

Kendrick, Christopher, ed. *Critical Essays on John Milton*. New York: Hall; London: Prentice, 1995.

Kenyon, J. P., ed. *The Stuart Constitution: Documents and Commentary*. 2nd ed. Cambridge: Cambridge UP, 1986.

Kermode, Frank. *The Romantic Image*. New York: Random, 1967.

Kermode, Lloyd. " 'To the Shores of Life': Textual Recovery in *Lycidas*." *Milton Quarterly* 31 (1997): 11–25.

Kerrigan, William. "The Politically Correct *Comus*: A Reply to John Leonard." *Milton Quarterly* 27 (1993): 147–53.

———. *The Prophetic Milton*. Charlottesville: UP of Virginia, 1974.

———. *The Sacred Complex: The Psychogenesis of* Paradise Lost. Cambridge: Harvard UP, 1983.

King, John N. *Spenser's Poetry and the Reformation Tradition*. Princeton: Princeton UP, 1990.

———. *Tudor Royal Iconography: Literature and Art in an Age of Religious Crisis*. Princeton: Princeton UP, 1989.

Klibansky, Raymond, Erwin Panofsky, and Fritz Saxl. *Saturn and Melancholy*. New York: Basic, 1964.

Knight, G. Wilson. *Chariot of Wrath: The Message of John Milton to Democracy at War*. London: Faber, 1942.

Knoppers, Laura Lunger. *Historicizing Milton: Spectacle, Power, and Poetry in Restoration England*. Athens: U of Georgia P, 1994.

———. "Imagining the Death of the King: Milton, Charles I, and Anamorphic Art." *Imagining Death in Spenser and Milton*. Ed. Elizabeth Jane Bellamy, Patrick Cheney, and Michael Schoenfeldt. Basingstoke: Palgrave, 2003. 151–70.

———. "Late Political Prose." Corns, *Companion* 309–25.

———. "Milton's *The Readie and Easie Way* and the English Jeremiad." Loewenstein and Turner 213–25.

————. "The Politics of Portraiture: Oliver Cromwell and the Plain Style." *Renaissance Quarterly* 51 (1998): 1283–319.

Knoppers, Laura Lunger, and Gregory M. Colón Semenza, eds. *Milton in Popular Culture*. New York: Palgrave, 2006.

Kolbrener, William. *Milton's Warring Angels: A Study of Critical Engagements*. Cambridge: Cambridge UP, 1997.

Kristeva, Julia. *The Sense and Non-sense of Revolt*. Trans. Jeanine Herman. New York: Columbia UP, 2001.

Krook, Anne K. "The Hermeneutics of Opposition in *Paradise Regained* and *Samson Agonistes*." *SEL* 36 (1996): 129–47.

Kushner, Tony. "Reflections on an America Transformed." *New York Times* 9 Sept. 2003, sec. 4: 15.

Labriola, Albert. "John Milton." *Dictionary of Literary Biography: Seventeenth-Century British Nondramatic Poets*. 3rd ser. Ed. M. Thomas Hester. Detroit: Gale, 1993. 153–89.

Lake, Peter. *Anglicans and Puritans? Presbyterianism and English Conformist Thought from Whitgift to Hooker*. London: Unwin, 1988.

Lancashire, Ian. In collaboration with John Bradley, Willard McCarty, Michael Stairs, and T. R. Wooldridge. *Using TACT with Electronic Texts*. New York: MLA, 1996.

Lanier, Douglas. "Encryptions: Reading Milton Reading Jonson Reading Shakespeare." *Reading and Writing in Shakespeare*. Ed. David M. Bergeron. Newark: U of Delaware P, 1996. 220–50.

"Larger Catechism." *Westminster Standard of Faith*. Glasgow: Free Presbyterian, 1995. 127–283.

Lawes, Henry. *Sitting by the Streams: Psalms, Ayres and Dialogues*. Cond. and perf. Anthony Rooley. Perf. Consort of Musicke. Hyperion, 1984.

The Lawes Resolutions of Womens Rights; or, The Lawes Provision for Women. London, 1632.

Leishman, J. B. " 'L'Allegro' and 'Il Penseroso' in Relation to Seventeenth-Century Poetry." *Milton, Modern Judgements*. Ed. Alan Rudrum. London: Macmillan, 1969. 58–93.

Leonard, John. "Milton's Vow of Celibacy: A Reconsideration of the Evidence." *Of Poetry and Politics: New Essays on Milton and His World*. Ed. P. G. Stanwood. Binghamton: Medieval and Renaissance Texts and Studies, 1995. 187–202.

————. "Saying No to Freud: Milton's *A Mask* and Sexual Assault." *Milton Quarterly* 25 (1991): 129–40.

————. " 'Trembling Ears': The Historical Moment of 'Lycidas' " *Journal of Medieval and Renaissance Studies* 21 (1991): 59–81.

Lessing, G. E. *"The Lacoön" and Other Prose Writings of Lessing*. Ed. W. B. Ronnefeldt. London, 1895.

Levi, Peter. *Eden Renewed: The Public and Private Life of John Milton*. New York: St. Martin's, 1996.

Lewalski, Barbara Kiefer. Forum response. Lewalski, Shawcross, and Hunter 143–54.

————. "How Radical Was the Young Milton?" Dobranski and Rumrich 49–72.

————. *The Life of John Milton: A Critical Biography.* Oxford: Blackwell, 2000.

————. "Milton and the *De Doctrina Christiana*: Evidences of Authorship." *Milton Studies* 36 (1998): 203–28.

————. "Milton: Political Beliefs and Polemical Methods, 1659–60." *PMLA* 74 (1959): 191–202.

————. *Milton's Brief Epic: The Genre, Meaning, and Art of* Paradise Regained. Providence: Brown UP, 1966.

————. Paradise Lost *and the Rhetoric of Literary Forms.* Princeton: Princeton UP, 1985.

————. *Protestant Poetics and the Seventeenth-Century Religious Lyric.* Princeton: Princeton UP, 1979.

Lewalski, Barbara Kiefer, John Shawcross, and William B. Hunter. "Forum: Milton's *Christian Doctrine.*" *SEL* 32 (1992): 143–66.

Lieb, Michael. "*De Doctrina Christiana* and the Question of Authorship." *Milton Studies* 41 (2002): 172–230.

————. *Milton and the Culture of Violence.* Ithaca: Cornell UP, 1994.

————. *Theological Milton: Deity, Discourse, and Heresy in the Miltonic Canon.* Pittsburgh: Duquesne UP, 2006.

Lieb, Michael, and Albert C. Labriola, eds. *John Milton: The Writer in His Works.* Spec. issue of *Milton Studies* 38 (2000): 1–320.

Lieb, Michael, and John T. Shawcross, eds. *Achievements of the Left Hand: Essays on the Prose of John Milton.* Amherst: U of Massachusetts P, 1974.

Liljegren, S. B. *Studies in Milton.* Lund: Gleerup, 1918.

Lipking, Lawrence. "The Genius of the Shore: Lycidas, Adamastor, and the Poetics of Nationalism." *PMLA* 111 (1996): 205–21.

Literature Compass. 2005–06. Blackwell Publishing. 7 Apr. 2002 <www.blackwell-compass .com/subject/literature/>.

Lodge, David. *Small World: An Academic Romance.* London: Secker, 1984.

Loewenstein, David. " 'Fair Offspring Nurs't in Princely Lore': On the Question of Milton's Early Radicalism." *Milton Studies* 28 (1992): 37–48.

————. *Representing Revolution in Milton and His Contemporaries: Religion, Politics, and Polemics in Radical Puritanism.* Cambridge: Cambridge UP, 2001.

Loewenstein, David, and James G. Turner, eds. *Politics, Poetics, and Hermeneutics in Milton's Prose.* Cambridge: Cambridge UP, 1990.

Makin, Bathsua. *An Essay to Revive the Ancient Education of Gentlewomen, in Religion, Manners, Arts and Tongues.* Rudrum, Black, and Nelson 425–33.

Marcus, Leah S. "The Earl of Bridgewater's Legal Life: Notes toward a Political Reading of *Comus.*" *Milton Quarterly* 21 (1987): 24–34.

————. "John Milton's Voice." *Unediting the Renaissance: Shakespeare, Marlowe, Milton.* London: Routledge, 1996. 177–227.

————. "Justice for Margery Evans: A 'Local' Reading of *Comus.*" Walker 66–85.

————. "The Milieu of Milton's *Comus*: Judicial Reform at Ludlow and the Problem of Sexual Assault." *Criticism: A Quarterly for Literature and the Arts* 25 (1983): 293–327.

――――. "Milton's Anti-Laudian Masque." *The Politics of Mirth: Jonson, Herrick, Milton, Marvell, and the Defense of Old Holiday Pastimes*. Chicago: U of Chicago P, 1986.

Marshall, William, illus. *Eikon Basilike: The Portraiture of His Sacred Majestie in His Solitudes and Sufferings*. London, 1649. Frontispiece.

Martin, Catherine Gimelli. "Dalila, Misogyny, and Milton's Christian Liberty of Divorce." Martin, *Milton* 53–74.

――――. "The Feminine Birth of the Mind: Regendering the Empirical Subject in Bacon and His Followers." *Francis Bacon and the Refiguring of Early Modern Thought: Essays to Commemorate the Advancement of Learning (1605–2005)*. Ed. Martin and Julie Robin Solomon. Burlington: Ashgate, 2005.

――――, ed. *Milton and Gender*. Cambridge: Cambridge UP, 2004.

――――. "The Non-Puritan Ethics, Metaphysics, and Aesthetics of Milton's Spenserian Masque." *Milton Quarterly* 37 (2003): 215–44.

――――. "The Sources of Milton's Sin Reconsidered." *Milton Quarterly* 35 (2001): 1–8.

Martz, Louis. *Milton: Poet of Exile*. New Haven: Yale UP, 1986. Rev. ed. of *Poet of Exile: A Study of Milton's Poetry*. 1980.

――――. *Poetry of Meditation: A Study of English Religious Literature of the Seventeenth Century*. New Haven: Yale UP, 1954.

Marvell, Andrew. "On Mr. Milton's *Paradise Lost*." *Andrew Marvell: The Complete Poems*. Ed. Elizabeth Story Donno. New York: Penguin, 1972. 192–93.

Masterman, J. Howard B. *The Age of Milton*. London: Bell, 1897.

Mayhew, Jonathan. *A Discourse concerning Unlimited Submission and Non-resistance to the Higher Powers. . . .* Bailyn, *Pamphlets* 204–47.

Mazzaro, Jerome. "Gaining Authority: John Milton at Sonnets." *Essays in Literature* 15 (1988): 3–12.

McColgan, Kristin Pruitt, and Charles W. Durham, eds. *Arenas of Conflict: Milton and the Unfettered Mind*. Selinsgrove: Susquehanna UP, 1997.

McColley, Diane. *Milton's Eve*. Urbana: U of Illinois P, 1983.

McCullough, Peter. *Sermons at Court: Politics and Religion in Elizabethan and Jacobean Preaching*. Cambridge: Cambridge UP, 1998.

McGrath, Alister. *In the Beginning: The Story of the King James Bible and How It Changed a Nation, a Language, and a Culture*. New York: Doubleday, 2001.

McGuire, Maryann Cale. *Milton's Puritan Masque*. Athens: U of Georgia P, 1983.

McLoone, George H. "Milton's Twenty-Third Sonnet: Love, Death, and the Mystical Body of the Church." *Milton Quarterly* 24 (1990): 8–20.

Mendle, Michael. Rev. of *Representing Revolution in Milton and His Contemporaries*, by David Loewenstein. *Renaissance Quarterly* 55 (2002): 775–79.

Merian, Matthäus. *The Bible: In Word and Art*. Amsterdam, 1630. Rpt. New York; Arch Cape, 1988.

Metzger, Bruce. *The Bible in Translation: Ancient and English Versions*. Grand Rapids: Baker Academic, 2001.

Miller, Nancy Weitz. "Chastity, Rape, and Ideology in the Castlehaven Testimonies and Milton's Ludlow Mask." *Milton Studies* 32 (1995): 153–68.

Milton, John. *Complete English Poems, Of Education, Areopagitica.* Ed. Gordon J. M. Campbell. London: Dent; Rutland: Tuttle, 1993.

———. *The Complete Poems.* Ed. John Leonard. London: Penguin, 1998.

———. *Complete Poems and Major Prose.* Ed. Merritt Y. Hughes. New York: Odyssey, 1957. Indianapolis: Hackett, 2003.

———. *The Complete Poetry of John Milton.* Ed. John Shawcross. New York: Anchor, 1971.

———. *Complete Prose Works of John Milton.* Ed. Don M. Wolfe et al. 8 vols. New Haven: Yale UP, 1953–82.

———. *Complete Shorter Poems.* Ed. John Carey. Longman Annotated English Poets. London: Longman, 1971.

———. "An Epitaph on the Admirable Dramaticke Poet W Shakespeare." *Mr. William Shakespeare's Comedies, Histories, and Tragedies.* London, 1632. A5r.

———. *John Milton's Complete Poetical Works Reproduced in Photographic Facsimile.* Ed. Harris Francis Fletcher. 4 vols. Urbana: U of Illinois P, 1943–48.

———. *John Milton: Selected Prose.* Ed. C. A. Patrides. Columbia: U of Missouri P, 1986.

———. *John Milton: The Major Works.* Ed. Stephen Orgel and Jonathan Goldberg. Oxford: Oxford UP, 2003. Rpt. of *John Milton.* Oxford: Oxford UP, 1991.

———. *A Maske Presented at Ludlow Castle.* London: Humphrey Robinson, 1637.

———. *Milton's Samson Agonistes.* Ed. A. W. Verity. Cambridge: Cambridge UP, 1892.

———. *Milton's Sonnets.* Ed. E. A. J. Honigmann. London: Macmillan, 1966.

———. "On *Shakespear.* 1630." *Poems of Mr. John Milton, Both English and Latin, Compos'd at Several Times.* London, 1645. B6r.

———. *Paradise Lost.* Ed. Scott Elledge. 2nd ed. New York: Norton, 1993.

———. *Paradise Lost.* Ed. Barbara Lewalski. Oxford: Blackwell, forthcoming.

———. *Paradise Lost and Other Poems.* Ed. Edward Le Comte. New York: Signet, 2003.

———. *The Poems of John Milton.* Ed. John Carey and Alastair Fowler. New York: Norton, 1972.

———. *The Poetical Works of John Milton.* Etchings, mezzotints, and copper engravings by William Hyde. London: Astolat, 1904.

———. *The Poetical Works of Mr. John Milton.* Illus. Louis Chéron. London, 1720.

———. *The Riverside Milton.* Ed. Roy Flannagan. Boston: Houghton, 1998.

———. *Samson Agonistes: A Dramatic Poem.* Illus. Robert Medley. Norwich: Mell Clark, 1979.

———. *Selected Prose.* Ed. David Loewenstein. Barbara Lewalski, gen. ed. Oxford: Blackwell, forthcoming.

———. *Shorter Poems.* Ed. Stella Revard. Barbara Lewalski, gen. ed. Oxford: Blackwell, forthcoming.

———. *A Variorum Commentary on the Poems of John Milton.* Merritt Y. Hughes, gen. ed. 4 vols. New York: Columbia UP, 1970.

———. *The Works of John Milton.* 18 vols. New York: Columbia UP, 1931–38.

Milton-L Home Page. Ed. Kevin J. T. Creamer. 7 Apr. 2006 <http://www.richmond.edu/~creamer/milton/index.html>.

Milton Reading Room. Ed. Thomas Luxon. 7 Apr. 2006 <http://www.dartmouth .edu/~milton>.

Mitchell, W. J. T. *Iconology: Image, Text, Ideology.* Chicago: U of Chicago P, 1986.

Mohamed, Feisal G. "Confronting Religious Violence: Milton's *Samson Agonistes.*" *PMLA* 120 (2005): 327–40.

More, Thomas. *A Dialogue of Sir Thomas More. Wherein Be Treated Divers Matters, As of the Veneration and Worship of Images.* London: [William Rastell], 1529.

———. *Utopia.* Trans. and ed. Robert M. Adams. 2nd ed. New York: Norton, 1992.

Mueller, Janel. "The Mastery of Decorum: Politics as Poetry in Milton's Sonnets." *Critical Inquiry* 13 (1987): 475–508.

"A Muse of Fire." *The Story of English.* Prod. William Cran. Dir. John Pett. BBC. Videocassette. Films, Inc., 1986. Program 3 of *The Story of English.*

Nardo, Anna K. *Milton's Sonnets and the Ideal Community.* Lincoln: U of Nebraska P, 1979.

The New Oxford Annotated Bible, New Revised Standard Version with the Apocrypha. 3rd ed. Ed. Michael D. Coogan. Oxford: Oxford UP, 2001.

Nicolson, Adam. *God's Secretaries: The Making of the King James Bible.* New York: Harper, 2003.

Nicolson, Marjorie. *John Milton: A Reader's Guide to His Poetry.* New York: Farrar, 1963.

Nietzsche, Friedrich. *Twilight of the Idols; or, How to Philosophize with a Hammer.* Trans. Richard Polt. Indianapolis: Hackett, 1997.

Norbrook, David. *Poetry and Politics in the English Renaissance.* Rev. ed. New York: Oxford UP, 2002.

———. "The Politics of Milton's Early Poetry." Patterson, *John Milton* 46–64.

———. *Writing the English Republic: Poetry, Rhetoric and Politics, 1627–1660.* Cambridge: Cambridge UP, 1999.

Norbrook, David, and H. R. Woudhuysen, eds. *The Penguin Book of Renaissance Verse, 1509–1659.* London: Penguin, 1992.

Norton, David. *A History of the English Bible as Literature.* Cambridge: Cambridge UP, 2000.

Nyquist, Mary. "The Genesis of Gendered Subjectivity in the Divorce Tracts and in *Paradise Lost.*" Nyquist and Ferguson 99–127.

Nyquist, Mary, and Margaret W. Ferguson, eds. *Re-membering Milton: Essays on the Texts and Traditions.* New York: Methuen, 1987.

Onions, C. T., ed. *Samson Agonistes.* By John Milton. London: Marshall, 1905.

Orgel, Stephen. *The Jonsonian Masque.* Cambridge: Harvard UP, 1965.

Orgel, Stephen, and Jonathan Goldberg. Introduction. Milton, *John Milton: The Major Works* ix–xxxii.

Ovid. *The Metamorphoses.* Trans. Charles Martin. New York: Norton, 2005.

Pagels, Elaine. *Adam, Eve, and the Serpent.* New York: Random, 1988.

Panofsky, Erwin. *Studies in Iconology: Humanistic Themes in the Art of the Renaissance.* New York: Harper, 1972.

"Paradise Lost." *Testament: The Bible and History.* Dir. John Romer. Videocassette. Films for the Humanities, 1988.

Parker, William Riley. *Milton: A Biography.* 1968. 2nd ed. Ed. Gordon Campbell. 2 vols. Oxford: Clarendon P, 1996.

———. "Milton's Last Sonnet." *Review of English Studies* 21 (1945): 235–38.

———. "Milton's Last Sonnet Again." *Review of English Studies* 27 (1951): 147–52.

Parry, Graham. *The Seventeenth Century: The Intellectual and Cultural Context of English Literature, 1603–1700.* New York: Longman, 1989.

Parry, Graham, and Joad Raymond, eds. *Milton and the Terms of Liberty.* Cambridge: Brewer, 2002.

Patrides, C. A., ed. *Milton's "Lycidas": The Tradition and the Poem.* Rev. ed. Columbia: U of Missouri P, 1983.

Patrides, C. A., and Raymond Waddington, eds. *The Age of Milton: Backgrounds to Seventeenth-Century Literature.* Totawa: Barnes, 1980.

Patterson, Annabel. " 'Forc'd Fingers': Milton's Early Poems and Ideological Constraint." *"The Muses Common-Weale": Poetry and Politics in the Seventeenth Century.* Ed. Claude J. Summers and Ted-Larry Pebworth. Columbia: U of Missouri P, 1988. 9–22.

———, ed. *John Milton.* Longman Critical Readers. New York: Longman, 1992.

———. " 'No Meer Amatorious Novel'?" Loewenstein and Turner 85–101.

Pechter, Edward. "When Pechter Reads Froula Pretending She's Eve Reading Milton; or, New Feminist Is but Old Priest Writ Large." *Critical Inquiry* 11 (1984): 163–70.

Petrarch, Francesco. *Rime sparse. Petrarch's Lyric Poems: The* Rime sparse *and Other Lyrics.* Ed. and trans. Robert Durling. Cambridge: Harvard UP, 1976. 35–583.

Phillips, Edward. "The Life of Mr. John Milton." Darbishire 49–82.

Phillips, John [attrib.]. "The Life of Mr. John Milton." Darbishire 17–34.

Pollock, Frederick, ed. *Table Talk of John Selden.* By John Selden. London: Selden Soc., 1927.

Poole, Matthew. *Annotations upon the Holy Bible.* London, 1683. 3rd ed. 1696.

Poole, William. "Two Early Readers of Milton: John Beale and Abraham Hill." *Milton Quarterly* 38 (2004): 76–99.

Pope, Alexander. *The Poems of Alexander Pope: A Reduced Version of the Twickenham Text.* Ed. John Butt. Cambridge: Yale UP, 1966.

Pope, Elizabeth P. *"Paradise Regained": The Tradition and the Poem.* Baltimore: Johns Hopkins UP, 1947. New York: Russell, 1962.

Porter, Charlotte, and Helen A. Clarke, eds. "The Prometheus Stories as Treated by Aeschylus, Shelley, Goethe, Milton, and Byron." *Poetic Lore: A Quarterly Magazine of Letters* ns 9 (1897): 589–606.

Potter, Lois. *A Preface to Milton.* London: Longman, 1986.

Pound, Ezra. *The ABC of Reading.* New York, Doubleday, 1960.

———. "Notes on Elizabethan Classicists." *Make It New.* New Haven: Yale UP, 1935. 95–121.

Prince, F. T. *The Italian Element in Milton's Verse*. Oxford: Clarendon, 1954.

The Putney Debates. Rudrum, Black, and Nelson 1238–60.

Radzinowicz, Mary Ann. *Toward Samson Agonistes: The Growth of Milton's Mind*. Princeton: Princeton UP, 1978.

Rajan, Balachandra, and Elizabeth Sauer, eds. *Milton and the Imperial Vision*. Pittsburgh: Duquesne UP, 1999.

Rambuss, Richard. *Closet Devotions*. Durham: Duke UP, 1998.

———. "Sacred Subjects and the Aversive Metaphysical Conceit: Crashaw, Serrano, Ofili." *ELH* 71 (2004): 497–530.

Reynolds, Samuel Harvey, ed. *Table Talk of John Selden*. By John Selden. Oxford: Clarendon, 1892.

Ricks, Christopher. *Milton's Grand Style*. Oxford: Clarendon, 1963.

Rivers, Isabel. *Classical and Christian Ideas in English Renaissance Poetry: A Students' Guide*. Boston: Allen, 1979.

Roethke, Theodore. *The Collected Poems*. New York: Anchor, 1974.

Rogers, John. *The Matter of Revolution: Science, Poetry, and Politics in the Age of Milton*. Ithaca: Cornell UP, 1996.

Rosenblatt, Jason P. *Torah and Law in* Paradise Lost. Princeton: Princeton UP, 1994.

Rosendale, Timothy. "Milton, Hobbes, and the Liturgical Subject." *SEL* 44 (2004): 149–72.

Rubin, Gayle. "The Traffic in Women: Notes on the 'Political Economy' of Sex. *Towards an Anthropology of Women*. Ed. Rayna R. Reiter. New York: Monthly Review, 1975. 157–210.

Rudrum, Alan. "Milton Scholarship and the *Agon* over *Samson Agonistes*." *Literature Compass* 1.1 (2004). 6 Apr. 2006 <http://www.blackwell-synergy.com/toc/lico/1/1>.

Rudrum, Alan, Joseph Black, and Holly Faith Nelson, eds. *The Broadview Anthology of Seventeenth-Century Verse and Prose*. Peterborough, ON: Broadview, 2000.

Rumrich, John. "Milton's Arianism: Why It Matters." Dobranski and Rumrich 75–92.

———. *Milton Unbound: Controversy and Reinterpretation*. Cambridge: Cambridge UP, 1996.

———. "The Provenance of *De Doctrina Christiana*: A View of the Present Controversy." *Milton and the Grounds of Contention*. Ed. Mark R. Kelley, Michael Lieb, and John T. Shawcross. Pittsburgh: Duquesne UP, 2003. 214–33.

Rushdy, Ashraf. *The Empty Garden: The Subject of Late Milton*. Pittsburgh: U of Pittsburgh P, 1992.

Sagaser, Elizabeth. "Flirting with Eternity: Teaching Form and Meter in a Renaissance Poetry Course." *Renaissance Literature and Its Formal Engagements*. Ed. Mark David Rasmussen. New York: Palgrave, 2002. 185–206.

Sandler, Florence. "Icon and Iconoclast." Lieb and Shawcross 160–84.

Scanlan, Robert. "Director's Note." *Milton's* Samson Agonistes. 92nd Street Y, New York City, 21 Apr. 2003. Program insert.

Schwartz, Regina. *Remembering and Repeating: On Milton's Theology and Poetics*. Chicago: U of Chicago P, 1993.

Selden, John. *De Diis Syris*. London, 1617.

————. *De Jure Naturali et Gentium juxta Disciplinam Ebraeorum*. London, 1640.

————. *De Synedriis et Praefecturis Juridicus Veterum Ebraeorum*. 3 vols. London, 1640.

————. *John Selden on Jewish Marriage Law: The "Uxor Hebraica."* Tr. Jonathan R. Ziskind. Leiden: Brill, 1991.

————. *Opera Omnia*. Ed. David Wilkins. London, 1726.

————. *Uxor Ebraica*. London, 1646.

Sellin, Paul R. "Further Responses." *Milton Quarterly* 33 (1999): 38–50.

————. "John Milton's *Paradise Lost* and *De Doctrina Christiana* on Predestination." *Milton Studies* 34 (1996): 45–60.

Sensabaugh, George F. *Milton in Early America*. Princeton: Princeton UP, 1964.

Shakespeare, William. *Mr. William Shakespeares Comedies, Histories, and Tragedies*. London, 1632.

————. *Shakespeare's Sonnets*. Ed. Stephen Booth. New Haven: Yale UP, 1977.

Shawcross, John T. Forum response. Lewalski, Shawcross, and Hunter 155–62.

————. "The Genres of *Paradise Regain'd* and *Samson Agonistes*: The Wisdom of Their Joint Publication." *Milton Studies* 17 (1983): 225–48.

————. *Milton: A Bibliography for the Years 1624–1700*. Binghamton: Medieval and Renaissance Texts and Studies, 1984.

————. *Milton, 1732–1801: The Critical Heritage*. London: Routledge, 1972.

————. *Rethinking Milton Studies: Time Present and Time Past*. Newark: U of Delaware P, 2005.

————. "The Temple of Janus and Milton Criticism in the New Millennium." *ANQ* 15.4 (2002): 20–29.

————. *The Uncertain World of* Samson Agonistes. Cambridge: Brewer, 2001.

Shea, Christopher. "Was [Milton's] Samson a Terrorist?" *Boston Globe* 3 Nov. 2002: D5.

Shelley, Mary. *Frankenstein; or, The Modern Prometheus*. 1818. 2nd ed. Ed. D. L. Macdonald and Kathleen Scherf. 1999. Peterborough ON: Broadview, 2001.

Shelley, Percy Bysshe. "Prometheus Unbound." *Shelley's Poetry and Prose*. 2nd ed. Ed. Donald H. Reiman and Neil Fraistat. New York: Norton, 2002. 202–86.

Shoaf, R. Allen. *Milton, Poet of Duality*. New Haven: Yale UP, 1985. Gainesville: UP of Florida, 1993.

Shoulson, Jeffrey. *Milton and the Rabbis: Hebraism, Hellenism, and Christianity*. New York: Columbia UP, 2001.

Showalter, Elaine. *Teaching Literature*. Malden: Blackwell, 2003.

Shuger, Debora K. *The Renaissance Bible: Scholarship, Sacrifice, and Subjectivity*. Berkeley: U of California P, 1994.

Shullenberger, William. "The Profession of Virginity in *A Mask Presented at Ludlow-Castle*." Martin, *Milton* 77–94.

Sidney, Philip. *Astrophil and Stella*. *The Poems of Sir Philip Sidney*. Ed. William A. Ringler, Jr. Oxford: Oxford UP, 1962. 163–264.

Sims, James H. *The Bible in Milton's Epics*. Gainesville: U of Florida P, 1962.

Skerpan-Wheeler, Elizabeth. "*Eikon Basilike* and the Rhetoric of Self-Representation." *The Royal Image: Representations of Charles I*. Ed. Thomas N. Corns. Cambridge: Cambridge UP, 1999. 122–40.

Skinner, Quentin. *Visions of Politics*. Cambridge: Cambridge UP, 2002.

Smectymnuus. *An Answer to a Booke Entituled,* An Humble Remonstrance. London: I. Rothwell, 1641. London: Nathanial Butter, 1641.

Smith, Nigel. *Literature and Revolution in England, 1640–1660*. New Haven: Yale UP, 1994.

Smith, Robert Metcalf. *The Variant Issues of Shakespeare's Second Folio and Milton's First Published English Poem: A Bibliographical Problem*. Folcroft: Folcroft Lib., 1975.

Sokol, B. J. "'Euripedes' *Alcestis* and the 'Saint' of Milton's Reparative Twenty-Third Sonnet." *SEL* 33 (1993): 131–47.

Southwell, Robert. *The Poems of Robert Southwell*. Ed. James H. McDonald and Nancy Pollard Brown. Oxford: Clarendon P, 1967.

Speght, Rachel. *A Muzzel for Melastomus*. Rudrum, Black, and Nelson 397–400.

Spenser, Edmund. *The Faerie Queene*. London: Penguin, 1987.

———. *The Yale Edition of the Shorter Poems of Edmund Spenser*. Ed. William A. Oram et al. New Haven: Yale UP, 1989.

Sperber, Dan, and Deirdre Wilson. *Relevance: Communication and Cognition*. Oxford: Blackwell, 1986.

Spitzer, Leo. "Understanding Milton." *Essays on English and American Literature*. Ed. Anna Hatcher. Princeton: Princeton UP, 1962. 116–31.

Sprott, S. E. *A Maske: The Earlier Versions*. Toronto: U of Toronto P, 1973.

Steinberg, Leo. *The Sexuality of Christ in Renaissance Art and in Modern Oblivion*. 2nd ed. Chicago: U of Chicago P, 1996.

Stephen, Leslie, and Sidney Lee, eds. *The Dictionary of National Biography*. 22 vols. Oxford: Oxford UP, 1998.

Sterne, Laurence, and Harold H. Kollmeier, eds. *A Concordance to the English Prose of John Milton*. Binghamton: Medieval and Renaissance Texts and Studies, 1985.

Stevens, Paul. "Milton's Janus-Faced Nationalism: Soliloquy, Subject, and the Modern Nation State." *Journal of English and Germanic Philology* 100 (2001): 247–68.

———. "Subversion and Wonder in Milton's Epitaph 'On Shakespeare.'" *English Literary Renaissance* 19 (1989): 375–88.

Stone, Lawrence. *The Family, Sex, and Marriage in England, 1500–1800*. Abr. ed. New York: Harper, 1979.

Taylor, G. C. *Milton's Use of Du Bartas*. Cambridge: Harvard UP, 1934.

Theocritus. *Idylls*. Trans. Robert Wells. New York: Penguin, 1989.

"The Thirty-Nine Articles of Religion." Ed. Gavin Koh. 29 Nov. 1999. 28 Nov. 2006 <http://www.members.tripod.com/~gavvie/39articles/articles.html>.

Thompson, Craig R. *The Bible in English, 1525–1611*. Washington: Folger Shakespeare Lib., 1958.

Toner, Robin, illus. "Restoration: What It Used to Be Just Ain't What It Used to Be." *New York Times* 7 Jan. 2001, late ed., sec. 4: 1.

Turner, James Grantham. *One Flesh: Paradisal Marriage and Sexual Relations in the Age of Milton*. Oxford: Clarendon; New York: Oxford UP, 1987.

Tuve, Rosemond. *Images and Themes in Five Poems by Milton*. Cambridge: Harvard UP, 1957.

Tyacke, Nicholas, ed. *England's Long Reformation, 1500–1800*. London: UCL, 2003.

Tyndale, William. *An Answer to Sir Thomas More's Dialogue*. [Antwerp], 1530.

Urban, David V. " 'Out of His Treasury Things New and Old': Milton's Parabolic Householder in *The Doctrine and Discipline of Divorce* and *De Doctrina Christiana*." *Milton's Legacy*. Ed. Kristen A. Pruitt and Charles W. Durham. Selinsgrove: Susquehanna UP, 2005. 208–19.

Vaughan Williams, Ralph. *Hodie: A Christmas Cantata*. 1954. Cond. Richard Hickox. Hayes: EMI, 1990.

Vergil. *Aeneid*. Trans. H. Rushton Fairclough. 2nd ed. Ed. G. P. Goold. Vol. 1. Cambridge: Harvard UP, 1999.

———. *The Eclogues: Dual Language Edition*. Ed. Guy Lee. New York: Penguin, 1984.

———. *Virgil: Eclogues, Georgics, Aeneid*. Ed. and trans. H. Ruston Fairclough. 2 vols. Cambridge: Harvard UP, 1960.

Verity, A. W. Introduction. Milton, *Milton's* Samson Agonistes vii–lxvi.

Voice of the Shuttle. Ed. Alan Liu. 7 Apr. 2006 <http://vos.ucsb.edu/>.

Walker, Julia M., ed. *Milton and the Idea of Woman*. Urbana: U of Illinois P, 1988.

Wallerstein, Nicholas. " 'The Copious Matter of My Song': A Study of Theology and Rhetoric in Milton's *Paradise Lost* and Twenty-Third Sonnet." *Pacific Coast Philology* 30 (1995): 41–59.

Ward, John. *God Judging among the Gods*. London, 1645.

Whateley, William. *A Bride-Bush: or, A Direction for Married Persons*. London, 1623.

Wilding, Michael. *Dragon's Teeth*. Oxford: Clarendon, 1987.

———. "John Milton: The Early Works." *The Cambridge Companion to English Poetry: Donne to Marvel*. Ed. Thomas N. Corns. Cambridge: Cambridge UP, 1996. 221–40.

Willey, Basil. *The Seventeenth Century Background*. New York: Columbia UP, 1934.

Williamson, Marilyn L. "A Reading of Milton's Twenty-Third Sonnet." *Milton Studies* 4 (1972): 141–50.

Wilson, A. N. *The Life of John Milton*. New York: Oxford UP, 1983.

Wittreich, Joseph Anthony, Jr. *Feminist Milton*. Ithaca: Cornell UP, 1987.

———. *Interpreting* Samson Agonistes. Princeton: Princeton UP, 1986.

———. " 'Reading' Milton: The Death (and Survival) of the Author." *Milton Studies* 38 (2000): 10–46.

———. *Shifting Contexts: Reinterpreting* Samson Agonistes. Pittsburgh: Duquesne UP, 2002.

———. " 'Strange Text!' '*Paradise Regained* . . . to Which Is Added *Samson Agonistes*.' " *Poems in Their Place: The Intertextuality and Order of Poetic Collections*. Ed. Neil Fraistat. Chapel Hill: U of North Carolina P, 1986. 164–94.

Wolfe, Don M. *Milton in the Puritan Revolution*. New York: Nelson, 1941.

Wolleb, Jean. *The Abridgement of Christian Divinitie: So Exactly and Methodically*

Compiled, That It Leads Us, As It Were, by the Hand to the Reading of the Holy Scriptures, Ordering of Common-places, Understanding of Controversies, Cleering of Some Cases of Conscience. London, 1650.

Woodhouse, A. S. P. "The Argument of Milton's *Comus*." *University of Toronto Quarterly* 11 (1941): 46–71.

———. *The Heavenly Muse: A Preface to Milton.* Ed. Hugh MacCallum. Toronto: U of Toronto P, 1972.

Woods, Suzanne. " 'That Freedom of Discussion Which I Loved': Italy and Milton's Cultural Self-Definition." Di Cesare 9–18.

Worden, Blair. "Milton and Marchamont Nedham." Armitage, Himy, and Skinner 156–80.

———. "Milton, *Samson Agonistes*, and the Restoration." *Culture and Society in the Stuart Restoration.* Ed. Gerald MacLean. Cambridge: Cambridge UP, 1995. 111–36.

———. "Milton's Republicanism and the Tyranny of Heaven." *Machiavelli and Republicanism.* Ed. Gisela Bock, Quentin Skinner, and Maurizo Viroli. Cambridge: Cambridge UP, 1990. 225–46.

Wordsworth, William. *The Major Works: Including* The Prelude. Ed. Stephen Gill. Oxford: Oxford UP, 2000.

Wroth, Mary. *The Poems of Lady Mary Wroth.* Ed. Josephine A. Roberts. Baton Rouge: Louisiana State UP, 1983.

Zagorin, Perez. *Ways of Lying: Dissimulation, Persecution, and Conformity in Early Modern Europe.* Cambridge: Harvard UP, 1990.

Zillman, Lawrence John, ed. *Shelley's "Prometheus Unbound": A Variorum Edition.* Rev. ed. Seattle: U of Washington P, 1960.

Zimmerman, Shari A. "Disaffection, Dissimulation, and the Uncertain Ground of Silent Dismission: Juxtaposing John Milton and Elizabeth Cary." *ELH* 66 (1999): 553–89.

INDEX OF NAMES

Abrams, M. H., 10
Achinstein, Sharon, 8
Aers, David, 11
Alciato, Andrea, 7
Alexander, 182
Alpers, Paul, 51
Ames, William, 112
Ammons, A. R., 159
Anderson, Benedict, 29
Anger, Jane, 36
Antipater, 182
Apuleius, 215
Armitage, David, 9, 120n5
Arnold, Matthew, 175
Arthos, John, 27
Askew, Anne, 52
Astell, Mary, 36
Atwan, Robert, 110
Aubrey, John, 112
Augustine, 15, 210

Bacon, Francis, 40, 50, 243
Bailyn, Bernard, 135
Baker, Herschel, 4
Bal, Mieke, 35
Balaam, 182
Barker, Arthur E., 8, 42, 45
Barker, Jane, 36
Bauman, Michael, 240n8
Bayley, John, 200
Bayne, Peter, 202
Beale, John, 202
Bear, Risa, 6
Behn, Aphra, 36, 49, 51
Belsey, Catherine, 7
Benet, Diana Treviño, 9, 27, 28
Bennett, Joan, 45, 100
Bennett, Judith M., 154
Berger, Harry, Jr., 167
Berger, Joseph, 200
Beza, Theodore, 138n1
Bible, 6, 11n3, 43, 45, 46, 35, 110–13, 229, 237
Bion, 175
Black, Joseph, 4, 36, 40n2
Blake, William, 64–65, 73n4, 174, 203
Bloom, Harold, 169
Boehrer, Bruce, 10, 22, 176, 177, 178n3
Boesky, Amy, 87n4
Book of Revelation, 197
Borges, Jorge Luis, 48
Bowra, C. M., 8
Braden, Gordon, 143

Bradford, Richard, 7
Bradshaw, John, 5
Brathwaite, Richard, 153
Breasted, Barbara, 10, 152
Brennan, Gillian, 34n2
Breton, Nicholas, 36
Brisman, Leslie, 158
Brown, Cedric, 10
Brown, Christopher, 67, 223
Browne, Thomas, 36, 52
Bruce, F. F., 111
Bryson, Michael, 6
Bunyan, John, 52
Burke, Kenneth, 203
Burke, Seán, 24
Bush, Douglas, 7–8
Bush, George H. W., 222–23
Bush, George W., 222–23
Butlin, Martin, 64
Bynum, Caroline Walker, 151n7
Byron, George Gordon, Lord, 174

Caesar, 182
Calamy, Edmund, 104
Calvin, John, 231
Campbell, Gardner, 22
Campbell, Gordon, 3, 5, 10, 24, 28, 237, 240n4
Carey, John, 3, 73n5, 102n1, 174n1, 200, 241n12
Carroll, Clare, 4
Cary, Elizabeth, 36
Cavendish, Margaret, 36, 49, 50
Chaney, Edward, 27, 28
Chaplin, Gregory, 35
Chapman, Alison, 21
Charles I, 7, 26, 30, 42, 115, 135, 136, 197, 198, 220, 221
Charles II, 223, 224, 242
Chaucer, Geoffrey, 50, 51, 52, 140, 160
Cheke, John, 99
Cheney, Patrick, 87n2
Chéron, Louis, 67–68
Chidley, Katherine, 36
Christ, 21, 42–45, 63, 64, 74, 78, 87n1, 113, 116, 140–43, 145–50, 177, 180, 182, 183, 191, 204n2, 224, 226, 228, 229, 231, 232, 235, 240n2. See also Jesus
Christine de Pisan, 36
Christopher, Georgia, 112
Cinquemani, A. M., 27, 28
Clarke, Helen, 204n1
Cleaver, Robert, 153

Cleveland, Charles D., 5
Clinton, Bill, 222–23
Coffey, John, 179
Coleridge, Samuel Taylor, 174
Collinson, Patrick, 112
Comenius, 39
Congreve, William, 51
Cook, Eleanor, 87n3
Cooper, Thomas, 224
Corns, Thomas N., 3, 5, 7, 8, 9, 11, 26, 27, 193, 216, 237, 240n4, 244
Corregio, Antonio da, 151n6
Cowley, Abraham, 50, 110
Cowper, William, 48
Crane, Mary Thomas, 122
Crashaw, Richard, 63, 148–49, 151n5
Cromwell, Oliver, 7, 26
Cummings, Robert, 4

Daniell, David, 111
Danielson, Dennis, 7, 8, 9
Darbishire, Helen, 24, 113n1
David, J. C., 243
Davie, Donald, 113
Davies, Stevie, 8
Davis, J. C., 243
Davis, Matthew, 22
Demosthenes, 183
De Quincey, Thomas, 203
Derrida, Jacques, 114, 169
Deuteronomy, 42, 43, 166, 229, 230, 231
Di Cesare, Mario, 27
Dickens, A. G., 112
Diekhoff, John, 24
Dietz, Michael, 10
Diodati, Charles, 143
Dobranski, Stephen, 9, 20, 23n1, 59, 165n1
Dod, John, 153
Donne, John, 52, 63, 110, 146
Drake, Judith, 36
Dream of the Rood, 52
Dryden, John, 36, 49, 51, 52, 110, 174
Du Bartas, Guillaume, 210n1
Duran, Angelica, 7, 20
Durham, Charles, 9
Dürer, Albrecht, 159
Dylan, Bob, 156
Dzelzainis, Martin, 26

Edward, Lord Herbert of Cherbury, 36
Edwards, J. M., 175
Edwards, Thomas, 100, 116, 120n4
Egerton, Alice, 153, 154
Egerton, John, 152, 153
Egerton, Frances, 153
Egerton, Sarah Fyge, 36
Elijah, 182
Eliot, T. S., 120n1, 166

Elledge, Scott, 9, 174n1, 236
Ellison, Ralph, 203
Emerton, J. A., 111
Empson, William, 8, 28, 201
Engel, Adam, 52, 200
Escobedo, Andrew, 20
Euripides, 44
Evans, J. Martin, 10, 24, 26, 27, 143
Everyman, 51
Exodus, 208
Ezell, Margaret, 178n2

Fairclough, H. Rushton, 180
Fallon, Robert, 24
Fallon, Stephen, 8, 24, 26
Featley, Daniel, 100
Felltham, Owen, 36
Fenton, Elijah, 87n2
Ferguson, Margaret, 8, 9, 92, 175
Ferguson, Moira, 36
Fincham, Kenneth, 112
Fish, Stanley, 8, 9, 10, 11, 73n5, 126, 195, 200, 217, 239
Fishbone, Alan, 204n2
Fisher, Alan, 179
Fixler, Michael, 9
Flannagan, Roy, 3, 6, 10, 11n1, 102n1, 121, 163, 168–69, 174n1, 193, 236
Fletcher, Angus, 159
Fliegelman, Jay, 48
Fortescue, John, 136–37
Foucault, Michel, 170
Fowler, Alastair, 10, 102n1
Fox, Margaret Fell, 36, 37
Foxe, John, 226
Franklin, Julian H., 138n1
French, J. Milton, 24
Froide, Amy M., 154
Frost, Robert, 156
Froula, Christine, 8, 10
Frye, Roland M., 9, 62, 170n1
Fulk, Mark K., 22
Furman-Adams, Wendy, 5, 20

Galations, 229
Gallagher, Philip J., 166
Gardiner, Anne Barbeau, 234n3
Gay, David, 49, 112
Genesis, 208, 228, 230
Ghabra, Shafeeq, 201
Gibson, Mel, 141
Gideon, 182
Gilbert, Roger, 156
Gilbert, Sandra, 35, 152
Gilfillan, George, 202
Goldberg, Jonathan, 3, 24, 121, 170n1
Goldsmith, Oliver, 49
Graff, Gerald, 236

Graves, Robert, 25
Gray, Thomas, 52
Greenberg, Lynne, 21
Gregerson, Linda, 10
Gregory, E. R., 10, 87n2
Gross, Kenneth, 140
Grossman, Allen, 10
Grotius, Hugo, 38, 41n3
Grünewald, Mathias, 64, 73n4
Gubar, Susan, 35, 152
Guillory, John, 146, 163
Guttenplan, D. D., 52, 73n5, 200

Hale, John, 50, 237, 240n4
Halkett, John, 35
Hall, Joseph, 105
Haller, William, 112
Halley, Janet, 11
Halpern, Richard, 145, 150
Hamilton, Newburgh, 204n2
Hammond, Gerald, 86, 87n5
Handel, George Frideric, 6, 201
Hanford, J. Holly, 7, 144, 174n1
Hardy, Nathaniel, 100
Harrington, James, 243, 245
Hartlib, Samuel, 38–39
Haskin, Dayton, 84, 112, 234n1
Haug, Ralph, 206–07
Hausknecht, Gina, 36, 38
Hawkes, Terence, 169
Healey, John, 210
Heaney, Seamus, 80
Helgerson, Richard, 8
Henderson, Katherine, 40n1
Heninger, S. K., 6
Henrietta Maria, 197, 223
Henry VIII, 229
Herbert, George, 52, 110
Herman, Peter C., 21, 35, 218
Hexter, J. H., 203
Hill, Christopher, 8, 26, 27, 57, 102n2, 110,
    193, 241n10
Hill, Elizabeth K., 87n3
Hill, G. B., 173
Himy, Armand, 9, 120n5
Hinks, Dennis, 240n1
Hobbes, Thomas, 41n4, 234n3
Hodge, Bob, 11
Hodges, Margaret, 52
Holderness, Graham, 34n2
Hollander, John, 87n3
Holmes, David I., 237, 240n4
Holstun, James, 243, 244
Homer, 183
Homily on Obedience, 132–33
Honigmann, E. A. J., 87n2, 102n1, 102n2
Hotman, François, 138n1
Huckabay, Calvin, 5

Hughes, Merritt Y., 3, 102n1, 110, 121,
    168–69
Hume, Patrick, 110
Hunter, William B., 4, 7, 151n3, 235–36, 237,
    241n9, 241n10
Huntley, John, 11, 206
Hyde, William, 68–70

Illo, John, 11, 23, 212, 213, 214, 215
Ingram, Randall, 10
Ingram, William, 5
Ireton, Henry, 220–21
Isaiah, 45
Isocrates, 213

James I, 26, 136, 220
Jauss, Hans Robert, 166
Jefferson, Thomas, 142
Jeremiah, 45, 242
Jesus, 22, 43, 66, 117, 131, 142, 146–50, 164,
    179–84, 185–88, 215, 235, 239. *See also*
    Christ
Job, 180, 182
John, 182
Johnson, Samuel, 22, 35, 49, 52, 158, 173,
    174, 202, 204n3
Jokinen, Anniina, 6
Jones, Edward, 87n2
Jonson, Ben, 50, 51, 161, 165n3
Jordan, Constance, 4
Josipovici, Gabriel, 42
Judges, 66, 145, 190, 197

Kahn, Victoria, 10
Kean, Margaret, 48
Keats, John, 52, 92, 156–57, 159
Kedourie, Elie, 29
Kelley, Mark R., 194
Kelley, Maurice, 235
Kendrick, Christopher, 9
Kenyon, J. P., 199n2
Kermode, Frank, 120n1
Kermode, Lloyd, 10
Kerrigan, William, 9, 24, 87, 155
King, Edward, 27, 74, 78, 173–74, 176, 177
King, John, 199n1
Klibansky, Raymond, 159
Knight, G. Wilson, 201
Knoppers, Laura Lunger, 8, 11, 23, 49, 179,
    223, 224, 227, 242
Kolbrener, William, 21, 120n5
Kollmeier, Harold H., 5
Kristeva, Julia, 177
Krook, Anne K., 191
Kushner, Tony, 203

Labriola, Albert C., 5, 20, 24, 193
Lake, Peter, 112

Lancashire, Ian, 188n1
Lanier, Douglas, 10, 164, 165n3
Lanyer, Aemelia [Amelia Lanier], 36, 52
Lares, Jameela, 21
Laud, William, 196, 197
Lawes, Henry, 6, 51
The Lawes Resolutions of Women's Rights,
    152–53, 154
Leapor, Mary, 52
Le Comte, Edward, 3
Lee, Sidney, 5
Leishman, J. B., 50
Lely, Peter, 223–24
Leonard, John, 3, 23, 24, 26, 155
Lessing, G. E., 73n2
Letter to the Hebrews, 66, 191
Letterman, David, 116
Levi, Peter, 5
Lewalski, Barbara, 3, 5, 22, 26, 27, 82, 113,
    147, 162, 179, 180, 182, 206, 236, 237,
    238–39, 240n6
Lewin, Jennifer, 21
Lieb, Michael, 9, 24, 193, 239, 240n3, 240n8,
    241n11, 241n12
Liljegren, S. B., 27, 28
Lipking, Lawrence, 43n1
Liu, Alan, 6
Locke, John, 48
Lodge, David, 166
Loewenstein, David, 3, 8, 9, 22, 26, 179
Luther, Martin, 231

Macrobius, 46
Makin, Bathusa, 36, 37, 39, 40n1
Malachi, 232
Mantegna, Andrea, 63–64, 73n4
Marcus, Leah S., 10, 152
Mark, 43, 179
Marlowe, Christopher, 48, 50
Marshall, Stephen, 104
Marshall, William, 224, 225
Martin, Catherine Gimelli, 20, 35, 38, 40
Martz, Louis, 24, 141, 180
Marvell, Andrew, 202, 204n3
Mary, Queen of Scots, 136, 226
Masterman, J. Howard B., 202
Matthew, 43, 76, 168, 179, 190, 215, 237,
    239, 240n5
Mayhew, Jonathan, 135–36
Mazzaro, Jerome, 10
McColgan, Kristin Pruitt, see Pruitt, Kristin
McColley, Diane, 35, 40
McCullough, Peter, 112
McGrath, Alister, 111
McGuire, Maryann Cale, 9
McLoone, George H., 87n2
McManus, Barbara, 40n1

Medley, Robert, 70–71
Melville, Herman, 47
Mendle, Michael, 200
Merian, Matthäus, 67
Metzger, Bruce, 111
Mikics, David, 21
Miller, Nancy Weitz, 152
Milton, Deborah, 142
Mitchell, W. J. T., 73
Mohamed, Feisal, 200
Monck, General George, 242
Montagu, Mary Wortley, 51
More, Thomas, 49, 108, 242, 243–44, 245
Mornay, Phillipe du Plessis, 138n1
Moseley, Humphrey, 59
Moses, 182, 208, 229, 233
Mueller, Janel, 99
Mundia, Constancia, 36

Nardo, Anna K., 82, 98
Nelson, Holly Faith, 4, 36, 40n2
Newcomen, Matthew, 104
New Testament, 38, 43, 45, 111, 113, 172,
    190, 191, 228, 230, 233
Nicolson, Adam, 111
Nicolson, Marjorie, 7, 26
Nietzsche, Friedrich, 169
Norbrook, David, 4, 8, 26, 120n5, 213
Norton, David, 111
Nyquist, Mary, 8, 9

Old Testament, 38, 66, 111, 113, 117, 172,
    182, 191, 228, 229, 230, 233, 242
Onions, C. T., 200
Orgel, Stephen, 3, 8, 24, 121
Ovid, 98, 164, 176

Pagels, Elaine, 35
Pagitt, Ephraim, 100
Palmer, Herbert, 100
Panofsky, Erwin, 72n1, 159
Parker, William Riley, 5, 27, 28, 45, 87n2, 100
Parry, Graham, 8, 9
Patrides, C. A., 4, 8, 9, 26, 113, 173
Patterson, Annabel, 9–10, 11, 24, 26
Paul, 43, 213, 230
Pechter, Edward, 8, 11
Perloff, Marjorie, 47
Perry, Curtis, 21, 60n1
Petrarch, 93
Phillips, Edward, 141
Phillips, John, 112, 113n1
Phillips, Katherine, 36
Piombo, Sebastiano del, 151n6
Plato, 182, 183
Pollock, Frederick, 137
Poole, Matthew, 45, 46n1

Poole, William, 202
Pope, Alexander, 50, 52, 175
Pope, Elizabeth P., 182
Porter, Charlotte, 204n1
Potter, Lois, 7
Pound, Ezra, 42, 48
Powell, Mary, 85, 87n2, 87n3, 228
Prince, F. T., 9
Pruitt [McColgan], Kristin, 9
Prynne, William, 100
Psalms, 45
Pullman, Philip, 48
The Putney Debates, 218, 220–21

Quilligan, Maureen, 170n1

Radzinowicz, Mary Ann, 9, 82, 195, 241n10
Rainsborough, Thomas, 221
Rajan, Balachandra, 9
Raleigh, Walter, 50
Rambuss, Richard, 5–6, 21, 139, 146, 151n7
Raymond, Joad, 9
Rembrandt van Rijn, 66–67, 73n4
Revard, Stella, 3
Reynolds, Samuel Harvey, 44
Richard II, 136
Richard III, 226
Ricks, Christopher, 9
Ripa, Cesare, 159
Rivers, Isabel, 19, 112
Roethke, Theodore, 175
Rogers, John, 151n1
Romans, 229
Rooley, Anthony, 6
Rosenblatt, Jason, 20, 190, 234n1
Rosendale, Timothy, 234n3
Rubens, Peter Paul, 66
Rubin, Gayle, 153
Rudrum, Alan, 4, 11n2, 36, 40n2
Rumrich, John, 8, 9, 21, 24, 151n5, 180, 240n4
Rushdy, Ashraf, 9

Sagaser, Elizabeth Harris, 21, 89
Salter, Mary Jo, 92, 175
Sandler, Florence, 226
Sauer, Elizabeth, 9, 21
Saxl, Fritz, 159
Scanlan, Robert, 200
Schwartz, Louis, 210n2
Schwartz, Regina, 9
Selden, John, 38, 43–44, 46, 137
Sellin, Paul R., 240n6, 240n7
Semenza, Gregory M. Colón, 49
Sensabaugh, George F., 135
Shakespeare, William, 50, 51, 55, 80, 92, 160, 161–65, 169

Sharp, Joane, 36
Shawcross, John T., 3, 5, 9, 21, 23n1, 87n1, 191, 202, 236, 241n9
Shea, Christopher, 52, 200
Shelley, Mary, 48, 202
Shelley, Percy Bysshe, 175, 202
Shoaf, R. Allen, 22, 185
Shoulson, Jeffrey, 22, 190
Showalter, Elaine, 47, 51
Shuger, Deborah, 8
Shullenberger, William, 35
Sidney, Philip, 52, 80, 84, 175, 245
Sims, James H., 110, 111
Sir Gawain and the Green Knight, 49
Skerpan-Wheeler, Elizabeth, 21, 224
Skinner, Cyriack, 113n1
Skinner, Quentin, 9, 120n5
Sloane, Thomas, 87n2
Smith, Nigel, 8, 112, 120n5
Smith, Robert Metcalf, 57
Socrates, 182
Sokol, B. J., 87n2
Southwell, Robert, 52, 63
Sowernam, Esther, 36
Speght, Rachel, 36, 37, 40
Spenser, Edmund, 80, 85, 140, 148, 165n4, 175, 199n1, 245
Sperber, Dan, 139
Spitzer, Leo, 87n2
Sprott, S. E., 8
Spurstow, William, 104
Stallworthy, Jon, 92, 175
Steinberg, Leo, 21, 149, 151n7
Stephen, Leslie, 5
Sterne, Laurence, 5
Stevens, Paul, 11, 12, 226
Stevens, Wallace, 156, 157
Stone, Lawrence, 8
Sumner, Charles, 235, 241n12
Swain, Kathleen, 5
Swift, Jonathan, 50, 51
Sylvester, Joshua, 210n1
Szelzainis, Martin, 26

Tarquin, 136
Tasso, 180
Tayler, Edward, 25
Taylor, G. C., 210
Theocritus, 175
Thompson, Craig R., 111
Toner, Robin, 222
Turner, James G., 9, 35
Tuve, Rosemond, 9
Tweedie, Fiona J., 237, 240n4
Tyacke, Nicholas, 112
Tyler, Margaret, 36
Tyndale, William, 108

Urban VIII, 28
Urban, David V., 23, 237

Van Dyke, Anthony, 7, 66, 223
Vaughan Williams, Ralph, 6, 73n3
Vergil, 175, 179–80, 185
Verity, A. W., 204n2

Wace, 49
Waddington, Raymond, 8
Walker, Julia M., 40
Walker, Robert, 7, 223–24
Walker, William Sidney, 241n12
Wallerstein, Nicholas, 87n2
"The Wanderer," 49
Ward, John, 100, 101
Warner, Susan, 47
Whateley, William, 153
Wieder, Laurence, 110
Wilding, Michael, 8
Wildman, John, 220–21
Willey, Basil, 8
Williams, William Carlos, 50
Williamson, Marilyn L., 87n2

Wilmot, John, earl of Rochester, 36
Wilson, A. N., 5
Wilson, Deirdre, 139
Wittreich, Joseph A., 9, 22, 24, 35, 73n5, 189,
    194, 195
Wolfe, Don M., 3, 8–9
Wolleb, Jean, 112
Woodcock, Katherine, 85, 87n2, 87n3
Woodcock, Matthew, 23
Woodhouse, A. S. P., 42
Woods, Suzanne, 28
Woolf, Virginia, 35
Worden, Blair, 11, 12
Wordsworth, William, 52, 81–82, 156, 157,
    175
Woudhuysen, H. R., 4
Wroth, Mary, 85

Young, Thomas, 104

Zagorin, Perez, 9, 232
Zillman, Lawrence John, 204n1
Zimmerman, Shari A., 11, 23
Zwingli, Huldrych, 231

INDEX OF WORKS BY MILTON

Ad Patrem, 16, 51

Animadversions upon the Remonstrants
Defence against Smectymnuus, 32, 103–09

"Another on the Same," 16, 51

An Apology for Smectymnuus, 17, 24–25

Areopagitica, xi, 4, 16, 17, 18, 21, 22, 32, 33,
37, 38, 39, 42, 43, 49, 52, 58, 100, 101,
114–20, 126, 185, 194, 201, 211–17, 236,
242

"At a Solemn Musick," 16, 20, 74–75

"At a Vacation Exercise," 4, 16, 142, 143

Colasterion, 25, 97, 98, 99, 100, 109

Comus (A Mask Presented at Ludlow Castle),
xi, 4, 6, 8, 9, 15, 16, 17, 19, 20, 21, 26, 35,
37, 38, 51, 54, 58, 65, 85–86, 109, 126,
130–31, 145, 150, 152–55, 156, 163, 191,
194, 195–96

"Damon's Epitaph" ("Epitaphium
Damonis"), 16, 20, 31, 58

De Doctrina Christiana, see On Christian
Doctrine

Defense of Himself, 25

The Doctrine and Discipline of Divorce, 16,
17, 18, 22, 25, 37, 38, 39, 42–43, 54, 58,
97, 100, 101, 128, 166, 194, 196, 212,
228–34, 237

Eikonoklastes, 4, 17, 23, 155, 194, 196, 201,
211, 222–27

elegy 6 ("To Charles Diodati"), 16, 142–43,
155

"An Epitaph upon the Marchioness of
Winchester," 16

"The Fifth Ode of Horace," 4

First Defense of the English People, 30,
201

Heimbach, Peter, Letter to, 30

History of Britain, 20, 31, 34n4, 101–02

In Quintum Novembris, 26

The Judgment of Martin Bucer, 58, 97,
100

"L'Allegro" / "Il Penseroso," xi, 4, 6, 16, 17,
21, 50, 62, 88, 93–95, 107, 156–60

"Letter to a Friend," 17, 28

Likeliest Means to Remove Hirelings, 113,
184

Lycidas, xi, 4, 16, 17, 31, 50, 58, 74, 78–79,
171–74, 175–78, 191

"Mansus," 20, 31

A Mask, see Comus

Nativity Ode, see "On the Morning of
Christ's Nativity"

Of Education, 17, 38, 39, 50, 52, 53, 58, 109,
111, 242

Of Prelatical Episcopacy, 103–09

Of Reformation, 4, 27, 28, 32, 33, 103–09,
112, 126, 199

On Christian Doctrine (De Doctrina
Christiana), 3, 17, 22, 35, 44, 45, 74, 107,
112, 180, 201, 235–41

"On Shakespeare," 4, 16, 20, 21, 54–61, 81,
161–65

"On the Death of a Fair Infant," 36, 48,
140–41, 142

"On the Morning of Christ's Nativity," 4, 6,
16, 17, 18, 20–21, 46, 52, 54, 62, 63–65,
74, 77–78, 88, 95, 109, 139–44, 145–51,
157, 158, 204n2

"On the New Forcers of Conscience," 4, 16,
106, 120n2

"On the University Carrier," 16, 51

"On Time," 16

Paradise Lost, xi, 3, 7, 15, 18, 20, 24, 35, 37,
38, 39, 40, 46, 48, 52, 54, 62, 63, 64, 65,
81, 84, 95, 106, 107, 112, 115, 117, 119,
122, 129, 145–46, 150, 151n2, 156,
157–59, 162, 167, 179–80, 181, 185, 186,
187–88, 189, 190, 191, 194, 198, 201, 209,
210n1, 211, 214, 215, 219, 223, 227, 228,
229, 233, 236, 238, 244

Paradise Regained, xi, 16, 17, 20, 22,
52, 60, 107, 112, 130–31, 147, 148, 158,
179–84, 185–88, 189–93, 196, 203, 227,
231, 232, 236, 238

"The Passion," 16, 52, 142, 146, 148, 150,
151n4, 164, 185–88, 189–93

"A Postscript," 103–09

Prolusions, 17

The Ready and Easy Way to Establish a Free
Commonwealth, xi, 7, 17, 22, 44, 51,
121–25, 132, 196, 215, 219, 242–45

The Reason of Church Government, 4, 16,
21, 22–23, 25, 29, 103–09, 126–31, 196,
201, 205–10, 211

Samson Agonistes, xi, xii, 4, 5, 9, 15, 16, 17, 20, 22, 24, 35, 40, 45, 49, 51, 52, 60, 62, 65–72, 109, 129, 189–93, 194–99, 200–04, 227, 228, 229, 233

The Second Defense of the English People, 17, 20, 25, 28, 30, 40, 97, 101, 121–25, 128, 155

"Song: On May Morning," 4

sonnet 1 ("O Nightingale"): 16, 82–83

sonnet 2 ("Beautiful Lady"): 16, 82

sonnet 3 ("As on a Rugged Mountain"), 16, 82

sonnet 4 ("Diodati, e te'l dirò con maraviglia") 82

sonnet 5 ("Per certo i bei vost' occhi") 82

sonnet 6 ("Giovane piano, e semplicetto amante") 82

sonnet 7 ("How soon hath Time"), 4, 16, 20, 36, 48, 64, 74, 75–76, 81, 82, 83–84, 88, 89–91, 130, 142, 143, 165n2

sonnet 8 ("Captain or Colonel"), 4, 16, 36, 51

sonnet 9 ("Lady that in the prime"): 36, 130

sonnet 10 ("To the Lady Margaret Ley") 36

sonnet 11 ("A Book was writ"): 21, 36, 97–102

sonnet 12 ("I did but prompt the age"), 4, 21, 36, 97–102, 130

sonnet 13 ("To Mr. Henry Lawes"), 4, 16

sonnet 14 ("When Faith and Love"), 36

sonnet 15 ("On the Lord General Fairfax"), 4, 36

sonnet 16 ("To the Lord General Cromwell"), 4, 36, 84, 220

sonnet 17 ("To Sir Henry Vane the Younger"), 36, 84

sonnet 18 ("On the Late Massacher in Piemont"): 4, 16, 52, 84, 107

sonnet 19 ("When I consider how my light is spent"): 4, 16, 20, 22, 36, 48, 64, 74, 76–77, 81, 84, 88, 91–92, 130, 166–70, 232

sonnet 20 ("Lawrence of vertuous Father"), 87n1

sonnet 21 ("Cyriack, whose Grandsire"), 36, 84

sonnet 22 ("Cyriack, this three years day"), 36

sonnet 23 ("Methought I saw"), 4, 16, 21, 36, 80, 84, 85–86, 87n1, 88, 92–93

The Tenure of Kings and Magistrates, xi, 17, 21, 22, 26, 101, 121–25, 132–38, 218–22, 232, 242

Tetrachordon, 17, 38, 97, 98, 99, 100, 101

"To Sir Henry Vane the Younger," *see* sonnet 17

"To the Lord General Cromwell," *see* sonnet 16

A Treatise of Civil Power, 120n3, 193

"Upon the Circumcision," 16, 146, 228, 229, 233

Modern Language Association of America

Approaches to Teaching World Literature

Joseph Gibaldi, series editor

Achebe's Things Fall Apart. Ed. Bernth Lindfors. 1991.

Arthurian Tradition. Ed. Maureen Fries and Jeanie Watson. 1992.

Atwood's The Handmaid's Tale *and Other Works.* Ed. Sharon R. Wilson, Thomas B. Friedman, and Shannon Hengen. 1996.

Austen's Emma. Ed. Marcia McClintock Folsom. 2004.

Austen's Pride and Prejudice. Ed. Marcia McClintock Folsom. 1993.

Balzac's Old Goriot. Ed. Michal Peled Ginsburg. 2000.

Baudelaire's Flowers of Evil. Ed. Laurence M. Porter. 2000.

Beckett's Waiting for Godot. Ed. June Schlueter and Enoch Brater. 1991.

Beowulf. Ed. Jess B. Bessinger, Jr., and Robert F. Yeager. 1984.

Blake's Songs of Innocence and of Experience. Ed. Robert F. Gleckner and Mark L. Greenberg. 1989.

Boccaccio's Decameron. Ed. James H. McGregor. 2000.

British Women Poets of the Romantic Period. Ed. Stephen C. Behrendt and Harriet Kramer Linkin. 1997.

Brontë's Jane Eyre. Ed. Diane Long Hoeveler and Beth Lau. 1993.

Emily Brontë's Wuthering Heights. Ed. Sue Lonoff and Terri A. Hasseler. 2006.

Byron's Poetry. Ed. Frederick W. Shilstone. 1991.

Camus's The Plague. Ed. Steven G. Kellman. 1985.

Cather's My Ántonia. Ed. Susan J. Rosowski. 1989.

Cervantes' Don Quixote. Ed. Richard Bjornson. 1984.

Chaucer's Canterbury Tales. Ed. Joseph Gibaldi. 1980.

Chaucer's Troilus and Criseyde *and the Shorter Poems.* Ed. Tison Pugh and Angela Jane Weisl. 2006.

Chopin's The Awakening. Ed. Bernard Koloski. 1988.

Coleridge's Poetry and Prose. Ed. Richard E. Matlak. 1991.

Collodi's Pinocchio *and Its Adaptations.* Ed. Michael Sherberg. 2006.

Conrad's "Heart of Darkness" and "The Secret Sharer." Ed. Hunt Hawkins and Brian W. Shaffer. 2002.

Dante's Divine Comedy. Ed. Carole Slade. 1982.

Defoe's Robinson Crusoe. Ed. Maximillian E. Novak and Carl Fisher. 2005.

DeLillo's White Noise. Ed. Tim Engles and John N. Duvall. 2006.

Dickens' David Copperfield. Ed. Richard J. Dunn. 1984.

Dickinson's Poetry. Ed. Robin Riley Fast and Christine Mack Gordon. 1989.

Narrative of the Life of Frederick Douglass. Ed. James C. Hall. 1999.

Early Modern Spanish Drama. Ed. Laura R. Bass and Margaret R. Greer. 2006

Eliot's Middlemarch. Ed. Kathleen Blake. 1990.

Eliot's Poetry and Plays. Ed. Jewel Spears Brooker. 1988.

Shorter Elizabethan Poetry. Ed. Patrick Cheney and Anne Lake Prescott. 2000.

Ellison's Invisible Man. Ed. Susan Resneck Parr and Pancho Savery. 1989.

English Renaissance Drama. Ed. Karen Bamford and Alexander Leggatt. 2002.

Works of Louise Erdrich. Ed. Gregg Sarris, Connie A. Jacobs, and James R. Giles. 2004.

Dramas of Euripides. Ed. Robin Mitchell-Boyask. 2002.

Faulkner's The Sound and the Fury. Ed. Stephen Hahn and Arthur F. Kinney. 1996.

Flaubert's Madame Bovary. Ed. Laurence M. Porter and Eugene F. Gray. 1995.

García Márquez's One Hundred Years of Solitude. Ed. María Elena de Valdés and Mario J. Valdés. 1990.

Gilman's "The Yellow Wall-Paper" and Herland. Ed. Denise D. Knight and Cynthia J. Davis. 2003.

Goethe's Faust. Ed. Douglas J. McMillan. 1987.

Gothic Fiction: The British and American Traditions. Ed. Diane Long Hoeveler and Tamar Heller. 2003.

Hebrew Bible as Literature in Translation. Ed. Barry N. Olshen and Yael S. Feldman. 1989.

Homer's Iliad *and* Odyssey. Ed. Kostas Myrsiades. 1987.

Ibsen's A Doll House. Ed. Yvonne Shafer. 1985.

Henry James's Daisy Miller *and* The Turn of the Screw. Ed. Kimberly C. Reed and Peter G. Beidler. 2005.

Works of Samuel Johnson. Ed. David R. Anderson and Gwin J. Kolb. 1993.

Joyce's Ulysses. Ed. Kathleen McCormick and Erwin R. Steinberg. 1993.

Kafka's Short Fiction. Ed. Richard T. Gray. 1995.

Keats's Poetry. Ed. Walter H. Evert and Jack W. Rhodes. 1991.

Kingston's The Woman Warrior. Ed. Shirley Geok-lin Lim. 1991.

Lafayette's The Princess of Clèves. Ed. Faith E. Beasley and Katharine Ann Jensen. 1998.

Works of D. H. Lawrence. Ed. M. Elizabeth Sargent and Garry Watson. 2001.

Lessing's The Golden Notebook. Ed. Carey Kaplan and Ellen Cronan Rose. 1989.

Mann's Death in Venice *and Other Short Fiction.* Ed. Jeffrey B. Berlin. 1992.

Marguerite de Navarre's Heptameron. Ed. Colette H. Winn. 2007.

Medieval English Drama. Ed. Richard K. Emmerson. 1990.

Melville's Moby-Dick. Ed. Martin Bickman. 1985.

Metaphysical Poets. Ed. Sidney Gottlieb. 1990.

Miller's Death of a Salesman. Ed. Matthew C. Roudané. 1995.

Milton's Paradise Lost. Ed. Galbraith M. Crump. 1986.

Milton's Shorter Poetry and Prose. Ed. Peter C. Herman. 2007.

Molière's Tartuffe *and Other Plays.* Ed. James F. Gaines and Michael S. Koppisch. 1995.

Momaday's The Way to Rainy Mountain. Ed. Kenneth M. Roemer. 1988.

Montaigne's Essays. Ed. Patrick Henry. 1994.

Novels of Toni Morrison. Ed. Nellie Y. McKay and Kathryn Earle. 1997.

Murasaki Shikibu's The Tale of Genji. Ed. Edward Kamens. 1993.

Pope's Poetry. Ed. Wallace Jackson and R. Paul Yoder. 1993.

Proust's Fiction and Criticism. Ed. Elyane Dezon-Jones and
    Inge Crosman Wimmers. 2003.

Novels of Samuel Richardson. Ed. Lisa Zunshine and Jocelyn Harris. 2006.

Rousseau's Confessions *and* Reveries of the Solitary Walker. Ed. John C. O'Neal
    and Ourida Mostefai. 2003.

Shakespeare's Hamlet. Ed. Bernice W. Kliman. 2001.

Shakespeare's King Lear. Ed. Robert H. Ray. 1986.

Shakespeare's Othello. Ed. Peter Erickson and Maurice Hunt. 2005.

Shakespeare's Romeo and Juliet. Ed. Maurice Hunt. 2000.

Shakespeare's The Tempest *and Other Late Romances*. Ed. Maurice Hunt. 1992.

Shelley's Frankenstein. Ed. Stephen C. Behrendt. 1990.

Shelley's Poetry. Ed. Spencer Hall. 1990.

Sir Gawain and the Green Knight. Ed. Miriam Youngerman Miller and
    Jane Chance. 1986.

Song of Roland. Ed. William W. Kibler and Leslie Zarker Morgan. 2006.

Spenser's Faerie Queene. Ed. David Lee Miller and Alexander Dunlop. 1994.

Stendhal's The Red and the Black. Ed. Dean de la Motte and Stirling Haig. 1999.

Sterne's Tristram Shandy. Ed. Melvyn New. 1989.

Stowe's Uncle Tom's Cabin. Ed. Elizabeth Ammons and Susan Belasco. 2000.

Swift's Gulliver's Travels. Ed. Edward J. Rielly. 1988.

Thoreau's Walden *and Other Works*. Ed. Richard J. Schneider. 1996.

Tolstoy's Anna Karenina. Ed. Liza Knapp and Amy Mandelker. 2003.

Vergil's Aeneid. Ed. William S. Anderson and Lorina N. Quartarone. 2002.

Voltaire's Candide. Ed. Renée Waldinger. 1987.

Whitman's Leaves of Grass. Ed. Donald D. Kummings. 1990.

Wiesel's Night. Ed. Alan Rosen. 2007.

Woolf's To the Lighthouse. Ed. Beth Rigel Daugherty and Mary Beth Pringle. 2001.

Wordsworth's Poetry. Ed. Spencer Hall, with Jonathan Ramsey. 1986.

Wright's Native Son. Ed. James A. Miller. 1997.